Global Diversities

In collaboration with the Max Planck Institute for the Study of Ethnic and Religious Diversity.

Series Editors: **Steven Vertovec**, Director at the Max Planck Institute for the Study of Religious and Ethnic Diversity and Honorary Joint Professor of Sociology and Ethnology, University of Gottingen, Germany and **Peter van der Veer**, Director at the Max Planck Institute for the Study of Religious and Ethnic Diversity and Professor-at-Large at Utrecht University, The Netherlands.

Over the past decade, the concept of "diversity" has gained a leading place in academic thought, business practice, politics and public policy across the world. However, local conditions and meanings of "diversity" are highly dissimilar and changing. For these reasons, deeper and more comparative understandings of pertinent concepts, processes and phenomena are in great demand. This series will examine multiple forms and configurations of diversity; how these have been conceived, imagined and represented; how they have been or could be regulated or governed; how different processes of inter-ethnic or inter-religious encounter unfold; how conflicts arise and how political solutions are negotiated and practiced; and what truly convivial societies might actually look like. By comparatively examining a range of conditions, processes and cases revealing the contemporary meanings and dynamics of "diversity," this series will be a key resource for students and professional social scientists. It will represent a landmark within a field that has become, and will continue to be, one of the foremost topics of global concern throughout the 21st century. Reflecting this multi-disciplinary field, the series will include works from Anthropology, Political Science, Sociology, Law, Geography and Religious Studies. The series publishes standard monographs, edited collections and Palgrave Pivot titles, for shorter works that are between 25,000 and 30,000 words.

Titles include:

Tam T. T. Ngo and Justine B. Quijada
ATHEIST SECULARISM AND ITS DISCONTENTS
A Comparative Study of Religion and Communism in Eurasia

Susanne Wessendorf
COMMONPLACE DIVERSITY
Social Relations in a Super-Diverse Context

Steven Vertovec
DIVERSITIES OLD AND NEW
Migration and Socio-Spatial Patterns in New York, Singapore and Johannesburg

Forthcoming titles:

Jin-Heon Jung
DEFECTION AND CONVERSION
The Christian Encounters of North Korean Migrants and the South Protestant Church

Laavanya Kathiravelu
MIGRANT DUBAI
Building a Global City

Tatiana Matejskova and Marco Antonsich
GOVERNING THROUGH DIVERSITY
Migration Societies in Post-Multiculturalist Times

Fran Meissner
SOCIALISING WITH DIVERSITY
Making Sense of Urban Superdiversity

Monika Palmberger
HOW GENERATIONS REMEMBER
Contested Memories in Post-War Bosnia and Herzegovina

Maria Schiller
EUROPEAN CITIES, MUNICIPAL ORGANIZATIONS AND DIVERSITY
The New Politics of Difference

Junjia Ye
INEQUALITY IN THE GLOBAL CITY
Division of Labour and the Politics of Cosmopolitanism

Global Diversities
Series Standing Order ISBN 978–1–137–37750–0 (hardback) and
978–1–137–37751–7 (paperback)
(*outside North America only*)

You can receive future titles in this series as they are published by placing a standing order. Please contact your bookseller or, in case of difficulty, write to us at the address below with your name and address, the title of the series and one of the ISBNs quoted above.

Customer Services Department, Macmillan Distribution Ltd, Houndmills, Basingstoke, Hampshire RG21 6XS, England.

Atheist Secularism and its Discontents
A Comparative Study of Religion and Communism in Eurasia

Edited by

Tam T. T. Ngo
Research Fellow, Max Planck Institute for the Study of Religious and Ethnic Diversity, Germany

and

Justine B. Quijada
Assistant Professor of Religion, Wesleyan University, United States

Selection, introduction and editorial matter © Tam T. T. Ngo and Justine B. Quijada 2015
Individual chapters © Contributors 2015

All rights reserved. No reproduction, copy or transmission of this publication may be made without written permission.

No portion of this publication may be reproduced, copied or transmitted save with written permission or in accordance with the provisions of the Copyright, Designs and Patents Act 1988, or under the terms of any licence permitting limited copying issued by the Copyright Licensing Agency, Saffron House, 6–10 Kirby Street, London EC1N 8TS.

Any person who does any unauthorized act in relation to this publication may be liable to criminal prosecution and civil claims for damages.

The authors have asserted their rights to be identified as the authors of this work in accordance with the Copyright, Designs and Patents Act 1988.

First published 2015 by
PALGRAVE MACMILLAN

Palgrave Macmillan in the UK is an imprint of Macmillan Publishers Limited, registered in England, company number 785998, of Houndmills, Basingstoke, Hampshire RG21 6XS.

Palgrave Macmillan in the US is a division of St Martin's Press LLC, 175 Fifth Avenue, New York, NY 10010.

Palgrave Macmillan is the global academic imprint of the above companies and has companies and representatives throughout the world.

Palgrave® and Macmillan® are registered trademarks in the United States, the United Kingdom, Europe and other countries.

ISBN: 978–1–137–43837–9

This book is printed on paper suitable for recycling and made from fully managed and sustained forest sources. Logging, pulping and manufacturing processes are expected to conform to the environmental regulations of the country of origin.

A catalogue record for this book is available from the British Library.

A catalog record for this book is available from the Library of Congress.

Contents

Acknowledgments		vii
Notes on Contributors		viii
1	Introduction: Atheist Secularism and Its Discontents *Tam T. T. Ngo and Justine B. Quijada*	1

Part I Genealogies

2	God and the Vietnamese Revolution: Religious Organizations in the Emergence of Today's Vietnam *Jayne S. Werner*	29
3	The Socialist Interregnum and Buddhist Resurgence in Laos *Grant Evans*	54
4	Conflict and Coexistence of Church and State Authorities in (Post)Communist Poland *Agnieszka Pasieka*	70
5	Secularization without Secularism: The Political-Religious Configuration of Post-1989 China *Ji Zhe*	92
6	North Korea's Culture of Commemoration *Heonik Kwon*	112
7	Was Soviet Society Secular? Undoing Equations between Communism and Religion *Sonja Luehrmann*	134

Part II Creative Destruction

8	Apologetics of Religion and Science: Conversion Projects in Contemporary China *Dan Smyer Yu*	155
9	Perun vs Jesus Christ: Communism and the Emergence of Neo-paganism in the USSR *Victor A. Shnirelman*	173

10 Conversion to Be: The Christian Encounters of
   North Korean Migrants in Late Cold War Korea   190
   Jin-Heon Jung

11 The Role of Religious Art in Post-Communist Russia   210
   Clemena Antonova

12 Chinese Socialism and the Household Idiom of
   Religious Engagement   225
   Adam Yuet Chau

13 Awkward Secularity between Atheism and
   New Religiosity in Post-Soviet Kyrgyzstan   244
   Mathijs Pelkmans

References   256
Index   285

Acknowledgments

First and foremost we must thank the Max Planck Institute for the Study of Religious and Ethnic Diversity, and Peter van der Veer, Director of the Department of Religious Diversity, for supporting and funding the workshop: Religion and Communism: Comparative Perspectives, May 5–6, 2011, that gave rise to this volume. We would like to thank all the participants at the workshop, both those who have contributed chapters to this volume, and those who, for various reasons, have not, but whose comments shaped the conversation. Foremost among these are Chris Hann and Catherine Wanner, as well as Jualynne Dodson, Anca Sincan, Chenyang Kao, Torsten Lofstedt and Yuqin Huang. Our colleagues at the Institute provided much intellectual stimulation and support for which we are deeply grateful. We would particularly like to thank Jie Zhang, and all the staff at the Institute, who made running the workshop possible, as well as enjoyable.

In addition, Tam Ngo would like to thank Richard Madsen and Hue-Tam Ho-Tai for their helpful and insightful comments on the first draft of the introduction. Likewise, Justine Quijada would like to thank her colleagues at Wesleyan University, particularly Elizabeth MacAlister and Mary-Jane Rubenstein, for their comments on the introduction. Last but never least, she would like to thank her family: Roberto, Eva and Esme, for always being there for her.

Notes on Contributors

Clemena Antonova's research is undertaken at the intersection of art history and religious studies with a focus on Eastern Orthodox and Russian material. At present, she is working on her second book project, which analyzes aspects of the religious philosophy of the Russian thinker Pavel Florensky (1882–1937). She is a senior research associate at the Centre for Patristic and Byzantine Cultural Heritage at the Theology Faculty, Sofia University, Bulgaria, and the Religious Contributor on Orthodox Christianity for *Faithology.com*.

Adam Yuet Chau is University Senior Lecturer in the Anthropology of Modern China in the Department of East Asian Studies at the University of Cambridge, UK. He is the author of *Miraculous Response: Doing Popular Religion in Contemporary China* (2006) and editor of *Religion in Contemporary China: Revitalization and Innovation* (2011). He is interested in developing better ways of conceptualizing Chinese religious culture. One of his out-reach ambitions is to stop people from asking the question "How many religions are there in China?" He is currently working on book projects investigating the idiom of hosting (*zuozhu*) and forms of powerful writing ("text acts") in Chinese political and religious culture.

Grant Evans (1948–2014) was Senior Research Fellow in Anthropology at the École Française d'Extrême-Orient, Vientiane, Laos. For many years he was Professor of Anthropology at the University of Hong Kong. He has written widely on Laos including, *The Last Century of Lao Royalty: A Documentary History* (2011), *A Short History of Laos* (2003), *Politics of Ritual and Remembrance: Laos since 1975* (1998) *Red Brotherhood at War: Vietnam, Cambodia and Laos since 1975* (1990).

Jin-Heon Jung is a research fellow and the Seoul Project coordinator at the Max Planck Institute for the Study of Religious and Ethnic Diversity in Germany. His research interests focus on religion and nationalism in Korea, refugee migration and human rights, urban aspirations and political movements. He is an editor of *Building Noah's Ark for Refugees, Migrants, and Religious Communities* (2015) with Alexander Horstmann, and completing a monograph on North Korean migrants' Evangelical Encounters.

Ji Zhe is Associate Professor at INALCO (Institut National des Langues et Civilisations Orientales) in Paris, France, and an associated research fellow at GSRL (Groupe Sociétés, Religions, Laïcités). Ji's main study areas are religious modernity in China and contemporary evolutions of Buddhism in China and France. He edited a collective volume entitled *Religion, Éducation et Politique en Chine Moderne* (2011) and guest-edited with Vincent Goossaert a special issue of *Social Compass* on Buddhism in post-Mao China (2011).

Heonik Kwon is Senior Research Fellow in Social Science and distinguished research professor of Social Anthropology at Trinity College, University of Cambridge, United Kingdom. He has served as an external advisor to the Army of the Republic of Korea for its forensic anthropological taskforce as well as to South Korea's Truth and Reconciliation Commission. His work in Vietnam resulted in *After the Massacre* (2006, Geertz Prize) and *Ghosts of War in Vietnam* (2008, Kahin Prize), while his work in Korea has been published in *The Other Cold War* (2010) and *North Korea Beyond Charismatic Politics* (2012) with Byung-Ho Chung. He is currently completing a book on Korea's civil war experience seen in the context of family genealogical histories.

Sonja Luehrmann is Assistant Professor of Anthropology at Simon Fraser University in Vancouver, Canada. Drawing on ethnographic and archival methods, her research engages questions of human transformability. Her book *Secularism Soviet Style: Teaching Atheism and Religion in a Volga Republic* (2011) deals with Soviet atheist propaganda and post-Soviet religious revival in the multi-religious Volga region of Russia. Her forthcoming book *Religion in Secular Archives: Soviet Atheism and Historical Knowledge* deals with the methodological and epistemological problem of studying religious practice through the militantly secularist lens of Soviet-era archival documents.

Tam T. T. Ngo is a research fellow at the Max Planck Institute for the Study of Religious and Ethnic Diversity in Goettingen, Germany. Her work focuses on the relation between media and various forms of religiosity in Vietnam during the socialist and post-socialist eras. Since 2011, she has conducted two ethnographic projects; one on social memory of the 1979 Sino-Vietnamese Border War in China and Vietnam (known in English as the Third Indochina War), and another on Human Bones, Telepathy and the Politics of Reconciliation in Post-Revolutionary Vietnam. She is currently working on a book entitled *The New Way: Protestantism and the Hmong in Contemporary Vietnam*.

Agnieszka Pasieka is postdoctoral fellow at the Polish Academy of Sciences (2012–2015). Drawing on her sociological and anthropological training, her work focuses on religious and ethnic pluralism, church-state relations, and the role of religion in nationalist movements. She is the author of *Hierarchy and Pluralism: Living Religious Difference in Catholic Poland* (2015).

Mathijs Pelkmans is Associate Professor of Anthropology at the London School of Economics, United Kingdom. He has carried out extensive ethnographic research in Georgia and Kyrgyzstan since 1995. He is the author of *Defending the Border: Identity, Religion and Modernity in the Republic of Georgia* (2006) and editor of *Conversion after Socialism: Disruptions, Modernisms, and Technologies of Faith in the Former Soviet Union* (2009) and *Ethnographies of Doubt: Faith and Uncertainty in Contemporary Societies* (2013).

Justine B. Quijada is an assistant professor in the Department of Religion, Wesleyan University, United States, where she teaches on secularism, shamanism and the social scientific study of religion. Her work focuses on religious revival in the Republic of Buryatia, Russian Federation. She is currently completing a book manuscript entitled *Opening the Roads: History through Ritual in Post-Soviet Buryatia*.

Victor A. Shnirelman is a senior research fellow at the Institute of Ethnology and Anthropology at the Russian Academy of Sciences, Russia. He is one of the leading Russian anthropologists specializing in the politics of ethnicity, nationalism, race discourses, and social memory in Soviet and post-Soviet Russia and the former Soviet republics – newly independent states. His books in English include: *Who Gets the Past? Competition for Ancestors among Non-Russian Intellectuals in Russia* (1996); *The Value of the Past: Myths, Identity and Politics in Transcaucasia* (2001); *The Myth of the Khazars and Intellectual Antisemitism in Russia, 1970s–1990s* (2002). His recent two-volume book in Russian deals with the ideology and practice of the "new racism."

Jayne S. Werner is a research scholar at the Weatherhead East Asian Institute, Columbia University, and Professor Emerita of Political Science at Long Island University, both United States. She is the editor of *Sources of Vietnamese Tradition*, with John Whitmore and George Dutton (2012). She specializes in Southeast Asian politics, history and culture, with a specific focus on Vietnam's political, social and cultural change from the colonial period up to the present. She has written on the history and politics of the Cao Dai, gender and the family, the Vietnam War, religion and politics, state-society relations and the politics of reform (Doi Moi).

Dan Smyer Yu is Distinguish Professor and Founding Director of the Center for Trans-Himalayan Studies at Yunnan Minzu University and a core member of the Transregional Research Network (CETREN) at the University of Göttingen. Prior to this faculty appointment he was a research group leader at Max Planck Institute for Religious and Ethnic Diversity and a New Millennium Scholar at Minzu University of China. He is the author of *The Spread of Tibetan Buddhism in China: Charisma, Money, Enlightenment* (2011) and *Mindscaping the Landscape of Tibet: Place, Memorability, Eco-aesthetics* (2015). His current research interests are religion and ecology, landscape and emotionality, transboundary state effects, hydraulic politics, climate change and heritage preservation, Buddhism and peacebuilding, and comparative studies of Eurasian secularisms.

1
Introduction: Atheist Secularism and Its Discontents

Tam T. T. Ngo and Justine B. Quijada

Twenty years ago, a poor peasant who lives about 30 kilometers west of Hanoi survived a strange illness that almost killed her. Since then, she claimed that every night in her dreams she met Uncle Ho, who taught her "the way of Ho Chi Minh". When she woke up, she wrote down these teachings, using a popular Vietnamese traditional poem form. Very soon, a growing crowd began to gather around her, honoring her as the Master (Thầy), and seeking healing and moral teaching. Such was the birth of the Ho Chi Minh religion. Today, the Ho Chi Minh religion has thousands of followers in thirteen provinces in North, Central and South Vietnam. Followers of this religion worship Uncle Ho as the "Jade Buddha of the Nation" (Ngọc Phật Nước Nam) and follow the teachings in the "Book of Prophecies", a compilation of the Master's poems. A bronze statue of Ho Chi Minh is venerated in the halls of the religion's main temples, which are adorned with the national flag of Vietnam and the communist hammer-and-sickle flags. Once initiated into the religion, followers are required to replace ancestral and Buddhist altars in their home with a Ho Chi Minh altar, similar to the decorations in the temples. Ritually, the religion has adopted all national and communist holidays, such as Independence Day (September 2), Reunification Day (of north and south vietnam, April 30), International Labor Day (May 1) and the annual commemoration of war casualties (July 27), as their own celebrations. On some of these occasions, followers in different places organize themselves into units and hold processions on the street, or to the Ho Chi Minh Mausoleum in Hanoi, using a typical socialist style of processions such as "reporting achievement to uncle Ho".

Vietnamese government authorities have become alarmed by the movement and want to suppress it. The problem is, however, it is not easy to suppress a popular movement whose followers do exactly what the state has told them to do. For the last four decades, Ho Chi Minh has been venerated by the state as the founding father of the nation. A mausoleum was built for him, government offices venerate his statues, people were encouraged to worship his pictures in their home, his thoughts on virtually all matters of life and politics were cited the way Christians cite bible verses. Ho Chi Minh's home village became a popular pilgrim destination, and his biography is sanitized of any human and worldly details. His morality is promoted as the model for all national citizens to follow. In short, he was made a god in the religion of Vietnamese nationalism. This puts the state in an awkward position, since the members of the Ho Chi Minh religion are ostensibly doing exactly what the state wants them to. However, their apotheosis of a political leader reveals the contradictions in the state's own tactics. The state has turned to denouncing the movement for abusing the name of the nation's father to lure and exploit the masses into violating Vietnamese religious laws. Lately, the government's headache intensified when followers formally invited different government officials to join them in celebration of "Uncle Ho's" ritual occasions.

What is remarkable about this example is that it is really not that remarkable. Despite the widespread perception that communism and atheism are inseparable, throughout the communist and post-communist world, religious and political imaginaries are intimately intertwined. In China, Mao's mangos became political relics (Chau, 2010). On the steppes of Siberia, Buryat Buddhists explain the 1937 purges as a result of Stalin's karmic debts (Humphrey, 2002b). In contrast, shamans in Siberia explain their shamanic callings as a genetic inheritance (Quijada, 2009), Buddhists use forensic analysis to confirm miracles (Quijada, 2012), and in Moscow faith healers wear white lab coats and wield machines that produce aura analyses (Lindquist, 2006), showing that atheist scientific forms have migrated into religious practices. And yet, atheism was central to communist ideology, so central that Smolkin-Rothrock, for example, has argued that one of the pivotal moments in the USSR's collapse was the decision to officially celebrate the 1000 year anniversary of Christianity in Russia.[1] While this may seem like a contradiction, in fact, it is precisely *because* atheism was so central to the communist project that atheism's others, superstition and religion, were essential to the communist experience.

What is surprising instead is that it has taken so long to come to this realization. The past twenty years have produced a considerable amount of scholarship on what appeared to be a florescence of religion after the fall of the Soviet Union. The result is a rich tapestry of data that shows the intimate intertwining of religious practices and communist governance, complicating Cold War understandings of communism.[2]

The end of the Soviet Union, which occurred at the same time as transformative economic reform in China, was a socio-political watershed moment. The Cold War was over in practice, but the interpretive frameworks of the Cold War continued, and still continue, to influence scholarship about these territories. It is time to reassess what the past twenty years have taught us about the relationship between religion and communism, and leave behind, once and for all, the ideological assumptions of Cold War scholarship (see also Rogers, 2005). Once we do so, it becomes clear that state-sponsored atheism is best understood as one variant of the global experience of secularism.

We are not alone in viewing Soviet state-sponsored atheism as a form of secularism. Catherine Wanner (2007) and Sonja Luehrmann (2011b), for example, have both explored Ukrainian and Russian state atheism specifically as a form of secularism through detailed and focused case studies. Comparative studies have also treated the Soviet experience as a form of secularism in Russia and the Ukraine (Wanner, 2012), and Central Asia (Hann and Pelkmans, 2009). The research on religion under and after communism by the Max Planck Institute for Social Anthropology under the direction of C. M. Hann has produced a rich array of case studies in the only context that bridges both Eastern European and Asian experiences of communism, but the theoretical framework of these studies focus more on civil society and economic transformation than on secularism (Hann, 2000; 2006; 2010a; 2010b). While studies of the former Soviet Union tend to be limited to the temporal and geographic boundaries of the Soviet experience, studies of secularism in China, in contrast, locate secularization within the historical experience of colonialism and modernization, underplaying the peculiarities of communist secularism (Mayfair Yang, 2008; Goossaert and Palmer, 2011). The authors in this volume draw on the insights of all these authors, attempting to synthesize these approaches.

The intertwined relationship of communism and religion deserves our attention not only because it promises to offer greater insight into communism as a political system, but because it promises to offer greater insight into secularism as a global phenomenon. Beginning with Casanova (1994) there has been an ever-growing body of literature about secularism, challenging the Weberian assumptions that dominated 20th Century social science. A new body of literature, taking up Asad's call to reconsider secularism (2003) has produced a vibrant body of work that explores secularism as a cultural system in its own right, rather than as merely a backdrop for political action, defined by the absence of religion (see for examples Mack, 2009; Warner et al., 2010; Calhoun et al., 2011a).³

As Calhoun et al. put it, secularism "is not in itself neutral. Secularism should be seen as a presence" (2011b, p. 5). Secular values, such as the separation of church and state, or religious freedom as a human right, are increasingly shown to be grounded in very Western and Protestant conceptions of what religion is and does. Mahmood (2006) for example, through an analysis of the International Religious Freedom Act, shows how secular practices presume and thereby create certain kinds of religious subjectivities as normative.

This new research has presented compelling new perspectives that have deeply influenced all the contributors in this volume. We argue, however, that in order to fully see secularism's "presence" as a global, rather than a Western phenomenon, we must bring the communist experience into the picture. As Calhoun et al. note, the ideology of secularism has shaped the academic study of it, producing theoretical blind spots that we are only now beginning to fill (2011b, p. 4). Whether we choose to define secularism philosophically as framing religious belief and practice, as Charles Taylor does (2007), or anthropologically as a project of power in the Foucauldian sense, as Talal Asad (2003) does, secularism is a state of being that exists primarily in the West, and that is inextricably linked to democracy and modernity. Theories of "our" secular age have, until recently, been limited to the historical experience of Western Christianity, leaving large parts of the Christian world (including Eastern Christianity) and other religions out of the picture entirely. There are good reasons for this. Secularism, as it is conventionally understood, grew out of the European Reformation and the Enlightenment, and as a result Protestant ideas are fundamental to its logic. Most notably, Western post-Enlightenment secularism privileges the idea that religion ought to be about belief, rendering practices secondary. This assumption becomes less and less applicable, the further secularism spreads from its European point of origin, and like its alter-ego "religion", colonial and communist empire-building projects have spread secularism around the globe. Or at least this is how the dominant narrative of secularism would have us understand the process. However, both the European Reformation and the Enlightenment were, to a large degree, a response to the changing horizons of European expansion and colonialism. The idea of "religion" as an abstract concept describing an area of human endeavor (rather than Christian truth, for example) developed as much out of the colonial encounter as out of the

Protestant Reformation. Secularism, as an ideology that posits that some spheres of life should be separate from religion, requires that religion be defined as a field of human endeavor, rather than as truth. "Belief" becomes the privileged form of religion out of a comparative project that posits "our belief" as superior to "your (Catholic/heathen) practice". Therefore, we argue, not only is secularism a global phenomenon now, it has been one since the very beginning.

Not surprisingly, a considerable amount of new critical research is focused on one of the fault-lines of Western secularism: the presence of Islam in Western Europe (Göle, 2006; Fernando, 2010; Roy, 2007; Al-Azmeh, 1993; Lewis, 1993; Goody, 2004), while the other focuses on states such as Turkey (Çınar, 2005) or India (Madan, 1998), where secular principles are perceived to have been imposed on non-secular subjects either by modernizing reformers or colonial powers (Göle, 2008; Nandy, 1988; Tambar, 2009). This work is important and extremely valuable, but it risks re-inscribing the ideological formations that underpin secularism, and paints Islam as its only "other", a particularly troubling conceptualization, because of all religious practices, Islam most clearly matches a secular definition of religion as being about belief. To avoid this mistake a number of scholars have pursued an "interactionist" approach to study how secular principles have evolved in non-Western contexts (Van der Veer, 2001; Chatterjee, 2006; Bhargava, 2010). Secularism presumes that religion ought to be a form of belief, but many forms of religious practice cannot or should not productively be considered forms of "belief". What of religions that foreground practice and that posit multiple-inflected selves? Clearly, "religion" is a concept that developed out of imperial projects of knowledge production (Asad, 1993; Smith, 1998; Van der Veer, 2001; Gottschalk, 2013). Local concepts that are sometimes translated as "religion", like *dharma* or *jiao* (teaching) have connotations that are quite different from "universal religion". If the world ever was moving towards increasing secularism, the resurgence of public religion, in radically new forms, in recent years has proven that we need a more nuanced understanding, a new history if you will, of secularism. We want to enter into this debate by bringing a previously unconsidered geographical area to the table: the so-called Second World of the former and current communist countries. We contend that a new comparative understanding of secularism cannot be generated without attention to Western secularism's twin: state-sponsored atheist secularism.

Regardless of its recently burgeoning growth, the scholarship on secularization and secularism until today still largely remains within the Western world. For instance, while Casanova (1994) does examine the role of Catholicism in the transformation of Poland into a postcommunist society, his comparative work remains entirely within the Western, Christian world. The same is true for another major contribution to the study of secularism by the philosopher Charles Taylor. In his seminal book *A Secular Age*, Taylor (2007) explicitly limits his analysis to Western Europe and the USA. As Chris Hann (2010a) observes, very little effort has been expended on studying secularism in East Asia, which, drawing on non-Western roots, is quite different from the patterns of European history. We indeed know very little about how older political traditions that have come to be seen as secularism shaped the socialist experience. There have recently been some attempts in historical sociology to make comparisons between Western and non-Western secularisms by focusing on imperialism. For instance, Peter Van der Veer (2001) suggests that the project of European modernity should be understood as part of what he has called "interactional history". That is to say that the project of modernity, with all of its revolutionary ideas of nation, equality, citizenship, democracy and rights, developed not only in Atlantic interactions between the United States and Europe, but also in interactions with Asian and African societies as they came within the orbit of imperial expansion. Instead of the oft-assumed *universalism* of the Enlightenment, he proposes to look at the *universalization* of ideas that emerges from a history of interactions. Enlightened notions of rationality and progress, which are intimately intertwined with secularism, are not simply invented in Europe and accepted elsewhere, but are both produced and spread through the expansion of European power. Examining secularism in India and China, for instance, uncovers some of the peculiarities of this universalization by showing how it is inserted into different historical trajectories in these societies (Van der Veer, 2011). While Van der Veer focuses on imperial encounters, what is missing from his, and other discussions, is the comparative analysis of one of the major transformative international movements of the 20th Century: Communism.

This void is a product of the Cold War and its discursive effects (Chari and Verdery, 2009). During the Cold War the secular West, and particularly America, was figured as a champion of religious freedom in contrast to the repressive atheism of communist states (Grimshaw, 2011). This role might seem contradictory for a secular state, but is in fact, the logical result of the way in which secular discourse defines religion as a matter of privatized and internalized belief. This type of individualized and privatized religion is not only compatible with, but is best protected by a separation of church and state. Martin Luther argued for such a separation, in the interest of protecting religious faith, as early as 1523 (Luther, 1991). As the enlightenment progressed, however, internal belief came to be understood as separate and exempted from the kind of rational, logical debate that should characterize the public sphere of politics and government (Calhoun et al., 2011b, p. 7). Within the growing discourse of Western secularism, the sphere of private belief needed to be protected from politics, just as politics needed to be protected from irrational private belief. Marx's approach to secularism developed from this same ideological ground, accepting the definition of religion as privatized belief, with all that this entailed, but resisting the argument that this belief could be safely bracketed from politics.[4] By protecting religion through the separation of church and state, the United States became the champion of religious freedom. In contrast, it was a popular Cold War argument that Communism was "like a religion". This statement reveals the post-Enlightenment assumption that religion is irrational, and therefore best kept out of the political sphere, an assumption that reveals the shared philosophical roots of liberal and communist politics. Within Cold War discourse, communism was liberal secularism's evil twin, which, like fascism, blurred the appropriate boundaries between "irrational belief", which belonged in the private conscience of the individual, and "rational statecraft" which is the realm of political debate.

However, both liberal secularism and communist atheism are ideal-typical political visions. In practice, both secular and atheist states invoke ideas about transcendent power, creating slippages that disturb the neat division between "rational statecraft" and "irrational religion". The existence of state-sponsored atheist secularism within the parameters of the Cold War has transformed not only the religious practices of those living under atheist regimes, but the political valence of religion around the globe. For example, the Cold War has produced a militant anti-communism in dominant forms of both Catholicism and Protestantism that continues to inflect international politics and debates over the freedom of religion as a universal human right. A closer examination of the relationship between communism and religion has the potential to contribute significantly to the debate on secularism and religion as a global phenomenon.

Assertions and assumptions

State-sponsored atheist secularism, a political project that dominated half the globe for most of the 20th Century, is not usually considered a form of secularism because of the prevailing discourse about religion in Communist states. This discourse rests on three assertions: Religious practice was forcibly repressed by communist regimes, communist ideology can be considered akin to a religion, and communist nationality politics turned religious practice into an expression of ethno-national identity. A close examination of the realities of religious life in communist countries complicates these assumptions, revealing them to be not so much wrong, but merely limited and limiting. These generalizations originally arose to help make sense of a flood of social changes, but now, like most simplifications, they obscure more than they reveal, and it is time to revise them.

Assumption #1: Communism repressed religion

The prevailing scholarly narrative about secularism has omitted communist varieties of secularism in large part because of the assumption that communist states repressed religious practice. If Western secularism seeks to separate church and state, and relegate religion to the private sphere, then Communism seeks to eradicate religion completely. This view is not wrong so much as incomplete and insufficient. It takes communist ideology at face value, rather than examining the historical facts, and ignores the shared ideological heritage of the Enlightenment that produced both Western secularism and its communist counterpart.

In theory, Marx posited that religion, the "opium of the people", was fundamentally incompatible with communism. Following this party line, Communist party leaders from Lenin to Mao Ze Dong declared that religion would be eradicated. None succeeded, and most expended far less effort and resources in the attempt than might be expected given the ideological importance of atheism. In practice, as the authors in this volume show, communist parties from Poland to Vietnam repressed, but also negotiated with, accommodated and sought to co-opt and control religious institutions. We agree with Hann (2010a) that while atheism was everywhere propagated as an integral part of Marxist-Leninist-Maoist ideology, we can find hardly any communist countries in which all religions were formally abolished. Even the most extreme attempts, the Cultural Revolutions of Stalin and Mao, and Cambodia under Pol Pot, were short lived and could not be sustained in the long-term. Even today, in China and Vietnam, the state condemns most popular practices as "feudal superstition" while giving legal recognition to some form of Christianity and Buddhism to function, albeit under strict controls. Many states in the communist world have tried to replace religious rituals with secular rituals, but we are aware of only few cases of success (such as the *Jugendweihe* in Eastern Germany by Peperkamp (2010), and Rajtar (2010)). In other cases, including that discussed by Shnirelman in this volume, secular rituals inadvertently promoted religious forms of practice. The chief feature of socialist secularization, as Hann (2010a) asserts, was the state's aggressive propagation of scientific atheism, but the degree to which this can be considered to be successful, and how that success would even be measured, remains a complicated question (Peperkamp, 2010; Husband, 1998; 2000; Powell, 1975; Young, 1997). Smolkin-Rothrock (2010) in fact, asserts that in the later years of the Soviet Union anti-religious activists attempted to create secular rituals because they came to realize just how unsuccessful attempts to promote scientific atheism had been.

Under conditions of suppression and state co-optation, practitioners often found ways to circumvent officially recognized forms of religion, and as a result "popular" religion, freed of institutional control, often flourished (Dragadze, 1993; See Wanner, 2012; Chau, 2005 for excellent examples). As Peris (1998) and Husband (2000) argue, in Russia, social reforms were far more effective in changing people's behavior than anti-religious propaganda ever was. More importantly, this assumption views power as a top-down repressive force. Since Foucault, however, we have come to see power as a creative force. Foucault has argued that power "doesn't only weigh on us as a force that says no; it also traverses and produces things, it induces pleasure, forms knowledge, produces discourse" (1984, p. 61). Anti-religious repression throughout the communist world was, as Dan Smyer Yu phrased it in his contribution to this volume, destructively creative. State-building efforts targeted major religions because these were rival institutions, but religious practices are not limited to merely what people do inside state-recognized (or alternately, un-registered opposition) churches. Religious practice has always been a slippery target, escaping and eliding the eye of the state and analyst alike.

As Werner, Grant, Pasieka, Shnirelman, Chau, Zhe and Smyer Yu (all this volume) show, in order to establish itself as the dominant national ideology in Asian and Eastern European countries, communism regulated the discourses, practices and institutionalization of atheist secularism in a way that absorbed rather than excluded religion as a presence within the public sphere. Various forms of religious practices, knowledges, and movements were monitored and utilized to serve a public demonstration of what the replacement of religion (communism) would look like. Communist states established their authority and legitimation through the controlled inclusion of religions and appear-like-religion movements in the public sphere. Other forms of practices, that might be considered religious, or superstitious, or examples of "folk culture" escaped the eye of the state and flourished in margins, supplanting institutionalized religious practice, sometimes becoming state-sanctioned forms of ritual. Rather than expressing "belief" many of these practices persist despite, or perhaps as forums to express doubt, skepticism and creative re-appropriation of tradition. Some bypass the question of belief altogether. Although external observers and internal participants alike may debate the intentionality of participants in state-sponsored rituals, and debate the "authenticity" and "sincerity" of these rituals, we must be careful not to fall into a very secularized definition of religion as "being about private belief", or we too risk seeing religion only as the communist state did. As the chapters of this volume show, it is time to rethink communist repression, and ask what forms of religious activity the exercise of state power created.

Assumption #2: Communist ideology is like a religion

A common argument in the existing literature is that religious practices provide an alternative modernity and moral structure with which to counter either the communist state or the "ideological vacuum" of the post-communist society. This argument has many forms, but all rest on the presumption that post-communist religion fills a need previously filled by communist ideology. For example, in a project that looks at religion in post-socialist societies, Chris Hann (2010a, p. 9) argues that modernity was achieved under socialism in the Soviet Union and most other socialist states. In his view, the ending of socialism has made some people in these societies turn to what they perceived to be modern forms of religion. Second, according to Hann (2010a, p. 10), across Eurasia, a shift away from the centralized political economy of socialism to the principle of the market makes it very hard for societies to find a common moral foundation on which to resist and overcome the anomie of the market. Socialist aspirations to forge a new, secular, unitary moral order clearly failed. In the wake of this failure, the disorder of the present phase has presented unprecedented short-term opportunities for faith communities of all kinds.

The argument that post-communist religious practice fills an "ideological vacuum" replicates communist ideology that posits religion and ideology as filling the same function. Marxism defined religion as an ideology, a false set of beliefs explaining the world, a set of beliefs that would be replaced with scientific atheist truth. Religion was thereby discursively located in the past, and negatively paralleled to the communist ideology that would herald a utopian future. Religion and communism filled the same social function, and one would replace the other. When post-Soviet subjects assert that religion fills the "ideological vacuum" left by the fall of the Soviet Union, or the abdication of socialist economic policy, they are merely flipping the argument that had been made by Communist states, that scientific atheism would replace religious belief. Scholars, however, cannot accept this assertion uncritically.

Just as recent literature has conceptualized Western secularism as a project, so too should state-sponsored atheist secularism be considered a project. As such, state-sponsored atheism should be considered a work-in-progress rather than a monolithic ideology whose collapse would produce a "vacuum". In all post-socialist societies, personal memoirs and recently made available historical documents show anything but a picture of a successful socialist modernity, a transformation "from underdeveloped agrarian economies into industrial, scientifically advanced economies" (Hann, 2010a, p. 8). It was exactly the fact that these societies had not fully achieved socialism that provided the legitimation for relentless state-run social engineering projects and political campaigns that deeply transformed citizens' lifestyles, among them the campaign to eradicate religion and superstition. The replacement theory that Hann advocates here also does not explain how religions survived during the communist period and whence their modern forms in the post-socialist period came.

What makes these arguments sound compelling is that they are often offered by post-communist religious practitioners. How can we discount the testimony of our ethnographic interlocutors? We cannot. However, when Ukrainian evangelicals (Wanner, 2007), members of Protestant House Churches (Fenggang Yang, 2005; Bays, 2003; Smyer Yu this volume) and Buddhist temples in China (Fisher, 2008) and Buryatia (Quijada, 2009) state that religion provides an alternative ideology to communism, we must read this statement not as theory but as a political statement made in a particular political context. We must read it as a critique that stems from within the hegemonic discourse of the socialist modernist project. Communist ideology defined religion as a false ideology destined to be replaced by atheist truth. Within this ideology, scientific atheism is figured as progressive and modern, and bringing this awareness to the "backward" masses justified state intervention, and often, state violence. Communist ideology defined religion as its antithesis, its counter-ideology, and this understanding of religion remains hegemonic in the popular consciousness. We must revisit the statements of post-communist believers within the context of this history.

Several contributors to this volume reexamine the ways in which communist ideology and religion are discursively constructed to resemble each other, both by the state and by believers. Dan Smyer Yu argues most convincingly that communism should be considered "religionish", Jin-Heon Jung shows how North Korean Christian converts see Christianity as comparable to North Korean Juche ideology, and Victor Shnirelman explores the slippery slope from state-sponsored folklore into neo-paganism, implying that the divide between state ideology into religion is easily bridged. Both Heonik Kwon and Ji Zhe's chapters also examine state rituals that evoke religious moods and motivations in the interest of state power, but their arguments serve more to parallel communist and liberal democratic forms of governance than to support the view that communism should be treated as a religion. Sonja Luehrmann, who tackles the question head on in her chapter, convincingly argues that communism and religion represent completely different forms of transcendence, but at the same time her data reveals productive similarities in the way both religion and communism enable a transformation in subjectivity through self-disciplining practices, a theme that can also be found in Jung's chapter. Adam Chau argues that communism is more like a religion than the practices scholars usually call "religion" and suggests that "religion" is ultimately an unproductive way of thinking about ritual and secularization in China. Pelkmans argues that secularization in Central Asia during the Soviet period is more far-reaching than usually considered, not because religion has not revived there, but rather because secular ideas about what constitutes "appropriate" forms of religion continue to be defined by Soviet secularist values. In contrast to all of these, Ji Zhe, in his critique of the current regime in the People's Republic of China, argues that contemporary Chinese communism is a form of secularization without secularism, meaning that it has lost all ideological coherence in favor of the realpolitik of maintaining power. The implication of this argument, of course, is that communism, and by extension, politics, ought to be something one can believe in.

Assumption #3: Religion in currently and former Communist countries is an expression of ethno-national identity

Another strong theme that runs throughout all the chapters is the enduring strength of the nation-state form. Despite the predominance of internationalism in Communist rhetoric, the secular project, like the communist project, most often took the political form that dominated the 20th Century: that of the nation. Much of the existing literature on religious movements in communist and post-communist countries focuses on the relationship between religion and ethno-national identity. Within this paradigm, religious practice is presented as an expression of ethno-national identity set in opposition to the secular atheist state. This assertion often links the repression of ethno-nationalism to the repression of religious practices. This argument is far more prevalent in the literature on the religious revival in the countries of the former Soviet Union, but finds a welcome echo in the current rejection of Christian conversion among ethnic minorities or acceptance of "traditional" religions by Asian communist governments, such as Laos and Vietnam (Ngo, 2009). In the case of the Soviet Union, post-1989 analysts quickly realized that despite intense centralizing efforts, Soviet nationality policies fostered the very national identities that the regime sought to have "wither away" (Suny, 1993; Slezkine, 1996; Martin, 2001; Hirsch, 2005). However, because the Soviet government had co-opted so many of the potential sources of national and ethno-national imaginaries through stylized demands for a "national costume", "national literature" or "national arts", religion became the one area of pre-Soviet life where ethno-national identity could be found free of Soviet influence. Or at least such was the widespread perception of the post-Soviet religious boom. As with the other two assumptions, this narrative is not so much wrong, as incomplete. It presumes a false separation between state secularism and ethno-national religion rather than a co-constitutive relationship and is therefore in need of re-evaluation.

The nation-state form continues to be fundamentally important to religion in communist and formerly communist countries, but ethno-national identities are only one element of this. More important is the link between secularism and state-building. For it is in the national form that post-Soviet religion takes that we see the fundamental relationship between secularism and nationalism. As Asad states:

> Secularism is not simply an intellectual answer to a question about enduring social peace and toleration. It is an enactment by which a political medium (representation of citizenship) redefines and

transcends particular and differentiating practices of the self that are articulated through class, gender and religion. (2003, p. 5)

Processes of state formation are, however, decidedly different from one society to the next. The separation of church and state in the United States enabled religious dissenters to practice their religion freely without interference of the state and made a Tocquevillean civil society possible. Forms of church-state separation are quite different in Western European societies, such as Britain, France, Holland and Germany (Casanova, 1994).

Again, these histories are a far cry from what happened under communism. Communism did not allow a separation of church and state, since the state sought to occupy all social space. State sponsored atheism and the atheist rituals through which it was enacted were central to transcending local identities in the creation of a greater communist society. Communist secularism was crucial to communist state-building, and therefore secularism remains crucial to nation-building in the post-Soviet period (see Pelkmans, Shnirelman and Chau this volume). When religious forms could be linked to anti-colonial state-building projects, they were often co-opted or re-imagined as "national culture". Where religious practices undermined these projects, they were denounced as dangerous foreign influences (Wanner, 2007; Ngo, 2010; 2011) or internally subversive superstitions (see e.g. Chau, 2005; Kaplonski, 2008). The chapters in this volume suggest that ethno-national forms of religious practice must be considered in relationship to state-building projects. These state-building processes are constitutive of and determine the form and shape of communist and post-communist ethno-national identities, which are then embodied in religious practices.

These three assumptions, that communism repressed religion, that communism is like a religion, and that post-communist religion is an expression of ethno-national identity, have to date determined the narratives that are available for understanding the varieties of religious practice in current and formerly communist countries. This discourse was formed under the ideological conditions of the Cold War, and came to fruition in the early 1990s, immediately after the collapse of the Soviet Union. In an immediate response to enormous social change, these assertions productively served to orient scholarship, but they are based on a simple view of power as repressive rather than productive, and uncritically adopted certain presumptions from the Cold War, most notably, the assumption that religion and communism were separate and in opposition, rather than co-constitutive phenomena. Since then, there has been a veritable flood of new research, both historical and ethnographic, on religious practices in the communist and formerly communist world, and a host of social, political and economic changes in these same countries. It is time to re-evaluate and complicate this paradigm.

Atheist secularism as historical project

It is our contention that state-sponsored atheism, which developed from the historical roots of the European Enlightenment, is a form of secularism and produced forms of secularization. Just as we have come to see modernity not as a single monolithic teleology, but rather a variety of local modernities (Eisenstadt, 2000), we should view secularism not as a monolithic teleology but rather as a variety of local secularisms, each a local form produced through the interaction between religious practices, political reform and state-building. It is our hope that this volume sparks a conversation that will re-evaluate the relationship between religion and communism, and that this re-evaluation will, in turn, provide new perspectives for research on secularism.

The study of secularization and secularism seemed almost dead in the 1980s and 1990s, but it has been revived with a vengeance in the last decade as an almost natural counterpoint to the study of "religious revival", political religion and so-called fundamentalism, of which the Chicago Project on Fundamentalism is probably the best example.[5] While the Fundamentalism project still had a sense that fundamentalism was a violently reactionary response to the secularization of the world, subsequent scholarship has developed new perspectives on religion and secularization, particularly through the Social Science Research Council's The Immanent Frame project (see above).

Jose Casanova began the process of dismantling the secularization thesis with his now classic book *Public Religion in the Modern World* (1994). He argued that the three propositions of the secularization thesis – namely, the decline of religious beliefs, the privatization of religion, and the differentiation of secular spheres and their emancipation from religion – should be looked at separately in a comparative analysis. He comes to the conclusion that comparative historical analysis allows one to get away from the dominant stereotypes about the United States and Europe and to open a space for further sociological inquiry into multiple patterns of fusion and differentiation of the religious and the secular across societies and religions. This means moving away from teleological understandings of modernization. Or perhaps better, it means questioning that telos by recognizing its multiplicity and its contradictions. Casanova's intervention can be understood as building on the Weberian project of comparative and historical sociology but going beyond it by avoiding the reduction of civilizations to essences that can be compared, thereby avoiding a Hegelian evaluation in terms of "lack" or "deficit" in the world-historical process of modernization and rationalization.

Recently, in his effort to conceptualize the relationship between Christianity and the state in Asia, Bryan Turner (2009) expands his scope of analysis to communist secularization. Secularization, according to Turner, has developed into two powerful forms; secular liberalism and the rise of consumerism in the West and communist secularization in the Soviet Union and Asia, especially in China and Vietnam. As Turner sees it, liberal secularization was the unintended outcome of modernization, whereas communist secularization was the consequence of state policies. In a sense, Turner argues, both forms of secularization may have now come to an end and we are now confronted instead with two forms of re-sacralization.

Turner's argument mistakenly equates secularization as societal process with secularism as a political project. Moreover, regardless of being aided by modernization or by state policies, this historical process seems to be clearly delineable with a beginning and an end: the disenchantment and the re-sacralization of the societies in question. However, liberal secularism in the West is less of an "unintended consequence" of modernization than Turner thinks. Recently, for example, Çinar et al. (2012, p. 8) argue that secularism in India, Turkey, Egypt and Lebanon legitimizes itself by way of limited inclusion of religion in the public sphere. Rather than a total exclusion or suppression of religion from political life, secular states in these countries exerted their control over the production and framing of religion in ways that justify the existence and hegemony of secularism. Çinar et al. show that contrary to the assumption that secularism replaces religion, secularism instead produces, redefines and controls religion in order to establish itself as the norm. A similar process can be observed in Russia, China, Vietnam, Laos and elsewhere in the communist and post-communist world.

In this volume, however, we insist that it is necessary to distinguish between secularization as a process and secularism as a project (Casanova, 2009). Doing so reveals that both Western secularism and communism shared ideological presumptions and a teleology of modernization, while at the same time allowing us to see the productive differences in how these shared ideologies were implemented under different local conditions. As Sullivan (2005) argues, any state engaged in defining and recognizing religion, whether to restrict it or to protect it, asserts control over religious practice. In her analysis of *Warren v. Boca Raton*, Sullivan convincingly demonstrates that the dominant secular view of religion as internal belief is so pervasive in the United States court system that it produces forms of religious repression akin to those seen in communist countries. The mechanisms by which the state recognizes, defines and delimits forms of religious practice may be different, but the underlying logics are not.

Modernization theory, an academic reflection of Western and colonial political practice, saw secularization as part of modernization, an inevitable result of the process of societal development. The secularization theory has three propositions – namely, the decline of religious beliefs, the privatization of religion, and the differentiation of secular spheres and their emancipation from religion. In other words, modernization of the economy and the state bring about the secularization of society. In theory, this does not require political intervention, unless one assumes that religious forces form an obstacle to modernization. However, the discursive construction of religion as potentially anti-modern, shared by both Western secularism and communism, opens the door to state violence.

Communist ideology shares a similar vision of modernity, but rejects gradual evolution and advocates speeding up the process of modernization through revolution. Communist activists intended to forcefully liberate those people who are perceived to be under the sway of religion. Moreover, Marxism defined religion as a smokescreen that enables the ruling classes to maintain their power, and as such, religion was a direct threat to the state's modernizing project. Despite Marx's predictions, communism took power in predominantly agrarian societies where the process of privatizing religion had not or not yet occurred. Since communist ideology presumed that religion was a form of privatized belief, communist revolutionaries sought to change these agrarian societies, and thus had to attack religion. Within a communist teleology, this project is a central part of the entire transition from feudal society to a modern society. They sought to transform societies based on kinship and community into a society that is structured around classes, so that the communist revolution through class struggle could continue. Since Eastern European and Asian societies did not have the expected class divisions prior to communism, class had to be created before it could be abolished.

Secularism as a project is carried by political actors (intellectuals, social movements and the state) who want to actively limit the role of religion in society, control it or even radically remove it. In the communist world, secularism has been a forceful ideology when carried by political movements, like the Communist Party, that capture both the imagination and the means to mobilize social energies. The socialization of secular values surely has been of paramount importance for secularist projects in communist states, but not only there. Education is key to secularization, both communist and Western. In the Soviet Union, legal freedom of religion was limited to adults, and the religious education of minors was illegal. State education became the medium through which young people learned that religion is backward and that communism is progressive. Ongoing struggles over the role of religion in public schools throughout Europe and North America reveal the importance of public secular education to state-building projects.

However, much of the struggle between religious movements and secular movements is about finding possibilities for early socialization outside of state schools. The production of youth culture is a particularly important site for constructing and contesting secularism. The communist party in both Europe and Asia was very successful at promoting youth culture with youth unions, Pioneers, the Komsomol and so forth, all of which have their own rituals. These communist youth movements have their parallels in the United States as well, with Boy and Girl Scout movements. Religions have their own youth movements, often global in scale, linking religious groups in Western secular countries to those in communist or previously communist ones. In communist countries religious youth organizations that competed with communist ones were severely repressed. In the post-socialist period in Eastern Europe Catholic and Protestant youth movements have contested both the values of the communist period as well as the new consumerism of the market economy. It is in this space that new views of secularity arise that are different from the earlier communist ones, but also do not completely partake in capitalist market ideologies either.

Despite shared ideologies, across the communist world from Eastern Europe to Asia, secularism has been interpreted and institutionalized in unique ways in diverse contexts. Therefore, it is necessary to investigate secularism not only as an abstract concept, but as a political project that has acquired quite distinctive and sometimes contrary meanings in practice in specific local contexts. There is no use in drawing generalizations and abstract conceptualizations of a triangle love affair between religion, communism and secularism. Instead, we seek to study secularism as practice, not only in the political realm but also in the context of daily life, thereby escaping pre-existing assumptions when it comes to understanding the sphere of influence of religion in the communist world.

One such assumption is the distinction between public and private spheres, where similar discourses often can reveal productive differences (Gal and Kligman, 2000). Colonial and communist modernization theories shared a vision of what public religion looks like. This becomes evident particularly in the Chinese case, where Communist reform projects built on previous colonial modernization projects (see Mayfair Yang, 2008; Goossaert and Palmer, 2011). European secularism as a project always had the church as a clear target, but in the case of Asian societies this target first had to be created, because Buddhism and Taoism are interwoven with popular practices that do not have a clear, church-like structure. Buddhism and Taoism had to be organized in church-like public organizations to be able to control or eliminate them. The creation of these organizations was done by modernizing religious reformists themselves, and the process began in the colonial period, long before the Communist Party took power. Buddhist and Taoist leaders were eagerly engaged in building religious associations, which they saw as crucial to the modernization of their respected religions. The Chinese case shows that secularism is not simply anti-religious in these societies, although there are anti-religious elements in it, but that it simultaneously attempts to transform religion into moral sources of citizenship and national belonging. The masses have to be reeducated to realize their emancipatory potential, and religions can be used as state apparatuses to perform this reeducation.

Although, in theory, all forms of communism sought to eradicate or limit religion, the unexpected richness of religious life under communism demonstrated by the authors in this collection proves that power is always productive. The following chapters show that defining, co-opting and appropriating religion and religious forms was central to Communist political practices and political imaginaries. However, while religion is an important element in the production of these imaginaries, it can never be entirely contained by a secularist frame. It may produce linkages outside of the nation-state as world religions do; it may produce alternative visions of the moral state and thus become dangerous for secularist control, as in millenarian movements that have emerged in post-Soviet Russia and in China after the demise of Maoism. Precisely because secularism is a project, not a process, it is bound to be incomplete and is bound to produce contradictions that it itself cannot explain.

The objects of comparison

This volume grew out of discussions between colleagues at the Max Planck Institute for the Study of Religious Diversity in Gottingen, Germany. We too, were trained within traditional area studies limits, but as we discussed our work, we quickly realized that we were researching similar phenomena from very different frames of reference. This volume is the result of a workshop designed to take this dialogue further.

The workshop included both senior scholars and new voices in the study of religion and communism. All of the workshop participants met for three days, read and discussed each other's papers, sometimes argued, sometimes agreed and then returned home to rewrite their contributions. The result is a collection of essays that truly represents the current state of debate in the field.

The essays do not speak with one voice. Instead, they contest and interrogate each other, provoking as many questions as conclusions. Each essay makes its own contribution to the common discussion by examining different aspects of religion under and after communism, including the impact of religious institutions on communist governance; the influence of communist forms of governance on religious practices; the role of ritual, both religious and secular, in maintaining the communist state; political inflections in personal conversion experiences; and the different ways in which secularization and the secular can be reflected in religious practices, from Buddhist philosophers arguing for the scientific value of their faith, to Russians venerating icons in state art galleries. It is our hope that the following chapters will spark new perspectives on religion, communism and secularism, and provide the beginnings of a new conversation. The current chapters focus on Soviet (Poland, Russia, Kyrgyzstan) and Maoist (China, Vietnam, Korea, Laos) forms of secularism found on the Eurasian continent. For the most part, Soviet refers to European and Maoist refers to Asian, but Siberia, Mongolia and Central Asia, which are all firmly past the Urals, but nonetheless Soviet, remind us that neither ideology nor geography can be rigidly divided.

We use the terms communist and post-communist instead of socialist and post-socialist since we want to focus on the Communist Party and the Communist State. Many scholars of socialist and communist societies use the term "communism" to refer to ideology, and "socialist" to refer to the actual lived experience of state socialism, drawing on these regimes' own assertion that communism was the goal towards which they were working, but had not yet achieved (Verdery, 1996). Although our data is drawn from lived socialism, the comparative project is defined by a shared interest in communist ideology. It is a shared ideology that makes these states comparable. From the start we need to be clear that in comparing Europe and Asia we have countries like China, Vietnam, Laos and North Korea that still have communist regimes, while some of the countries of the former Soviet Union, in Eastern Europe and Central Asia have been post-communist for 20 years. One might argue that some Asian countries are communist in name only ("socialism with Chinese characteristics" as Deng Xiaopeng had it), or that many countries of the former USSR are democratic in name only. However, it is precisely the comparison of these differences that promises to yield productive results. All of these countries have experienced a history of communist social engineering and subsequent market reforms. We wish to keep the question of whether or not individual countries are "communist" or "post-communist" open, and ask what elements of continuity and change in the regime are relevant to religious practice? Given different political and economic situations, widely different cultural histories and the presence of widely different religions, the similarities between Asian and European examples are all the more striking, allowing us to see more clearly the relationship between communism and religious practice.

Chapter outline

The essays in this volume are organized into two parts, which draw on the contradictions produced by secularism as a project, revolving around the idea that secularism and religion co-constitute each other. Part I, Genealogies, examines the way in which religion was central to the process of state formation in communist countries and challenges us to rethink what we know about communist atheism. Sometimes this took the form of negotiations and compromises between communist parties and religious institutions (Werner, Pasieka, Ji and Grant), between communist and religious intellectual elites (Werner), through the use of ritual (Kwon and Ji) and transcendent ideals (Kwon and Luehrmann), for nation and communist-building processes.

Jayne Werner's chapter "God and the Vietnamese Revolution: Religious Organizations in the Emergence of Today's Vietnam" re-evaluates the development of socialism in Vietnam as a post-colonial movement, arguing that the Communist Party found itself in an uneasy alliance with anti-colonial religious movements like the Cao Dai. She convincingly argues that this was not merely a *realpolitik* stance, but rather a structural necessity in a colonized state. As an anti-colonial movement,

Vietnamese socialism sought to defend and liberate the nation, thereby opening a space to accommodate any religious movement that could claim national status. She therefore argues that the Communist Party's accommodation of religion after 1986 is a return to previous policy rather than a break with socialist ideals.

In Chapter 2, Grant Evans argues that socialist revolution had little impact on religion in Laos. Like Vietnam, the Laotian communist movement was an anti-colonial one, and so rather than ban Buddhism, which represented national culture, the communist state sought to "purify", co-opt and reform it, thereby making the national religion worthy of a new civilized socialist state. Although there were some perfunctory attempts to restrict practice immediately after the revolution, like most communist states, the Laotian Communist Party politicized and co-opted religion, but did not succeed in banning it. The speed with which Buddhism returned to a central position in Laotian national space after the revolution shows how little impact communist reform had.

Both chapters highlight, however, the close link between communism's civilizing mission and religious reform. In both these cases communism was an anti-colonial movement, and liberating the nation from the false consciousness of colonialism was more important than liberating the people from the false consciousness of religion, except in the case of internal minority populations, who, throughout the communist world, bore the brunt of socialism's civilizing impulse.

Agnieszka Pasieka's chapter provides a re-evaluation of the standard narrative about communism and Catholicism in Poland. She challenges the "resistance narrative", arguing that during the Soviet period the Catholic Church and the Communist Polish State in fact worked together quite closely, the church negotiating privileges in exchange for supporting state policies. Once again, we see co-optation and co-existence rather than outright suppression. Pasieka argues that we must re-evaluate the question of belief and practice, and the supposition that religious practice is inevitably nationalist and anti-communist. She argues that pre-Soviet Poland was more secular than post-Soviet Poland, and that it would be a mistake to interpret the population's desire for church-sanctioned life cycle rituals as a rejection of secular values or a blind support for the policies of the Catholic Church.

Her chapter is particularly interesting when read in conjunction with Ji Zhe's discussion of the current situation in China, raising interesting questions of chronology. Ji argues that the post-1989 Chinese state not only does not repress religion, but actively fosters co-opted forms of religious practice, while at the same time suppressing religious forms that do not conform to state ideals. Unlike Pasieka, who is looking back at Soviet-era Poland, Ji is critiquing a state that is currently in power. Both, however, argue that the Communist state is not a secular state, but rather seeks to use the power of religious organizations in its own service. Ji ultimately concludes that China has achieved secularization without secularism because, although religious practice has been reduced, there is no ideological underpinning that might define the relationship between church and state.

Like Ji, Heonik Kwon examines state rituals, specifically the national cemetery of war heroes in North Korea. He argues that North Korea is better understood through 19th century nationalist practices, rather than as a communist regime. By comparing commemorative practices in Vietnam and Korea he brings our attention not only to classic nationalist practices, but also to the role of gender in constructing the nation. His chapter addresses the same question raised by both Pasieka and Ji: how should we understand ritual? If we define religion as a matter of belief, which so much literature on secularism does, then one could argue that religious ritual is an expression of belief, and state ritual is merely an obligation. But if we accept this argument we are left with another question: why is state ritual so important to the maintenance of state power? If we argue, in contrast, that ritual is effective because it is a form of practice, rather than a question of belief, because it brings about states of being, then familiar boundaries between religious ritual and state ritual collapse.

In the final essay in Part I, Sonja Luehrmann also compares state and religion, not through ritual, but by comparing ideas of transcendence. Communism did, she argues, elicit and engage in a lot of "faith talk" but Luehrmann convincingly shows that if we consider levels of transcendence, communism cannot be considered a religion. Communist ideology placed faith in the actions of human beings, requiring no appeals to powers outside of the human world. Drawing on Luckmann's ideas of levels of transcendence, Luehrmann argues that despite many similarities in form between Soviet practices and post-Soviet religion, Soviet social practices evoked and privileged "medium" transcendence, whereas religion evokes "great" transcendence. Like the previous authors in this section, she gives us a new perspective from which to interrogate secularism.

In Part II, Creative Destruction, examines how secular notions of the religious have intersected with popular practice to produce new forms of religiosity. Drawing on the Foucauldian view of power as a productive force, these essays examine communist religious suppression not as a form of negative authority, but of productive and creative force that lead us to new definitions of both religion (Smyer Yu, Jung, Chau and Shnirelman) and secularism (Antonova, Luehrmann and Pelkmans), or both.

In Chapter 8, Dan Smyer Yu, in contrast to Ji Zhe, argues that communism in China should still be considered to be "like a religion" in its conversionary impulse and utopian eschatology. During the Cultural Revolution, Smyer Yu argues, communism cleared away traditional religious practices in the name of countering superstition, and the result opened the field for Christianity, which looks like what Maoist ideology presumed a religion should look like, and for Buddhist modernism, whose practitioners argue for the compatibility of science and Buddhism. He ultimately argues that neither Christianity nor modernist Buddhism would have a place in contemporary China if it were not for the anti-religious policies and propaganda of the Communist Chinese state.

Similarly, Victor Shnirelman credits the Soviet government with the creation of the Russian neo-pagan movement. The standard narrative is that the Soviet Union sought to turn religions into manifestations of national cultural heritage. In this instance, however, the reverse happened. In order to replace religious holidays, the Soviet state encouraged people to celebrate pagan Russian holidays as forms of "cultural heritage", thereby unwittingly transforming what had been considered merely "cultural heritage" into a neo-pagan religious movement. This neo-paganism, originally formed as government-sponsored anti-religious activism, in some cases transformed into virulently nationalist ideologies that challenge the state in the name of the ethnic nation.

Returning to the distinction between human and divine transcendence discussed by Luehrmann, Jin-Heon Jung's chapter explores the similarities between North Korean Juche ideology and South Korean evangelical Christianity, as they are perceived by North Korean refugees. He examines the conversion experiences of North Korean migrants who convert to Christianity while traveling through an extended "underground railroad" that takes them through China, and sometimes southeast Asia, on their way to South Korea. He convincingly shows that their personal religious experiences can only be understood within a Cold War framework that casts North Korea's state atheism as evil, and South Korea's secular separation of church and state as divinely sanctioned. Despite embracing the narrative of a pilgrim's progress to describe their flight from North Korea, many of these migrants are deeply ambivalent about the similarities they see between North Korea's Juche ideology and the demands of their new Christian faith. As in Smyer Yu's chapter, communist, and in this case Cold War anti-communist ideological structures, shape personal religious experiences.

Focusing on icons in Russia, Clemena Antonova also pushes us to consider new places to examine what secularism might be. Icons, which can be considered "iconic" of Russian Orthodox Christianity, were targeted for "secularization" by the early Bolshevik state. Icons were removed from churches, reclassified as art and manifestations of "national culture", and placed in secular state museums. Here we see again the centrality of the idea of the "nation" to the transformation of religious practice into the cultural heritage of the nation. Communism's civilizing mission could not escape the national form. However, these icons are now being worshipped in state galleries. Arguing not only that Bolshevik policy failed to recontextualize the icon, Antonova, through a reappraisal of the theories of pre-revolutionary Russian thinker Pavel Florensky, suggests that perhaps the form of the icon resists recontextualization.

Returning to China, Adam Chau pushes us to reconsider secularization and secularism from a new methodological standpoint. The study of secularism has, he argues, been too long trapped within the paradigm of church/state relations, which is not helpful in a place like China, where the idea of a "church" simply doesn't fit the religious forms of popular practice. Rather, Chau urges us to consider the household as the primary unit of religious practice in China and to examine how state policy changed the way in which the household can engage in activities that might be considered (by both householders, the state and/or researchers) as religious, thereby giving researchers a new lens with which to think about the idea of secularization.

In the final chapter Mathijs Pelkmans returns us to the question of religion as national culture in post-Soviet Kyrgyzstan. By examining arguments over Protestant missionaries and new Islamic sects, Pelkmans shows us that although defining Islam as "national culture" helped to foster a post-Soviet religious revival, it also, perhaps ironically, continues to foster secular attitudes about the proper role of religion in society that are strikingly similar to those found in liberal democratic secular states.

We see this collection as a first step in a larger dialogue, an attempt to assess where 20 years of scholarship on communism and religion has brought us, and where we should go from here. Although we tried to include a broad selection of perspectives from Asia and Europe, there is much of the communist world that is not represented here, including African socialisms and Cuba. However, we hope that the arguments made by the contributing authors are enough to show that a study of communism, in all its multiplicities, is an integral part of the study of secularism, and that the conversation is worth continuing.

Notes

1. Victoria Smolkin-Rothrock, April 7, 2014, "Lessons from the Land of Godlessness: How Atheism Changed the Spiritual Life of Soviet Society," Lecture at Center for Humanities, Wesleyan University, Middletown, CT. http://www.wesleyan.edu/humanities/current_theme/lecture_smolkinrothrock.html.
2. Given the geographical breadth of the socialist experience, this literature is far too extensive to be cited comprehensively here. We direct the interested reader to the combined bibliography at the end of this volume, and the area-specific citations of each chapter.
3. In addition to traditional publications we would like to draw the reader's attention to the Social Science Research Council's Immanent Frame project, which has produced a wide array of new perspectives on secularism as a "presence": http://blogs.ssrc.org/tif/.
4. See, for example, Marx's famous essay on The Jewish Question (Marx, 2002).
5. http://www.press.uchicago.edu/ucp/books/series/FP.html.

Part I
Genealogies

2
God and the Vietnamese Revolution: Religious Organizations in the Emergence of Today's Vietnam

Jayne S. Werner

Religion has been curiously absent in the conversation about the postcolonial construction of socialism and the Communist state in Vietnam.[1] Yet I would argue that religion has been integral to the transformation of Vietnam's modern social and political landscape, first under French colonialism and then during the historical evolution of Vietnam's long anti-imperialist struggle. The resurgence of religion under post-1986 economic reform or *Doi Moi* thus marks less a radical departure from the past than an evolution from Vietnam's own particular history of colonial modernity. Vietnam differs from China, where society was "saturated" with socialism, and the Soviet Union where socialism was gradually drained by dissidence and economic and political stagnation.[2] During the French colonial period, religious communities in Vietnam claimed the allegiance of substantial segments of Vietnam's peasant and urban population, played an important role in the struggle against colonialism and foreign intervention, and established themselves as part of Vietnam's national landscape before the Communists gained complete control over Vietnam in 1975.

When the country was reunited in 1975, it seemed initially as though "religion" would have little place in Vietnam's socialist future. Yet by 1990, Vietnam witnessed a resurgence of religious practices, including increased activity at pagodas, temples, churches, village shrines and festivals, ancestor worship and clan rites, as well as the proliferation of mother goddess and spirit possession cults under the rubric of "popular religion." Of course this was in part due to the new cultural and religious policies introduced by the *Doi Moi* state in the early 1990s. The government officially recognized the initially proscribed religions of the

Cao Dai, the Hoa Hao, several Protestant groups and many popular religious associations. (Catholicism was never prohibited; 7–8 percent of the population is currently Catholic.) By the 1990s, religion was deemed officially to be compatible with socialism and religious subjectivity was embraced as part of national subjectivity by the Communist government.[3] Indeed, religion, popular culture, and the newly emergent cult of Ho Chi Minh have now become ways to legitimate the Vietnamese state and the post-revolutionary transition to a market economy.[4]

Yet the manner in which the *Doi Moi* state is managing the boundaries between religiosity, secularity, and national belonging is linked to the history of anti-colonialism and war communism in Vietnam and not only stems from the challenges of the market economy. In addition, the party's cultural and religious policies have evolved over the years, shaping how "religion" would be incorporated into "the nation" and how the nascent nation-state would deal with the various communities within its fold. Vietnamese Marxist ideology was less class-oriented than Maoist China; the ruthless suppression of religion was never an option for the embattled Communist party. The front policies of the Viet Minh during the French war and the National Liberation Front (NLF) during the American war included religious communities as part of the "great unity" policy, already prefiguring the accommodationist stance *Doi Moi* Vietnam would adopt after 1986. Even Ho Chi Minh's 1930 program of the Vietnamese Communist Party (renamed the Indochinese Communist Party [ICP] later that year) incorporated the national bourgeoisie.[5] The party's first statement on culture (1943) attempted to <u>decolonize</u> culture rather than proletarianize it as such, making it more national, scientific, and mass-based, that is, popular. Despite the later efforts of Marxist cultural theoreticians to enforce a secular and class line, Vietnamese Communism was not theoretically inflexible towards religion. In practice, Vietnamese Communists were conflicted towards religion, at times allying with religious groups and at others in open conflict with religion.

The first section of this chapter outlines the simultaneous emergence of the communist movement and modern religious movements and institutions during the colonial period in Vietnam, examining how both were shaped by the conditions of colonialism and the struggle for independence against the French and then the US. Both the Communist Party and religious groups competed with each other for the allegiance of the peasantry and the urbanizing classes, were ideological rivals, and positioned themselves in different ways towards the colonial state. The second section outlines the relations between the religious communities and the ICP during the fight for independence, including the shifting cultural and religious policies of the party/state. Finally the paper considers the heroic and cultic discourses that were essential to the success of war communism in Vietnam and the party/state's newly imagined community as it sought to consolidate its power in the north, and then in the south, following the collapse of South Vietnam (1975). These discourses drew on popular cults and worship practices which associated heroes with divine and supernatural powers.

Religion, communism, and modernity in colonial Indochina

It is often forgotten that the Communists and the religious parties were the main ideological and political contenders in colonial Indochina for political prominence during the critical years of the 1930s and 1940s.[6] These were the years that set the stage for the alignment of forces which competed for power in the nascent nation-state. The Indochinese Communist Party (ICP) was founded in 1930 by Ho Chi Minh, who presided over its first congress and its initial Program of Action. The ICP quickly became a major secular political force in colonial Indochina. The Vietnam National Party (VNQDD) suffered a crippling setback after its failed uprising at Yen Bai in 1930. Bui Quang Chieu's Constitutionalist Party was restricted to a small circle of educated urban elites, located mostly in the south. Other parties were never able to compete with the Communists in terms of mass adherence, ideological appeal, geographical range, and international contacts. The exception were the religious parties, particularly the Cao Dai, founded in 1926 and the Hoa Hao, founded in 1939, and possibly the Buddhist revival movement. The Catholic Church, representing 10 percent of the population, was highly organized. Closely associated with the colonial state, Catholicism was introduced into Vietnam in the early 16th century by Jesuit priests but flourished after the French conquest in 1885. Catholic priests aided the French in the pacification of the Tonkin delta, and converts to the faith rose to prominent positions in the colonial regime.[7]

In contrast to the favored status of Catholicism, Marxist parties and the new religious groups were either outsiders or pariahs in the colonial system. The French *Surete* or colonial police ruthlessly suppressed the Communists and kept a tight surveillance on the others. Nonetheless, during the 1920s and 1930s a veritable explosion of new political and religious activity occurred in response to the challenges presented by colonialism. New ideas and understandings of politics, nationalism, secularism, religion, and the nation-state had emerged in French Indochina, having been introduced by colonial modernity and Asian modernists in Japan and China. Despite French restrictions and repression, the political arena was crowded with political ferment and new religious groups as well as revivals of existing religions, which offered new solutions to Vietnam's cultural and social, and after 1930, economic crisis.[8] The Catholic Church was caught up in this ferment but turned to the right, distancing itself from Marxist ideology and the other religious parties.[9]

During the 1930s, the ICP attracted many urban, educated young people to its ranks for its anti-colonial platform, Leninist methods of organization, and rejection of gradual change through political reform within the colonial system. All the new groups, especially the Marxist parties, sought social and cultural change as well as political and ideological progress. Arrayed against the ICP were the Cao Dai, the Hoa Hao, and the renewal of Buddhism. Like the ICP, these three religious movements took on modern accoutrements such as situating their doctrines in sacred texts (which they began to publish in abundance)[10], setting up national organizations, using religion as a tool to mobilize large masses of people, refashioning new definitions of religious subjectivity and the collectivistic community, assimilating political ideology into religious discourses, voicing their concerns about national progress, and proclaiming universalistic religious principles.

The Cao Dai and Hoa Hao were the largest of the groups and were based in southern Vietnam. The Cao Dai claimed ½ million peasant followers by World War II (out of a total population of four million for Cochinchina in 1936).[11] In its temple architecture, organization, religious terminology, texts, and rituals, as well as congregational mode of participation, the Cao Dai modeled itself on the Catholic Church. The Cao Dai cult was centered on the worship of the Jade Emperor, Ngoc Hoang Thuong De, while also based on a syncretic Taoist, Buddhist, and Confucian set of beliefs. Its sacred texts consisted of "spirit writings" from séances conducted by its priestly caste, most of whom were practiced mediums.[12]

The Cao Dai believed that the Creator or the Jade Emperor had chosen Vietnam as the site to save mankind from destruction, and that the Cao Dai incorporated the entire corpus of the world's religious teachings. If mankind refused to heed these teachings, the gates of heaven would be closed forever. The religion was officially known as the Great Way of the Third Period of Salvation (*Dai Dao Tam Ky Pho Do*), the third period being the last opportunity given to mankind to save itself. The Cao

Dai promoted a new "morality" which would lead disciples from their personal failings and difficulties into a new community of well-behaved and well-ordered believers.[13]

The Cao Dai closely fit Prasenjit Duara's model of a "redemptive society" which embraces apocalyptic salvationist discourses and entails the "moral transformation of ordinary people," "extinguishing worldly desires while engaging in virtuous action."[14] As with other East Asian syncretic popular movements such as the White Lotus, the Yiguandao, the Daoyuan, and the Hongwanzihui (Red Swastika Society), the syncretism of the Cao Dai was aligned with modern discourses of universalistic redemption and a global model of religious citizenship. As with these religious societies, "syncretism" in the Vietnamese three-religions (*tam-giao*) tradition in the Cao Dai was molded into a new model of subjecthood compatible with modern notions of citizenship.

Duara argues that the secularity of the 20th century East Asian state and the abeyance of the imperial rites associated with the Emperor and the court had a profound influence on the spiritual landscape of East Asian countries, contributing to the proliferation of Chinese and Japanese syncretic sects in the late 19th century and early 20th century. He suggests that a kind of "traffic" between imperial state cultures and these sects took place, thereby altering religious subjecthood among adherents of the new religions.[15] In colonial Indochina, not only was the colonial state secular, and the sacred rites discontinued by the imperial court, but the politico-religious power of the Emperor had been superseded by the French Governor General and his minions, all hailing from a foreign land. Religious rites had lost their political-institutional mooring, while colonialism shunted "religion" aside from the state, redefining it as a separate category from "society." It was into this space that new types of religious movements such as the Cao Dai, the Hoa Hao, and the modern Buddhist movement were able to step in, very successfully redefining themselves vis-à-vis the colonial state.[16]

Like the Cao Dai, reform-minded Buddhists in the 1930s sought to reinvent and revive Buddhism "for this world," attempting to make it more relevant to the modern age. Buddhism needed to be compatible with modern science and secularism, relevant to national concerns, and serve as a way to cope with the social and cultural crisis. Many Buddhist revivalists linked the nation's destiny to a reinvigorated Buddhism, seeing Buddhism's public activities as a way to promote the religion while also serving the country. Monks and pagodas had come under attack for their "superstition" and corruption, and Buddhism in general was criticized for being ill-equipped to provide the spiritual and philosophical foundation for national progress. Buddhists in the mainly Mahayana tradition promoted stricter standards for monks and nuns; changes in monastic life; translations of sutras and texts from Chinese into the national romanized script, *quoc ngu*; the development of lay instruction as a way to encourage the popularization of Buddhist principles; and education, charity, and publication initiatives.[17] In doing so, urban Buddhists were consciously adopting the model of the Catholic Church.[18] The Buddhist revival was strong in southern Vietnam although it also spread to the center and the north. The monk Tri Hai, a leader of the revival in the north, called for enlightenment through Buddhism as a way to lift Vietnam's populace from ignorance and dependence on others.[19]

The Hoa Hao, founded in 1939, practiced a Buddhistic cult, emphasizing home worship. Led by the charismatic Huynh Phu So, the Hoa Hao grew out of a century-old tradition of Buddhist millenarianism among the southern peasantry, while it also stressed the Buddhist dharma, filial piety, and self-cultivation.[20] The Hoa Hao eschewed an elaborate sangha (there are very few Hoa Hao temples) and elaborate Buddhist ritual statuary. There were about 300,000 Hoa Hao adherents by the early 1940s.[21] Sermons left by Huynh Phu So, who died in 1947, were collected as written texts and published for adherents, constituting the basis of Hoa Hao leaders' spiritual authority.[22]

Like the Buddhists and the Cao Dai, Huynh Phu So's religious teachings were infused with political ideology. One of the most important texts in the Hoa Hao canon, "The Way to Practice Religion and Rules for Everyday Life" (1945) demonstrates Huynh Phu So's emphasis on national progress and concerns for the world at large. Among the fundamental precepts Hoa Hao Buddhists were (and are) obliged to know are the "four debts of gratitude" to one's ancestors and parents, to the country, to the Buddhist Three Treasures, and to one's compatriots and humanity. In this text, Huynh Pho So claims "it is our duty to defend our country if we want our life to be sustained and our race to survive. Let us help safeguard our country making it strong and prosperous. Let us try to liberate our country from foreign domination. We are safe only when our nation is strong and wealthy."[23]

Communist leaders in the 1930s were quite aware of the ideological and organizational challenges posed by the reinvention of Buddhism and the rise of the Cao Dai, and later the Hoa Hao.[24] Both the communists and the new religious groups had national political agendas, appealed to the same peasant groups for their mass base, and drew from the new urbanizing elites for their leaders. As Alexander Woodside argues, the Communists, Buddhists, Cao Dai, and Hoa Hao all searched for "equivalence with the West," were interested in new techniques, and incorporated new ideas of egalitarianism and Western science, but the Communist advantage lay in their promotion of mass literacy and social-economic solutions. That is, their concerns were social as opposed to moral.[25] The colonial regime ruthlessly repressed Communist organizations but tolerated the Buddhist revival movement and closely monitored Cao Dai and Hoa Hao organizing and recruitment. Although the Communists had many advantages over the religious groups, the Communists did not have a clear field, and would need to deal with the religious communities, including Catholicism, as they prepared to fight the French for control of Indochina. Religion would not remain external to the construction of what would become the nation and constitute the independent state. As Shawn McHale has shown, the dynamic and vigorous religious debates of the 1930s had a life of their own, and shaped modern Vietnamese consciousness.[26] This would become even more apparent as the struggle turned into two long wars against France and then the US. Indeed, the religious communities, including Buddhism and Catholicism, would also become involved in the national liberation struggle.

The long wars (1945–1975) and the party's united front policies

Although initially it was not party policy to form alliances with the religious communities (because the party pursued the Comintern-dictated proletarian line), that changed with the adoption of the united front policies of the party, particularly with the creation of the Viet Minh Front for the Liberation of Viet Nam in 1941. The Viet Minh was created by Ho Chi Minh and ICP leaders to unite all patriotic organizations behind the party for armed struggle to achieve national liberation in the wake of the Japanese takeover of Indochina (1941–1945). The party had first adopted a united front ("from above") policy in line with the 7th Congress of the Comintern and the Popular Front in France in 1936, calling for democratic reforms within the colonial political system, when it adopted "legal" forms of struggle.[27] During this period, the party dropped the class line and the radical policies which had marked the uprisings associated with the Nghe-Tinh soviets (1932) and their brutal repression by the colonial military.

In the 1930s, the party and the Cao Dai recruited followers in many of the same areas of the Mekong delta (by 1938, peasant membership in Communist organizations in the south was estimated to be about 20,000).[28] But during World War II, the Cao Dai broke off contact with the Viet Minh, adopting a pro-monarchist and pro-Japanese stance. However, in 1945, as the Viet Minh assumed power throughout the country, both the Cao Dai and the Hoa Hao joined the Viet Minh in a coalition government in Saigon which was formed on September 10, 1945 (with approval from party headquarters in the north). This short-lived government faced many challenges, not the least of which was the prospect of the returning French, but in the rural areas, sectarians, including Catholics, generally cooperated and even allied with the Viet Minh.[29]

With the re-entry of French forces in the fall of 1945 and their rapid deployment in Saigon and throughout the Mekong delta, the Viet Minh government fell and the sectarian forces pulled back. Although Huynh Phu So had initially allied with the Viet Minh government in the south, other elements of the Hoa Hao were in league with the Trotskyites, the Buddhists, and the Democratic Party. On September 8, 1945, 15,000 Hoa Hao followers marched to Can Tho and tried to take control of the Western Mekong delta. Viet Minh forces vigorously counterattacked. In bitter fighting, the Viet Minh massacred almost 3000 Cao Dai in Quang Ngai in August, 1945. Armed clashes persisted between the Viet Minh and Cao Dai to the north of Saigon and in Tay Ninh. By 1947, both the Cao Dai and the Hoa Hao withdrew from their alliance with the Viet Minh and concluded pacts with the French to establish "base areas" in their respective regions of control. The French returned *Ho Phap* Pham Cong Tac, the exiled Cao Dai leader, from Madagascar where he had been detained during the war, and permitted both sects to retain their military forces. The Viet Minh arrested Huynh Phu So in 1947 and executed him.[30]

Yet the sects did not prove to be reliable partners of the French Expeditionary Corps. Accommodations were often reached with Viet Minh forces on the ground. Sect-controlled areas were not easily pene-trated by Viet Minh forces, but this did not always actually work to the disadvantage of the Viet Minh, although it complicated Communist strategy, to be sure.[31] The party, nonetheless, remained in a weak position in the south up until 1953, just before Dien Bien Phu (May 1954).[32]

Despite overt hostilities on the ground, Viet Minh policy toward the religious groups during the first Indochina war was based on anti-colonialism and the united front approach. In September 1945, Ho Chi Minh persuaded four Vietnamese Catholic bishops to support the Viet Minh government in the north. Tens of thousands of Catholics joined

Viet Minh organizations at the start of the first Indochina War.[33] In 1946, the Viet Minh created the Lien Viet (Vietnamese Alliance) Front as an umbrella organization to group the religious communities, political parties, and individuals into one organization, appealing to all of them to oppose the French on patriotic grounds. But by the late 1940s, most Catholics had left the Lien Viet and the Viet Minh, as the French offered them semi-autonomy in their own regions of control. Catholic-based militias fiercely protected the dioceses of Phat Diem and Bui Chu in the Tonkin delta (80 percent of Catholics lived in the north or center before the 1950s). Similar arrangements were concluded with the Hoa Hao and the Cao Dai, who controlled large swaths of territory in the Mekong delta with their own military forces. Despite the enmity between the Hoa Hao and the Communists following the execution of Huynh Phu So, the Viet Minh did not give up on reaching an accommodation with the Hoa Hao in the western Mekong delta. In fact some party accounts criticized local cadres for being too passive and lenient vis-à-vis the Hoa Hao, especially when the French kept giving them arms.[34]

In 1949 the Viet Minh tried to reach a secret truce with the Cao Dai but failed. Le Duan (to become Secretary General of the Party from 1960–1986), the cadre who dealt with *Ho Phap* Pham Cong Tac, stated that the Viet Minh aimed to "work with eminent men, intellectual and religious elements, political parties, and ethnic minorities, which possess different ideas from us, but which are determined to struggle for Union and Independence for the Country and to denounce the diabolical ruses of the colonialists who are pitting Vietnamese against Vietnamese."[35] By then, however, working out an effective plan with the religious groups for control of the south was beyond the Viet Minh's grasp.[36]

The party's official policy was the united front and anti-imperialism, in alliance with the national bourgeoisie During the First Indochina War, and this entailed a new doctrinal definition of "culture." The party undertook major efforts to redefine and reorient Vietnamese "culture" during the l940s in order to aid the liberation struggle. Truong Chinh, the Party's chief theoretician from the early 1940 until the late 1980s, defined culture as a form of ideological struggle, asserting that there needed to be a "cultural revolution" in order to achieve national liberation.[37] For the party's theoreticians, culture would compete vigorously with class for the soul of the Vietnamese revolution. Truong Chinh's cultural goals were to overhaul the "obscurantist," mystical, and anti-scientific elements in Vietnamese culture, including religion.[38] Religion and parts of Vietnamese culture were imbued with "feudal customs" and mores, facilitated by colonialism. The party approach was to construct a new culture and a "new life" in the countryside which would take "industry, thrift, integrity, and uprightness" (*can, kiem, liem, chinh*) as its standard bearer (the slogan comes from Ho Chi Minh).[39] Costly village rituals such as marriage ceremonies, funerals, festivals, and banquets needed to be curtailed and simplified. In developing national culture, the objective was to rid Vietnamese culture of its sense of inferiority and backwardness, and to raise the cultural level of the masses. Marxism would be used as the compass, but the goal was to use these new guidelines in reconstructing Vietnamese culture for nation building.[40]

Truong Chinh insisted the first task in cultural change was to decolonize the existing culture, which he viewed as overly influenced by French and Chinese civilization. Vietnamese culture needed to develop its own authority and independent spirit and become more "autonomous." The way to do this was to develop a spirit of collective sacrifice and heroism, forging "a nation in struggle." Culture would thereby become more popular, less elitist, and more "progressive."[41] Truong Chinh urged cultural workers to create broad unity in culture to support the revolution, helping to "create [new] Vietnamese values." As Kim N. B. Ninh argues, this new cultural policy of building up the nation was not a tactical move on Truong Chinh's part.[42]

In urging Vietnamese culture to become more national, Truong Chinh and the ICP created an opening for religion to be included in the national community. In his two most important statements on culture in the 1940s, Truong Chinh nowhere suggested that religion was not part of the national community. Quite the contrary, in "Marxism and Vietnamese Culture," he railed against the French for their crimes against religion: "the French aggressors are destroying and making a mockery of culture in our land. They burn, kill, plunder property and rape women in the most savage manner. They demolish statues of gods, shatter crucifixes and even slay bonzes and priests and rape Catholics and Buddhist nuns...They trample on religion and drag human dignity through the mud...Their war of aggression is at the same time a war of cultural destruction."[43]

The critique of religion as "superstition" (*me tin*) only appears once in this text, although it would later be used to justify state actions against religion. Attacking religion as "superstition" was originally not a part of Truong Chinh's discourses. Truong Chinh saw culture as a national problem, not a class problem, and in doing so, left the door open for religion. In addition, despite Truong Chinh's socialist realist approach to the arts and letters, he applied a unity policy and the united front for groups in society. Truong Chinh's concept of using culture, including religion, for nation building would be a theme picked up and further developed under *Doi Moi*.

Over the course of the evolution of Vietnamese socialism, the tensions between class and culture/nation-building shifted according to the challenges at hand, with class assuming a more overt and violent character during struggles over land reform and war policy in the south. Yet culture and unity polices were never eclipsed by class. During the American war (1960–1975), the party reinstituted the united front strategy, as during the French war. Following the Geneva Agreements of 1954 and the temporary division of Vietnam for purposes of military regroupment along the 17th parallel, Ngo Dinh Diem was installed first as Premier (1955) and then elected as President of the Republic of Vietnam (creating the state of South Vietnam in 1956). Ngo Dinh Diem's regime was heavily reliant on over 700,000 Catholics who fled the north after the Geneva Agreements, constituting a political bloc which was "crucial to the American strategy of building an anti-communist Republic of Vietnam."[44] Diem's first moves were to repress any armed and organized groups that presented a threat; his initial military campaigns were to destroy the military forces of the Cao Dai and the Hoa Hao. Those which escaped hid in the Plain of Reeds and the jungle and periodically attacked the posts of the Army of the Republic of Vietnam (ARVN). Meanwhile, in the north, the Democratic Republic of Vietnam issued a major policy directive on religion, Decree 234-SL, in part to stem to flow of Catholic refugees streaming to the south, which guaranteed freedom of religion, the right to religious instruction and training, and non-interference in religious groups' internal affairs.[45]

In 1956, Ngo Dinh Diem initiated an "exterminate the communists" campaign targeting Viet Minh cadres who remained in the south after the Geneva Accords. No longer able to count on protection from the north and advised not to pursue armed struggle, Viet Minh elements went into hiding.[46] From 1957–1959, portions of the Cao Dai and Hoa Hao forces, as well as sections of the Viet Minh driven underground, joined forces to stage low-scale attacks on the Diem regime and the ARVN. Coordinated military units among the sects and party cadres carried out "concerted uprisings," as a hedge against Diem's repression. In doing so, according to a Communist Party source, these mixed units rekindled the revolutionary movement in the south and comprised the bulk of forces of the initial southern liberation movement, which would be named the National Liberation Front.[47] Furthermore, these initiatives, along with other concerted uprisings, forced the hand of the party in the north, leading to the adoption of a new line, permitting armed struggle in the south.⁴⁸ In 1960, the Third Congress of the party formally established the National Liberation Front, and the armed religious groups were incorporated into the Peoples Liberation Armed Forces in 1961.

The National Liberation Front included leaders from the Cao Dai, the Hoa Hao, Catholics, and Buddhists. The NLF actively sought to win religious adherents over to the cause and recruit religious leaders into party organizations. A captured NLF document, dated 1962, stated: "We must increase our actions among religious groups and increase our organizational work. Religious leaders should be won to our cause. Pay particular attention to Catholics, Caodaists, and Hoa Hao Buddhists in Soc Sai [a major town in the Mekong delta] ... Unmask the enemy scheme of using religion to divide the people ... Help the religious to maintain their principles, repair pagodas, temples, and churches. Enable the people to carry on their prayers, attend mass and religious ceremonies. Absolutely do not use pagodas, temples, and churches for meetings and do not post slogans, slips, or banners inside or out of them."⁴⁹

As the revolutionary movement gained traction in the south, class struggle and radical land reform were generally suspended in areas where religious communities were potential allies, although there were exceptions to this rule.⁵⁰ But the Front was accused of faking its religious alliances, when real power was held by the Communist party.⁵¹ Indeed, Le Duan's priorities, after he became General Secretary of the party (1960–1986) and controlled war policy, were to complete the communist revolution in the south (as opposed to building socialism in the north), topple the Saigon regime, and reunite the two halves of Vietnam, as recent research has shown.⁵²

Ngo Dinh Diem's rigid posture towards the religious communities, except the Catholic Church which received favored status under his regime, eventually contributed to his downfall. Since the 1930s, Buddhism had been gathering force as a unified movement, bringing pagodas into wider affiliated networks, organizing youth chapters (there were 1000 youth chapters with 70,000 members in South Vietnam in the 1960s),⁵³ establishing study groups, devising new programs of social and religious activism, and producing a new generation of monks. As Pham Van Minh notes, the Buddhist revival movement of the 1930s laid the groundwork for the 1960s Buddhist struggle movements against Ngo Dinh Diem and Nguyen Cao Ky.⁵⁴ In the 1960s, Diem's favoritism toward the Catholic Church increasingly persuaded Buddhists that Diem was trying to make Catholicism the state religion. Alarmed by the destruction wreaked by US bombing of South Vietnam and US military operations on the ground, Buddhists saw Ngo Dinh Diem as a symbol of foreign intervention. These concerns awakened a wide-spread feeling of national identity in the south mobilized around Buddhism, reflected in the graphic image of the self-immolation of the monk Quang Duc in 1963.[55]

The Buddhists formed the backbone of what was known as the "third force" between the polarized extremes of the military governments allied with the US and communism. Many monks saw the NLF as a nationalist organization and followers of the Viet Cong as reacting against foreign intervention.[56] Thich Nhat Hanh favored an immediate cease-fire and political compromise to the conflict, arguing that US military intervention and the continued violence were counterproductive.[57] Diem's government fell in October 1963, replaced by a succession of ineffectual military regimes, which the Buddhists continued to attack as illegitimate because they were propped up by US military power. In 1966 Buddhists staged a large-scale uprising in the northern part of South Vietnam led by the monks at An Quang pagoda. A section of the ARVN under General Nguyen Chanh Thi broke off and supported the Buddhists, presenting the Saigon government under Nguyen Cao Ky with a supreme challenge. Aided by a sizeable contingent of US Marines, Ky quelled the uprising, which if successful, could have led to the secession of the five northern provinces, including Danang and Hue.[58]

The shaky government in Saigon stabilized, for the time being, and staged elections. Nguyen Van Thieu became the last President of the Republic. But again, protest under the banner of religion considerably weakened his government in the wake of the 1973 Paris Accords concluded between North Vietnam and the US, with the withdrawal of US troops in 1973. This time it was the Catholics who took the lead in organizing protests against the US-backed Thieu regime. Father Tran Huu Thanh, a popular priest, led an anti-corruption campaign against Thieu in 1974–1975. He was joined by Redemptorist priest Father Chan Tin, who protested the human rights abuses of the regime and the continued violence of the war.[59]

In sum, the ICP and its later incarnations (renamed the Vietnam Workers' Party in 1951) faced an uphill battle in its struggle to achieve an independent state in the face of militarily superior foreign forces which tried to prevent the Communists from coming to power. In the long wars against the French and then the US, the Vietnamese Communist Party relied on a policy of anti-colonialism and a united front strategy towards the religious communities. Extremist approaches tended to backfire. Postures of flexibility towards religion permitted the party to reap political benefits, particularly during the American war, when religious groups directed their concerns towards stopping the unrelenting war and bringing an end to foreign intervention.

Indeed, it was the religious communities which were responsible for undermining the Saigon governments during the American war. The Buddhist struggle movement led to the toppling of Ngo Dinh Diem in 1963, the first and arguably the most successful regime in the Republic, and the Catholics critically wounded another, that of Nguyen Van Thieu. Buddhists and Catholics championed peace, an end to US military intervention, and repairing the body politic. In doing so, they undermined the military solution pursued by the US and its Vietnamese allies, kept the Saigon governments from gaining political legitimacy, and hastened the end of the war. The Second Indochina War not only consisted of the military conflict between the US and the NLF and the North Vietnamese army, but ultimately rested on the question of the political legitimacy of the Saigon governments. These military governments relied on force, and their alliance with the US, not internal politics, for staying in power. The religious groups skillfully used political means to strengthen the visibility and the legitimacy of those who favored peace. By the end of the American war, most of the population of South Vietnam favored a cessation to continued military hostilities. This weariness no doubt aided the Communists in their takeover of the south in 1975. After the fall of Ngo Dinh Diem, the Cao Dai and Hoa Hao in large part sided with the Saigon government, although some elements of the Cao Dai tried to maintain a more neutral posture. But even in these communities, the yearning for peace and an end to the violence was palpable to observers who visited them.[60] The voices of national identity, cast in religious terms, had kept the option of peace and an end to the US military presence alive.

The cult of the heroic in war communism and the reform period

While the religious communities were staking a claim to membership in the national community, the Communist party itself was not immune to its own brand of religiosity. In fact, the party relied on heroic discourses implicitly associated with supernatural powers in the narratives they constructed about the nation. Confucian modernists first introduced these discourses as part of their own nation-building efforts. Early nationalists such as Phan Boi Chau and other leaders of the anticolonial movement had turned local deities such as the Trung sisters and Tran Hung Dao (the Vietnamese general who fended off the 13th century Mongol invasion), worshipped at temples both in Hanoi and in the Red River delta, into heroes and heroines. These "feudal" heroes were transformed into "national" heroes, highlighting the greatness of the ancestral land and the people's resistance against foreign aggression. The Communist movement adopted these narratives, adding to them the unique "revolutionary spirit and morality" of the Vietnamese people. After independence, and with the advent of *Doi Moi*, these discourses shifted to a state-supported cult of Ho Chi Minh, who became enshrined as the prime hero and patron saint of the revolution and the nation, providing one of the primary props of the party's legitimacy to rule. The national cult of Ho Chi Minh has now become the official ideology of the regime.

The cult of the hero served several purposes for the Communist state, besides mobilizing the population for two wars against foreign occupiers. It was also a way for the fledging state to insert its power into the villages and build on the tradition of imperial state-penetration of local power structures. The local population had a tradition of honoring and deifying cultural heroes and designating sacred places as "heroic" land. The imperial state had long sought to control the designation of village tutelary deities; in doing so, it could oversee the process of extracting wealth from the local population.[61] Building on this tradition, the Communist movement inserted new state discourses into local communities linking heroism to patriotism and suggesting that local people, that is, peasants, could be heroes. What distinguished the Vietnamese revolution was that it was a "peasant revolution" in official discourse, one of ordinary people with an extraordinary heritage, who could call upon their national greatness in fighting for a just cause. In this way mythical heroes were connected to everyday heroes, both representing national identity, and with the ICP encapsulating the singular essence (*quoc tuy*) of the Vietnamese national character.[62]

The new state used war heroism in part to construct its political order, unify the national community, and inculcate a sense of civic morality. The exemplary society was based on displays of public virtue, associated with meritorious feats, signified by grades, titles, and awards. Revolutionary virtue drew some of its ideas drawn from Confucian precepts, while Marxism added concepts of merit and egalitarianism. The ICP devised new heroes of the people such as soldier martyrs (*liet si*), emulation heroes, labor heroes, army heroes, and "new heroes."[63] Emulation movements were used as early as 1947 to motivate the population to join party organizations and "build a new life" at the local level.[64] The state used the greatness of the ancestral land (*to quoc*) and the heroism of its people to reconstruct the historiography of the nation along the theme of resistance to foreign aggression, in a post-colonial attempt to recover Vietnam's long past in its official history.[65]

In the wake of the collapse of the world-wide communist bloc in the late 1980s, the commemoration of Ho Chi Minh (d. 1969) as a national hero/deity would become particularly useful to the party as it started to promote his cult and Thought. After Vietnam adopted market reforms in 1986, Marxism lost its usefulness and authority as the ideological framework of the regime. The state turned to nationalist and cultural discourses to fill the vacuum. New cultural policies introduced in the early and mid-1990s sought cultural authenticity and to "build a progressive Vietnamese culture saturated with national identity."[66]

Adopting economic development as the overriding goal, the reform era (instituted in 1986) has used "culture" as the ideological force behind economic progress.[67] The *Doi Moi* state discovered that heroes, religiosity, and worship – ethics and "culture" – could be important for a modern and civilized society, as well as ways to strengthen national pride and identity.[68] As such, the *Doi Moi* state ritually engages with war martyrs, revolutionary heroes, and the "charismatic dead" for political legitimacy.[69] Starting in the late 1980s, the cult of Ho Chi Minh began to emerge all over Vietnam, simultaneously and spontaneously, from the bottom-up, alongside the veneration of other national defense heroes, worshipped in pagodas and temples from north to south.[70] Ton Duc Thang (1888–1980), another founder of the Indochina Communist Party, has also become mythologized as a revolutionary hero. My Hoa Hung, An Giang province, Mekong delta, his native village, inaugurated a shrine and museum to his memory in 1988. Ton Duc Thang's official biography features his exemplary character; his cult, akin to a religious rite, is a "testament to the ethical and spiritual ethos of revolutionary virtue." Visitors praying at his shrine come to "call up" his tutelary spirit, according to Christoph Giebel.[71] The idea that exceptional individual behavior is associated with supernatural power was already widely accepted in Vietnamese culture, easily transferring over to Ho Chi Minh and other leaders. They simply joined similar historic figures venerated by the population for their actions to protect the national community. Linkages between the ancestors, the family, the nation-state, and in terms of Ho Chi Minh, Uncle Ho's benevolence, had long been promoted by the party/state.[72]

Thus the "reenchantment" of society that has occurred under *Doi Moi* has been intimately linked to the politics of reform.[73] The *Doi Moi* state and the Communist party have invested in hero worship and the revival of national culture to maintain control in the face of rapid social and economic change.[74] Alongside the cult of Ho Chi Minh is the expanding cult of Tran Hung Dao (the 13th century general who repulsed the Mongols) which has become very popular with the market economy and is big business in Hanoi. According to a recent study, Saint Tran's cult dignifies the hero worship of Ho Chi Minh, while Ho Chi Minh lends credence to the saint's cult.[75] As times are uncertain and people seek "luck" and fortune in business, Saint Tran's cult is being transformed during the reform era. Tran Hung Dao is considered efficacious for bringing "spirit favor" (loc) to business activities and preventing disturbances by ghosts and spirits; he fights off demons and directs the souls of the nether worlds. Although most of the mediums who incarnate Saint Tran are men, women can be empowered by serving as mediums for him, breaking out of their domestic role and reconnecting to the public sphere as they had done during the wartime/socialist past.[76]

Thus recent research is documenting the shifting spiritual landscape in Vietnam. Scholars have also noted the expansion of spirit-calling and mediumistic cults in urban centers like Hanoi, while others have focused on popular pilgrimage sites in the south frequented by women merchants from Ho Chi Minh city.[77] Changing Buddhist, Catholic, and Cao Dai rituals as interpreted by their officiates and adherents is richly documented in a new collection of essays.[78] The cult of Princess Lieu Hanh and "Mother worship" have experienced a "rebirth" in the north as the state moves to claim popular religion as part of Vietnam's traditional heritage.[79] As Kristen Enders puts it, "mediumism" and all religious practice "thrives within a field of tension between the Party-state's vision of a modern nation-state...and the effects of greater state tolerance, economic transformation and enhanced consumerism."[80]

Furthermore, Heonik Kwon poignantly shows how kinship commemoration practices, particularly in central Vietnam, have been transformed in order to deal with the traumatic losses and divisions of the war.[81] Grieving families have eschewed state narratives of war death in order to reconcile and account for the ghosts of soldiers lost on both sides of the Cold War divide, often soldiers from the same family who fought for both the Communists and the Saigon regime. Similarly, in northern villages, families have sought to reclaim the moral space of the war's legacy by constructing their own rituals and spiritual paths apart from state narratives.[82] The dramatic rise of Christian evangelism among the ethnic minorities in the highlands in the 1990s raises questions of rapid conversions, transnational linkages, new technologies, and perceived ethnic discrimination.[83]

From suppression to engagement: 1975 to *Doi Moi*

Immediately following the end of the war (1975), however, the Communist regime took a hard-liner stance toward all religious organizations and religious activity. Religious organizations suspected of having worked with the US or Saigon regime were deemed to be anti-revolutionary, reactionary, and engaged in "superstitious" activities. From 1975–1988, almost all religious groups were suspected of foreign ties and were caught up in post-liberation surveillance and "depoliticization" efforts. During this period, Vietnam moved quickly to control all organized religious activity, counteract any religiously-based opposition, and restrict the growth of religious organizations. Several hundred Catholic clergy and Buddhist monks who had worked with the Americans or the Thieu regime were imprisoned. The son of Cao Dai dignitary Ho Tan Khoa, *Ho Phap* Pham Cong Tac's successor at the Cao Dai Holy See in Tay Ninh, staged a rebellion, with arms smuggled in from Thailand, against the regime in 1984. The plot was quickly uncovered, and the principals were executed.[84] The Hoa Hao hierarchy was disbanded, although the dispersed and home-based Hoa Hao community remained relatively intact. The government shut down virtually all the orphanages, welfare associations, clinics, and schools run by all the religious groups. Religious ordination and Catholic priests declined precipitously, while Buddhist monks dropped from 30,000 to 10,000.[85] Only one Catholic seminary was in operation in the early 1980s. Ordination of priests among the Cao Dai was effectively halted with the outlawing of spiritism, which was used to select new dignitaries.[86]

The state's repressive approach was coupled with controlling religious groups through "patriotic organizations," new bureaucratic structures, and tightly regulated religious legislation. The Hoa Hao, Cao Dai, and Buddhist Sangha were all reorganized at the top level to ensure they complied with the religious and political policies of the government. A 1977 directive on religious activity confined all religious activities (including propagation) to religious institutions and required government approval for education, training, ordination, publications, and pilgrimages. The Vietnamese Buddhist Association (Giao-Hoi Phat Giao Viet Nam) was established in 1981 to serve as the official Buddhist national organization, which was not universally accepted among Buddhists. The An Quang Unified Buddhist Church (UBC) based in Hue refused to join the VBA, constituting a nucleus of Buddhist "dissidents" against the regime which persists to this day. The regime did not attempt to create a similar organization for the Catholics or to discourage Catholics from attending mass. But Catholics were subject to discrimination and surveillance, especially the Catholic hierarchy. However, the state was less restrictive towards the Catholic Church than the other religions; the church was able to "preserve its internal unity and its ties with the Vatican."[87]

This started to change with *Doi Moi*. Although the religious communities have not recovered their pre-1975 status, their prospects notably improved after 1986. There are now eight Catholic seminaries which ordain new priests every year. The Vatican and the Vietnamese government are on the verge of establishing diplomatic relations; President Nguyen Minh Triet paid a visit to Pope Benedict in 2009. Buddhist pagodas affiliated with the Vietnamese Buddhist Association are thriving. The Catholic Church is growing and continues to gain new adherents, especially in the south.[88]

In 1994, the government Committee for Religious Affairs identified the Cao Dai and Hoa Hao as indigenous religions (*ton giao noi sinh dac trung*), as opposed to the "imported" religions of Catholicism and Buddhism.[89] By 1997, the government had recognized seven branches of the Cao Dai; in 1999 the state officially recognized the Hoa Hao. In the mid-1990s, 700 Cao Dai temples, 20,000 Buddhist pagodas, and 6,000 Catholic and 500 Protestant churches dotted the landscape of Vietnam. Government estimates of religious adherence included 5 million Catholics; 2.5 million Cao Dai, 1.5 million Hoa Hao, ½ million Protestants, and 50,000 followers of Islam.[90]

Nonetheless, the state continues to be ambivalent about "superstition" and the revival of mediumism. Some "spirits" are deemed legitimate and others not; some cults are superstitious, others not. Over the past decade, the state has moved to incorporate "popular religion" as part of the national patrimony, including some forms of mediumism and the occult arts. In some cases, spirit mediums are regarded as bearers of Vietnamese culture. They are not so considered in the case of the Cao Dai, where spirit calling continues to be outlawed. In 2006, the Ministry of Culture organized spirit possession cults as part of an effort to promote "favorable elements" of cultural identity."[91] This followed a change in the Ordinance on Belief and Religions, issued in June 2004, which legalized ancestor worship, hero worship, folk beliefs, and other religious beliefs which represent the "fine historical, cultural values and social ethics [of Vietnam]."[92] The state finally lifted these quintessential "superstitious" practices because popular religious activities, diffuse in nature, constitute no real institutional challenge to the regime. In effect, the state can control popular religion and substantiate it as part of "national tradition." The government now touts ancestor worship as central to national "belonging", that is, the religious identity of Vietnam.[93]

In recent years, however, tensions have escalated among Catholics, Protestants, Buddhists, and the government over land disputes, worship services, evangelism, and human rights.[94] Protestant evangelism among the Hmong in the northwest and the hill tribes in central Vietnam is subject to heavy restrictions.[95] The government continues to monitor, supervise, and reserve the right to "manage" all religious organizations and activity. Religionists chafe at this interference and have learned to live with it, to varying degrees.[96] The government's position is that religionists must be good citizens first and then they are "free" to hold and practice any belief they wish.

Conclusion

Historically speaking, viewed from the perspective of the long span of communist-religious interactions from the colonial period to the present, the tensions between religion and communism in Vietnam only in part consisted of opposing ideologies, atheism versus supernatural belief, competition for the same constituencies, and institutional competition. They have principally been a product of colonialism and foreign intervention and the emergence of Vietnam as a modern nation-state. Colonialism altered the relationship between religion and national identity in Vietnam. During the long struggles against foreign powers, from the 1930s to the 1970s, the communist movement could ill afford to alienate the religious communities in its midst; it needed to guard against, to the extent possible, their concluding cast-iron alliances with foreign occupiers. The party had to contend with the religious communities on its road to power. Once in power, however, the state sought to curtail the power of organized religion and restrain its "political" activities. With the advent of reform in 1986, religion returned in force and vitality to the cultural landscape of Vietnam, and the party once again found itself in league with the supernatural. Yet this was not such a difficult transition to make; the party had already relied on heroic discourses in mobilizing the population to fight two wars and to implant the cult of Ho Chi Minh firmly in the nation's consciousness. And, both the party and the new religions had emerged from the crucible of French colonialism. Even Catholicism, so bitterly opposed in the past, had earned its stripes as a patriotic national community. With the advent of reform, the party finally acknowledged that religion was part of the national patrimony and as such, could be appropriated as "national culture" which it now depended on for political legitimacy.

Notes

1. I would like to thank David Marr, Shawn McHale, Justine Buck Quijada, and John Whitmore for their close readings of this paper and comments. A revised version of this paper was presented to the Yale Council on Southeast Asia Studies Seminar Series, November 28, 2012. Thanks to Erik Harms and Ben Kiernan and the other participants for their observations and feedback.
2. As described by Stephan Feuchtwang (2001, p. 196).
3. The Communist party started to change its position on religion in 1990, with the adoption of a Politburo resolution stating that "faith and religion are needed by a segment of the population" and that "religion is a long-term issue" (Nguyen Ming Quang, 2005, p. 137). In 1991 a decree on religious activities led to a relaxation of government restrictions on religious groups and practices, while it also started a process of codifying and regulating religious organizations. In 1992 the new Constitution of the Socialist Republic of Vietnam reaffirmed that all citizens had the right to religious belief and non-belief.
4. See Pham Quynh Phuong (2009, p. 271).
5. Sophie Quinn-Judge (2002, pp. 158, 180). When the VCP changed its name to the ICP in October, 1930, it moved closer to the proletarian line of the Comintern, viewing the bourgeoisie as a class enemy.
6. For instance, William Duiker vaguely suggests the main ideological rival to the ICP during the 1930s was "Confucianism" rather than the religious groups as such. See Duiker (1976, pp. 47, 95, 287–290).
7. See David Marr (1986).
8. Huynh Kim Khanh characterizes this period as the beginning of a "fundamental political disaggregation of Vietnamese society," which would last for decades (1982, pp. 38–53).
9. See Charles Keith (2012, pp. 200–207). Also David Marr (1981, pp. 82–88).
10. See Shawn F. McHale (1995, p. 338).
11. Jayne Werner (1980, p. 108).
12. Aside from a rich cultural tradition of spirit possession, early Cao Dai leaders drew their religious inspiration and authority from local Sino-Vietnamese Minh masters who were the "guardians of the Jade Emperor's knowledge in the south." They were also influenced by the early 20th century Western theosophy movement. See Jeremy Jammes (2010, pp. 359–362).
13. Dai Dai Tam Ky Pho Do (1966) comprises the canonical texts of the Cao Dai religion.
14. Prasenjit Duara (2008, p. 48).
15. Ibid., pp. 43–54.
16. Some modernist intellectuals such as Tran Trong Kim tried to resuscitate a modern form of "Confucianism," but these efforts did not present viable alternatives in the l930s. See Shawn McHale (2002, pp. 397–431).

17. Elise DeVido (2007, pp. 250–297).
18. Marr (1981, pp. 304–306).
19. Tri Hai (1938).
20. Hue Tam Ho Tai (1983).
21. Werner (1980, p. 108).
22. A useful edition of these texts is Giao-Hoi Phat Giao Hoa Hao (1966).
23. Dutton, George, Jayne Werner, and John Whitmore (eds) (2012, p. 440). In the same text, Huynh Phu So pointedly cautions adherents against the godless Communists: "[until] recently, many people believed that the red color we used to use for worship had been appropriated by those who worked against the rules and the ideals of the Buddha. This is why we adopted brown as our color. Furthermore, monks use brown to symbolize their taking holy orders. Since brown is the combination of all the other colors, it symbolizes the harmony of humankind with out distinction in race or individual. This is why we use brown where we worship to represent Buddha's sublimity."
24. Nam Moc, a long-time party member, commented in the retrospective volume (1985) on Truong Chinh's *De cuong van hoa* (Theses on Culture), that in the late 1930s and early 1940s the ICP was so preoccupied with dealing with the sects that it did not have time to work on a cultural policy. See Truong Chinh, "De cuong ve van hoa Viet Nam" (Theses on Vietnamese Culture) (Truong Chinh, 1985, p. 86; Kim N. B. Ninh, 2002, p. 26). See also Tran Van Giau (1975, pp. 187–188), who devotes an entire chapter to the Cao Dai, claiming that the religious sects assumed the character of political parties during the 1930s and early 1940s, given the absence and prohibition of real political parties by the colonial regime.
25. Alexander Woodside (1976, pp 182–200).
26. Shawn McHale (2004).
27. Werner (1980, pp. 117–118).
28. Ibid., p. 108.
29. Tensions in the southern Viet Minh military command led by hard-liner Nguyen Binh contributed to the defection of religious groups from the Viet Minh military forces. See Christopher Goscha (2002, pp. 29–57).
30. Shawn McHale, pers. comm.; Werner (1980, pp. 122–125).
31. The sects controlled over ½ the population in Cochinchina during the first Indochina war (Werner, 1980, p. 108).
32. Ibid., pp. 125–127.
33. Marr (1986, p. 126).
34. Elliott (2003, p. 149).
35. Werner (1980, p. 127). This approach may have been taken to offset Nguyen Binh's ruthless retaliations against the sects after they left the united front. See Goscha, op. cit. Some Cao Dai and Hoa Hao had maintained relations with the Viet Minh, however. In addition to forming alliances, the united front policy targeted various organizations for infiltration. This did not work with the Catholics in Phat Diem, who resisted all Communist tactics. The Viet Minh desecrated and destroyed Buddhist pagodas in the north, although the extent is unknown (David Marr, pers. comm.).
36. The Viet Minh's heavy-handed approach in the south backfired. Their main goal was to achieve a unified control of the south and prevent a divided, balkanized Resistance (Shawn McHale, pers. comm.).

37. Truong Chinh issued two major statements, "Theses on Culture" (1943) and "Marxism and Vietnamese Culture" (1948) which defined the party's position on culture until 1986. These statements have been interpreted in a variety of ways, but I would suggest a new angle: a post-colonial reading (Truong Chinh, 1985). There is no reference to class struggle in this first statement on culture (Truong Chinh, 1977).
38. Truong Chinh defined culture as follows: "Culture is a very vast domain that encompasses literature, art, science, philosophy, customs, religion and more besides" (1977, p. 205). He believed that culture strongly influenced "material life."
39. Shaun Malarney (2002, pp. 57–64).
40. Truong Chinh (1977). Truong Chinh's socialist realist prescriptions for artists and writers to serve politics and awaken the "masses" were written in the context of waging a war. In this sense, socialist realism works were to be used for anti-colonialist purposes.
41. Ibid.
42. Kim N. B. Ninh (2002, p. 42).
43. Truong Chinh (1977, p. 248).
44. Marr (1986, p. 127). Two-thirds of the Catholics in the north fled south, according to Keith (2012, p. 7).
45. Peter Phan (2014). At the same time, the regime was confiscating large landholdings and other properties of Catholics, Buddhists, and other religious groups.
46. Werner (1980).
47. Jayne Werner (1976, pp. 471–488).
48. David W. P. Elliott (2003, pp. 227–229).
49. Werner (1980, p. 129).
50. As David Elliott notes, in one village in My Tho Province, the NLF initiated a religious extermination campaign (*phong trao diet dao*) where they closed Cao Dai temples and dismantled Cao Dai altars in adherents' homes (2003, p. 83). In My Tho in general, the hostility among the Cao Dai, the Hoa Hao, Catholics, and Communists limited the growth of the NLF there.
51. Elliott (2003, p. 274).
52. Nguyen Lien Hang T. (2012).
53. Pham Van Minh (2002, p. 167). Elise DeVido concurs, arguing that the Buddhist revival movement from 1920–1951 laid the organizational and conceptual foundation for Vietnamese national Buddhism (2007, p. 262).
54. Pham Van Minh (2002, pp. 169, 171).
55. Don Luce and John Sommer (1969, pp. 105–118); George McT. Kahin (1987, pp. 148–150); Robert J. Topmiller (2002, pp. 44–47).
56. Kahin (1987, pp. 415–416); Topmiller (2002, p. 138).
57. Thich Nhat Hanh (1967).
58. Luce and Sommer (1969, pp. 118–137); Kahin (1987, p. 432); Topmiller (2002, pp. 71–91).
59. Jayne Werner (1974).
60. As I discovered in 1972 in a research trip to Tay Ninh.
61. Georges Boudarel (1991, pp. 128). See also Dutton, Werner, and Whitmore (eds) (2012).

62. Benoit De Treglode (2002, pp. 28, 33, 53). Even during the Land Reform, the most radical phase of Vietnamese Communism (1954–1956), some village worship cults and festivals remained in place, as in the Red River delta village where I conducted field work in 1995–1996.
63. Ibid., p. 24.
64. Ibid., pp. 136–153.
65. Patricia Pelley (2003, p. 47).
66. Pham Quynh Phuong (2009, p. 146).
67. Cheng, Grace Ming-Hui (2002).
68. See Katrin Louise Jellema (2007).
69. See Shaun Malarney (2007, pp. 505–537).
70. Malarney (2002).
71. Christoph Giebel (2001, pp. 77–105).
72. De Treglode (2002, p. 388); Pelley (2003, pp. 115–118).
73. One of the first collections to address the "reenchantment" of Vietnam was Philip Taylor (ed.) (2007).
74. Intellectuals and academics in Vietnam have lent their cachet to this enterprise, by elevating "folklore" studies to a popular new topic of study.
75. Pham Quynh Phuong (2009, p. 161).
76. Ibid.
77. See Kristen Enders (2011); Philip Taylor (2004).
78. Le Hong Ly va Nguyen Phuong Cham (2008).
79. Olga Dror (2007).
80. Kristen Enders (2011, p. 121).
81. Heonik Kwon (2006).
82. Malarney (2002).
83. See Ngo Thi Thanh Tam (2011).
84. Including Ho Thai Bach, the son of *Bao Dao* Ho Tan Khoa. *Bao Dao* Ho Tan Khoa was forced to step down, and the top echelons of the Cao Dai were disbanded. Many dignitaries went back to their native villages. Interview with Vu Quang, Director, Committee for Religious Affairs, Hanoi, July 25, 1994; Interview with Le Quang Vinh, Deputy Director of the Committee for Religious Affairs, Ho Chi Minh City, August 24, 1994. Also Sergei Blagov (1996, pp. 278–280).
85. Marr (1986, p. 131).
86. Spirit session ceremonies were conducted by high-ranking dignitaries who invoked the Jade Emperor or another deity, with the assistance of a medium using a beaked basket (*co but*), to write down messages which were then transcribed by the dignitary. Spirit messages constituted the main spiritual authority of the Cao Dai.
87. Stephen Denney (1990, p. 390). All monks were and are officially required to affiliate with the government-controlled VBA.
88. See Tom Fox (2011). Cardinal Pham Minh Man, Archbishop of Ho Chi Minh city, told Tom Fox in 2011 that in his archdiocese there were 5000–7000 new adult baptisms every year, in part because of the influx of migrants to Ho Chi Minh City. In 2010, there were 3 archbishops, 44 bishops, 4000 priests, and 26 dioceses in Vietnam, and the priesthood had increased by more than 50 percent, compared to the previous five years. See US Department of State (2010), Country Report for Vietnam, September 13, 2011.

89. Interview with Vu Quang, Director, Committee for Religious Affairs, Hanoi, July 25, 1994. Vu Quang also told me that the party recognized that religion was a "spiritual necessity" for many people in Vietnam.
90. Interview with Vu Quang, Director Committee for Religious Affairs, Hanoi, July 25, 1994. When I interviewed Le Quang Vinh (Deputy Director of the Committee) in Ho Chi Minh city in August, he said it was not true that the government had declared the Cao Dai to be "illegal," only its "administrative committee" (i.e. the ruling councils of the Cuu Trung Dai and Hiep Thien Dai, the two main dignitary organizations). The government's policy towards the Cao Dai was to persuade them to "return to the source" (of their religion) and be a "religion" rather than a "political organization." But in effect he also admitted that the sect needed to reorient itself to the state by making accommodations to the national community as defined by the Socialist Republic of Vietnam. Once the Cao Dai (and any religious organization, by implication) accepted these terms, the state would "recognize" them. Le Quang Vinh noted, with approval, that the Tay Ninh branch of the Cao Dai had added Ho Chi Minh to its pantheon of saints and included some of his writings in their scriptures. Cao Dai branches which adopted "religion and country" as their slogan were viewed favorably by the government.
91. Pham Quynh Phuong (2009, p. 158).
92. Nguyen Minh Quang (2005, p. 178).
93. Jellema (2007, p. 596).
94. News services such as the BBC and RFA (in Vietnamese) and *Asia Times Online* covers these issues and incidents religiously.
95. For the Hmong see Ngo Thi Thanh Tam (2011).
96. See Peter Phan (2014).

3
The Socialist Interregnum and Buddhist Resurgence in Laos

Grant Evans

Communist revolutionaries in general have been hostile to religion, especially after seizing power. This mandate comes in part from a tendentious reading of Marx and Engels' statement in the *Communist Manifesto* that "religion is the opium of the people," and arises from the fact that communist revolutionaries have usually been radical modernists, on the side of science and progress and against "backward feudal beliefs." In an earlier essay on Buddhism and revolution in Laos I referred to this attitude as "secular fundamentalism" (Evans, 1998a), and in Asia we have seen outbursts of it in China during the Cultural Revolution and during the brief reign of Pol Pot in Cambodia. While less extreme versions of this attitude have been the broad standpoint of communism, its national and local manifestations have been very different from one another. The dethroning of the Christian church's worldly authority by science in Europe gave secular fundamentalism there a sharp and uncompromising edge. Faced by an almost monolithic monotheism, its target was clear and unambiguous. Elsewhere, however, revolutionaries were immersed in societies where beliefs and practices were diverse and boundaries were ambiguous.

For instance, in the small Asian state of newly independent Laos, the declaration in its first constitution in 1948 by the Royal Lao Government (RLG) that Buddhism[1] was the state religion may seem like the promulgation of a kind of monotheism, yet the religion itself is nothing of the kind because the Buddha is not a god in Buddhist theology. The establishment of Buddhist institutes by the French colonialists (1893–1947), or the setting up of a Ministry of Religion and the centralization of the Buddhist *sangha* (the order of monks) by the RLG (1947–1975), all suggested a modernizing drive for uniformity in beliefs and practices, but such desires were continually subverted by the religion's popular practice. Besides local diversity Buddhism cohabited or blended with beliefs in spirits and "angels," *thevada*. Furthermore, although Buddhism had been declared the state religion and the King its protector, only a little over half of the population were Buddhists and they were overwhelmingly ethnic Lao. Besides Buddhism, people of Chinese or Vietnamese descent practiced what has been referred to as "Chinese religion,"[2] and some upland groups, like the Hmong, followed practices derived from it. Beyond that, diverse ethnic groups practiced what many like to refer to as "animism," usually centered on various forms of ancestor worship. These practices are most likely to be viewed as backward superstitions by the Buddhist majority, but this view derives as much from these peoples' inferior social status as the intrinsic nature of the beliefs and practices.

Unlike in East Asia where certain forms of Confucianism in particular periods had produced a tradition of religious skepticism, no such tradition is discernable in the societies practicing Theravada Buddhism. The king as the protector of Buddhism sometimes led movements of renewal in the *sangha*, especially when monks were not following its rules and magical practices threatened to swamp the teachings of the Buddha (Tambiah, 1977, pp. 162–164). A famous case being the Lao King Photisarath (r. 1520–1548) who issued a decree against the worship of *phi*, spirits, but this may have been directed as much against the protective spirits of Tai[3] chieftains who he was in the process of subduing as it was concerned with Buddhist doctrine. During the 19th century Buddhism in the Siamese (Thai) Kingdom spawned a reform movement, the *Thammayut*, led by royalty "that emphasized the rationalistic side of the religion [and] arguably became the cultural expression par excellence of proto-nationalism" (Ishii, 1986, p. 136; also Reynolds, 2006). But although this was backed by the state it had relatively little influence on the popular practice of Thai Buddhism (McDaniel, 2008, p. 105). Thammayut monks found their way to Laos, but because a central sangha did not exist as a result of the wars that had destroyed the Lao kingdoms in the 18th and 19th centuries there was no central institution to "capture," and so any impact of this movement was local at best. In Laos there was no direct indigenous response by Buddhism to the challenges posed by modern science to its cosmology, at least until the middle of the 20th century.

Only in the 1920s did the French colonialists begin a reorganization of Buddhism, and they established Buddhist Institutes in the 1930s. Although the French Orientalists who were engaged in this "renovation" of Lao Buddhism favored a rationalist doctrine not unlike the

Thammayut, they were wary of the latter as it was seen as an instrument of Siamese influence and expansion in Laos. Many Lao monks received training in Thailand, but it seems that few of them were influenced by the Thammayut. A key figure in the Lao Buddhist Institute in Vientiane, Maha Sila Viravong, had been ordained in a Thammayut temple in Thailand, and according to Kourilsky (2006) this influenced his work in the Institute. Yet, as he argues, Maha Sila's approach was "ambivalent" and he did not reject the strong ritual components of Lao Buddhism.[4] In 1960 Bong Souvannavong, leader of the Lao National Union party and a local intellectual, published his *Doctrine Lao ou Socialisme Dhammique*, which proposed a rationalist version of Buddhism as the basis of democratic politics. He attacks the division of the monks into sects of Mahanikay (traditional Lao Buddhism) and the Thammayut because it destroyed Lao "solidarity" (1960, pp. 82–83), and he also criticized beliefs in *Thevada* (angels) and their alleged influence on human affairs: "The 'Thevada' is in reality a man like you and me who lives in the same terrestrial globe" (1960, p. 84). Belief in their magical powers is "contrary to the principles of Buddhism." His views, however, had little impact, and perhaps reflected the influence on Bong of the French Orientalists and colonial administration's view of Buddhism as a "moral code" and a source of social and political stability (see Kourilsky, 2006, pp. 61–63).

In the 1950s, as the "communist threat" loomed in the East, Bong was considered a "leftist" by the American supporters of the RLG because he had allied himself with the communist front the *Neo Lao Hak Sat* (NLHS, Lao Patriotic Front) in elections in 1958. He broke with them soon after, and his "Doctrine Lao" was anti-communist. Nevertheless, Bong's views on Buddhism were not all that different from those espoused by the revolutionary NLHS. Phoumi Vongvichit who was the NLHS spokesman on religious affairs spoke of the "deep influence of Buddhist Philosophy on the minds, feelings and ideology of the Lao people. The pagoda is the cultural centre of the Lao village," and he called monks "the intellectuals of the countryside" (1969, pp. 26–27).[5] During the revolutionary struggle the NLHS espoused freedom of belief and claimed to protect Lao Buddhism from outside influences: "To oppose all acts of sabotage by the US imperialists and their henchmen against Buddhism, such as distorting Buddhist catechism, controlling Buddhist monks and forcing them to serve criminal schemes, destroying pagodas or using them to preach decadent American culture, sowing discord among the various Buddhist factions, etc." (cited in Brown and Zasloff, 1986, p. 221). Prior to the revolution in late 1975 Buddhism was but one aspect of Lao culture that had to be protected from foreigners. Indeed, the broader social and cultural changes that came in the wake of Laos being drawn into the wider Vietnam War in the 1960s and 1970s was a source of anxiety for many, and monks were among the intellectuals forced to reflect on these changes. Given the centrality of Buddhism to Lao nationalism, it is not surprising that some monks were attracted to the anti-foreign nationalism of the NLHS.

The base areas of the revolution were in the sparsely populated mountains inhabited mainly by non-Buddhist ethnic groups. Among them unostentatious ritual activity was allowed, but shamanism was discouraged. Among Buddhists ritual expenditure was discouraged and laymen were told to devote themselves to the revolution rather than religion. Some "rationalization" of Buddhism occurred, but this was not emphasized, and monks were asked to not be burden on the people and to preach the cause of "liberation," and were important in literacy campaigns. A Lao Buddhist Fellowship organization was set up in 1961 by the revolutionaries, and this would take over the reins of the Sangha after 1975. When King Sisavang Vatthana visited the revolutionary headquarters at Vieng Sai in May 1975 as an act of reconciliation between the two sides in the civil war, Buddhist ceremonies were held to welcome him.

While the NLHS made propaganda out of any attempts by the RLG to direct Sangha affairs before the December 1975 revolution, it asserted complete control over the monkhood after taking power. The monarchy was abolished, the supreme patriarch of Buddhism was also abolished in early 1976, and adherence to Buddhist sects was outlawed. With the lapse of the RLG constitution Buddhism was no longer the state religion, and when a new constitution finally appeared 16 years later it was not restored to its former status either. The government, in accordance with an old script, set about purifying Buddhism. Maha Thongkhoun Anantasountone told Brown and Zasloff in 1980: "We prohibit spectacles, and those things that violate the principles of Buddhism. We wish to purify the practice of Buddhism and return to our genuine tradition" (1986, p. 227). A Department of Religious Affairs was set up as part of the NLHS, which in 1977 became the *Neo Lao Sang Sat* (NLSS, Lao Front for National Construction).

People became poorer after the revolution as commerce ground to a halt and the state attempted to take control of the economy, and so people had less money for religious activities. Moreover the government called on them to be frugal, and monks, along with everyone else, were encouraged to become self-sufficient. Poverty placed restrictions on Buddhist offerings, and village officials often made it difficult for men to enter the monkhood. Restrictions placed on Buddhist activities varied across the country, but where they were severe it was often because non-Buddhist ethnic minority cadres were in charge. The teaching of Buddhism in schools was stopped, while everyone, including monks, had to attend "seminars" to learn the party line, and monks also had to help propagate it too. Attempts by the state to take control of the provisioning of monks quickly ran up against popular opposition because alms-giving was central to Lao Buddhist practice (Evans, 1993).

The new rulers of Laos set out to politicize the Sangha. In early January 1976, the leading radical Buddhist Maha Khamtan Thepbouali, author of the seminal tract *Buddhism and the Lao Revolution* (1975), said: "We hold that the country and Buddhism cannot be separated... Therefore, since Lao society is changing favourably, it is certain that Buddhist monks and novices will undergo changes... We will try our utmost to stamp out the vestiges of the old society and build a new, pure and bright one. In the religious sphere it is necessary to correct many mistakes such as Buddhist text-books which do not conform with the principles of Buddhism – textbooks compiled by capitalism and feudalism to hoodwink the people" (SWB, 21/1/76).[6] The Lao Buddhist Fellowship Organisation proclaimed at its first nationwide conference held in Vientiane on July 6, 1976: "In the social field, the Association will defend all fine customs and habits of the people and the good morality of religions, while eliminating superstitious practices and all other social evils left behind by the old regime... The spread of Buddhist morality must accord with the line and policies of the Lao People's Revolutionary Party" (SWB, 30/6/76). Later in the year Phoumi Vongvichit gave the new regime's keynote speech on Buddhism, where he said that in contradistinction to the "old regime which prohibited Buddhist monks from engaging in politics" the new regime encourages it. The Buddha's original path of learning, he claimed, led him to the same conclusion as communists: "the Lord Buddha gave up all his worldly possessions and became an ordinary person with only an alms bowl to beg food from other people. That meant that he tried to abolish the classes in his country and to create only one class – a class of morally conscious people who were respected by other people. It was in this way that the Lord Buddha became involved with politics" (SWB, 1/11/76). He requested that monks go out and preach in support of the state's developmental programs. There was in fact little room for dissent from members of the monkhood as NLHS monks now held firm control of the Sangha. Those who disagreed, like the former patriarch (*Sangkharat*), fled to Thailand as refugees.

Significantly, Phoumi situated himself and his government in the same position as the Theravada kings of old who, in their role as defenders of the faith, occasionally acted as purifiers of the Sangha. By retraining monks, the new regime, he said, "will help purify and make Buddhism in this country more scientific than in other countries." Interestingly, the LPDR's (Lao People's Democratic Republic) "scientific" hostility to "superstitious" practices gained endorsement for a while from modernist Buddhists in Thailand, the followers of Buddhadasa, who, according to Lafont (1982, p. 159) saw Lao Buddhism as "reverting to the Buddha's original teaching." The regime's emphasis on rationality was underlined in a brief message to Lao Christians in 1982 when Khamtan Thepbouali told them: "Under this regime, everybody has a right to his own religion. But be careful. Don't believe just anything. Choose a belief that has some foundation and logic. Christianity is a good example. It has a set of scriptures which you can study and understand" (cited by Peachey, 1983, p. 19).

It is very hard to assess the impact of the Thammayut monk Buddhadasa on Lao Buddhism. The Lao revolutionaries were ambivalent towards the sect, not unlike the French colonial Orientalists who were attracted by the Thammayut's interpretations of Buddhism, but repelled by the fact that they were closely allied to Thai royalty and the propagation of Thai culture. Yet Buddhadasa's sentiments concerning "superstition" accorded with the new regime. He wrote, for example: "The influence of the collective mental flow of many ignorant people can have enough power to possess the minds of foolish individuals...and accordingly develop in them the feeling that such things are true and so cause them to believe in ghostly and magical things...the thing *avijja* (ignorance) builds up such erroneous beliefs" (cited by Jackson, 2003, p. 107). No doubt some Lao monks and officials concerned with religion read him in Thai but did not refer explicitly to his teachings publicly. Only in 2009 did his small book on *Dhammic Socialism* appear in Lao.

Communist hostility to superstition arose directly from their claims to be progressive and scientific, but the communists were also hostile because magical practices are charismatic and most often practiced individually and independent of major institutions, and for that reason uncontrollable, except by direct suppression.

Monks who had previously engaged in activities such as fortune telling or dream interpretation either stopped or became much more circumspect after 1975. The vicissitudes of everyday life, however, did not disappear with the revolution and a variety of "shamans" were available for consultation, in particular the *nang tiam*, mostly women who were possessed by mainly royal or powerful figures from the past. In the aftermath of the revolution some of these people were sent off for "re-education," or their activities were stopped by local authorities, especially the usually yearly congregations of these women which revolutionaries saw as equivalent to witches' covens. Yet as happened so often in post-revolutionary Laos the suppression was uneven. *Nang tiam* told Monique Selim (1997, p. 311), that after 1975 "The *phi* (spirits) hid themselves as they were scared of being arrested" or, "the *phi* have been sent to seminar" (re-education camps). Another *nang tiam*, however, explained that she was protected by her spirit: "After 1975 it was difficult. One day the militia and the soldiers came to arrest me because what I was doing was not allowed, but my *nya pho* (her spirit) stopped the soldier from arresting me; and so the soldier never arrived, he fell ill, his stomach swelled up and he couldn't heal it" (Selim, 1997, p. 312). I attended a gathering of *nang tiam* in a suburb of Vientiane in mid-1986, when one could feel the first breezes of reform communism, and many people had come to watch or consult their spirits. The women, while in a trance, dressed as men, smoked and danced with swords and provided advice to their devotees. However, I was chased away by a young soldier who said he did not want me to make "propaganda for the BBC," that is, propaganda that would show how backward and superstitious the new Laos still was.

Selim's research on women factory workers, done in the early 1990s when market reforms were in full swing and the shackles had started to be taken off everyday life, documents how former revolutionaries who had only been preoccupied with politics had "rediscovered the spirits" over 1988–1989 (1997, p. 302). Problems in one factory, for example, were diagnosed as being a result of not making the proper offerings to the earth spirits, and so an altar was constructed for them by these revolutionaries.

Moving away from the lowland Lao Buddhists, Vanina Bouté has given a fascinating account of the religious reforms introduced by the NLHS among the Phou Noy, speakers of a Tibeto-Burman language in the northern province of Phong Saly who claim to have been Buddhists for two hundred years. Before the imposition of strict NLHS control over the province in the 1960s, their Buddhism was combined with a strong cult of ancestral worship conducted by a *chao cham* or *maphê* but this was suppressed with the help of revolutionary monks. "The permanent altars dedicated to the ancestors and the *maphê* were the main targets; the first were burned, as were the costumes, jewellery and ritual accessories of the latter. The Lao compelled the villagers from there on to succour their ancestors at the temple, especially during the festivals devoted to the dead (*khao phadapdin* and *khao salak*)" (2008, p. 581).

The role of the *chao cham*, however, did not disappear, and a syncretism has evolved in which the monks and such "spirit specialists" preside over ancestral rituals (Bouté, 2008, p. 591).

Olivier Evrard's study of the Khmou is very similar, though here the revolutionaries accompanied by monks began their program of "exorcism ceremonies to 'expel the spirits back to the forests'" after 1975 (Evrard, 2008, p. 545). In one village he studied it began in 1977: "This ritual, carried out house by house, was finished in 1992 with a collective ceremony carried out by monks to expel the village spirit" (Evrard, 2008, p. 546). They did not follow this, however, by building a temple in the village, although monks have been used to create sacred spaces in the village. Only during Lao New Year do they attend ceremonies in a neighboring village. Interestingly a young Khmou who has left the village and married a Lao offered a replica of the neighboring village's Buddha to his natal village. Its incorporation into the village, argues Evrard, was accompanied by invoking "Buddhist legends and particular elements of Khmou mythology" producing a kind of syncretism rather than some straightforward conversion. Nevertheless this village's experience "shows how the articulation operated historically between the two cosmologies of the Khmou and Lao, and the inclusion of the indigenes in the political and symbolic space of the Lao" (2008, p. 548).[7]

My own research among the non-Buddhist Black Tai in Houaphan province, long under revolutionary control, asked whether there had been "reform or revolution in heaven?" (Evans, 1991). Here too reform intensified in the 1960s, the old aristocratic families had been deposed and the main rituals which reinforced their power abolished. Black Tai cosmology is more or less modelled on earthly power relations and so "heaven" had also been stratified. Initially I was told that equality now reigned there following the revolution, but it transpired that this view very much depended on whom one was talking with and that the former elite were not giving up their privileges. A more fluid conception of heaven was now available to Black Tai. This is a change that most probably would have happened with the expansion of any modern state and the compromising of chiefly privileges, though perhaps at a slower pace.

Prior to the revolution, emphasis was placed on Buddhism by the NLHS as a central part of Lao culture. In the immediate post-revolutionary period the whole society was subjected to political indoctrination, and the party set out to build socialist man and socialism. Emphasis fell on doctrinal purity in both politics and religion, and "superstition," almost by definition, was impure as there was no doctrine to purify. With the collapse of communism globally over 1989–1990 we saw a rapid shift back to the traditional pillars of legitimacy in Laos (Evans, 1998b; 2002), and this included the reassertion of Buddhism's cultural centrality and the valorization of many other ritual practices as part of Lao culture. A key symbolic act was the replacement in 1992 of the hammer and sickle in the national emblem with an icon of the That Luang, the central national Buddhist stupa of Laos.

A constitution was finally endorsed in 1991 whose article 30 stated that "Lao citizens have the right and freedom to believe or not to believe in religions." The latter phrase can be seen as a last shadow of socialist religious policy. In reality the government threw itself behind a reinvigoration of Lao Buddhism, in particular Buddhist education, which recommenced in Lao schools as a form of moral education. In September 1998 the Prime Minister promulgated a constitution for the Lao Sangha Administration. The Lao government promoted Buddhist moral education as a way of solving social problems. Indeed, according to a monk, Phra Santisouk (2004) writing on "Buddhist Teachings and Life" in the party paper, *Pasason*, it could solve every sort of problem, developmental, managerial, illness and so on. The Propagation of Buddhism Committee of the Lao Buddhist Fellowship Organization (LBFO) has set out to encourage the formation of meditation centers (not unlike a similar movement in Thailand), with Vat Pa Luang in Vientiane as its guiding center. This was led by Phramaha Pan Anantho who studied *Vipassana* meditation at Wat Mahathat in Thailand, an important Thammayut center.[8] And a kind of socially engaged Buddhism has become possible with monks involved in projects to help at-risk youth, and those with HIV. However, Ladwig (2008, p. 483) argues that while some monks have been taking their cue from engaged Buddhism in Thailand, they are constrained by the political system in Laos that inhibits civil society activity and by the strict control of the Sangha by the NLSS.[9]

Very recently young monks who have been trained overseas have begun to publish books that deviate from the standard recitations of modern Lao history under the LPDR. *Buddhism in Laos: A Study from the Ancient up to the Present*, published a by a Savannakhet-based monk D. P. Dhammikamuni in 2010, provides an unusually sympathetic treatment of Buddhism under the Royal Lao Government, and is unusually critical of post-1975 policies. "In 1975 when the Kingdom changed into a Republic the education of students of the Pali language in our Sangha disappeared and in its place there was simply the standard secular education... studying the *dhamma* or studying Pali was only a very small part and was not strict. Simply speaking, the old system was thrown out in its entirety and completely changed into the new system. It was a huge mistake in the education of the Lao sangha at this time ... this situation for the sangha's education took away the foundations for individual learning and meant that most monks and novices did not understand the *dhamma* and did not understand Pali which is the language of Buddhism" (2010, pp. 321–322). As we have seen, this situation changed rapidly in the 1990s and in 1998 "there was the revival of the sangha university at Vat Ong Teu [Vientiane] which had been closed" (2010, p. 322), and Pali schools began opening across the country after 2005.

One of the effects of the attenuation of Buddhist learning between 1976 and 1991 was that monks had to turn to Thailand to acquire and revive Buddhist learning, as in the case of Dhammikamuni himself, who also then went on to study at Buddhist Universities in India.[10] What they tended to encounter was the "rationalist" version of reform Buddhism, of which the Thammayut are an example, and this fitted with the ideology of the LPDR. Thus Dhammikamuni expresses views similar to Buddhadasa or Phoumi Vongvichit when he writes: "Lao people in general are strong Buddhists in a traditional way and they respect the Buddhist sangha highly. However, in their everyday practice they still believe in evil spirits along with many angels, *thevada*. Thus we can say that it is a kind of Buddhism mixed with the worship of evil spirits" (2010, p. 304). This attitude, however, must remain a minor stream within Lao Buddhism despite the fact that it accords with government propaganda, and despite mass education where adherence to superstition is criticized.[11] It is unlikely to gain traction until the composition of the Lao population shifts from being overwhelmingly rural.

In another publication on *Buddhism and Democracy* (c. 2010. interestingly only published in English) Dhammikamuni is heavily reliant on Thai and Indian Buddhist tracts. In the light of the changing political climate within Laos perhaps what is significant is that throughout the book the United States is seen as being in the "vanguard of democratic reform" (c. 2010, p. 88). It is an intriguing Buddhist intervention into Lao political debate.

Buddhism has become the de-facto religion of the Lao state since the 1990s and the work of the Religious Affairs Department of the NLSS is overwhelmingly oriented towards Buddhism, its strengthening and expansion. Certain publications claim that 90 percent of the Lao population are Buddhists,[12] although this is obviously an exaggeration. Nevertheless, I suggest, that such a percentage is the implicit aim of the government. While there are no explicit missionary plans for ethnic minorities, one of the aims of the LBFO is to send monks and novices to establish Buddhist teaching where there is none (Khamyad, 2006, p. 167). The establishment of temples by minority peoples are reported favorably in the press. For example, an article in the Party paper *Pasason*, entitled "The Various Minorities of Sekong Province Are Coming to Believe in Buddhism," reports on the "positive influence" by lowland Lao on minority communities who have established temples in Sekong:

> Today there are five villages... that have agreed to invite monks to carry out prayer rituals to wipe out spirit beliefs, for example the Alak village of Ban Nawa Saen, and the Taliang village of Ban Don Muang... these various villages now lead lives much like lowland Lao and believe in Buddhism... In the future they intend to build more temples in villages that do not have them because the people have a desire to follow Buddhism.[13]

In the last decade the government has swung increasingly behind a missionary Buddhism because of the spread of revivalist forms of Christianity among Khmou, Hmong and others. Buddhism is seen as a unifying force in Laos whereas Christianity, which is "foreign" is divisive, especially as these groups often refuse to have anything to do with the NLSS, and therefore are considered illegal. While the LPDR loudly proclaims its multi-ethnicity, one perspective which has not changed is the centrality of Lao culture to their conception of national unity. Phoumi Vongvichit argued long ago "Thai-Lao culture is representative of the cultures of all nationalities living on Lao territory. This ancient and rich culture is the most developed in all Laos. It has played in the past and it will play in the future a decisive role in the evolution of Lao culture" (1969, p. 26). Buddhism, of course, is central to that vision of Lao culture and is accordingly the "default" religion in Lao discourse.

There have been many statements concerning the relationship of Buddhism and nationalism in Laos in the last two decades, but I will take Saykham Champaouthoum's 2004 article in the Party's newspaper, *Pasason*, entitled "The Lao People and Buddhism," as representative. He argues: "The facts of Lao history show that the Lao people have respected Buddhism for a very long time... For this reason Buddhism and the Lao nation are one and the same, and Buddhist teachings have a role in society, culture, customs, traditions, and even up to the management of the country it has a place. Lao society therefore has become a Buddhist society." Almost all the yearly celebrations are Buddhist, he says, and "Polite behaviour in Lao society is almost completely derived from Buddhist teachings...and Buddhism is the basis of culture...Thus being a Buddhist and being a Lao cannot be separated." He only just stops short of saying that if you are not a Buddhist then you are not a Lao, which would, of course, excommunicate from the nation a large swathe of people, especially ethnic minorities.

One of the paradoxes of the government and the LBFO's commitment to a reform style of Buddhism is that it is in fact likely to hamper its spread. As Craig Reynolds has pointed out so clearly, "One of the reasons Buddhist cosmography fitted so well into mainland Southeast Asian societies is that it included a place for the creatures of animism. One kind of spirit (Pali *peta*; Sanskrit *preta*) that dwells below the terrestrial level between the demons (asura) and the animals is none other than the *phi*, or ghosts, of the departed dead in popular Siamese [and Lao] Buddhism" (2006, p. 165). Popular Buddhism's tolerance of indigenous beliefs and practices has been one of the secrets of its success to date. Indeed as we have seen from Bouté's study above, this mingling of beliefs has been maintained, albeit in a new form, despite campaigns against "superstition."

A modern urban and educated society may demand more "rational" forms of Buddhism,[14] such as the extraordinary Thammakai movement in Thailand that Donald Swearer equates with other "new mass religious movements" and is very influential among university students (2009, p. 139), but Laos is still a long way from that.[15]

A nationalist agenda has completely eclipsed any socialist agenda in Laos. This began with the collapse of communism globally and has intensified year by year since then. Marxism-Leninism is an ideology that justifies the maintenance of power by the Lao People's Revolutionary Party (LPRP), and the Leninist party has shown that it is well equipped to ensure a smooth transition to capitalism – an historical outcome foreseen by no-one.[16] The Lao government and its society differs little from the various developmental regimes that one can find across Asia today. The main differences are residual – that is, the continuity of the one-party state, and the continuing restrictions on civil society organizations, although these too are slowly loosening. Certainly within the LPRP lip-service is still given to Marxist-Leninist ideology, but its main purpose seems to function in a sectarian way by having people within the party commit themselves to an esoteric belief system, and therefore it acts as a way of disciplining dissent within the party, or put another way, of producing conformism. This is now mixed with heavy doses of developmental nationalism in which the party is seen as main means of protecting the nation and bringing prosperity.

Lip-service also continues to be paid to socialist ideology in Sangha education. Khamyad (2006, pp. 222–223) informs us that the monks "broker information from the party down to the people. In seminars, monks are told that Buddhism and socialism have much in common. For example, they espouse that all human beings are equal, that they are all brothers, and that as a body they live and work together without individual ownership of property. Monks are encouraged to approach the Marxist ideal of a future communist society...Both Buddhism and socialism aim to end suffering and work towards true happiness." But today we hear few references to socialism or to government policy in the context of monks' sermons, and the younger intellectually oriented monks make little attempt to directly align their views with socialism or Marxism.

Ladwig has written "that some of the central roles once occupied by the temple have been taken over by other institutions in the course of the successive expansion of the modern nation-state: schooling, healthcare and administration, but also the composition and transmission of art (literature, fine arts etc.) are today less and less incorporated into the religious sphere as they often were in the past" (2008, p. 471). However, there is nothing specifically communist in these changes, as similar policies by any other modern state would have the same impact.

Perhaps we can say that the state's promotion of a "rational" reform style of Buddhism has accelerated the penetration of these ideas into the monkhood in advance of the actual social changes that would normally support such a shift in religious practice among the population at large. Indeed one could argue that the most important social change under the LPDR has been the expansion of secular education, and this has surely had a much greater impact on people's perceptions of religious cosmologies than any more targeted propaganda by the government.

"Superstition," of course, remains the *bête noir* of government propaganda and Lao people generally are sensitive to any suggestions that what they do or believe in is superstitious. As a general rule practices that are encompassed by Buddhism, such as the rocket festival, the ubiquitous *baci* ceremony, or even *phi ban* (village spirit) rituals, are clearly exempted from the charge of superstition. And there is a large grey area of Lao practices associated with spirits, such as the *nang tiam* we encountered earlier in the essay, which may or may not attract such criticism. Certainly the reform monks would attack such practices, but many people do not. And then there are "real" superstitious practices that no-one really defends, such as the notorious case of a Lao man who killed his three-month pregnant wife in order to use the fetus to produce what is known as a *luk lort*, a potent spirit that could bring him fortune.[17] The story captivated the public in early 2011 because the man refused to reveal where he had buried the fetus, presumably because he did not wish others to find and use it. But normally "superstition" is a term most often used with reference to the beliefs and practices of Laos' non-Buddhist ethnic minorities. Such "superstitions" are considered symptomatic of "backwardness" and in need of reform or suppression because they retard the country's progress. Minorities are aware of this general disdain, and when they enter the education system, and when they migrate to urban centers, there is a great deal of pressure on them to be discreet about their religious practices. One strategy to "upgrade" their beliefs has been to appropriate the term "religion" and thus call their beliefs *sasana phi*, spirit religion, or alternatively to brand it as *sasana pham*, Bhrammanistic religion. The latter has been associated with the various courts of Southeast Asia and its practice very visible in Laos through the medium of Thai television and its coverage of royalty there. But it is also visible through the ceremonies conducted by Thai movie and pop stars where they seek the blessings from, for example, Ganesha (a cult which has grown in popularity over recent years). However, this "upgrading" has met with a lukewarm response from the Buddhist Lao.

The higher place of Buddhism in Lao society and the many public rituals associated with Buddhism press on young members of minority groups to merge upwards and become part of the larger Lao-centered culture and to at least nominally convert to Buddhism. Some groups can resist these cultural pressures better than others, such as the Hmong. But they have been susceptible to Christian conversion. One of the attractions of this conversion is that they "upgrade" to a world religion, but one that is not controlled by the Lao.[18]

Laos has joined the Asian economic boom, and Buddhism has been an immediate beneficiary of the wealth generated in the form of temple building and renovation and in terms of the laity's ability to support the monkhood. We might say that Buddhism is booming in Laos, and that the socialist interregnum of late 1975 to 1991 has faded away barely leaving any trace on its practice.

Notes

1. That is, Theravada Buddhism (School of the Elders) which is also predominant in Sri Lanka, Thailand, Myanmar and Cambodia. It is claimed that its teachings are closer to the teachings of the historical Buddha compared to the Mahayana found in East Asia, which has evolved new teachings.

However, Thai historian Prapod questions whether one can use the term "Theravada Buddhism" which he says was really invented by German and British Indologists and Buddologists in the 19th and early 20th centuries: "if we examine the early Indian context, there is no 'pure' or 'primitive' aspect of any of the religions, and certainly no 'ism' existed. Since all religions in India emerged from the same social background, they can be said to be Indian. The same moral, philosophical, and intellectual foundation pertains to all Indian religions. In the rush to differentiate these religions, scholars used the tool of 'isms.' However, if by religion we mean what is actually practiced by the masses, then these differences were scarcely felt by the people" (2010, pp. 188–189).
2. A variable mix of Confucianism, Taoism and Buddhism (Mahayana).
3. Tai (unaspirated) refers to a broad ethno-linguistic family that includes both Buddhist Thai (of Thailand) and Lao as well as non-Buddhist groups.
4. Kourilsky (2006, p. 5) uses François Bizot's term "tantric Theravada" to describe Lao and Thai Buddhist practice.
5. Phoumi said of the Thammayut: "In spite of support given by the American imperialists, this sect has remained weak and has made its influence felt only in a few pagodas in the suburbs of Vientiane, in Lower Laos, and especially in Champasak province" (1969, p. 27).
6. SWB = BBC Summary of World Broadcasts.
7. Both Bouté and Evrard are concerned to show the "agency" of the Phou Noy and the Khmou in their interaction with the dominant Lao and to show that there is not some simple one-way conversion of these peoples. No doubt this is true in the short term, but looking at the spread of Buddhism over the long term in this part of Asia we see a lot of local syncretisms in the creation of Buddhist adherents, as documented so well by Charles Archaimbault's many studies in Laos, and by Bizot (2000). These studies concern religious change in rural areas in the past and present. However, migration to cities and modern education creates a new dynamic which we shall come to further on.
8. See Dhammikamuni (2010, pp. 305–306) on Phramaha Pan for his work in this regard. Swearer (2009, pp. 178–183) discusses the importance of meditation for the revitalization of Buddhism in Southeast Asia.
9. See Swearer (2009, pp. 141–159) for a discussion of the situation in Thailand.
10. In 2005 there were "monks and novices going for Bachelor and Masters Degrees in places like Thailand, India, Myanmar, and Sri Lanka. Today, there are 392 monks and novices studying in foreign countries, most of whom go to Thailand" (Khamyad, 2006, p. 172).
11. Another similar text criticizes: "the belief in high gods (*thevada chao*) who can do anything, and in smaller gods in their hundreds or hundreds of thousands, which are thought to have power and influence and are able to supernaturally create various things. When a person wants something they go to beg for it from the gods, or when they fear things they ask for protection." And, of course, sacrifices of animals to such gods are condemned (Siripanyo, 2009, pp. 14–15).
12. Khamyad's (2006, p. 200) claim is based on a Lao Tourist Authority brochure!
13. *Pasason*, January 26, 2004.

14. Some intellectuals have expressed opinions not unlike those of Rationalist Societies in Europe. So one researcher in the Ministry of Culture was reported in the *Vientiane Times* claiming that "'The teachings of all religions and rituals are based on scientific causes and reasons,' he said, adding that there was no superstition in the world that did not have some scientific basis. Mr Some said that it was because of his study of socialism...Socialism encouraged people to believe in the truth, facts, and science" (Ekaphone, 2005). But such views are rare.
15. Swearer (2009, p. 140) cites Sanitsuda Ekachai who says: "Dhammakaya, then, could be viewed as a capitalist version of Buddhism aimed at urban Thais who are used to comfort, convenience, and the instant gratification found in consumer society."
16. This is discussed in greater depth in my revised and updated *Short History of Laos*, which is in-press.
17. Articles from January 17 and 18, 2011, in the *Vientiane Times* document the case.
18. On this process of conversion see Ngo Thi Thanh Tâm's (2010) discussion of the Hmong in northern Vietnam. I am not aware of any similar research in Laos, but see Evans (2004, p. 23).

4
Conflict and Coexistence of Church and State Authorities in (Post)Communist Poland

Agnieszka Pasieka

Introduction

In April 2010, a few days after the crash of the Polish President's plane in Smolensk, the Cardinal of Cracow announced that the president and his wife would be buried in the cathedral crypt in the Wawel Castle, which arguably constitutes the most significant part of the national heritage. Various objections were raised against the decision. It provoked strong protests among intellectuals, politicians, and, last but not least, inhabitants of Cracow, who only a few months earlier opposed the idea of bestowing the Honorary Citizenship of Cracow on President Lech Kaczyński. The government did not take any stand, considering that the issue should be dealt with by the cardinal and family members. Eventually, the burial took place as planned by the cardinal.

In 1935, the then Cardinal of Cracow decided on his own to move the coffin of an important Polish statesman, Marshall Józef Piłsudski, to a new crypt without consulting the state authorities. As a result, a big conflict erupted, involving the president, mass media, civil society organizations, and even Vatican authorities. Members of parliament demanded breaking off the concordat, and people wrote letters of protest to both the Church and state authorities. The most extreme voices demanded divesting the cardinal's citizenship and expelling him from the country. Eventually, the cardinal had to write an official apology to the president, which was later formally approved by parliament.

Obviously, both cases had a complex socio-political background and one must be careful while drawing comparisons between the 2nd and the 3rd Polish Republic. At the same time, there are (at least) two reasons that make this comparison insightful for an understanding of the relation between the Catholic Church and the Polish state. First, it is important to point out that the events of 1935 are hardly imaginable in present-day Poland. Today, not only does the state prevent any possible confrontation with the Church but it often gives up its own prerogatives under the pressure of the episcopate. In the last two decades, numerous debates on the state's functioning and citizens' rights constituted a perfect exemplification of this fact. Importantly, the Church's influence on politics was criticized not only from the position of the defenders of a secular country's worldview and pluralistic public sphere, but by legal representatives who cautioned against the violation of constitutional rights. Assessing the realization of the concordat and the impact of the Church on state matters, they spoke about a "step backward" in comparison with interwar Poland (Winiarczyk-Kossakowska, 2010). Second, many scholars of Polish Catholicism stress that the processes occurring in interwar Poland were evidence of the country's increasing secularization; had it lasted, the importance of Catholicism in Poland would diminish (Casanova, 2001; Ramet, 1998). What begs the question, therefore, is the role of the 45 years of communist regime in shaping post-1989 church-state relations, and namely the issues if and how the communist period influenced today's manifestations of religion in Poland.

Attempting to answer this question, I find it crucial to go beyond the repeatedly mentioned issue of the Church's support for the democratic opposition and its role in abolishing communism. For this – no doubt true – fact tends to be portrayed in a simplified manner, functioning as an analytical shortcut in investigations of postcommunist reality. Concurrently, this observation means the necessity to go beyond the studies of Polish Catholicism, which focus on Romantic national-religious discourses and argue about church-nation alliance in the 19th century independence struggles, reproducing the discourse of a 'Catholic nation' instead of attempting to deconstruct it and inquiring into the societal response to it (cf. Porter, 2001). Such works tend to disregard the fact it was Positivism rather than Romanticism that brought about a new understanding of a 'Polish nation' and – even if indirectly - reinforced ethno-religious bonds (cf. Walicki, 1999; Porter, 2000) as well as ignore the problem of a 'respectively constructed' link between religion and nationhood (cf. Zubrzycki, 2010). Instead, they provide an analytical scheme, according to which the church-society alliance had a long tradition, dissident movements had romantic roots, and the continuity of religious nationalism in postcommunism constitutes the proof of 'Polish exceptionality.' Consequently, due to a tendency to highlight 'cultural' rather socio-political factors, vast areas of the phenomenon of Polish Catholicism remain unexplored.

The reason why a critical engagement with the argument on 'Polish exceptionality' is so important is the fact that it perfectly reflects profound ambiguities which characterizes the discourse on secularization and secularism, understood, respectively, as socio-historical process and as a worldview (Casanova, 2009). In numerous scholarly works (e.g. Bruce, 2010) and textbooks (e.g. Bowen, 2010), the Polish case epitomizes the strength of national-religious bonds. Such a categorization rarely takes into account the very problematic nature of the idea of 'religious' and 'religiousness' or recognize the extent to which 'religious' symbols and beliefs might have been secularized for the purpose of serving national needs (Zubrzycki, 2010, p. 613). By imposing a reading of religious-national connection, it also imposes an understanding of what religion is or how it is supposed to be understood. This, in turn, has an impact on the approaches to secularization, manifested, for instance, in the conviction that strong church-state relations preclude secularization.

Henceforth, in my attempt to deconstruct the idea of 'Catholic Poland,' I find it necessary to problematize the relation between church, and state and society, or rather: church representatives, state actors, and "average" people.[1] What is observable, in my view, in the studies of both communist and post-communist Poland is a strong focus on "church/state discourses," "religious/national narrative," while the question of the people's answer to those is often ignored. This fact becomes even more important if one takes into consideration that people's answers, expressed in public opinion polls, often demonstrate disapproval to the church/state decisions and challenge some taken-for-granted images. I guess that while many people, scholars or not, had a chance to learn about the Polish Church-opposition alliance under communism, it is less likely that they heard that in the tough period of the 1980s only a small part of the Polish population believed that the Church supported the dissidents.[2] Similarly, today's vision of "Catholic Poland," in which the Church plays a prominent political role, is commonly quoted without further analysis of the voices of the Polish population that disapprove of this role. In other words, what will constitute the focus of my attention is the question of what should be actually understood as "Catholic Poland." It is often pointed out that the Polish state is secular (constitutionally guaranteed division) but the society is very religious (high number of practices and religious declarations). However, an analysis of the contemporary situation may bring completely different conclusions: in many dimensions of public life it is rather difficult to speak of church-state division, while the society represents in fact a model of "pick and choose religiosity," that is, it accounts for secularization rather on the micro than on the macro level (Dobbelaere, 2002).

In order to address all these issues, I present ethnographic evidence from a religiously and ethnically diverse village in Southern Poland, where I carried out a year-long fieldwork between 2008 and 2009. Due to both fieldsite location (scarcely inhabited borderland with Slovakia) and its heterogeneity, this region constitutes a quite peripheral context. While such areas are rarely taken into account in the study of Polish Catholicism, I suggest it is precisely the region's "marginality" and "specificity" to make it an appropriate setting for studying the "mainstream." First, anthropological contributions have by now proven the "margins" as spaces which reflect best mainstream policies as well as the flows against them (Das and Poole, 2004). Second, due to the presence of several religious communities, the site permits us to study how Catholics position themselves, understand and evaluate their religion and the Church in confrontation with other communities. Finally, it enables us to show how "religious others" perceive and experience the dominant religion. Notwithstanding the importance of all these issues, in this chapter I focus mainly on the first two aspects, starting with a brief historical overview.

Religious life under communism

The village I am describing here is inhabited by ca 1100 people. It is the seat of the regional government and other locally important institutions. Along the main road, there are situated, one next to another: the school, the village leader's house, the Centre for Social Assistance, the post office, the District Council, and two churches: a relatively small, old wooden shrine belonging to the Greek Catholic community and a huge, new stone Roman Catholic church towering over all other buildings. The church is visible in the entire district even by night due to a big red crucifix, made of fluorescent bulbs, installed on the church tower. Until the mid-1940s, a vast majority of the population was of Ruthenian ("Lemko") origins and practiced Greek Catholicism. In 1947, Polish authorities expulsed the local population and settled in their place Polish Roman Catholics.[3] New inhabitants took over the Greek Catholic shrine, and in 1951 a new parish was officially established. Some Lemkos managed to come back in the late 1950s, yet the Greek Catholic Church was banned throughout the entire communist period. After its reestablishment in 1989, Roman and Greek Catholics would use the church jointly, and since 2002 Roman Catholics have prayed in the newly built temple.

Despite the fact that my informants differed in terms of age and occupation, their memories of religious life under the communist period were strikingly similar. First of all, people would argue that religious practices under communism were as vivid as they are now, or even say that in the past they used to attend church more frequently. Secular rituals were hardly ever mentioned, whereas the narratives regarding religious ones, such as baptisms or weddings, constituted an important element of people's remembrances from communism, proving both personal attachment to those rites and their community-building character. Besides, inhabitants did not recall any problems regarding the performance of religious practices and stressed that the only people who – in theory – could not openly practice were state employees, yet also in their case the ban tended to be bypassed. They too remarked upon some high state officials who married or baptized their children secretly in their remote village.

Yet, people did distinguish between "good" and "bad" communist officials. The bad guys were the ones who attempted to control the population or who took their credo "seriously": they fought against the crosses in the public institutions and organized obligatory Marxism and Leninism classes. The good ones, instead, would help the church thanks to their connections, for instance organizing material for church renovations. Thus, some of state officials were described as strong church supporters. Many of my informants used to be Party members but few of them stopped attending church for this reason. On the one hand, this proves that the communist system meant first and foremost an economic and not ideological dimension to them, but on the other hand, it shows that church attendance was a traditionally rooted, community activity. This proves, too, that communism and Catholicism were in people's eyes "responsible" for and related to distinct spheres of people's lives. What needs to be stressed here is the fact that religious life under communism was not considered by my informants a relevant issue and recalling the times of the People's Poland they focused on other aspects, such as work and social life (Pasieka, 2015).

Hence, villagers were far from describing their religious practices under communism in terms of resistance or opposition against the system. And yet, it is precisely a "resistance narrative" to constitute a leitmotif in the exploration of Church-state-society relations before and after 1989. The period of communism is often seen as crucial for the construction of the bond between Catholicism and Polishness and as a key to understand the strong role of the Church in today's Poland. It is argued that the main reasons of this fact were (1) the process of homogenization of Poland, arising from war operations and postwar policies, and bringing as a result a population composed 90–95 percent of Catholics, (2) the Church's (support for the) opposition to the state, and (3) the communist state's failure to create a socialist national identity. Due to all these processes, the national identity was "catholicized" (Zubrzycki, 2001, p. 639). Such an interpretation is accepted by many scholars, who stress an exceptional independence of the Church in Poland in comparison with other countries of the former Soviet bloc (Ramet, 1990). Some of them emphasize the strong connection between Church and society, perceiving them as two agents acting against the state (Dudek and Gryz, 2003), while others emphasize the role of the Catholic religion as a symbolic reservoir, which provided the opposition with means of expression (Kubik, 1994). Notwithstanding the weight of these arguments, I contend that none permits to fully address the relation between communism and religion. Since the definitive element of this relation is the role of Catholicism in *opposing* communism, the issue regarding other possible "configurations" remains un-answered (in fact even un-asked). This is not to say that the Church did not play a role in the opposition, but to suggest that it might have played different roles, too, or that there might have been people who did not oppose the system but the religion did play a role for them. In other words, it invites us to look at those dimensions of the communist regime's period, which are passed over in the "oppositional" (and "romantic") narrative.

More precisely, such observations lead to a recognition of a twofold, changing nature of Church-state relations, which involved both conflict and coexistence (Eberts, 1998). Scholars observe that the Church was "a difficult and independent partner, but predictable and capable of compromise" (Dudek and Gryz, 2003, p. 372). Indeed, an analysis of church-state relations after 1945 suggests that every time the state "needed" the Church's support, it would negotiate with the episcopacy for privileges and concessions, which were to be exchanged for the "proper" content of pastoral sermons and letters. To give a few examples, in 1950 the condemnation of anti-communist partisans was exchanged for safeguarding the Church's properties and religious education; in 1956 and 1970 sermons calming down the protesting workers were promised for lessening the censorship policies; while in the 1980s the reluctance to support Solidarity's protests and voices inviting society to accept martial law turned into a boom of sacral buildings. This does not mean that the promises were necessarily kept; once the critical situation passed, the state would often withdraw declarations and sharpen the policies. Likewise, the positions of the clergymen were very diverse; there were more or less conciliatory priests, and the latter ones would often ignore the orders of the hierarchy and challenge the state on the local ground (see, e.g., Dudek and Gryz, 2003, pp. 98, 393, 403). Nevertheless, the very existence of such negotiations proves that the Church was an actor seriously taken into account by the state and that the latter was perfectly aware of its power (which also meant an awareness of how to instrumentalize it).

Seen in this light, the above account on the researched village does not seem to constitute an exceptional case, but an illustration of a widespread tendency to accommodate communism and religion (certainly, the character and degree of such an accommodation would vary in different contexts). Before discussing the present-day situation, it is necessary to describe in more detail a few patterns of "conflict-coexistence" relation, which may shed light on today's religious manifestations and the role of communism in shaping them.

Communism and Catholicism in Poland

In this section, I extend the discussion on "conflict and coexistence" by focusing on some similarities between communism and religion[4] and later on relating my argumentation to the frequently presented views on the bond between Catholicism and Polishness. What I aim to discuss here are communist discourses and practices that meant the re-shaping of well-known, socially accepted and rooted "ways of doing." A good exemplification of this process may be the introduction of "new" rites of passage, such as the ceremony of "name-giving" (secular baptism), "personal identity card ritual" (secular confirmation), and "individual conversation" as an alternative to the confession (Kubik, 1994, p. 38). Not only the form, but also the content of many rituals resembled the religious ones. Despite the activities of the Society for the Promotion of Secular Culture, none of the mentioned forms were widely accepted. Moreover, apart from introducing new rituals, the state attempted to secularize the institution of marriage and funerals, also in this case encountering big difficulties. Religious marriages resulted to be so popular that the authorities decided to make the civil marriage a condition for the religious one; in time, it became the best accepted among the secular rites. On the contrary, secular funerals found less acceptance, what Kubik explains (1994, p. 40) with the meritocratic ideology behind them, which contradicted the socialist idea of equality (cf. Buchowski, 2001, p. 42). All in all, not only did the state's rituals fail to substitute for the religious ones, but they made some non-religious people turn to religious rites, just because they disapproved of communist ones

(Chrypinski, 1990, p. 126; Dudek and Gryz, 2003, p. 9; Grabowska, 2001, p. 174). Importantly, in many cases these traditionally performed "religious" rituals were, in fact, secularized (often deprived of strictly religious content). Thus, taking into account the ritual-oriented character of the Polish religiosity (and Catholicism in general), it may be argued that new rituals were not necessarily seen with hostility, but rather judged as unnecessary and artificial.[5]

The second issue that I want to highlight is the religious and communist view of a "good life" and ideas of morality. Despite the fact that the materialistic doctrine and the formation of the "socialist man" were seen as contradictory and incompatible with the Catholic catechism, there were many conjunctions in both systems. Seemingly emancipated, communist morality was in many fields very prudish (Kula, 2003, p. 108). And although the Church highly criticized some of the state's policies (for instance the accessibility of abortions)[6], both actors found several fields of cooperation. In the 1970s, the Church and the communist regime fought against "social pathologies" and disapproved of "Western influences" in the sphere of culture and morality. Extensive correspondence between bishops and Party members prove a common concern with excessively liberal cultural performances and a need to limit their "potentially damaging" consequences. While bishops were asking the state authorities to block the staging of "immoral" theatre plays, the latter appealed to the clergymen: "Use letters and sermons to stigmatize, not the authorities, but writers and directors" (quoted in Dudek and Gryz, 2003, p. 348). Another very telling example is the vision of a Polish citizen as presented by the Church and the authorities. Similarly to the rulers of other Soviet bloc countries (Verdery, 1996), Polish communists integrated into their doctrine an ethnic-defensive ideology (Zaremba, 2001). As Kubik points out (1994, p. 122), the Church's vision of an ethnically and religiously homogeneous Poland, with Catholicism as its religion, was "'an image of Poland that mirrored the state's vision' and as such was problematic for non-Catholic anticommunists." Although the communists would make do without the religious component, both institutions were advancing the idea of "Poland for Poles." Furthermore, in promoting moral life, Church and state shared the use of certain discursive strategies (obsolete forms, hyperbole, authoritarian tone), which made their messages very rigid (Kubik, 1994, pp. 125–126)[7] and evoked resemblances between communist "langue de bois" and religious preaching.

Above mentioned examples are of course only a small segment of the vast field of Church-state relations. The dynamics of "conflict-coexistence" can be traced on different levels. On the one hand, many more parallels between communism and religion can be drawn; these regard issues as different as organization and functioning of institutions, character of beliefs, or iconographic representations (see Buchowski, 2001; Kula, 2003). On the other hand, there are plentiful examples of confrontations and clashes between Catholic and communist authorities, resulting in different attempts to silence the most rebellious priests (by the state and the Church authorities alike[8]). Besides, the complexity of religious phenomena makes it difficult to provide a clear-cut picture of religious life under communism. However, the herein described picture enables us, in my view, to draw a few important conclusions. I shall summarize them referring to above presented arguments regarding the reasons for the strong connection between Catholicism and Polishness.

First, although ethnic and religious homogenization of the Polish society is a fact, it is necessary to take into account internal pluralism within a single religious denomination and an ambiguous relation between religious declarations and faith: "Catholics" also include "cultural Catholics" or even "Catholic atheists." Communism furthered this process, leading to the reinforcement of ritualistic aspects of Polish Catholicism, even if it did so in an indirect way. This was the case in the above discussed failure of communist "rites de passage." Another example of such an indirect impact can be traced through the Church's "defensive policies," for instance the authorities' reluctance in adopting the reforms of the Second Vatican Council (1962–1965). The reason for that was the Polish primate's stand regarding the need of authoritarian, rather than conciliatory, ways of Church governing, as well as criticism towards the Council's reservations against popular devotion (Ramet, 1990, p. 4; 1998, pp. 289–290; Casanova, 2001, p. 103).[9] Second, the Church's support for the opposition was far from unambiguous, and thus it does not seem to be *the* explanation for the role of the Church; rather, it was a particular way of two systems' coexistence to result in a reinforced position of the Church. Moreover, when it comes to oppositional activities, general participation in religious practices did not necessarily deepen faith but reinforced – or rather created (Bjork, 2010)[10] – social-national ties, for religion served as a provider of "cultural schema" for acting (Kubik, 1994, p. 128). The very same reason is valid for the third argument, namely the state's failure to create a socialist national identity. Here, too, the institutions' coexistence resulted in mirror-like policies of Church and state. It regarded mainly the state's "borrowings" from religion, reflected in rituals, public ceremonies, visions of morality and nationhood.

To conclude, the views regarding the increased importance of Catholicism and the Church in Polish society need to be examined cautiously. While making such claims it is necessary to point out which kind of Catholicism and which functions of the Church were actually reinforced. Specifically, it is crucial to highlight a peculiar underpinning of the ritualistic aspects of the Polish religiosity, accompanied by the process of weakening state rituals. Understanding of this fact is necessary to comprehend the post-communist developments to which I turn in the following section.

Post-communism: powerful priests, powerless parishioners, and pious state officials

Contrary to other countries of the Soviet bloc, in which the churches regained social position as a result of the post-communist transformation, the Catholic Church in Poland gained a vast majority of privileges before the communist regime ended. In mid-1989, communist authorities, which had hoped for the Church's neutrality in the forthcoming elections, granted the Church a variety of rights.[11] Moreover, this legislation paved the way for further developments, continued by democratically elected governments throughout the 1990s (right- and left-wing alike). One of such developments was the concordat between the state and Vatican, which regulated their relations and confirmed the Church's privileges (1993). Noteworthy here is also the law on the restitution of Church property, dealt with by the so-called "Property Commission," which brought about numerous abuses and frauds.[12] It constitutes the best exemplification of the state's policies, which enabled the Church's agency to the detriment of the state's own prerogatives. Not only did the state lose the property, which hosted important institutions (schools, hospitals, offices), but a preferential treatment of the Church was seen as unjust by large groups of citizens. Ironically, some of the most scandalous decisions of the "Property Commission" were later mediated by an ex-communist secret service agent, who acted as a plenipotentiary of several dozens of orders and parishes.

While the property issue affected relatively few people (even if it outraged many more), other activities and campaigns undertaken by the Church and supported and/or enabled by the state authorities triggered more reactions, as they affected the lives of all Polish citizens. These were, for instance, the shaping of the Polish constitution, the broadcast law, the debates on abortion law, which took place in the 1990s and aimed – according to the Church – to "protect" Christian values and

Polish Catholics, and – according to the critics – to "impose" them on all citizens. Many scholars provide a thorough analysis of all those proceedings (Burdziej, 2005; Eberts, 1998; Kurczewska, 2005; Zubrzycki, 2001), evincing some fundamental patterns of contemporary Church-state-society relations. First, they prove that Polish Catholicism "left churches and entered the public forum" (Marody and Mandes, 2006, p. 58), acting as a political player and striving to influence state legislation. Moreover, once it participates in the game, it finds it hard to accept the democratic rules. A good example here may be the Church's attempts to ban abortion, as well as its insistence to forbid referenda on this matter. All this would not have been possible without the state's permission, which leads to the second point, namely the government's reluctance to use its own prerogatives. Referring to the just quoted example, under the pressure of the Church the government gave up the idea of a referendum on abortion (1991);[13] more recently, it withdrew, due to the Church's criticism, the proposal of refunds for "in-vitro" treatments. Negotiations and exchanges of "favors," well-known from the communist period, also continued. Not infrequently the state even overreached and acted for the sake of the Church's position, without even being asked to do so.[14] Third, few of those Church (or Church-state) activities can be said to be taken in the name of Polish Catholics. Continuing with the same example of a referendum on abortion, the National Committee for the Referendum was formed as about 80 percent of Poles were in favor of a liberal legislation, that is, opposed the Church's proposal (Ramet, 1998, p. 297; Roguska, 1999, p. 2; Eberts, 1998, p. 824). Generally, social acceptance of the Church's involvement in politics has been declining drastically since in the 1990s (Burdziej, 2005, p. 170). All in all, there evolves a picture of a peculiar triangle, composed of the powerful Church, the state that acts in its name, while both, in theory, act in the name of and for the good of the society.

The above remarks mirror the evidence I gathered in my fieldsite. As I have indicated in the earlier account, my informants considered the dynamics of religious life under communism neither important nor unusual. Today, on the contrary, they are very concerned about Church matters. The issue bothering them the most is the Church's financial power, represented in Poland by the chief of a Catholic radio station (*Radio Maryja*), known from the mass media for his ostentatious manifestation of wealth. Inhabitants often mentioned his example to illustrate social inequalities in Poland. Journalists' reports regarding the activities of the "Property Commission" only reinforced people's criticism towards the Church and the perception of clergymen as "those who made a pile" during the post-communist transformation. Since the majority of inhabitants do not think that their own situation improved, such "transformation winners" are regarded with reservation. For the very same reason, people are very critical towards ex-communists (the "bad" ones) who are today exemplary Catholics and the priests' best friends, occupying the first benches in the church. Moreover, many of my female informants disapprove of the Church's influence on the "in-vitro" legislation, perceiving it as an act which precludes people from having a family. Noticeably, such views on social justice, modesty, or value of the family demonstrate that people's moral ideas may be independent of the Church's teaching yet still relate to the Catholic dogma; in herein quoted cases it was the Bible, and not the priests' preaching, that people used to explicate their stands.

Nevertheless, most people's concern with the Church is due to the controversial Roman Catholic parish priest (hereinafter: Priest), whom I dedicate my attention to in the following. The Priest has been the head of the parish for over 15 years. He has the biggest parish in the whole district (approximately 800 people) and doubtlessly is the best-known Roman Catholic priest in the area. The 50-year-old, self-confident clergyman with a sharp tongue owes his fame to two factors: his busy "social life" and the financial empire he managed to build. As to the first one, there was no person in the district who would not inform me about the Priest's love affairs and children conceived in these relations. Actually, the only element that varied in the stories was the number of the Priest's children: some people spoke about two, some about five (the latter, hearing from me that other inhabitants spoke only of two, were saying: "Yes, it's true, two in our village and three others in neighboring ones"). Although these kinds of stories may seem mere gossiping and their truthfulness could be put into question, the very existence of such narratives is very helpful in understanding how the power of the Priest is perceived. The villagers would not tell me that the Priest had a child with Mrs. X, but they would find it important to tell the whole story in detail. Telling me about his relationship with female parishioners, they recounted his vulgar way of speaking and insolent behavior, which, in their view, was evidence of how powerful he felt. They always depicted him as a cold, calculating person who can offend others without fearing consequences and can "buy" others' silence and consent (for instance paying his lovers' husbands for "adopting" illegitimate children or paying to the bishop, i.e., sharing with him the money gained through the selling of the parish's land). The latter point leads to the nub of the matter – the financial power of the Priest.

In order to understand this point, one must go back to the 1990s. When the Priest moved to the parish, the Roman Catholics still worshiped with Greek Catholics. It is worth mentioning that it was the Priest who dictated the timetable of services, and sometimes the Greek Catholics were not able to finish their mass, because the Roman Catholic procession was already waiting at the entrance. However, in the mid-1990s the church was given back to the Greek Catholics and the Priest decided to build a new one instead of using jointly the Greek Catholic one. He encouraged people to donate money for the construction of a new church; although the church was finished several years ago, "voluntary" donations have never ceased and even today[15] every parish member (and every family member) is supposed to pay 20 złotych [5 euro] per month (apart from the money given during Sunday collections). All in all, this brings a huge sum of money, which, according to the villagers, is not included in the parish's records. The new church is four times bigger than the Greek Catholic shrine; moreover, it was built too close to the latter, which forces Greek Catholics to adapt the hours of their mass to the Roman Catholic ones. If they held services at the same time, they might hear the Priest instead of their clergyman because the new church is equipped with an outside megaphone.

Having finished the construction of the church, the Priest involved himself in other kinds of activities. He bought an abandoned building nearby the church, renovated it, and opened a pension for tourists. The pension has its own name, and the villagers claim that it is not the property of the parish, but that it belongs to the Priest. Once again, I need to emphasize that the account of the Priest's pension was not referred to me as a trivial curiosity, but it was presented through a detailed story. Inhabitants did not simply tell me that he bought that place, but said that he paid 260,000 złotych [65,000 euro] for it; that once he realized he had collected sufficient money, he put everything into the bag and sent his domestic help with the money to the district's office; that the clerks in the office did not know what to do with the bag – they have no safe because nobody ever comes unexpectedly with such an amount of money. At a different occasion, people also told me that the church tower recently became a source of additional income for the parish or, some would insist, for the Priest, due to a mobile company's radio mast installed there. This kind of story corresponds with the above-mentioned characteristics of the powerful priest clergyman who demonstrates his possibilities. Nobody really knows whether the pension and radio bring income only to the Priest, but they do imply it is so and stress that the donated money goes into his own pocket. His lifestyle – expensive car and holidays abroad – only reinforces such an image.

Besides, comparisons of the Priest with other local clergymen, who do not impose on parishioners such big payments and delegate financial issues to specially elected committees, fuels people's discontentment.

Obviously, a question to follow must be an attempt to understand why parishioners pay for the church and whether they are able to challenge the Priest. At the same time, this attempt should shed light on what can be perceived as schizophrenic behavior: recurrent complaints on milking money and the Priest's immoral behavior, on the one hand, and tacit acceptance of the situation and continuation of religious practices, on the other. Such ambiguity has been highlighted by many scholars studying folk religion, who see anticlerical comments as a widespread phenomenon and a pattern of popular religiosity (Badone, 1990; Riegelhaupt, 1984). Importantly, anticlericalism does not mean for them a rejection of religion, but rather a negotiation of the limits of the Church's power. As Riegelhaupt puts it, "anticlericalism, at the village level, may thus be seen to contribute to a structural, emotional, and psychological ambiguity (...) a balanced stand-off in the acceptance and rejection of Catholicism" (1984, p. 111). Therefore, while the coexistence of contradictory patterns of religiosity should not come as a surprise, the herein analyzed case suggests that "the limits of the Church's power" are hardly negotiable by parishioners. When asked about the possibility to challenge the Priest's dominance, the parishioners' answer was a decisive "no." They always explained to me that there were only few people who rejected the Priest's practices. A group disagreeing with the Priest's activities wrote several letters to the bishop in which they expressed their concern with his conduct. However, the letters did not bring any results. As my informants explained, the bishop is a good friend of the Priest, so he would never remove him from the parish. Seeing the Priest and bishop whispering while walking shoulder to shoulder during some religious ceremonies, it was hard for me not to recall their words.

Nevertheless, my informants provided me with other examples, which proved that the foundation of the Priest's power not only lies in the hierarchy's support. Some time ago, after the Priest had placed on the church door a list of parishioners who had not paid their monthly donation, one villager (obviously one who had been on the list) tore it off and threatened the Priest with a trial for defamation. The list disappeared, but a few weeks later the villager's son was informed that he was not admitted to confirmation. This kind of "payback" is the most common strategy applied by the Priest: performance of rituals – baptisms, marriages, and most of all funerals – remains his most powerful tool. Moreover, as the following examples demonstrate, he is able to use it in many different ways. First, depending on how obedient the family of parishioners is, he performs the rituals for them with more or less solemnity. For example, if the family of the deceased pay well, he accompanies the coffin to the cemetery; if the family does not, he participates only in some part of the ceremony and holds a special sermon, speaking as much as possible about the deceased's "dark sides," for instance emphasizing that a drunkard's way to heaven is not an easy one. It must be stressed that all those rites of passage are of high importance for the community – it is not (only) the question of belief or faith, but social representation, image in the society, tradition and, last but not least, dignity. Therefore, having a decent marriage or having their children admitted to the First Communion is of the highest importance for the villagers. Hence, whenever we discussed the issue of financial abuse and protest (or rather lack thereof) against the Priest's practices, people always repeated that they have to think about their relatives, their children's future, and so on. Second, performance of rituals means for the Priest the possibility of an additional income. Therefore, other than a family's (mis)conduct, what also influences the performance of rituals is the sum the family is ready to pay. According to the villagers, the Priest requests so much money for marriages and funerals that many people can hardly afford it. They also stress that while marriage is a deliberate choice and the couple is prepared for the costs, a funeral is often an unexpected expense. It is thus a shame that instead of supporting the family of the deceased, the Priest puts an additional burden on them. For all these reasons, there have been cases of "post-mortem" conversions in the district, simply because Orthodox and Greek Catholic priests ask no or very little money for a funeral. Furthermore, inhabitants complained of a lack of solidarity in the village: they maintained that the Priest has a group of "agents" who denounce to him those people who are critical of him, and that denounced people may "pay consequences."

Hence, if the Priest's power lies in his role as ritual performer, what needs to be inquired is: where does the power of the ritual lie? There are two plausible answers to this question, the first regarding Catholicism as such and, the second one, its Polish variant. First, many studies on Catholicism have proved strong attachment to and dependence on rituals. Although such a statement risks to simplistically juxtapose intellectually, cognitively oriented religious traditions and performative, ritual-centered ones, ethnographic inquiries confirm that the attachment to rituals should not be seen as mindless repetition but rather as community-building practices, rooted in the local socio-cultural landscape. Just because one aim of such rituals it to make people follow the beaten track, even a slight change regarding the rituals' form or content may provoke resistance. Such cases were documented by many scholars researching Catholicism. For instance, Halemba (2015) described the case of a Ukrainian Greek Catholic community that did not agree on ritual modifications and taught new priests how to properly perform rituals, while Brettell (1990) emphasized insistence on locally accepted forms of religious practices by Portuguese peasants. Switching to my case study, it is useful to bring up another example of parishioners' protest against the Priest. Some years ago, a dispute flared up after the Priest restructured a historic chapel despite the people's harsh objections. As a result, one of the inhabitants put up banners made of paper sheets in the trees reprimanding the Priest, and some people started to attend services in a different parish.[16] In other words, what was unacceptable for people was a modification of a local tradition. This fact is also informative about the importance of rituals and of priests as their performers, as well as of the significance given to the "proper" form of those practices. Besides, the above remarks should not obscure all those people for whom religious rituals are strictly connected with religious beliefs; these were the people who would tell me they go to church not for the Priest but for God and what is important is participation in a Holy Mass and not the performer.

The second explanation for the importance of rituals refers to the perception of secular rites of passage in Poland. Arguably, neither the communist state nor the authorities of the 3rd Polish Republic provided the people with an alternative to religious ceremonies that would be held in high regard. Of course, everyone has a choice and can marry in the district's office or be buried by a lay clerk, but, in my informants' view, this kind of ritual is seen as not solemn enough. Such an approach is not limited to the countryside but is wide-spread in the cities, among middle class men and "Catholic atheists"; yet, while towns and cities observe a growing popularity of secular rituals, this process is much slower in the countryside. Religious rituals continue to be chosen, sometimes out of religious conviction, but sometimes as, in fact de-secularized practices, which have become the "way of doing things."

Such a picture of religious (or "religious") practices is drawn by many contemporary scholars, who highlight a contradiction between high popularity of religious rituals and people's selective use of the Church's teaching and its application in everyday life. According to Marody and Mandes (2006, pp. 60–61), reinforced in the communist times, Catholic rituals continue nowadays to play an important role due to the weakness of secular rituals. They explain the persistence of religious practices by observing that due to a different path of the modern nation-state formation, the Polish state did not colonize the public sphere; not in the 19th century, not under the communist regime, and not today. They also mention (2006, p. 61) that "a brief period of national independence [1918–1939 – A.P.] was simply too short to result in the formation of a modern national identity." At this point, it is worth coming back to my initial remarks regarding the comparison between the 2nd and the 3rd Polish Republic and the question of the "in-between" role of communism. Leaving aside other political aspects,[17] I would like to remark that despite a strong connection between the Church and the state, political life in interwar Poland was more independent from the Church's demands. Clashes between religious and secular authorities were common at both national and local levels (Bender, 1992, p. 545). Although the privileged position of Catholicism was guaranteed by the constitution and concordat, there was a distance between state and Church authorities, and the position of the Church in Poland was weak in comparison to the countries like Italy or Spain. Likewise, anticlerical stands among different strata of population were increasing; liberal intelligentsia spoke against Catholic morality while peasants and workers were very critical of the clergy's high financial situation (Majka, 1968, p. 203; Chrypinski, 1990, pp. 125–126).[18] Moreover, historians emphasize that although the main political parties were (in more or less extreme way) nationalistic, they did not need the Church for the realization of their policies. Thus, it is probably justified to repeat after Casanova (2001) and Ramet (1998) that had it not been for WWII and communism, the importance of Catholicism in Poland might have substantially decreased. This is because communism resulted in a paradoxical outcome: simultaneous rupture and continuation. Although patterns of religiosity varied through decades (Grabowska, 2001, p. 173),[19] it can be argued that in many cases communism stopped the process of secularization and "turned" many non-religious people into Catholics (even if "cultural Catholics" or Catholics "by opposition"), and at the same time it contributed to the petrification of certain practices and behaviors. In the final section, I demonstrate how this petrification of practices translates into a petrification of the socio-political status quo.

Church, state, and society: a peculiar triangle or a vicious circle?

Discussing the developments in post-communist Poland, I have observed that both the Church's political engagement and that the state's tendency to give in under the Church's pressure are strongly criticized by Polish citizens. However, analyses of people's opinions regarding Church and religion reveal many contradictions and paradoxes (Marody and Mandes, 2006, p. 59). Despite critique of the Church's pre-electoral propaganda, people's approach to the Church and Catholic values continues to be one of the key criteria of political standpoints and choices (Roguska, 1999, p. 6; Grabowska, 2001, p. 178). Moreover, people's criticism and lack of acceptance for the Church's social position and imposition of Catholic values are only expressed verbally and rarely translate into practices. This may, at least partly, explain politicians' conviction about the need to side with the Church. In the last two decades, politicians from left and right would strive for the Church's favor and always stress their Catholic identity in electoral campaigns.

Observations from my fieldsite clearly show these contradictions. To begin with, the Priest is often called "the second district leader," and the local government considers him to be someone to take into account. The village leader, although highly disapproving of the Priest's practices and providing me with many examples of the Priest's abuses, which he defines as "mental power," would not miss a single Sunday mass or forget to pay his share. When asked about the reasons for that, he would give me a "common" explanation: it was due to his son who was preparing for the confirmation, or his public image among the inhabitants. Justifying his position, he would remind me that even the district leader, despite being Orthodox, frequently attended mass. The reason for that was, in his view, the elections; the district leader needed the Priest's support to be re-elected. Although it is hard to believe that the views of this unpopular and highly criticized clergyman could be so influential, the village leader confirms what has been said about Poland in general: the apparent contradiction between the critique of the Church and the importance of religious factors for people's political choices.

As to the district leader, he would not tell me openly his reasons for attending Catholic mass, but he hinted at it, stressing the importance of being on good terms with the Priest for the overall benefit of the district. He asked me, too, not to write about the Priest's "love affairs," again for the sake of protecting the good name of the village. During one of our talks I had an opportunity to listen to one of his phone conversations with the Priest. The district leader was giving the clergyman advice on how to deal with some issues in the regional office. He was advising the Priest to mention his name to the clerks, which would supposedly facilitate the proceedings. It is not about the content, after all, it could be assumed that the commune leader simply helped the Priest to arrange some things which would be beneficial for the parish, but about the polite, nearly submissive tone in which the man, generally a very outspoken and self-confident person, talked to the Priest. I believe that observed stands of the local state's representatives, parishioners' accounts, and the Priest's activities well illustrate earlier observations about a "particular triangle," or rather prove this triangle to be a vicious circle.

To wrap up, narratives and attitudes of the studied community illustrate some large-scale phenomena: ways of accommodating communism and Catholicism, attachment to traditional religious practices, and perception of the Church's influence. Financial controversies and the issue of the sacral "building boom" also resemble nation-wide debates. The reasons for the Priest's strong position are harder to interpret, as they depend on multiple factors: folk Catholicism's specificities (ritualism, anticlericalism), networks of power, Church-friendly legislation, and specific local factors, such as the presence of "religious others." However, to conclude, it is worth recalling the words of a Catholic philosopher (nota bene priest) who claimed that in the common perception powerful priests, due to their privileged position and access to political power in today's reality, are often treated as successors of the local Party secretaries (Tischner, interviewed by Hayden, 1994). Stories about the Priest's "agents," conviction about his "omnipotence," and contacts with different levels of (Church and state) authorities cannot but bring into mind such resemblances. I am of course far from claiming that the above-described picture reflects the situation in the Polish countryside in general, even if it may resemble other ethnographic accounts on Poland. Doubtlessly, other studies and other researchers could elsewhere find examples of perfect cooperation and respectful priest-parishioners relations (I myself assisted in many different cases of other researched villages), as well as divergent approaches to communism. I believe, however, that at least some of depicted patterns have been wide-spread in Poland for decades, and this study "from the margins" accounts for their powerfulness.

Conclusions

My chapter has inquired into the relation between communism and religion by focusing on the relation between the Catholic Church, state authorities, and Polish society. Presenting some general patterns of their relations and illustrating them through the examples from my field research, I strove to argue several issues. First, I suggested that the explanation regarding the role of the Church in the opposition against the communist system does not provide a full picture of religious dynamics in both communist and post-communist times. Second, I spoke about the often paradoxical role of communist ideology and regime, which, although indirectly and "accidently," contributed to the reinforcement of some religious practices. Third, I showed that although post-1989 Poland was built on the rejection of the communist system, nowadays Church-state relations are marked in different ways by the residue of the previous system. And finally, comparing Church-state relations and religious life in the interwar period with today's manifestations, I argued that had it not been for the communist period, the importance of Catholicism in Poland might have substantially decreased.

An element linking all these dimensions was my focus on the ritualistic aspects of Polish religiosity. Conviction about their importance has been shared for decades by many scholars of the Polish religious landscape (e.g., Majka, 1968; Strassberg, 1988; Grabowska, 2001). Demonstrating the rift between "theory" and "practice" (or "Sunday" and "everyday" identity) in Polish religiosity and highlighting the role of rituals as "restoring moral order," Marody and Mandes go as far as to say "the only possible alternative interpretation is that the majority of the Polish society is cynical" (2006, p. 63). Yet another explanation of the rituals' function in the Polish context is, so to say, the long-term weakness, and weakening, of the state rituals. The fact that their popularity has recently been growing may serve as an argument in support of this explanation and in the future will probably open up new fields of analysis.

Most importantly, in comparing church-state relations and religious life in the interwar period with their manifestations today, I argued that had it not been for the communist period, the importance of Catholicism in Poland might have substantially decreased. However, I demonstrated that the last statement is not necessarily tantamount with the lack of secularizing tendencies. In her re-examination of religious nationalism, Zubrzycki observes that the Polish case turns secularization theory on its head (2010, p. 614). Questioning the argument about the strength of Catholicism in Poland under communism, she demonstrates (ibid.) that the public function of Catholicism may be also read as its weakening, while its privatization is read as a (potentially) beneficial path for the Church. Yet it can be also said that, rather than turning secularization theory on its head, the Polish case – with its high number of ritual practices and behaviors and "picked and chosen" beliefs which are not necessarily mediated by the Church or related to the catechism – reveals internal contradictions which both secularization theories and the doctrine of secularism entail. It encourages us to take under scrutiny "the essentializing of 'the religious,' but also of 'the secular' or 'the political,' based on problematic assumptions of what 'religion' is or does" (Casanova, 2009, p. 1058). In other words, it reminds us that it is by taking a step back and recognizing manifold possible meanings of the notions of secular and religion (and even their possible congruence – see McBrian and Pelkmans, 2008), different functions of "religious" and "secular" practices, and varied constellations and sources of belief and non-belief, that we can come to understand the experiences of secularization. While such an approach to secularism and secularization may appear as distinctively anthropological (Cannell, 2010), it constitutes quite a task. For many, the very discussion on "secularization in Poland" sounds like an oxymoron.

Notes

1. The notions of "church" and "state" are applied here as analytical categories. Speaking of church-state relations, I mean the relations between religious and political authorities, which interact through the processes of decision-making, debates, and negotiations. Obviously, an exhaustive analysis would require breaking these categories into smaller units and highlighting the diversity of, often contradicting, standpoints and interests among both clergy and politicians.
2. Twenty-four percent of Poles claimed that the Church supported the state; 6 percent saw it as an ally of the opposition, while 29 percent said that it supported sometimes the state and sometimes the opposition (Darczewska, 1989).
3. Expulsions constituted a part of the communist regime's assimilation policies. A detailed discussion of this issue goes beyond the scope of this paper.
4. Buchowski rightly points out that such a comparison could be drawn between religion and other social formations, yet in the case of communism, "due to its open ideological ambitions, the analogy is more pronounced" (2001, p. 53).
5. Similar observations can be made also with regard to public rituals, such as state ceremonies and national holidays. Due to the implied connection of nationhood and religion in Poland, many of such celebrations meant competition over the definition of nationally relevant festivities (see Main, 2004). Besides, while the church kept the continuity of the traditionally celebrated days (e.g. the anniversary of 1918 independence, celebrated on November 11), the state was attempting to substitute them with new celebrations (e.g., the Holiday of the Rebirth of Poland established to commemorate the Soviet "liberation" of Poland, celebrated on July 22).
6. Abortion is unaccepted by the Catholic Church in general, but the Polish episcopate used it as a persuasive tool in the religious-national narrative; the clergy would define it as a "genocide of the Polish nation" or the "policies known from the WWII." Such argumentation is still present today.
7. The language of John Paul II is often contrasted here, as less rigid and closer to everyday life of the people, and therefore successful in reaching the masses.
8. The most dramatic example is the priest Jerzy Popiełuszko, author of courageous sermons, who was killed by the secret service in 1986. Before he was murdered, the regime was using different measures to frighten him, while the Polish primate disapproved of this teaching and was planning to send him for studies to Rome (cf. Dudek and Gryz, 2003, pp. 412–415).
9. An analogical case took place in the 19th century; it is often claimed that due to the period of partitions (1795–1918) the Polish Church did not fully

experience Enlightenment, as it was focused on the preservation of national identity. Hence, it is possible to see it as a long-term process, which reinforced the importance of rituals and brought about the opinion of the Polish church and Polish religiosity as "not blessed with intellectuality." This opinion is repeated by both lay and church scholars, who point out scarce theological preparation of the clergy and a lack of Polish theological contributions (Bocheński, 1932; Majka, 1968). As to the faithful, researchers stress that "a low level of religious knowledge has always been one of the main characteristics of Polish Catholicism" (Piwowarski, 1976, p. 318).

10. It is debatable to which extent this connection was perceived by society, and to which extent it was assumed by the religious and communist authorities. In his astute study, Bjork challenges the idea regarding the importance of Catholicism in maintaining national identity and claims that the relation between Catholicism and Polishness was not strong and that it was rather to be created than to be reinforced (2010, p. 148).

11. For example, status as a legal entity; the right to freely conduct pastoral work and owe publishing houses, TV, radio, and the like; property tax release; state's insurance for clergymen; state's financing of Catholic schools (Dudek and Gryz, 2003, p. 437; Eberts, 1998, p. 820). Dudek and Gryz observe (2003) that the communist government gave to the Catholic Church more than right-wing governments in other countries did.

12. To give but some examples, the value of restituted property often was many times higher than it was supposed to be; Catholic authorities attempted to regain even such property taken from the Church under different regimes and in different circumstances (i.e. not only the ones confiscated by communists); the Commission did not have to justify its decision, which moreover could not be appealed to. Only recently, the Constitutional Tribunal and the prosecutor's office decided to control the Commission's operations and decisions, yet in the meantime the Commission ceased to exist.

13. The decision was taken by the right-wing government. Arguably, people's discontentment with this decision led to the victory of left-wing parties in 1993, which, however, did not manage to change the legislation (Eberts, 1998).

14. An example here may be the state acting to prevent the public manifestations of other religious groups (Pasek, 2006).

15. That is, at the time of my fieldwork in 2008 and 2009.

16. People indeed have a chance to go to a different church. Some do so, some would but do not have means of transport, while some claim they want to pray in their *local* parish.

17. No doubt relevant, but going beyond the scope of this paper (e.g. policies towards the minorities, anti-Semitism, or authoritarian turn in 1926).

18. It is worth citing Piwowarski's hypothesis regarding the role of communism for religiosity. He claims that by abolishing some of church's privileges (big estates, no taxation) the communist regime eradicated the causes of prewar anticlericalism. He concludes: "Thus Socialism is favourable in this sense for religiosity in Poland" (1976, p. 317). A similar point is made by Casanova (2001, p. 103).

19. Grabowska observes that religiosity declined in the 1960s and then increased in the 1970s, while in the 1980s many adult non-believers converted to Catholicism (2001).

5
Secularization without Secularism: The Political-Religious Configuration of Post-1989 China
Ji Zhe

Contemporary China: secular or post-secular?

Although atheist secularism is generally considered to be an uncontested characteristic of Communism, the contemporary revival of religion in the People's Republic of China (PRC) leads us to question that assumption. Since the beginning of the 1980s, religions, both traditional ones and new movements, have progressively reappeared and have even thrived in China. During the past two decades, thousands of temples, monasteries, and churches have been rebuilt or reopened; millions of people have gathered together in religious sites for various festivals; and religious symbols and references have become omnipresent in social and cultural life, from Internet to cinema. In 1997, the Chinese government (Information Office of the State Council of the PRC, 1997) recognized that there are over 100 million followers and more than 85,000 authorized religious sites of the five legal religions (Buddhism, Taoism, Islam, Catholicism, and Protestantism). Some recent non-official surveys showed that there could be up to 300 million religious believers in China, accounting for more than 31 percent of the adult population, in both urban and rural areas.[1] The accuracy of these statistics may be contested, since the religious identity of the Chinese is far from exclusive, and all existing surveys tend to be regional. However, no one can deny the increasingly religious nature of communist China at the beginning of the 21st century.

This revival could not exist without state toleration of religion. Furthermore, the role played by the State in this revival is not simply passive. In 1993, a new religious policy was established, centered on "actively guiding religions to adapt themselves to a socialist society." From then on, a great number of reconstructions and renovations of religious monuments (mostly Buddhist, but also of other religions) have been supported, initiated and even imposed by the government, and in particular by local authorities (Ji, 2004; 2011). At the central level, the government invests itself in the organization of religious gatherings, such as the triennial World Buddhist Forum since 2006 and the International Taoist Forums in 2007, 2011, and 2014. Yet, at the same time, it is also true that the Chinese Communist Party (CCP) has never ceased to suppress religion. Considerable efforts have been made by the Chinese government to control the personnel, monastic properties, and social influence of religion. The brutal crackdown on the new religious movement Falungong (法轮功) in 1999 is only one of the most dramatic examples. In each *Annual Report on International Religious Freedom* published by the US government, the records of the violations of religious freedom in the PRC are remarkable, especially on the issues of Tibetan Buddhism and non-official Christian churches. Is there an intelligible logic to the PRC's religious policy which explains this contradiction?

There is certainly more than one answer according to different conceptions of Chinese secularity. Richard Madsen (2009; see also 2011) sees a failure of Chinese religious policy in this contradiction. He argues that, since the end of the Cultural Revolution (1966–1976), China has entered into a post-secular period where religions are thriving and manifesting themselves in new forms. Facing this phenomenon, the CCP has even come to realize the defeat of its religious policy, essentially based on secularization theory and 19th century definitions of religion and superstition, and has begun to seek a post-secular theoretical foundation for its policy. Furthermore, Madsen points out that although this reorientation of policy allows more religious freedom than previously, it is a different freedom from that of the Western democracies. Here in China, despite its secularist Constitution, the State can be seen as having a religious spirit, considering itself as being at the head of religious followers, differentiating between true religion and "evil cults," and investing largely in public rituals redolent with religious symbols. On the other hand, whereas the Chinese government tends to export its indigenous religions, that is to say, Confucianism, Taoism, and Buddhism, it refuses to be open to external world religions, such as the global forms of Islam and Christianity. Hence Madsen suggests that the Chinese Party-State is reverting to a policy modeled on the sacral hegemony of the rulership of the Imperial age.

However, a contrary point of view has been put forward by Wang Gungwu, for whom China never departs from the way of secularism. Since the September 11 tragedy, he has argued in a series of lectures and articles (Wang, 2002; 2003) that China has been dominated by its Confucian secular values for most of the past two thousand years. In such a tradition, all public activity was essentially secular and it was not necessary to separate heavenly and earthly orders under the "rule by virtue." Therefore, if a godless communism conquered China in the 20th century, one of the reasons was that communist ideology and its scientism was supported by China's own worldly materialist traditions, even though communist secularism is much more fundamentalist than the earlier Chinese form. Under this hypothesis, Wang argues that the post-Maoist easing on religious policy is not yet sufficient to enable China to return to its earlier moderate secularism. If religion continues to be suspect and only state-approved doctrines and practices are allowed in this country, it is precisely because the residue of a fundamentalist secularism is still strongly present. Based on Wang's ideas, Zhao Litao (2010) has distinguished more explicitly three types of secularism: Chinese traditional secularism, according to which "religion was never allowed to develop into an independent source of power that could challenge and replace the secular state"; "modern secularism" imported from the West, which was the end-product of the separation of church and state, emphasizing secular values and institutions as the precondition for modernization; and thirdly, Communism as an extremist secularism. He argues that the relationship between religion and State in post-Mao China is characterized by the fading of the third form of secularism and the return and coexistence of the first and the second forms. According to him, the Chinese secularist tradition guarantees a syncretic and non-political nature to religious revival, while "modern secularism" explains the CCP's hostility and vigilance with regard to Tibetan Buddhism, Islam in Xinjiang, and non-official Christianity, which reflect the CCP's determination to put sovereignty and national unity ahead of religious freedom.

Thus we have two images of the Chinese political-religious situation: one is that of a religious State ill at ease in a post-secular age, the other is of a country in transition from a radical secularism to a hybrid and softer form of secularism. Each of these two views assumes that the separation of religion and State is central to secularism. However, for Madsen, the separation is aimed at the protection of religious freedom, while for Wang and Zhao, it promises the absolute superiority of the State with regard to religion. According to Madsen, post-Mao China has a tendency to return to the premodern governance model that only partially separates State from religion and indeed entrusts government with a supreme religious power, thus failing to adapt both to the religious revival situation and the context of globalization. In contrast, in the view of Wang and Zhao, neither the reappropriation by Chinese of their own tradition nor the state constraints of religions are inconsistent with secularism.

In spite of these divergences, however, these two views share something in common. They both seek the prototype of current Chinese political and religious realities in an imperial paradigm, by considering the religious oppression, toleration, and regulation strategies as an outcome of a specific ideological conviction. To a certain degree, both of them are culturally particularistic. In Madsen's speech, we can observe a slight shadow of the American liberal discourse of globalization, while Wang and Zhao's arguments remind us of the so-called "Asian values" that were briefly in vogue in the 1990s.

In this chapter, I suggest questioning Chinese contemporary secularity in a different way. Rather than trying to understand 21st century current affairs through pre-19th century history, I would like to situate the present Chinese political and religious configuration in terms of the post-89 conjuncture. I argue that, since 1989, the Chinese communist regime has been characterized by an unprecedented fear on the part of the Party-State of a potential crisis in sustaining its power, and a loss of ideological self-confidence. In this context, its religious policy is driven by purely instrumentalist reasons of Power, rather than by cultural convention or an ideological legacy. The suppression of religion is no longer in line with the communist atheist project, and the limited and selective toleration of religion by the State is not necessarily dictated by cultural tradition or national interests. In fact, it is difficult to reduce the political-religious configuration of contemporary China to merely "secular" or "post-secular," where religious revival coexists with an extreme secularization, but the public values to which both State and religion should adhere as a condition of a democratic secularism are still lacking.

Authority without authenticity: the post-ideological politics of the PRC

My starting point is that the year 1989 marked a pivotal moment for post-Mao politics in China. In the same year that saw in November the Berlin Wall fall amid cheers, the "Goddess of Democracy" raised by Chinese students on Tiananmen Square had already been crushed by tanks five months earlier. Far from arriving at the End of History, we were at the threshold of a new era where History was to diverge once again. From then on, the PRC cut itself off from what Huntington (1991) terms the "third wave" of democratization, and adopted a way which was atypical. From the economic point of view, a wild form of capitalism has bloomed, while the market remains deeply manipulated by the government and it is anything but liberal. As for politics, although the CCP is sometimes forced to give in at an administrative level when it is confronted by those it dominates, it remains wholeheartedly attached to the empty shell of "socialism," forbidding any public criticism of the regime, and never hesitating to resort to violence to maintain its power.

This post-89 regime in China is characterized by Xu Ben as neo-totalitarian (Xu, 2005a; see also Xu, 2005b; 2008). According to him, if Mao's regime from 1949 to 1976 is viewed as a kind of totalitarianism in its full meaning, the early reform period in the 1980s could be considered as post-totalitarian, which is characterized by a relative liberalization and a popular political enthusiasm for change. However, this period did not result in democratization. Since 1989, China has entered into a neo-totalitarian era that is an attempt to return to totalitarianism but is at the same time faced with the impossibility of completing such a return. Xu revealed a collection of social facts describing and analyzing the political, economic, and cultural aspects of this neo-totalitarianism. In a way which is directly related to our subject, the regime's ideological bankruptcy is underlined. On the one hand, the CCP no longer has confidence in its own ideology, which is still officially seen as a continuum from Marxist-Leninism and Maoism to present-day leaders' "theories." Meanwhile, it lacks the courage to engage itself in any deep ideological reflections, and debates and can only put forward superficial slogans designed to deceive both itself and others. On the other hand, haunted by the sentiment that it is reaching the end of its destiny and the insurmountable fear of the impending eruption of civil resistance, the Party-State tends to strengthen political control at all costs and considers the limited loosening of policies in the post-totalitarian period as signs of weakness and error.

In such an eschatological atmosphere, Xu argues, official ideology has lost its both social and moral validity. Unlike during the decades under Maoist totalitarianism, it is now neither "political gospel" nor moral norm. At the same time, it would seem that most people do not wish to voice public criticism or doubt concerning the regime as they did in some way during the post-totalitarian period, even though they are unhappy with events. Under omnipresent political surveillance and the economic pressure of everyday life, people in the neo-totalitarian era have developed a cynical attitude towards politics. Where possible, such as in private communications and anonymously in cyberspace, they may actively express their disgust with the regime in a satirical or jeering manner, but they will generally try to avoid direct and serious confrontation with the State's power. The CCP is well aware of the fact that it can no longer control people's minds, so it requires submission in appearance only, and contents itself with controlling the spread of dissentient ideas and forbidding people to speak the truth in public. Consequently, neo-totalitarian ideology has turned into a big "transparent lie." On one hand, the Party-State claims that the majority are faithful to its official discourses, and continues to make mannerist propaganda on a large scale. On the other hand, the people pretend to accept and even support this mendacious reality backed up by police force and media control. Both sides clearly see the other's dissimulation, but both of them keep formally playing the game of "pretending ignorance" with a show of sincerity and dignity, thus maintaining the non-ostensible agreement to never speak the truth in public.[2]

Although the pertinence of the term "neo-totalitarianism" is not incontestable,[3] Xu's arguments rightly outline that in post-89 China, the political authority is an authority without ideological authenticity. The fading of political conviction and trust results in not only disillusionment with the theological style politics of the earlier utopian and reforming communisms,[4] but also disenchantment with politics as a whole. For many Chinese, politics is no more a vehicle of transcendent concern and is not morally inspiring or enchanting any longer. The pre-1989 enthusiasm for political engagement has been replaced by general disappointment and indifference.[5] As for the Party-State, it is incapable of dealing with any political question on the level of meaning and value, so it attempts to translate social problems into economic problems, reducing politics to administrative and technological issues. Moreover, the neo-totalitarian leadership is no longer charismatic. None of the leaders of the post-89 generation can present himself as the embodiment of a certain sacred ideology; they are well aware that their role is only that of a temporary agent for the political and economic interests of certain groups of elites.

The CCP leaders certainly realize the vanishing of a value system, and desire to re-consecrate their authority as moral. A symptom of this anxiety is the continuous renewal of political slogans, such as "Three Represents" (*sange daibiao*, 三个代表)[6] in 2002, "Building a Party that serves the interests of the public and governs for the people" (*lidang weimin, zhizheng weigong*, 立党为民, 执政为公) and "Scientific Concept of Development" (*Kexue fazanguan*, 科学发展观) in 2003. In February 2005, a new slogan for the building of a socialist "harmonious society" (*hexie shehui*, 和谐社会) was launched, which has been credited to the former Chinese President and Party General Secretary Hu Jintao. During the 6th plenary session of the Central Committee of the 16th Congress of the CCP (November 2006) a "Resolution" was passed, which made "harmony" the major task of the time. Since then, and especially after the 2008 Beijing Olympic Games where the Confucian themes were present in the opening ceremonies, the slogan of harmony has been widely considered by both Western scholars and media, at least partially, as sign of the onset of a new political incarnation of Confucianism. Can this hypothesis be substantiated?

The slogan of *harm*ony: return of Confucianism or invasion of "river crabs"?

Despite the enthusiasm that the term "harmony" could give rise to in the West, however, little evidence can be found to prove that the CCP in ideological crisis tends to resort to Confucianism. In fact, the semantic tie between "harmony" and Confucianism is much looser than what is generally taken for, and it is hard to say people in China perceive anything "Confucian" from the current policy of "harmony."

First, "*hexie*"/harmony, which originally meant any simultaneous melodious combination of tones and was later employed to refer to social orders, is used in the sense of social integration in a way that is common, rather than exclusively Confucian. We cannot even find the word "*hexie*" in the *Analects* of Confucius. What we translate as "harmony" in the text of *Analects* comes from a single character "*he*," which is the first part of the term "*hexie*." From the etymological point of view, one of the earliest cases where the characters "*he*" and "*xie*" appeared together in the same sentence is the *Guanzi*, a collection of works attributed to Guan Zhong (管仲, about 725 BC–645 BC). Yet Guan Zhong is considered as being Legalist rather than Confucian. Of course, harmony is very much a key word in Confucianism, and is conceived as a human virtue and a social ideal. However, the same idea also exists in other religious philosophies, from Taoist to Buddhist. In reality, contrary to the wishful thinking discernible in the interpretations of some observers, in the social games surrounding the slogan, the Chinese never limit their arguments for harmony to Confucianism, but borrow from all kinds of traditional materials to cater to the Party-State's latest flavor of the month. When the President of the Taoist Association claimed that harmony is the fundamental idea of Taoism, Buddhist monks and pro-Buddhist lay scholars published a quantity of texts showing that Buddhism represents one of the best theoretical resources and practical models for building a harmonious society. Both claims can be justified, and the government has not pronounced itself in favor of either side.

Furthermore, even though the "harmony" slogan bears a certain semantic relationship to religious social values, it is by no means a religion-oriented or tradition-oriented reconstruction of ideology. If the slogan was advanced in 2005, it was because increasing social tensions resulting from the widening gap between the rich and the poor, the political authorities and the people, had reached a such a dangerous level that the government had to openly recognize a problem of "disharmony." According to official statistics, between 1994 and 2004, the phenomenon of "collective cases" (*qunti shijian*, 群体事件, that is to say demonstrations and attacks of all kinds against government bodies) increased by 22.2 percent a year, reaching 74,000 annually in 2004. The number of Chinese citizens involved in this kind of action grew from 730,000 to 3.76 million (Hu, Hu, and Wang, 2006). Therefore, the harmony slogan translates the increasing concern on the part of the Chinese leadership at the escalating social conflicts in the country, rather than a declaration in favor of a Confucian-inspired governance. Essentially, it has the same meaning as "*wending*" (稳定, stability) which is the foremost preoccupation of the regime and the central theme of official discourses since 1989.

Certainly, as I have tried to show in some of my other articles, there has been a revival of political Confucianism in China since the mid-1990s (Ji, 2005; 2008). Some intellectuals of this current of thought even propose reinstating Confucianism as a State Religion and substituting Confucianism for Marxist-Leninism and Maoism as the official ideology. Yet, it remains a purely theoretical construction limited to an intellectual field. It is nearly impossible to find an organic relation between this academic discursive game and the harmony slogan. Indeed, a dozen paragraphs drawn from Hu's discourses on harmony collected by the editor of a monthly published by the CCP Propaganda Department shows clearly that the original discursive context of Hu's "harmony" is wholly unrelated to Confucianism (Anonymous, 2005). When the harmony slogan was established during 2004–2005, Hu talked about "harmony" mostly by referring to official ideological terms such as Marxist-Leninism, Mao Zedong's thought and Deng Xiaoping's theory, and spoke of "stability and unity" (*anding tuanjie*, 安定团结). At best, Confucius was once mentioned when "tradition" was evoked in a highly vague manner (Hu, 2005).[7] Until now, there is no evidence that the CCP leaders would intend to ascribe their harmony policy to Confucianism. In reality, since Hu's successor Xi Jinping adopted "Chinese Dream" (*Zhongguo meng*, 中国梦) as his slogan at the end of 2012, the "harmony" slogan has begun to fade away.

As a Chinese speaker, it is not surprising for me to talk about harmony without thinking of Confucianism, since the word "*hexie*"/harmony is very common in the contemporary Chinese language. Language is a heritage. If a slogan on public affairs is to be invented, it is natural for it to make use of some traditional words, especially when a relatively elegant style is sought. It is interesting to point out that the harmony slogan is not really the first example with Confucian semantic implications. The objective of building a "relatively wealthy society"(*xiaokang shehui*, 小康社会) defined by Deng Xiaoping in the 1980s referred back to the notion of "*xiaokang*" which stems from the Confucian classics *Shijing* (*Book of Odes*) and the *Liji* (*Book of Rites*). The ex-General Secretary of the CCP Jiang Zemin also drew inspiration from Confucian vocabulary when he put forward the principle of "governing the country by virtue" (*yi de zhi guo*, 以德治国). If we go further, we will find that Mao used some typically Buddhist terms for his ideological construction, such as "*jiefang*" (解放, deliverance-liberation, which is still frequently used in current official discourses), "*juewu*" (觉悟, enlightenment-consciousness), and "*sixiang*" (思想, thought). However, any attempt to define Maoism as a return to Buddhism would be necessarily unconvincing.

Leaving aside the problem of etymology and hermeneutics, the real operation of the harmony policy does not correspond to Confucian virtues such as "*ren*" (仁, humanness) and "*yi*" (义, justice). On the contrary, Chinese neo-totalitarian harmony is alienating and violent. Any political criticism and protest is liable to be censored or sanctioned in the name of the maintenance of harmony. That is why in China, when something has been censored, or a given protest has been banned, one might say ironically "it has been harmonized." There are certain well-intentioned individuals who are seeking to combine the harmony philosophy with a more human governance, whether Confucian or modern democratic. However, what many Chinese perceive by the "harmony" politics is neither tradition nor democracy, but *harmful* "river crabs" (*hexie*, 河蟹), a word which sounds similar to "harmony" in Mandarin Chinese and is widely employed by Chinese netizens as a substitute for the latter. In 2009, when thousands of websites and blogs were closed down by the government, some Chinese netizens posted an innocent-seeming song on MV on line that immediately attracted more than a million viewers.[8] It tells the story of a herd of brave and smart "*caonima*"s (草泥马, which literally means "grass-mud horses," but sounds like an unprintable crude slang phrase showing people's anger and frustration over censorship) who fight back the invasion of "river crabs." Using semantic tactics, Chinese netizens rendered government censors totally ridiculous under the pretense of "harmony." [9]

Neo-totalitarian "spi-rituality": public sacrifice and staged power

Although ideologically, the Party-State does not seem to be returning to a traditional religious philosophy, in practice it invests substantially in ritual activities that imply a more ambiguous relationship with religions. Here the major question is not about "profane rites" associated with sports, politics, or judicial matters, like those we can observe more or less in any modern country, but about the appropriation of certain communal festivals, traditional rituals, and private religious practices, and the engineering of collective religion-related performances. In this respect, the most obvious example is the "public sacrifice" (*gongji*, 公祭) officially restored by Chinese authorities since the 2000s and even earlier, made to Confucius, the Yellow Emperor (*Huangdi*, 黄帝) and other national or local legendary heroes. Originally, public sacrifice means the rite of offering organized by and participated in by people outside the family of the dead, often in order to publicly worship and honor respected deceased or victims. In the current context, it refers above all to the ceremonies sponsored by the government, attended by one of more heads of the political authorities or their delegates, to commemorate legendary or religious figures. "Public" here means "official" (*guanfang*, 官方), as opposed to "popular" (*minjian*, 民间). This political engagement in cults recalls similar phenomena in Imperial times and during the Republican period (1912–1949). Does this reveal a real religious impulse on the part of the communist State?

Before dealing with this question, a brief overview of the contemporary evolution of the public sacrifice to Confucius would be revelatory. Qufu is a small city in Shandong Province, with about 60,000 urban inhabitants. As the birthplace of Confucius (551 BC – 479 BC), it contains numerous holy sites for Confucianism, especially the Temple of Confucius (*Kongmiao*, 孔庙) which resembles a veritable Confucian pantheon where the Master and 164 Confucian saints and sages are venerated. Since the 2nd century BC when Confucianism became the state religion-ideology, the cult of Confucius was regularly celebrated by officials and even emperors in the Temple of Confucius at Qufu. This tradition was largely preserved, with certain formal reforms by the republican governments of the first half of the 20th century, until 1948 when Qufu was occupied by the communist army. In 1966, once Mao's Cultural Revolution had begun, the Temple of Confucius and other historical sites at Qufu suffered extensive damage. Since 1982, the Temple has become a tourist site, managed firstly by the local committee of historical heritage, and latterly, since 1999, by the state-owned enterprise "Confucius Tourism Group, Ltd."

In 1984, the "Music and Dance for the Cult of Confucius" show was produced for the first time on stage, performed by a local opera troupe, as part of the tourist program of the annual "Festival of Confucian Culture," which takes place in September, around Confucius' birthday. For 20 years, this tourist festival and associated shows were kept, but no more than other contemporary festivals invented by local authorities using traditional cultural resources to promote tourism.[10] Things seemed to change in 2004. For the first time, the Mayor of Qufu was present at the gathering on Confucius' birthday and, as officials in the Imperial age, read a memorial text (*jiwen*, 祭文). The head of the municipal committee of the CCP also laid flowers at the Statue of Confucius. This ceremony is considered as the first public sacrifice to Confucius conducted by the Chinese government since 1948. Since then the ceremony has been celebrated in a "public" manner each year. In 2007, the "Festival of Confucian Culture" became an event co-sponsored by the Shandong province government and some State agencies on a national level, including the Ministry of Culture, the Ministry of Education, the Bureau of Tourism, and the Association of Overseas Chinese. Since then, the Governor of the province has replaced the Mayor of Qufu to read the memorial text.

The cult of Confucius at Qufu during the Festival of Confucian Culture is neither the first nor the only public sacrifice under the communist regime. In the 1980s and 1990s, the official rites to honor the Yellow Emperor, the mythical Ancestor of all Chinese and a civilizational hero, were resumed by the local authorities of Shaanxi province. Since the 2000s, this ceremony has been systematically organized, and attended by Party and State leaders of both provincial and national levels. Recent years have seen a tendency for the number of public sacrifices in the country to grow. There are nowadays for example the public sacrifices to Shun (舜, one of the first legendary sovereigns of ancient China,

23rd–22nd century BC) in Hunan, to Yu (禹, the successor of Shun) in Zhejiang, to Fuxi (伏羲, a legendry civilizational hero) in Henan, and to Lao-tzu (老子, 6th–5th century BC) in Gansu.

The restoration of public sacrifice certainly challenges the widely-spread conception of communist religious policy. However, its potential political and social implications should not be exaggerated. Even though there is a tendency to justify public sacrifice by some political discourses such as "patriotism" and "national unity," the initial and fundamental motive of the public sacrifice is rather economic.

Since the very beginning, the promotion of tourism and investment has been and is still the central aim of these public sacrifices, as the government has consciously recognized and emphasized in official documents.[11] We should not forget that the official cult to Confucius, the Yellow Emperor, and other legendary heroes always coincides with a series of trade consultation meetings, commercial promotion actions, and signing ceremonies of transactions arranged by the government. In this respect, public sacrifice is nothing more than an application of the policy formed in the 1990s, according to which "Culture builds the stage and the economy performs" (*wenhua datai, jingji changxi*, 文化搭台, 经济唱戏). After 1989, since it is impossible to legitimize the regime through political reform, economic growth has become the only real claim to legitimacy for the government. In this context, using mass gatherings in the name of culture – whether religious or not – to serve the economy is conceived as a privileged measure for officials to prove their capacity and successful governance. On the other hand, the Chinese government is directly involved in these economic activities. Almost all historical cult sites belong to the State and, in most cases, are run lucratively by the State. Therefore, public sacrifice is a very profitable operation for local authorities.[12]

It is thus not surprising that since the very beginning, public sacrifice in the PRC has been by nature a show, a "face project" (*mianzi gongcheng*, 面子工程),[13] a pretext for a series of spectacles for mass gatherings. A Taiwanese philosopher witnessed the ridiculous theatricality of the first public sacrifice to Confucius in 2004 (Gong, 2008, pp. 46–47): the actor-compere was dressed as a eunuch, a few men and women in theatrical costume acted and danced in an absurd manner in a supposed representation of the ancient rite, whereas no one cared that the offerings to Confucius were wrongly placed so that the Statue of Confucius was facing the rumps and tails of the scarified bull, ram and pig. In 2005, a Delegation of Kong's (the family name of Confucius) descendants were invited to attend the ceremony of public sacrifice. After four hours' wait in the rain, what they saw was a spectacle of "family sacrifice" performed by professional actors. Sébastien Billioud and Joël Thoraval (2009) have described how the inauguration ceremony of the Festival of Confucian Culture in 2007 took place in chaotic conditions, with a dense crowd, groups of high-ranking officials, among the advertisements of sponsors accompanied by the frenzied rock song of a young woman. They have pointed out that the rite of sacrifice is in itself extremely simple, which contrasts strikingly with the complex preparation, liturgy, and animal sacrifices offered to Confucius in Imperial China and even up into the contemporary era in Taiwan. According to them, the whole event represents the use and abuse of Confucius without Confucianism.

Billioud and Thoraval explain this kind of official rite devoid of ritual spirit by the "influence of a post-Maoist *habitus*." For me, it is a precise example of neo-totalitarian "spi-rituality" – a spirituality without spirit, which justifies and confirms itself by artificial shows. Indeed, the lack of piety and solemnity of public sacrifice has garnered criticism in China. However, the government organizers do not really care about these reactions because their purpose is neither to change people's morality by using religious rituals nor to re-embed a religious spirit in the political system. Besides the economic concern that is essential, Party officials enjoy much the ritual parties in the heart of some culturally important sites, where they honor themselves by pretending to honor legendary figures, and show to people that they are still "on the stage" (*zaitaishang*, 在台上, which in Chinese means "in power").

Rigid stability: the axis of state *Limitation* on religion

No matter how hypocritical the regime is, the restoration of public sacrifice seems notwithstanding to represent greater toleration on religious matters. All the same, it can be observed that alongside this toleration there are religious persecutions on a large scale and sometimes extremely violent, such as the campaign against the new religious movement Falungong since 1999, and the ongoing strict constraints on Christian "house churches" and "underground churches." How can this ambiguity in Chinese religious policy be understood? What is the principle of the State regulation of religion in this country?

In his study on the evolution of Chinese official discourses labeling heterodoxy in 20th century, David Palmer (2008) suggests that the category of "*xiejiao*" (邪教, evil cult) used in the anti-Falungong campaign marks a rupture from 50 years of socialist and secularist ideology: the oppressed religious groups are no longer criticized as feudal and counter-revolutionary, but defined by classical terms as heretical and demonic forces of chaos. Therefore, although the campaign uses all the classic instruments of propaganda and repression of a communist regime, it presents a return to the paradigm of traditional Chinese ideology, according to which the State is conceived of as the prime protector of the orthodox order incarnated by authorized religions. While this analysis may be pertinent to gaining some understanding of Chinese policy on so-called sectarian movements, it does not provide us with an answer as to why some other religious movements not labeled as an "evil cult" (e.g. non-official Christian churches), and sometimes even proper "orthodox" movements (e.g. popular Buddhist and Confucian movements), also suffer from political hostility and restrictions. Moreover, one can ask to what degree the current communist State consciously defines itself as the protector of the orthodox order, even though some imperial terminology seems to be coming back.

In fact, to seek a more global understanding of religio-political tensions in contemporary China, the understanding of domination logics in operation seems more significant than the recourse to traditional political culture. In fact, the ongoing State regulation on religion is related to a core task of neo-totalitarian politics: rigid stability (*gangxing wending*, 刚性稳定).[14] As we have mentioned above, since 1989, stability has become the foremost preoccupation and an absolute principle of the regime. Unlike democratic politics, this stability does not rely upon the rule of law, the separation of power, or any efficient institutional arrangement for social negotiation and equilibrium, but on a rigid negation of all dissidence and social movement for rights. By maintaining an absolutely stable order, the CCP is attempting to monopolize political power as long as possible. In such a context, for the government any kind of non-official social mobilization with political features is considered as dangerous, hence to be put down.

The timing of the Falungong event could be seen as a proof of this logic. Officially founded in 1992, Falungong emerged during the "*qigong* (气功) boom" in the 1990s and presented itself as a system of therapeutic education and exercises. From 1992 to 1998, though its rapid growth drew attention and was even criticized by some journalists and Buddhists as "anti-scientific" and "sectarian," it was allowed to develop freely, and it attracted millions of practitioners in the country. The crucial turning point was April 25, 1999, when the Falungong organized a silent demonstration of ten thousand people in front of Zhongnanhai (中南海), the residence compound of China's leaders in Beijing. It was not really a political protest, since the objective of the demonstration was only to demand the Central government's support in their dispute against criticism. Yet, the unauthorized gathering at the Capital was in itself highly offensive to the regime, which in the Chinese context is already symbolically anti-governmental. Besides, the demonstration was so well prepared that thousands of people assembled at short notice in Beijing from all over the country without the previous knowledge of the Secularity Bureau. The gathering lasted only a few hours, then the participants left in an orderly fashion without leaving any litter behind them. This extraordinary organizational capacity and disciplined attitude deeply frightened the authorities. Three months later, Falungong was suppressed and the anti-evil sect campaign started.

Consequently, the real reason for the banning of the Falungong movement may be not that, as claimed by the government, this religious movement is "evil" (doctrinal absurdity, swindling, negation of modern medical treatment, etc.), but its huge potential for mobilization. Another case concerning the Confucian revival serves to make this point clearer. Lujiang Cultural Education Center is a moral redemptive society founded by a Taiwanese Buddhist monk, Master Jingkong, in 2005 in his hometown Lujiang, Anhui province (Dutournier and Ji, 2009). Despite this Buddhist background, the mission of Lujiang Center is in line with popular Confucianism. It aims to transform the local society into a moral community in the Confucian sense – as the first step to changing the whole country – by the reintroduction of traditional virtues such as filial piety and ritual politeness, and to train young teachers from all over the country with popular Confucian texts and ideas. Politically, this Center is conservative and nationalist, where teaching staff pay great attention to incorporating the official discourses into their arguments and maintaining a good relationship with local authorities. However, in spite of all this, it was closed in December 2008 at a moment when the enterprise seemed to have a promising future. The order came from the "high" authority, and no reasons were given. However, a possible explanation is that the Center had violated the ban by displaying its capacity for mobilization and political ambition. During 2007–2008 it was focused on by the Chinese media and represented as a holy site of living traditional culture, changing the spirituality of local inhabitants, producing hundreds of "seed-professors," and receiving thousands of pilgrims. Moreover, Jingkong had too much to say about politics. In 2008, a series of DVDs in which he was interviewed was widely diffused in China. In his speeches, Jingkong talked directly about politics by taking the town of Tangchi (in Lujiang) reformed by his center as an exemplar of successful moral governance for China and the world, and even promised that if the CCP's leaders would only listen to his center's teaching, all of China's political and social problems would be solved.

To a certain degree, the problem of non-official Christianity is the same. The underground churches and house churches are forces for mobilization outside the government regulation framework of official patriotic Churches. Besides, for Chinese government, both of them are politically engaged. The Catholic underground churches give allegiance to the Vatican, which does not recognize the PRC. The Protestant house churches have close links with not only foreign Christian organizations, but also some famous dissidents, and therefore risk provoking insubordination to the Chinese government. Moreover, the debate on "religious freedom" and "human rights" is sometimes directly involved in the pro-Christian discourses, and is seen as a potential threat to political stability. If house churches have not been completely suppressed as Falungong in a political campaign, one of the reasons is that they are not yet considered by the CCP as an immediate great menace: these churches have neither a unified institution nor a supreme leader, which are crucial for any general mobilization at national level. Even though Christian believers grow in large numbers out of the official framework (a consensus estimate is 50–60 million), they are diffusedly affiliated with about one million churches (Li, 2011, p. 70). This does not mean, however, the loss of control. In fact, the government surveillance is omnipresent, and the police intervention may be intensive at the local level. It is not rare that house churches are banned in the name of "unlawful assembly" or "evil cult" (Yu, 2010b).

For the official institutions of the five legal religions, the State's intention to restrict their mobilization capacity is also evident. According to the *Regulations on Religious Affairs* revised in 2005, in principle only an authorized religious site is allowed to hold a religious activity. Any large-scale religious activities going beyond the capacity of the registered religious sites cannot be organized without the permission of the governmental Religious Affairs Bureau (RAB).

Actually, the only case when large-scale mobilization could happen is when religion is used by the government itself. Buddhism offers a good example in this respect. At the local level, Buddhism is above all used to promote tourism, as we have seen in the case of public sacrifice. At the level of the central government, the use is essentially political, especially in connection with Taiwan and Hong Kong affairs and international propaganda (Ji, 2011). In this case, the State has itself organized large-scale gatherings, extensively covered by the Chinese official media. In 2006, the first World Buddhist Forum was held in Hangzhou and Zhoushan, Zhejiang Province. It was the first large-scale international multilateral religious gathering hosted by the PRC since 1949. The Forum was co-organized by the official Buddhist Association and the China Religious Culture Communication Association (*Zhonghua zongjiao wenhua jiaoliu xiehui*, 中华宗教文化交流协会) newly founded in 2005. The latter presented itself as a non-profit social organization. Yet in reality, it was only a mask for the RAB of the central government, and its president was none other than the general director of the RAB Ye Xiaowen, and its administrative vice president and general secretary was, as expected, the RAB's vice director Qi Xiaofei. With this official background, the provincial parliament hall of Zhejiang was chosen as the principal meeting place, where more than 1000 Buddhist representatives from 37 countries and regions gathered. The main theme of the Forum was carefully defined as "A harmonious world begins in the mind," echoing the "harmony theory" of the Chinese government.

Similarly to public sacrifice, this kind of religious mobilization is of course not intrinsically "religious," but rather a governmental *imitation* of religious activity. Monks and lay Buddhists are reduced to the level of actors playing roles designated by officials in a political scenario dictated by the State. Even though the political utilization creates the opportunity for religion to be momentarily legally mediatized and publicized, it weakens the autonomy of the religious institution in the long run, since the latter has to adapt itself as closely as possible to the politically correct rhetoric and organize collective practices according to the demands of the State. Therefore, the main concern is still limitation rather than toleration.

Concluding remarks: secularization without secularism

Very briefly, I have tried to analyze some new phenomena of the Chinese political-religious configuration. Even though their complexity is far from being completely outlined, the facts presented here are enough to remind us that neither "secular" nor "post-secular" provide a suitable label for the contemporary neo-totalitarian situation. If we had to summarize Chinese secularity in such a context, I would like to propose referring to it as secularization without secularism.

First, what seems somewhat paradoxical is that an impressive religious revival and a radicalization of secularization coexist in post-89 China. Here secularization and the religious revival are not only uncontradictory, but have a certain relationship of cause and effect. On the one hand, neo-totalitarianism is no longer an applied "political religion" with an ideological authenticity, but a vulgar and disenchanted coercion of "transparent lies." Seen from this angle, neo-totalitarianism is a secularized form of Maoist totalitarianism, which appears to have lost the latter's utopian, charismatic, and transcendental dimensions. In such a context, regulation on religion does not operate for ideological reasons, but takes the form of a rational instrumentalism and a pragmatic utilitarianism, serving the ultimate objective of the regime: political stability. On the other hand, this political secularization generates a renewed form of religious secularization. Instead of the secularization under Mao's reign which was characterized by the direct seizing and violent destruction of religions, present-day secularization conforms more to its original juridical meaning, referring to the appropriation and use of religious material or symbolic properties by State power. Confronted by the State's total surveillance and direct intervention, any religion that tries to avoid clashing with the regime must seek its legitimacy in a limited secular realm, ranging from tourism to "soft power," and hence loses its autonomy with regard to politics and the "socialist" market economy. However, if the disenchantment of politics gives more place to religion in the marketplace of spirituality, it is precisely through government use of religions for economic and political ends that the latter are allowed to be legally rehabilitated and publicly expressed (Palmer, 2009; Ji 2004; 2011).

Second, the secularization we have observed is not accompanied by secularism, if we take the latter to refer to the democratic institutional arrangement in the political and juridical sense, aiming to secure the separation of religion and politics, freedom of conscience, and public norms to condition both State and religion. As we have pointed out, the slackening of religious repression does not result in a greater separation of politics and religion. Inasmuch as religion does not threaten the absolute political control on social mobilization, the neo-totalitarian Party-State no longer considers religion as an alien element by nature, but, on the contrary, as an instrument to be made use of. It manipulates religion, and if necessary, passes itself off as a religious actor. At the same time, the CCP is well aware that it can no longer successfully control people's minds as in the past, but it does all it can to forbid the explicit expression of dissidence. The consequence is devastating: in principle only official discourse is allowed in the public space, even though no one believes it. In such a false public space, religions lack both a common value and a reliable procedure to express their position and negotiate with the State.[15] At the most, religious actors strive in the aim of furthering development by catering to the State's likes or tastes, while the State reduces this negotiation to the level of a utilitarian exchange, neither admitting nor believing in any claim of value. In consequence, there is no room for a desirable secularism in the PRC, which should consist in founding the principle of governance on Public reason.

Notes

1. For a summary of the results of these investigations, see Vermander (2009). For an estimation of religious demography of the five recognized institutionalized religions in China, see Lai (2003).
2. It would be interesting to compare the Chinese neo-totalitarian state of mind with the late Soviet years. Cf. Yurchak (2006).
3. According to classical political studies, it may be more relevant to define Chinese post-Mao politics as authoritarian. From this point of view, only regimes such as the Stalinist USSR and Maoist China merit the term "totalitarianism." However, Xu's notion of neo-totalitarianism seems to me more interesting insofar as it breaks the illusion of the lineal progress of political freedom during the transition from totalitarianism to authoritarianism, reminding us of the retrogression of political reform in China after 1989. Here in the expression "neo-totalitarianism," "totalitarianism" refers to an ideal governmental principle rather than a political reality.
4. For a synthetic analysis of the theological style politics of the CCP and its post-Mao breakdown, see Goossaert and Palmer (2011, pp. 176–198).
5. It seems that the award of the Nobel Peace Prize to Liu Xiaobo, the Arab democratic uprisings, and the arrest of artist and activist Ai Weiwei in 2010–2011 have provided fresh stimulus for the mobilization of Chinese youth for democratization, but it is still too early to evaluate the consequences.
6. The "Three Represents" means the CCP should always "represent advanced social productive forces, represent the progressive course of China's advanced culture, and represent the fundamental interests of the majority."
7. For an analysis of the complexity and the ambiguity of the reference to traditional culture and Confucianism in Chinese official discourses in the 2000s, see Billioud (2007).
8. For a version of this song, see https://www.youtube.com/watch?v=01RPek5uAJ4 (last accessed March 17, 2015).
9. For more information about this event in Western languages, see for example Wines (2009) and Nivelle (2009).
10. For example, there are numerous new festivals related to "Buddhist Culture" in China since the 2000s. Cf. Ji (2004).
11. For example, see the emphasis on the economical use of Confucian Cultural Festival in the official program, cited by Feng (2005).
12. According to Chinese media, the income only from the entrance tickets to historical sites during the Confucian Cultural Festival amounts to millions of RMB (1 RMB ≈ 0.15 USD). During the public sacrifices to Yellow Emperor, only the businessman that made the largest donation can be the "principle priest" of the year. Since 2006, the price of this honor is about 5 million RMB,

which is always generously paid by a State-owned enterprise. In 2010, a local enterprise in Henan paid 1,060,000 RMB to be the first to burn incense (*shao touxiang*, 烧头香).
13. The project uses public resources to save the face of officials. It refers to a strategy to maintain a facade of stability and prosperity by engineering gigantic projects and holding grand celebrations. Cf. Cai (2004).
14. This concept has been advanced by Yu Jianrong (2010a) for analyzing the manners and effects of current Chinese governance.
15. Vincent Goossaert (2005) has pointed out that the separation of religion and politics in China is false, given the absence of genuine negotiations between the State and religious groups and the failure of the State to achieve a stance of political neutrality towards different religions.

6
North Korea's Culture of Commemoration

Heonik Kwon

The cemeteries of fallen soldiers, together with the Tomb of the Unknown Soldier, are important material and symbolic objects in the history of modern political life. In most cases, these sites of memory are regarded as an emblematic object that represents the authority and integrity of the nation-state. This is evident not only in Europe and North America, but also in many parts of the non-Western, postcolonial world. The same is true in revolutionary postcolonial societies such as postwar Vietnam. After the war against America was over in 1975, Vietnam's state authority sought to bring the confused central and southern regions into the fold of national unity by advancing the commemoration of revolutionary war martyrs as a principal civic duty. Its effort, in fact, went well beyond those of earlier European exemplars and brought the cemeteries of fallen soldiers and memorials dedicated to their memory to the center of postwar communal ritual lives and the village moral landscape.

North Korea is a striking exception to this fairly universal modern culture of war commemoration, or what is sometimes called modern civic religion. No publicly known cemeteries of fallen soldiers exist in North Korea, despite the fact that the country experienced one of the most violent civil wars of the past century – the Korean War (1950–1953) – as part of the global Cold War and during its formative era. This article will explore North Korea's culture of commemoration, questioning how the country's political order could sustain the devastating effects of a modern total war without resorting to what George Mosse (1991) calls the cult of the fallen soldiers and, in turn, what the absence of public war cemeteries says about the constitution of this order. The discussion will partly draw upon a comparison with the public culture of commemoration found in postwar Vietnam. The Vietnam War and the

Korean War share some common characteristics. Both were postcolonial political struggles fought in the age of the Cold War, and both were a civil war waged nevertheless in the form of an international conflict (Bradley, 2000; Cumings, 1981). In this respect, this article takes the absence of war cemeteries in postwar North Korea, in contrast to the abundance of these sites of memory in postwar Vietnam, as a point of departure for understanding the particularity of North Korea's political order and public authority. Before considering what is apparently absent in North Korea's material culture of commemoration, however, first we need to come to terms with what is abundantly present in this public cultural sphere.

The Manchurian tradition

One of the notable aspects of North Korea's public material culture of war commemoration is a pronounced hierarchy of value between two important episodes of armed struggle in the genesis of North Korean revolution. One of them is the nationwide experience of civil war in the postcolonial Cold War era in the early 1950s, and the other is a partisan warfare of a much smaller scale in the 1930s against Japan's colonial domination. North Korea's official historical narrative explains these two struggles in terms of victory over two separate forms of imperialism – Japanese imperialism and American imperialism. It also presents North Korea and its political leadership as having a unique honorable status, among other formerly colonized, newly independent nations in the 20th century, of having successfully fought against two powerful imperial forces of that century. Whereas North Korea's public culture and political literacy explain these two armed struggles in a scheme of continuum, the early partisan struggle against Japanese imperialism in the 1930s appears in them to be of greater esteem and authority compared to the collective struggle against American imperialism in the 1950s.

The eminent Japanese historian Wada Haruki explores the supremacy of the early partisan history in North Korea's statehood, coining the idea of North Korea's political system as a "partisan state" (*yūgekitai kokka*, in Japanese) (Wada, 1998; also Kwon, 2010a). The idea draws attention to the group of political actors who played a central role in the foundation of North Korea in the middle of the 20th century and to the career backgrounds of these formative actors in colonial times as members of an armed resistance group based mainly in Japanese-occupied Manchuria. One relatively small group of armed resistance fighters was led by the young Kim Il Sung and attracted considerable moral support from the large group of settlers of Korean origin in northeastern China (Armstrong, 2003, pp. 13–37; also Park, 2005). As is known, this group of originally Manchurian-based armed revolutionaries won the power struggle against other contending groups in the early years of state-building in North Korea after liberation from Japanese colonial rule in 1945, with strong support from the Soviet military who occupied the northern half of postcolonial Korea (the southern half was occupied by US forces) (Armstrong, 2003, pp. 222–239). It is also well-known that after the disastrous Korean War (disastrous for the people of Korea, but also for the North Korean leadership because it failed to liberate the southern half of Korea as had been anticipated), Kim and his former partisan group from the Manchurian era were successful in a power struggle against all other revolutionary factions. By the end of the 1950s, Kim's so-called Manchurian faction had risen as an unchallenged, singular political force in North Korea, and it remains so to this day (Suh, 1995, pp. 107–158). It is a generally held view among observers of North Korea that this group of now-aged former guerilla fighters (and their children and grandchildren) has been the principal power base on which the so-called personality cult of Kim Il Sung advanced in the postwar years. These people also contributed to building North Korea's people's army, in which they have held key posts, into an increasingly vital political force, after Kim's death in 1994, in support of Kim's designated successor, Kim Jong Il, and his so-called military-first socialist politics. In proposing the idea of partisan state, Wada describes how the above postwar political development of North Korea involved the sublimation of the history (and the myth) of the Kim Il Sung-led partisan group's armed anti-colonial resistance activity in Manchuria to the single most important, most sacred, and all-encompassing saga of the nation's modern history.

North Korean public art makes it crystal clear that the Manchurian legacy is the founding history of the country's sovereign political order. Interestingly, it also makes it abundantly clear that a towering moral hierarchy exists in the country's historical knowledge between the memory of Manchurian heroism and that of the Korean War experience. Most spectacular among numerous built objects in this respect is North Korea's national cemetery, the Graves of Revolutionary Martyrs. Standing on the hill Daesŏngsan on the outskirts of Pyongyang, the cemetery was first built immediately after the Korean War ended in July 1953 and underwent relocation and renovation in the second half of the 1970s and again in the mid-1980s. The timing of the cemetery's original construction may give the impression that the place should be a burial ground for North Korea's fallen soldiers of the Korean War. That is far from the case, however. North Korea has no state-instituted, recognized public cemeteries for the Korean War fallen soldiers, although it has a number of epitaphs, memorials, and museums dedicated to their memories. In fact, North Korea's national cemetery in Daesŏngsan has no trace of the country's collective Korean War experience or of the countrymen's tremendous mass sacrifice to that brutal, protracted civil and international war. Instead, the cemetery is reserved exclusively for a particular cohort of national heroes from a prewar history and from the era many years before North Korea existed – the so-called first generation of Korean revolution, which refers to the members of Kim Il Sung's Manchurian partisan group in the 1930s mentioned above.[1]

The above situation confused many foreign visitors to the Daesŏngsan cemetery. The cemetery is popularly known among South Koreans as the North Korean equivalent to South Korea's Hyŏnch'ungwŏn, the immaculately landscaped national war cemetery located at the heart of the crowded Seoul along the river Han. Although the national war cemetery in Seoul maintains graves of prominent patriotic figures from colonial times as well as graves for former heads of state, the place is primarily considered by the South Korean public as a place of rest for the fallen soldiers of the Korea conflict. The place also has a prominent Tomb of the Unknown Soldier, which, together with the chamber of names of missing soldiers and student volunteers, is regarded as keeping "the soul of the nation," according to the inscription on a memorial stone at the site. Being familiar with this material memorial culture, which is hardly unique to South Korea, many South Koreans, in coming to visit North Korea's national cemetery, expect that they would be seeing a Korean War-related cemetery of fallen soldiers (visiting this place is often an obligation for foreign visitors). Understandably, the experience frequently provokes confusion and reactions of surprise at the absence of the war dead in the national cemetery of a country, which the visitors know fought a highly destructive, mass-mobilized war just as South Korea did.

The above situation not only generates a disparity between South and North Korea in terms of war commemoration but also speaks of the fact that North Korea's war commemorative culture is an exception to the modern cult of the fallen soldiers. The last, invented in interwar Europe, has since become a nearly universal phenomenon in the modern world and a vital element in the moral order of modern nation-states. In the face of the mechanical mass death in the trench warfare of World War I, the Western European states invested huge efforts in memorial projects for fallen common soldiers and appropriated the universal experience of bereavement to strengthen national unity (Winter, 1995). Focusing on German public culture during the interwar period, Mosse (1991) describes how the sustenance of Germany's political order at the time was so intimately tied to what he calls the cult of the fallen soldiers. According to Mosse, this cult is an invention of modern nationalism, and the art of commemoration it empowers is, although adopting elements of traditional religious values and rituals, distinctly modern, inseparable from the principles of fraternity and equality central to modern political life. The cult has many facets, among which Mosse highlights the idea of glorious and joyous sacrifice – that the fallen soldiers sacrificed their lives voluntarily, without coercion, and "joyously" for the family and the nation. It draws upon diverse means of expression, including literature, art, and ritual. As to the literature, Mosse highlights the works of Friedrich Schiller, who glorified death in the battlefield as a sublime form of death that transcends the anxieties of life. For Schiller, the virtue of patriotic sacrifice lies not merely in its contribution to communal security and integrity, but in the fact that this death is free from the fear of death, the ontological condition of mortality, as Schiller says with his famous dictum, "Only the soldier is free." In the sphere of material culture, Mosse mentions the cemeteries of fallen soldiers as the most prominent cult object. Here the glorification of mass death is materialized in various monumental, inscriptive forms, such as the neo-gothic memorial towers. The structure of modern war cemeteries demonstrates the principles of equality and fraternity in a most vivid way. These places keep the bodies of fallen soldiers in simple and identical graves irrespective of the dead soldiers' differences in class, social status, region, and sometimes race. Their unity and equality in death embody the ideal of political fraternity and egalitarianism as individual citizens of a modern nation-state and bearers of equal rights and duties.

Since Mosse's seminal work, *Fallen Soldiers*, many other cultural historians of modern Europe have delved into the centrality of war commemoration in the making of modern nationalism and the nation-state (Gillis, 1994; Winter, 1995). This has been followed by a number of historians and anthropologists who write about the diffusion of what Mosse calls "the cult of fallen soldiers" to many newly independent, non-European nations during the turbulent process of decolonization in the mid-20th century. In writing about the experience of Zimbabwe, for instance, the anthropologist Richard Werbner states that war cemeteries provided a crucial theatrical arena "for proving the individual's subjection to the state, for asserting the state's encompassment of the personal identities of citizens, and for testing their identification with the nation" (1998, p. 2).

Similar observations have been made in regard of the Vietnamese experience of their civil and revolutionary war (1961–1975). The postwar Vietnamese state hierarchy put great emphasis on controlling commemorative practices and propagated a genealogy of heroic resistance wars, linking the death of a soldier in the Vietnam War (which is called in Vietnam the "American War") to a line stretching back from the French War to the legendary heroes of ancient victories. Every local administrative unit in Vietnam has a war martyrs' cemetery built at the center of the community's public space, and the reminder, "Our Ancestral Land Remembers Your Merit," is inscribed on the gothic memorial placed at the center. This construction of national memory, according to Patricia Pelley (2002), shifted the focus of commemoration from the traditional social units of family and village toward the state. As Shaun Malarney (2002) notes, however, the process was just as much about bringing the state into the living space of family and the community, ensuring that people felt and experienced a common national memory and revolutionary sentiment, even within the most intimate domains of life. Thus, the memorabilia of war heroes and revolutionary leaders replaced the ancestral tablets in domestic space, and the communal temples gave way to the people's assembly halls. In the latter, ordinary citizens and their administrators discussed community affairs and production quotas surrounded by the vestiges of the American War, in a structurally similar way to the pre-revolutionary time, when villagers and notables talked about rents for tenancy and the ritual calendar in the village's communal house, surrounded by the relics of their founding ancestors.

The Vietnam War and the Korean War share many common elements. The two nations were both liberated from colonial rule at the end of the Pacific War and subsequently experienced radicalized political bipolarization of society and national partition as part of the postcolonial process and the concurrent advancement of global Cold War conflicts. The wars they experienced were both in the form of a civil war, but waged nevertheless as an international and global conflict. Considering this historical fact and also the centrality of war commemoration in the progression of modern national politics noted earlier, it is surprising to observe a remarkable disparity between postwar Vietnam and postwar North Korea in the material culture of commemoration.

In Vietnam, the commemoration of the heroic dead from the era of the Vietnam War constitutes the central component of civic duty and morality. This was the case throughout the postwar years and continues to be so even today in the reform era. On national or local anniversaries for the "glorious victory in the liberation war," local residents and schoolchildren crowd the cemeteries of revolutionary war martyrs to clean the premises and lay flowers on their graves. The country's Communist Party committees, from Hanoi to the provincial and village level, hold mass rallies on these occasions and all other important public organizations, such as the local youth, labor, and women's associations, bring colorful wreaths to the cemeteries of war martyrs. Vietnamese art and music abounds with songs, poems, paintings, and sculptures dedicated to the meritorious sacrifice of these soldiers and partisan fighters of the American War; learning these songs and poems is an important part of the school education. All these vital national and local moral cultural activities focus on the cemeteries of war martyrs, which exist in all urban districts and rural communities of Vietnam, and they are made possible, in fact, by the physical presence of the material remains of the war dead in the intimate spheres of communal lives. North Korea also has a large body of songs and other cultural artifacts dedicated to the memory of its heroic soldiers from the time of the Korean War. In contrast to other societies that fought a revolutionary civil war, however, including Vietnam, these artifacts of memory exist in North Korea without what is, in other social contexts, the most important material cultural basis of public memory, the cemeteries of war martyrs.

I asked a number of other informants about the absence of war cemeteries in postwar North Korea. One particularly interesting conversation I had was with a prominent South Korean North Korea watcher. This expert works now in an academic establishment but used to be a close adviser to the South Korean administration on inter-Korean relations, what the South Korean administration calls national unification policies. The scholar contested the idea of absence, arguing that North Korea had a national cemetery just as South Korea did, and he pointed out the Deasŏngsan Graves of Revolutionary Martyrs and another relevant site, the Graves of Patriotic Martyrs in Hyŏngjesan (see below). He also cited a series of recent events relating to these important sites. These events included the visit of South Korean trade union leaders to Deasŏngsan in 2006 and the controversy this provoked in the South Korean public media. Some conservative South Korean reporters accused the union leaders of having violated the country's national security law, interpreting the visit as close to an act of benefiting the enemy. Their accusation was grounded in the alleged fact that people buried in the Deasŏngsan cemetery should be considered communist revolutionary elements rather than anti-colonial patriots. The union leaders countered this accusation, arguing that their decision to visit North Korea's national cemetery was in accordance with the broad national policy of inter-Korean reconciliation and rapprochement. The visitors also pointed out the earlier event in which delegates from North Korea came to South Korea's national cemetery in Seoul to make a gesture of tribute to the memory of "virtuous patriotic ancestors" buried there, referring to the activists of the colonial-era national independence movement. In detailing these events, the expert intended to say that national cemeteries exist in both political communities of Korea, and to convey his hope that in the future there would be a reciprocal recognition between South Korea and North Korea of their sacred symbols of national memory.

I agreed with the expert's emphasis on the imperative of reciprocal recognition between two Koreas and sympathized with his effort to highlight similarities between the two political societies, rather than their differences. I also recognize the importance of a sense of common prewar, colonial-era collective heritage in building up better relations between the two political communities. However, the expert's view clearly ignored the fact that a crucial structural difference exists between South Korea's national war cemetery and what he believed is North Korea's equivalent. The Graves of Revolutionary Martyrs in Deasŏngsan, as noted earlier, is no national cemetery in a conventional sense; no bodies of common fallen soldiers of a citizen's army are buried in that place. The other place the expert mentioned, the Graves of Patriotic Martyrs, has two individual graves for the soldiers of the People's Army martyred during the Korean War. As we will see shortly, however, it will be extremely difficult to call this place a modern war cemetery.

My interlocutors of North Korean origin offered a different view of the issue. Most of these recent refugees from North Korea, now settled in South Korea, were quite clear about the meaning of the Daesŏngsan cemetery – that the place was exclusively for Kim Il Sung's close comrades from the leader's Manchurian years and that the sacred burial ground had no connection with the Korean War – most of the old Manchurian-era heroes were dead by the time the war broke out. Our conversation clearly pointed to the fact that the cemetery was understood, in North Korean public knowledge, in a particular spatiotemporal scheme and according to a historical-genealogical order manifested in a concentric spatial form. According to this understanding, the sacredness of the cemetery comes from the fact that those buried in the premises were the "first generation" of North Korean revolution, and that these people were personally closest to Kim Il Sung and that they were the most loyal followers of Kim in his formative years. This meant that Kim had great personal affection for people buried in Deasŏngsan. As for the graves of the Korean War fallen soldiers, my informants told me that they had never seen or heard of a war cemetery existing in North Korea. In fact, many of them expressed surprise at my question, saying that the question had never occurred to them while living in North Korea. Some informants told me, however, about locally existing mass graves of Korean War dead. These places are where the local residents buried en masse, during the war, the bodies of the People's Army soldiers they had discovered in the vicinity. Some of these places developed into memorial sites after the war. In the immediate postwar years, these graves attracted steady visits from locals, which later prompted, in some communities, the local People's Committees to erect a wooden marker or a tombstone. In the city of Kyesŏng, close to the border with South Korea, a large mass grave exists on a modest hill at the city's historic quarter, which is now a favorite destination for foreign tourists. The tour guides in this place knew that the grave had been built for a certain number of North Korean army officers killed during the war. The grave looked well-preserved in the distance; however, the guides were not able to offer any more details about the place. Apart from these scattered examples, I failed to get a clear sense of North Korea's burial culture as to the Korean War fallen soldiers. I found no information about this in the large body of North Korean publications I surveyed; although I interviewed a large number of frequent visitors to North Korea and recent emigrants from the country, no one was able to say much about the whereabouts of North Korea's Korean War fallen soldiers.

Memorials for war martyrs

The Graves of Revolutionary Martyrs was first built in 1954, following a proposal submitted by Kim Il Sung to the Workers' Party assembly immediately after the end of the Korean War in July 1953. The cemetery brought together in one place about one hundred graves of Manchurian partisans which had been widely scattered around the country and in the northeastern region of China. Kim's intention to bring the remains of his old comrades into Pyongyang was to show, according to his instruction, which is today inscribed prominently in a memorial stone, that "the honorable revolutionary spirit of the martyrs of anti-Japanese revolution will be forever alive in the heart of our party and our people." However, it is unquestionable that his initiative had other objectives than purely paying respect to the memory of old revolutionaries. As mentioned earlier briefly in relation to the formation of North Korea's partisan state, the postwar years in North Korea were not only a time of forceful mass mobilization for economic recovery from the devastation of war, but also witnessed vicious power struggles and political purges within the Workers' Party. By the end of the 1950s, the Kim Il Sung-led Manchurian-faction won the power struggle, having purged (and neutralized, exiled, or executed) members of the contending factions: the indigenous Korean communist movement and the groups whose backgrounds and political orientations were closely in alliance with the Soviet or the Chinese communist movements. Charles Armstrong aptly calls this power struggle "centering the periphery," pointing to the fact that the struggle resulted in a group with a relatively marginal revolutionary credential, represented by Kim Il Sung, winning over all other historically more major streams of the Korean communist movement (Armstrong, 1995). The postwar decision to build the Graves of Revolutionary Martyrs close to the country's capital and to bury in it exclusively the heroes of the Manchurian partisan movement was, therefore, an important initiative to center the periphery and, for the part of Kim Il Sung and his Manchurian-faction comrades, to seize and consolidate power. Kim later reminisced in his memoir how grateful he felt to his old Manchurian comrades and to the unrelenting trust and fidelity they had shown to him. We previously saw how the stories of these old revolutionaries have been forcefully brought into North Korea's public culture since the 1970s, becoming a principal part of the sublimation of Kim's authority and the concurrent preparation for the succession of power. The concentration of the graves of the Manchurian partisans was an important episode in the consolidation of Kim's institutional power base and in the construction of his charismatic authority.

In this respect, it is important to recognize that North Korea's statehood in the postwar era was built up, in a crucial measure, on a culture of commemoration just as those of many other modern nation-states were in Europe and elsewhere. This culture of commemoration advanced immediately after a devastating war, one of the most brutal wars of the 20th century and one that claimed innumerable human lives. What is strikingly unique about the North Korean case is, however, the fact that the country's postwar culture of commemoration chose to engage with, rather than the mass destruction of the immediate past, a handful of martyrs from a generation before.

North Korea's postwar culture of commemoration did not (and probably could not) ignore the mass sacrifice of the Korean War entirely, however. Five years after the Daesŏngsan cemetery for Manchurian partisans was completed in 1954, North Korea built an epitaph in memory of the Korean War fallen soldiers on another hill near Pyongyang, now called Hyŏngjesan ("Hill of Brotherhood"). This initiative was based on a decision made by the Supreme People's Assembly, rather than by the Workers' Party, as was the case with the decision to erect the cemetery for Manchurian heroes, following a recommendation from Kim Il Sung and his "high political consideration of the revolutionary [war] martyrs" (Oh and Ha, 1989, p. 63). Named as the Tower of the People's Army Martyrs, the memorial was first completed in February 1959 and renovated later in 1968. The epitaph takes on a "bird" motif familiar to memorial art in other socialist countries and consists of a 24-meter-high neo-gothic tower with two lower horizontal wings on each side. The wings depict heroic battle scenes of the People's Army, including a scene from the Wŏlmido fight famous in the North Korean history of the Korean War. Contemporary North Korean memorial art history emphasizes that the cenotaph faces eastward. This emphasis probably relates to the fact that in the ensuing era, the authority and grace of Kim Il Sung were increasingly symbolized as the rays emanating from the rising sun. Some of the images depicted in the memorial's two horizontal wings were later replicated in the grandiose bronze sculptures of the Victorious Fatherland Liberation War Memorial, erected in Pyongyang in 1993. The city of Pyongyang also has a museum with a similar name: the Victorious Fatherland Liberation War Museum. This museum first opened in August of 1953, shortly after the Armistice agreement on July 27 that ended the three-year conflict. The museum that visitors see today, however, was built in 1974. The Victorious Fatherland Liberation War Memorial is formally dedicated to the memory of the Korean War fallen soldiers and patriotic citizens. However, the most honored object in this memorial complex is the stone where Kim Il Sung's hand-written dedication is inscribed: "Our People's Army and our people, inheriting the tradition of anti-Japan struggle, honorably defended our fatherland's freedom and independence against the allied imperialist forces during our great Fatherland Liberation War. Their heroic merit shall shine across ten thousand generations." The Victorious Fatherland Liberation War Museum, in its current form, is made to tell the story of North Korea's Korean War experience in a scheme of heritage from the heroic Manchurian anti-colonial armed struggle. The visitors to the museum, before they reach the displays about the Fatherland Liberation War (the Korean War), have to pass through several other exhibit halls. Most prominent of these entry halls are the hall reserved for Kim Il Sung and another one dedicated to the heroism of the Manchurian partisans.

The above shows one particular, exceptional element in the public culture of commemoration in North Korea compared to equivalent cultures found in other societies that experienced a mass-mobilized people's war. This element is better observed in memorial installations existing outside Pyongyang. North Korea's provincial towns also have museums where the locals have access to a displayed account of the revolutionary history. These museums are typically called the Kim Il Sung Museum of Revolutionary Historical Relics and, as such, incorporate the history of the Korean War as part of the great leader's long revolutionary career and as a modern-day manifestation of the tradition of the Manchurian partisan war. The incorporation of the Korean War history into the Manchurian partisan heritage history is also observable in the genesis of the Hyŏngjesan memorial for Korean War martyrs. This epitaph was opened to the public on February 8, 1959, the anniversary of the founding of North Korea's People's Army in 1948. The anniversary was changed in 1978 to April 25, however, for the claimed reason that the real origin of the People's Army should be traced instead to the founding of the Manchurian partisan army on April 25, 1932. The new birthday of the People's Army has taken on added significance in North Korea since 1996, when it became a national holiday together with the birthdays of Kim Il Sung and Kim Jong Il. This development in North Korea's postwar memorial art and commemorative calendar clearly shows that at the heart of the state's memorial projects for the Korean War and the Korean War fallen soldiers, there was actually the imperative to empower the Manchurian partisan legacy. In other words, the commemoration of the Korean War was primarily to sublimate the Manchurian legacy, functioning as a modern background against which the old legacy was to stand out. Subsequently, from the 1970s, the legacy was made into a full-blown, singularly meaningful, and all-encompassing founding historical episode, in view of which the national historical events in the following eras were given meanings retrospectively.

Crucial to this emerging process to center North Korea's national narrative along Kim Il Sung's biographical history was the establishment of the Daesŏngsan cemetery for Manchurian partisans in 1954. The cemetery was an important political instrument in Kim's early postwar power struggle; it continued to play a pivotal role in the subsequent era for the consolidation and eventual succession of his power and authority.

The heroic mother

The Graves of Revolutionary Martyrs has undergone two major renovations since it was originally built in 1954. The first renovation took place in 1975, three years after the celebration of Kim Il Sung's 60th birthday, and the second in 1985, three years after the leader's 70th birthday. Both of these major renovations are known to have been done under the guidance of North Korea's designated future leader, Kim Jong Il. The work of renovation was indeed an important part of the process of political succession; it was meant to be the appointed new leader's act of tribute to the memory of the country's founding revolutionary martyrs and, therefore, to the glory of their partisan leader. Thus it is depicted in North Korean literature that the renovation of the cemetery testified to Kim Jong Il's profound filial piety toward Kim Il Sung, as it meant to honor the people to whom the leader had deep affection. In fact, it is reported that Kim Il Sung was fond of telling foreign visitors how much he appreciated Kim Jong Il's affectionate care for the memory of his old comrades and how impressed he was by the young leader's deep respect to the founding generation of North Korean revolution. This was a very suggestive remark, considering that Kim Jong Il reportedly received strong support from the surviving members of Kim Il Sung's Manchurian partisan group along his apotheosis to North Korea's nominated future leader. Also notable was the fact that many descendants of the Manchurian partisans were in positions of influence, having had advantages in education and career opportunities thanks to their distinguished family backgrounds. It is broadly agreed among contemporary experts in North Korean affairs that these families of Kim Il Sung's Manchurian-era comrades were among the strongest supporters for Kim Jong Il (who had close personal ties with many of them) and today make up a most privileged group in North Korean society. It is not difficult to imagine, therefore, what the future leader's initiative to beautify the Graves of Revolutionary Martyrs, which were close in meaning to a family graveyard for the families of these martyrs, would have meant to these powerful families.

The 1985 renovation introduced another important element to the Graves of Revolutionary Martyrs. At the top summit of the hillside cemetery are found today the tomb and the bronze statue of Kim Jong Suk, Kim Il Sung's first wife and the birth mother of Kim's political successor, Kim Jong Il. The structure of the cemetery is such that visitors cannot miss the impression that Kim Jong Suk's tomb takes up the most honored, innermost location within the sacred space of the dead.

Her grave has in its back the magnificent stone sculpture of the flying Red Flag. Her bronze statue depicts Kim Jong Suk as the "Commander of the Northeast Anti-Japanese Army," an honorific reference for Kim Il Sung's Manchurian partisan group. Next to her statue, on both sides, stand the statues of Kim Hyung Gwon and Kim Chol Ju, Kim Il Sung's paternal uncle and his younger brother. In front, the Kim Jong Suk grave and statue open to the rows of graves and statues of other first-generation North Korean revolutionary martyrs, whose proximity to Kim's grave determines their variable ranks and significance in North Korea's national memory. In 2007, it was reported that the cemetery held about 150 graves, the majority of which were the graves of the Kim Il Sung's Manchurian partisan group members. This spatial organization of the cemetery clearly delivers the message that Kim Jong Suk should be remembered as the most esteemed leader of the Manchurian partisan army. Her esteem does not come from the fact that she held a commanding role in the army, which she did not, but relates to the same principle of degree of proximity to the partisan leader as that in the concentric spatial organization that the graves of other Manchurian heroes follow in relation to the grave of Kim Jong Suk.

Kim Jong Suk's towering presence in the pantheon of national heroes, in contemporary North Korea, is mainly associated with her public historical footing as the most loyal defender of the partisan leader (rather than her ties of marriage and blood to the leader and his successor). In public speech, Kim Jong Suk is referred to as "the unbending, unbreakable communist revolutionary who showed endless patriotic loyalty to the great leader of our revolution, Comrade Kim Il Sung".[2] She is also the "Mother of *Sŏngun*" ("military-first politics," North Korea's trademark politics in the era of Kim Jong Il) in today's North Korean public language, although the term "mother" in this context does not covey the sense of an inventor or creator as is often the case in the English language. The honorable status of the creator of *sŏngun* is instead relegated exclusively to the genius of Kim Jong Il in the early years of his rule. Although this has undergone some notable changes in recent years and the origin of this political form has been forcefully extended to the era of Kim Il Sung and even that of his earliest revolutionary experience, the genesis of the *sŏngun* idea remains strictly along a patrilineal political order of descent and allows no space for the Mother of *Sŏngun*.

Kim Jong Suk's place in military-first politics is not in the genealogy of the *sŏngun* idea but rather in the idea itself, as it were, as the most exemplary partisan fighter. She was the most faithful follower of the partisan leader and the most dedicated defender of the leader's life and authority; her footing thus makes up, today, the most shining, virtuous model persona in the *sŏngun* era, which the followers of this political guideline must look up to and try to learn from. We can say that Kim Jong Suk is the Mother of *Sŏngun* because her biography shows the exemplary way to be a proper and rightful citizen in the era of the military-first politics. The ideal of military-first politics is that all citizens of North Korea defend the country's revolutionary heritage with dedication and fidelity as strong as those which Comrade Kim Jong Suk once showed to Kim Il Sung. The idea postulates that the virtuous citizen of North Korea is one who not merely holds tight a gun in defense of the country's revolutionary heritage. According to this idea, the ideal citizen is like a gun, never wavering in face of the enemy's threat and being absolutely faithful to those who operate the means of violence. Kim Jong Suk is the Mother of *Sŏngun*, for she is the most shining ancestral partisan-warrior exemplar for all virtuous citizens of the military-first-era North Korea, whose vital purpose of life and primary duty as a citizen is, just it was for the Mother, to defend the great leader – his legacy and his hereditary authority. The North Korean song *Kim Jong Suk, Our Mother* says:

> The heavenly face we miss always,
> Looking up, it comes to embrace us.
> Your single-minded patriotic fidelity to the supreme leader
> Has blossomed all over our land as flowers under the sun.
> Our Mother Kim Jong Suk,
> We look up to you and we follow your steps.

The 1985 renovation of the Graves of Revolutionary Martyrs had two principal elements. On the one hand, it continued the objective of the earlier renovation in 1975, which was to strengthen the status of the First Generation revolutionary martyrs and therefore, according to what we discussed earlier, the authority of the partisan state. On the other hand, the renovation in 1985 sought to bring the memory of Kim Jong Suk to the vital center of the First Generation revolutionary heritage. This was also evident in the memorial projects that took place outside Pyongyang, particularly in Kim Jong Suk's natal home, Hoiryŏng, and other places in far northeastern region of Korea associated with her revolutionary footage. In Hoiryŏng, the town's Workers' Party authority mobilized workers and students to a construction work in the early 1980s, shortly before the renovation of the Cemetery of Revolutionary Martyrs commenced. The town's project focused on renovating the town's existing Kim Jong Suk statue and other memorial premises dedicated to her memory. When the work was completed, the townspeople saw that their familiar local hero dressed in traditional Korean costume had disappeared, giving way to a shining bronze statue wearing a military uniform. This change was, according to an observer, part of a broader change in North Korean women's public dress patterns (and the state's changing policy on the issue) from the predominant traditional dress (*hanbok*) in the postwar years to the combination of *hanbok* with military uniforms (Kim, 2010). It is observed that Kim Jong Suk was brought into this change as an iconic transitional figure from an exemplary, virtuous, traditional Korean woman (dressed in *hanbok*, and dedicated to her husband and children) to a new role model, both a virtuous woman and a dedicated defender of revolution and the revolutionary leader.

Heroic maternal icons have played an important role in other revolutionary traditions. One of the most well-known is probably the Soviet *mat' geroinya*, the Mother Hero Order awarded to mothers who bore and raised ten or more children. The entitlement of *mat' geroinya* was in practice in the Soviet Union from 1944 to 1991. In Vietnamese revolutionary history, the honor of "Mother of Vietnam" (*Ba Me Vietnam*) has a different meaning. This hero entitlement is awarded to mothers who lost all or many of their children (including those who lost their only child) to the revolutionary war against America. The postwar Vietnamese memorial landscape is dotted with monuments dedicated to the heroic maternal struggle during the war. Some of these monuments depict mothers who try to shield their children from the enemy's violence; others depict grieving and defiant mothers, who overcome the grief of losing their children to the enemy's violence to stand defiantly against the machinery of violence. Vietnamese mother icons are also powerful symbols of adoption and adoptive filial piety. The Vietnamese revolutionary war harnessed the image of motherhood as an important instrument of mass mobilization, particularly in southern Vietnam. Each southern and central Vietnamese village was supposed to be a "mother" in the ideology of the Vietnamese resistance war; expected to adopt, care for, and protect the volunteer soldiers sent from the north as if they were the village's own children. In urban areas, the powerful covert revolutionary networks encouraged women to forge intimate ties with young peasant soldiers conscripted by the southern regime, create a relationship of substitutive motherhood with the displaced youth, and work to dissuade them from following the wrong way (against the revolution). After the war was over, the commemoration of war continued to appropriate forceful symbolism of maternal sacrifice. As mentioned, mothers who lost many of their children to the revolutionary war were given the title of Heroic Mother of Vietnam, which came with modest state welfare benefits. The scheme operated within a broad affirmative system of revolutionary merit and welfare, which privileged the families of revolutionary martyrs in material and social terms, involving easier access to education and employment in public administration. Earlier we mentioned the centrality of the heroic war memory in postwar Vietnamese political lives and the materialization of this phenomenon in the war cemeteries built at the center of the postwar community. Heroic motherhood is integral to this sacred space. In Vietnamese war martyr cemeteries, mothers with a Mother of Vietnam title are buried along with the fallen soldiers (who are all categorically these mothers' children) and their graves take up prominent locations within the cemetery. On important national days, students and representatives of public organizations visit these tombs, clean the site and offer incense and flowers. The idea is that these mothers sacrificed their children to the honorable national cause, thereby losing the social basis on which they could be remembered and cared for as family ancestors, and that the society is therefore under moral obligation to care for their memory in place of their lost children, thanks to whom the society achieved independence and peace. The tombs of Mother of Vietnam, therefore, embody the morality of substitutive filial piety, performed by the society on behalf of the heroic mothers and in place of their own hero children.

The Mother of Vietnam takes up the most honored place in the Vietnamese cemetery of war martyrs; the Mother of Chosun is buried at the vital center of North Korea's sacred cemetery of revolutionary martyrs. The symbolism of these maternal heroes commonly encompasses the domestic and the public spheres, expressing the collective historical experience and public morality in terms of familial idioms and norms. However, a radical difference exists between these two forms of heroic motherhood. The Mother of Vietnam is bound up with the history of a violent war and mass human death and suffering. The icon is most prominently manifested in the cemetery of war martyrs, where the former in fact stands for a mother to all the fallen soldiers buried in the premises. It is also a channel through which the caring maternal feelings of the Mother of Vietnam (the structure of emotion demonstrated by the burial of hero-titled mothers in the war cemetery where their "children" are buried) are reciprocated by the collective actions of filial piety (visits and offerings made by the living members of the community where the cemetery is located). The Mother of Vietnam is therefore an important medium for commemoration of war, whose relevance is anchored in the historical reality of the Vietnamese revolutionary war as well as Vietnam's traditional norms of kinship relations, which highlight the Confucian ethics of filial piety. By contrast, the Mother of Chosun has no meaningful relationship with Korea's history of war or the history of mass human sacrifice it involved. The location of this icon is exclusively for colonial history and postcolonial memory. She is an important figure in North Korea's revolutionary politics of adoption, appearing as the principal care-giver for the orphaned children of the displaced population in Manchuria, as mentioned earlier, who are spiritually adopted by the nation's supreme paternal figure, Kim Il Sung.

The last provides some insights into the renovation of the Cemetery of Revolutionary Martyrs and the related efforts to empower the memory of Kim Jong Suk in the mid-1980s. Before the renovation, Kim Jong Suk's public image was largely that of a caring and benevolent mother, associated in North Korea's official historical narrative, particularly with the displaced orphans of the Manchurian Korean communities, and standing as the mediator between these revolutionary orphans and the nation's supreme anti-colonial hero and paternal figure of Kim Il Sung. After the renovation, however, her political motherhood came to incorporate the status of a militant. She became a partisan leader herself, and her revolutionary merit was then not merely as a substitutive mother for children adopted by Kim Il Sung but primarily as the most loyal partisan follower of Kim Il Sung, that is, the hero who was closest to the supreme leader in terms of interpersonal ties and therefore in terms of the intensity of loyalty. This is amply demonstrated in the recent literary and theatrical productions in North Korea depicting Kim Jong Suk as the Mother of Chosun. There are a large number of them, which typically describe the Mother of Chosun as the most loyal and dedicated defender, outstanding among her comrades from the Manchurian partisan group, of the supreme revolutionary leader.

Considering this, it then becomes clear why the Cemetery of Revolutionary Martyrs is such an important site in the political order and process of North Korea. The place embodies the main principles of the partisan state: the state's legitimacy in anti-colonial armed resistance and the empowerment of the members of the Kim Il Sung-led resistance group as the founding heroes of the state. The place also solidifies the morality of a family state. Kim Jong Suk, whose grave is at the cemetery's sacred center, represents all the virtues of patriotic family solidarity: she set the most preeminent exemplar of familial loyalty to the partisan leader in the latter's closest circle of relations – she took on the task of defending the center (the partisan leader) as her manifest destiny and singular purpose in life, and, therefore, she left a vital legacy for the era of military-first politics, wherein the citizen's supreme patriotic duty is once again to defend and protect the sovereign center. That Madame Kim has become the Commander of the Revolutionary Army in recent years is due precisely to the vital role that the Manchurian partisan army legacy plays in military-first politics. Just as Kim Jong Suk, the Mother of Chosun, devoted her life to the defense and protection of Kim Il Sung, so should her "children," the people of North Korea, dedicate their lives to the task of guarding and standing by the nation's new sacred center, which is the Dear Leader Kim Jong Il. According to this logic, appearing unabashedly in the literature about "the spirituality of military-first politics," the core spirit of this politics is, in a most concise yet lucid phrase, to follow faithfully Mother's footsteps and to turn her heroic revolutionary life to a re-lived drama in the present history enacted collectively by the soldiers of military-first politics.

The achievement of hereditary authority

The above development may be seen in light of questions involved in the succession of revolutionary charismatic power discussed by Max Weber (1947). As is well-known, Weber was most interested in charismatic authority among other types of political authority he discussed such as traditional authority and rational-bureaucratic authority. He saw charismatic authority as a dynamic form of moral and political power, unlike modern bureaucratic authority that he believed was static and ultimately alienating, and as having a revolutionary potential unlike traditional authority that he characterized as being stagnant and conservative. However, Weber was pessimistic about charismatic authority as a durable form of social and political order, doubting whether societies and collectives based on this form of authority were able to reconcile with "the conflict between the charisma of office or of hereditary status with personal charisma" (Weber, 1947, p. 370). The problem is basically about reconciling a highly personified charismatic authority with the imperative to reproduce the authority in the absence of the exemplary person. The routinization of charisma is basically a self-contradictory (if not self-defeating) process, for Weber, and a liminal process in which charismatic authority in transition would have to revert back to traditional authority or develop into a form of rationalized bureaucratic structure.

North Korea faced a similar kind of problem in the long process of the succession of power from the country's founding leader to its current leader; in this sense, Weber's thoughts on the historicity of charismatic authority are instructive for comprehending contemporary North Korean political process. The Graves of Revolutionary Martyrs was an important material object in building Kim Il Sung's charismatic power. For Kim, the cemetery meant a fulfillment of his debt to his loyal comrades from the Manchurian era. The leader's personal satisfaction was also a collective wish fulfillment. For the citizens of North Korea, the cemetery provides a home for the memory of the country's founding heroes and, more importantly, that of the most loyal, dedicated defenders of the Great Leader. As such, the place can be seen to embody the national memory and the soul of the political community, just as the cemeteries of fallen soldiers do in other modern nation-states, including South Korea. For this leader's successor, moreover, the Graves of Revolutionary Martyrs works remarkably well for the process of succession and for the related dynamic to advance the leader's personal charisma to a form of hereditary authority. It is through the successor's efforts and dedication that the great leader's wish to return the debt was fulfilled and, subsequently, that the political community was provided with a commendable site of national memory and civic morality. By this logic, Kim Jong Il performed a most exemplary patriotic filial duty to Kim Il Sung through the renovation of the graves: filial duty as the place is a tribute to the dearest wishes of the country's political father, and patriotic duty as the place honors the memories of the country's founding revolutionary heroes.

At the center of this important site of national memory, furthermore, lies the legacy of Kim Jong Suk, the most exemplary partisan and the birthmother of Kim Jong Il. The empowerment of her legacy helped facilitate the process of succession by displaying a bilateral character; that is, offering the successor a genealogical legitimacy from the maternal side as well as that coming from the patrilineal descent. However, it also helped to have the succession process break away from the structural problem inherent in the succession drama of charismatic authority, which is, according to Weber, the fundamental irreplaceability of the charismatic persona. By empowering the maternal icon, which is at the same time the iconic partisan, the child-successor came to be the exemplary filial-patriotic defender of the paterfamilias and his legacy rather than a substitutive leader in a bureaucratic-organizational sense or a new prince in a traditional, dynastic sense. By building the Graves of Revolutionary Martyrs, North Korea's new leader succeeded in presenting himself not merely as a descendant of the country's founding leader, but also as one of the country's most eminent partisan fighters and defenders of the leader. In other words, he created his entitlement to leadership by being both within and without the position of the irreplaceable Leader. Thus, the new leader came to personify the core spirit of military-first politics, which is the defense of national revolutionary heritage in the era of international crisis, as well as that of the military-first political philosophy, which advocates that the citizens of this era make up "ten million gun barrels" in the sacred defense. Through this artful transformation of the meaning of succession, in which the successor comes to occupy both the defunct position of power and the position of defender of this power, North Korea achieved a remarkable success in countering and resolving the formidable paradox involved in the succession of charismatic authority.

Notes

The research for this article received generous support from the Academy of Korean Studies (AKS-2010-DZZ-3104). An earlier version was presented at lectures in Yonsei University, South Korea, and at the University of Michigan at Ann Arbor. I thank Youngju Ryu for her kind invitation, and Tam Ngo and Peter van der Veer for their insightful comments.

1. The situation has changed recently, however. July 27, 2013, marked the 60th anniversary of the secession of fire after the three-year-long Korean War, and important public events took place in both South Korea and North Korea. Whereas the day is commemorated as Armistice Day in South Korea, for North Korea it is marked as the day of victory in its war against American imperial power. This year, the country, under the new third-generation supreme leader Kim Jong Un, celebrated Victory Day in a much more grandiose and focused way than had been the case under the previous leadership, calling it the Great Festival. Among the notable events was the opening of a new war museum in Pyongyang on July 27. Equally remarkable was the inauguration of the Cemetery of the Fatherland Liberation War Martyrs on July 25. Located on a modest hill in the outskirts of Pyongyang, Hyŏngjesan (Hill of Brotherhood), the Cemetery keeps the graves of 533 Korean War fallen soldiers, all heroes of the Democratic Republic of Korea. On July 29, Kim Jong Un left Pyongyang to pay a visit to another cemetery, the Cemetery of the Martyrs of the Chinese Volunteer Army in Hoichang County, where Mao Anying, Mao's eldest son, is buried (see Kwon, 2013). During the Festival, the North Korean state media went to great lengths to highlight both the country's dignity in defeating the mightiest imperial power of the 20th century and the majestic authority of North Korea's founding leader, who led the war efforts and thus enabled this collective dignity. They also emphasized the current leader's virtue – the virtue

of augmenting the founding leader's authority by enabling such majestic memorial projects as the Pyongyang museum and the Cemetery. An analysis of these new developments in North Korea's culture of commemoration requires a separate space.
2. This long reference to Kim Jong Suk is inscribed in the memorial stone on Osandŏk, in Hoiryŏng, erected in November 1978. Osandŏk is a small hill located at the center of the town, where in childhood, Madame Kim used to collect wild vegetables. According to North Korea's official biographical accounts of Kim Jong Suk, it was also on this hill that the young Kim nurtured her hatred of the Japanese and love of her country, after witnessing the pitiful scenes of dispossessed Koreans crossing the Tumen River in search of a better life in Manchuria.

7
Was Soviet Society Secular? Undoing Equations between Communism and Religion

Sonja Luehrmann

Socialist societies were dedicated to being secular in the sense of excluding gods and spirits from social dynamics, but their extraordinary promises also called for faith-talk. "In our radio show we heard from the workers of the wood-processing plant of the Mari Construction Trust. They talked about their faith in people, in the collective, their faith in the beautiful future of humankind: communism."[1] This line from an atheist radio show produced in an autonomous republic in Russia's Volga region in 1972 could have been recorded during almost any decade of Soviet rule, and probably in other socialist countries as well. An East German philosophical dictionary defines faith or belief as "holding something to be true although the grounds for it are insufficiently known, or not known at all" and notes that accepting the truth of facts and circumstances that lie beyond one's experience is part of everyday life. Rather than thinking of faith as necessarily religious, the dictionary asks readers to recognize the "orienting and mobilizing powers" of "the faith of progressive forces in the necessity and righteousness of their struggle, [...] in their strength and final victory" (Kosing, 1987, p. 224).

In this sense of trust in the unknown, appeals to faith were almost inevitable in a political system that asked people to participate in a radical transformation of lived experience. Socialist regimes where secular in the sense that they promoted "exclusive humanism" (C. Taylor, 2007) by combating institutions devoted to serving divinities and seeking to persuade people that only human beings created historical change (Husband, 2000; Powell, 1975). In the eyes of its builders, Soviet society was made secular through the mutual reliance on human hands and minds that sent people into space (Paert, 2004) and worked to secure a future of untold comfort, where no one would have to resort to "the illusory happiness of a human being who is deprived of actual happiness," as an atheist lecturer in the radio show paraphrases Karl Marx.

Critics have been quick to point out that communist humanism subordinates individuals to a society that transcends them, and that the deferred gratification of the promised communist future in many ways resembled religious promises of justice in the afterlife. The ubiquitous appeals to faith and to the enchantments of technology lead some observers to treat communism[2] as just another religion, whose discussion requires theological vocabulary. Scholars of the Soviet Union discuss the cult of leaders and heroes, practices of confession, and campaigns to uphold moral commandments – and in part, this quasi-religious language comes from the Communist Party's own terminology (Kharkhordin, 1999; Plamper, 2010; Tumarkin, 1983; 1994). But metaphors that assimilate communism to religion disguise what communist ideologues saw as a distinguishing feature of their faith: its focus on the humanly achievable rather than trust in divine help. This essay argues that the object of faith indeed makes a difference. Soviet secularization focused on diminishing commitments to the ultimate transcendence of immortal souls and miraculous helpers, instead redirecting people's strivings toward "medium transcendence." In Thomas Luckmann's (1985) terminology, this includes aspects of social life and experience that are inaccessible to an individual at a given point in time, but remain within the framework of the possible for the larger human community.

Especially in the later decades of the Soviet Union's existence, the smaller leaps of faith required for seeing one's role in the work targets for the current five-year-plan or feeling solidarity with citizens in other parts of the vast country increasingly eclipsed the grander, more mysterious promises of world revolution or religious salvation. Research on heavily secularized societies in 21st century central and western Europe shows evidence of a comparable reduction of the relevant scales of transcendence (Wohlrab-Sahr et al., 2009; Zuckerman, 2008). But Soviet history also reminds us that such resignation to the bounds of human life can be unstable and incomplete: periodic revivals of revolutionary enthusiasm brought more remote levels of transcendence back into play, as does the renewed interest in religiosity among parts of the post-Soviet population. When considering such resurgences, the analogy between communism and religion remains seductive, but limits our view of the historical dynamics of actually existing socialisms. Before outlining an understanding of collective encounters with transcendence that takes the Soviet quest to be secular seriously, I start with an example that illustrates why some people might want to consider communism as a religion, but also shows the limitations of that approach.

Thorns and briers: confession and faith in the end times

Confession, like faith, is a term that has been used to mark perceived analogies between European religious traditions and political ideologies such as communism. Through the work of Michel Foucault and others, the development of private confession in western Christendom (along with other "confessional genres" such as diaries of self-examination and conversion narratives) has been pinpointed as a religiously inspired source of the modern secular self (Foucault, 1976; Taylor, 1989). Although some scholars have tried to transpose this emphasis on intimate practices of individuation to the study of subjectivities created by Soviet socialist construction (Hellbeck, 2006), much of the literature about Soviet confessional practices emphasizes their collective framework. Instead of private confession, the public shaming and penance that remained widespread in Eastern Orthodox Christianity is said to have informed the practices of public critique and self-critique that culminated in the purges of the 1930s (Kharkhordin, 1999). Stalin-era citizens regularly had to confess to greater or lesser errors and shortcomings before their party cell, secret police interrogators, or before the infamous *troiki* (threesomes) of judges. Igal Halfin (2009, pp. 4–5) has argued that these confessional practices could bring individuals to formulate such grotesque accusations against themselves because they were less about shaping selves than about shaping a messianic collectivity that needed to root out evil once and for all in order to move toward a classless end of history. In histories of Soviet confessions as in the literature on western selves, terms borrowed from theology suggest that religious sensibilities and practices have traveled into a modern social life that only appears to be secular.

Consider, then, a scene that might well be read as proof of the irreducibly religious nature of public confession and the equally robust Russian predilection for group surveillance. It is around 3 a.m. on a Friday night in June; about 40 people are gathered in the run-down auditorium of a once-imposing cinema, built to hold more than 200. They have been there since 11 p.m., on their feet singing and praying for most of the time, sometimes sitting down and thumbing through their Bibles while listening to a preacher talk to them about the future of their community, about discipline, perseverance, and responsibility. They are all members of a Neo-Pentecostal church in Ioshkar-Ola, the capital of Marii El, a small and economically struggling autonomous republic on the middle Volga. Ranging in ages from college students to grandmothers, but with a stronger representation of people under 40 than in most Russian religious congregations, the most dedicated members of the Ioshkar-Ola Christian Center gathered once a month for an all-night prayer vigil, where they stayed awake from dusk until dawn to pray for the evangelization of their city and growth of their church.

This service in June 2005 was special, because there was a visitor: Pastor Maksim from Moscow, one of the assistant pastors at a church called Triumphant Zion, a Ukrainian mission where the pastor of the Christian Center had studied. Although the center had originally been founded by American missionaries, the pastor was now trying to forge close ties to Triumphant Zion and its mother church, the Embassy of God in Kyiv (Luehrmann, 2005; 2011b; Wanner, 2007). After four hours of hearing about God's great plans for the congregation, during which the participants were asked to repeat over and over "we believe," the faithful watched Maksim come back on stage after a song and announce that he wanted to pray for the church. He opened his Bible to Isaiah 27 and began to read:

> In that day the Lord with his hard and great and strong sword will punish Leviathan the fleeing serpent, Leviathan the twisting serpent, and he will slay the dragon that is in the sea. In that day it will be said: "A pleasant vineyard, sing of it! I, the Lord, am its keeper; every moment I water it. Lest any one harm it, I guard it night and day; I have no wrath. But should thorns and briers come up, I would set out against them, I would burn them up together." (Isaiah 27, 1–5, Revised Standard Version modified in accordance with the Russian Synodal Bible translation)

The church was the vineyard, explained Maksim, which God loved and guarded carefully, shielding believers from the devil. But should God find thorns and briers in His beloved vineyard, He would tear them out and burn them mercilessly. What was the meaning of thorns and briers? These were entanglements with the world, the pastor explained, as in the book of Genesis, where it was said that if someone is in the world, all his labor brings only thorns and briers. The task of the church was to tear out such undesired fruits before God brought judgment on the whole community. Maksim invited the congregation to do so through prayer, and suggested the spirit of bearing a grudge (*obida*) as the first "thorn" to be torn out. Finding no volunteers to pray about grudges, he said that he would give an example, and launched into the characteristic mix of praying in Russian and speaking in tongues that I encountered in many Russian Pentecostal churches. The spirit-inspired "tongues" manifested as strings of vocables interspersed between petitions in standard Russian, like the refrain of a song. People in the congregation supported the pastor with a steady low murmur of praying in tongues, and the praise-and-worship band occasionally punctuated his speech with music.

The prayer, delivered in accelerating tempo and loudening voice, announced that "we will tear out those thorns, we will not allow the devil to catch believers with grudge-bearing, we will pray for those who hurt us." A young woman eventually took over, shouting: "Lord, we repent, you with your power can tear out those briers, praise to you oh great God that you cleanse your beloved vineyard of all sin [interspersed vocables], thank you [vocables]." After an extended period of the whole congregation praying in tongues, Maksim performatively removed all grudges and invited someone to identify the next vice to be torn out, saying: "Give God the glory – may there be no more grudge in any of the believers here in this church, may this Word be our judge. Ok, you see how this is supposed to be done? Who would like to continue?"

A young man who played the electric guitar in the band suggested the next topic – the spirit of competition (*sopernichestvo*). Asked why this was a thorn, he explained that sometimes, as in the world, people in church were not happy for the success of others. They were happy to cry with a fellow believer if things were bad, "but if someone is rising up," advancing to a leadership position within the congregation, things became more difficult. "In the name of Jesus, we tear out this competition, we tear out this competition in the church, in the name of Jesus, we tear out this thorn, Lord God, you gave us this power, we tear it out, we forbid, and we accept in faith that we can be happy for others, we can be glad if you start raising someone up, we can be glad."

This prayer session continued for about an hour, and the thorns that were torn out all had to do with relations of authority and operational efficiency within the church – disobedience (*nepokornost' i neposlushanie*); greed and financial unfaithfulness (*srebroliubie*); cursing, idle chatter, and sarcasm (*skvernoslovie, pustoslovie, sarkazm*); religiosity (*religioznost'*, understood as a spiritless following of rules); negligence toward responsibilities (*nebrezhnost'*); independence and rebelliousness (*nezavisimost' i buntarstvo*); and indifference toward unsaved souls (*ravnodushie*). Almost all topics, except for cursing and religiosity, were suggested either by the pastor or another church leader, after which members of the congregation volunteered to pray about them. After the last prayer, a tea break was announced, and around 4:30 the congregation gathered again to hear Maksim expound the Embassy of God's teachings about evangelizing different spheres of society. Everyone went home to sleep around 6 in the morning.

Standing through the frenzy of people praying in human and spiritual language to be cleansed of flaws not unlike those that beset most workplaces, the thought came to my mind that this was what the Stalinist purges must have been like: loyal members of an organization picking up labels suggested from above and making them into self-accusations. One difference was that the prayer night was not about singling out individuals as carriers of the sins identified. The only exception was disobedience. The local pastor introduced this "thorn" and then called on his wife: "You should probably be the one to pray about that." The reference – slightly tempered by a jocular tone – was to gendered ideas about wives obeying their husbands as the faithful should obey their pastor. In general, it was the congregation – God's beloved vineyard – that was on trial rather than individual members, a situation made palpable by the presence of the guest from a larger and more influential church in Russia's capital city. But the individuals who prayed before the congregation also took the accusations upon themselves, modeling the individual effort that, in a logic similar to that of corporate training sessions on efficiency and responsibility (Dunn, 2004), was necessary to enable the church to live up to God's sense of its mission. A woman who volunteered to pray about rebelliousness, for instance, took this as an invitation to self-examination:

> The thing is that God sees our hearts. I've really experienced such a state, I repent of this, I beg the pastor's forgiveness, I have already said, Lord, that I see that this exists in me, give me repentance (*sokrushenie*), today I received repentance, I understood how wonderful that is, I don't need anything, I don't need independence, I just want to show my contrition to God.

This prayer night was not the only event in the congregation's life concerned with discipline and authority within the organization. A local man in his late 20s who had joined the church as a teenager and was younger than most of its members, the pastor had problems maintaining the kind of discipline he would have liked, and the congregation had lost members over his decision to align with Triumphant Zion and the Embassy of God. In line with the theories of Oleg Kharkhordin and others about continuities between Russian Orthodox and Soviet forms of self-making through collective surveillance, one might argue that such post-Soviet forms of collective confession are just one more phase in a back-and-forth between essentially similar religious and secular ways of enforcing obedience and conformity in a country that notoriously lacks substantive democratic traditions.

Analogies between communist and religious practices have a long intellectual pedigree, but the precise relationship between religious traditions and secular ideologies often remains poorly defined. The argument that communism was a certain kind of religion – a "political" or "substitute" religion, for example – emerged soon after the Bolshevik revolution in émigré circles. It was often connected to a comparison between communism and other forms of authoritarianism, such as German national socialism and Italian fascism. Depending on the observer's own stance toward religion, the intention was either to expose communism as a perverse reversal of centuries-old hopes (Berdyaev, 1932) or to emphasize the common irrationality and lack of legitimacy of "religion" as well as "totalitarianism" (Gurian, 1952; Voegelin, 1993 [1938]). In more recent work on modern authoritarian regimes as "political religion," the term "religion" stands for the capacity of ideological systems to become part of everyday practices and elicit emotional responses (Gentile, 1990). Kharkhordin takes the analogy one step further by claiming that not only can communist and religious approaches to collective authority be studied with the same tools, but they are actually manifestations of a single historical tradition that weaves back and forth between religious and secular contexts.

The juxtaposition between post-Soviet Pentecostals and Stalinist party cells illustrates one problem with this argument. If Kharkhordin and others are right, both groups embody a penchant for authoritarian collectivism rooted in Russian Orthodox traditions. But Bolshevik party discipline was arguably more deeply shaped by experiences in the late imperial revolutionary movement and western European exile than by exposure to Orthodox monastic practice (Service, 2002). Post-Soviet Pentecostals need look neither to communism nor Eastern Orthodoxy for authoritarian structures that discourage individual displays of independence. These principles are laid out in translated works of such US-trained evangelists as Larry Stockstill and Myles Munroe, whose model of cell-structured churches promises fast growth without diminishing centralized control (Luehrmann, 2011b; Martin, 2002). Even though the pastor of the Christian Center argued that the church's American founders had failed to appreciate the spiritual importance of proper respect and discipline, he did not look to Russian tradition for correctives. Rather, he advised his congregation to study the sermons of the Asian and African preachers who were frequent guests at seminars in Kyiv and Moscow.

Another problem with potential analogies between Russian religious culture and Stalinist purges is that by privileging high Stalinism as exemplary of communism per se, they eclipse the period that was formative for a good number of the people present in the Christian Center in 2005: the last decades of the Soviet Union's existence, most notably the long period of so-called "stagnation" when Leonid Il'ich Brezhnev was general secretary of the communist party (1964–1982). What united 21st-century Pentecostals and the secret police of the 1930s was perhaps the sense of participating in a time of change of millenarian proportions: Igal Halfin's (2009) reading of the records of interrogations and extorted confessions from the Great Purges emphasizes how the expectation of a radically new time led to demands for new degrees of loyalty and purity. In the Christian Center, sermons about becoming a disciplined group able to save many souls gained salience on the backdrop of prophesies about the imminent arrival of the Antichrist, embodied variously by the European Union or the United Nations. There are indeed structural analogies between both types of millenarian excitement. But taking them as evidence of the essentially religious nature of the Soviet state means treating the 1930s as emblematic of Soviet history as a whole, and drawing a direct line from there to the post-Soviet era. Along the way, one has to ignore the Khrushchev and Brezhnev periods, with their far less deadly and increasingly routinized techniques of bureaucratic control (Breslauer, 1982; Yurchak, 2006).

When we allow the later decades of Soviet history to take center stage, as they often do in the memories of post-Soviet citizens (Lemon, 2008), secularity appears as more than just another name for religious promises of salvation. Rather, it is a social condition that develops when the excitement about imminent salvation recedes into the background and is even politically discouraged. In other words, late Soviet society was increasingly secular because it shielded itself from destabilizing encounters with transcendence and urged people to place their faith in processes internal to society.

From political religion to secular faith: levels of transcendence

Analogies between religion and communism often rely on a particular definition of religion. Christel Lane's analysis of "secular ritual" in the

Soviet Union (1981), for instance, draws on Durkheimian understandings of religion as defined by a division between the sacred and the profane. Since it is the structural division that counts, not the content of either side, any society that holds something apart as sacred and non-negotiable counts as religious from this point of view. The only truly secular society would then be a radically Habermasian public sphere where everything is open to questioning through communicative reason (Habermas, 1962).

As Michael David-Fox argues, such a broad understanding of religion can be evocative, but ultimately fails to "take into account the novel nature of communism's appeal, its specific yet tension-ridden reliance on science as well as faith" (2011, p. 727). From a Durkheimian point of view, science may be just as sacred and non-negotiable as religion – after all, scientific discoveries themselves need to be taken on faith by most people (Giddens, 1991, pp. 88–89). To appreciate the demands and appeals of communism, we need definitions of religion and secularity that allow for distinctions between different objects of faith. In search of such a differentiated approach, I take inspiration from a somewhat unlikely source: Thomas Luckmann's conception of religion as "the socialization of encounters with transcendence" (1985, p. 26).

In a short essay entitled "On the Function of Religion," Thomas Luckmann argues that religion fulfills a universal function: establishing collective ways of dealing with inevitable experiences of transcendence in human life. He draws on phenomenological work by Alfred Schütz (1962), which explains the human capacity to imagine extraordinary realities by pointing to the shared experience of being born into a world whose orders precede us and will outlast us, and where we know many things and processes to be real, but out of our reach. Developing Schütz's idea of the inevitable experience of transcendence, Luckmann distinguishes three levels of transcendence: "small" transcendence refers to things only temporarily out of our reach, such as sounds coming from an adjacent room that help us imagine what is going on there, or an absent loved one whom we know to exist somewhere else. "Medium" transcendence refers to the interpersonal sphere, where an experience is not accessible to us at a given time, although we know it to be part of the humanly possible: young people have no personal experience of growing old, but they have seen others age and know that they themselves are moving toward that stage. Finally, "great" transcendence refers to spheres that are inaccessible to humans, but about which they speculate because of such experiences as dreaming and trance, which point to realities outside the sphere of human perception (Luckmann, 1985,

p. 29; Schütz and Luckmann, 1989 [1983]). Different from medium transcendence, about which an individual can form a picture from interacting with others and observing them, great transcendence remains a mystery, marked by a "border" beyond which lies something unknown (Luckmann, 1985, p. 30).

For Luckmann, religion encompasses all levels of transcendence, and he seems to think of religious history as a progression where increasingly specialized institutions focus on ever higher levels of abstraction. Applied to the case of communism, his definition could be taken to suggest that the utopian promise of a happy future is a way of mobilizing and harnessing the human striving to move beyond present reality, and toward a form of religion. But as Webb Keane (2010, p. 198) points out in an exploration of the themes of "absence" and "markedness" across the range of phenomena that researchers have called religion, different cultural settings vary in their choice of the sensory boundaries to which they devote special attention. Any kind of absence can potentially become an occasion for ritual and prayerful mediation, from the little transcendence of searching for lost property to the idea that an overarching mind has planned everything that happens in the universe. But in any given society, only some forms of absence are accorded ritual treatment.

Linking Keane's absences to Luckmann's levels of transcendence, one might add that although all absences can contribute to a sense that reality is always more than is immediately apparent, no human society treats all of them equally as pointing to larger worlds that cannot be fully known. From this point of view, the sphere of religion is limited to those forms of transcendence that demand specialized, marked practices of mediation because they contain elements that point beyond ordinary encounters between living human beings (see also Keane, 1997; Riesebrodt, 2007). On this background, secularization can be understood as a shift of collective attention away from previously relevant forms of transcendence, accompanied by new approaches to imagining and domesticating the unknown. Expressions of belief do not go away because they are part of the human predicament of living in a world that can never be fully known empirically (Rutherford, 2008). But processes of industrialization, promotion of science, and anti-religious struggle involve significant changes in the ways in which the empirically inaccessible is connected to everyday experience.

What exactly changes under secularization depends on the religious and cultural traditions that precede it. To describe socialist secularization in East Germany, a team of German sociologists uses Luckmann's concept of "medium transcendence" to discuss the focus on interpersonal virtues such as diligence, honesty, and friendship whose lasting effects can still be seen among residents of the eastern German states. Explicitly rejecting Luckmann's claim that such a commitment to socially bound transcendence is a form of religiosity, Monika Wohlrab-Sahr and her colleagues point out that it often goes together with disinterest in, or refusal to speculate about, such themes of "great transcendence" as life after death or the existence of divine beings. A retired physician who answered categorically that the only thing that comes after death is "ashes" became far more eloquent when remembering the mutual neighborly help between residents in her apartment bloc:

> All doors were open [...]. For years I brought our janitor's wife dinner on Sunday, this went without saying and I bought groceries for her [...]. And when I was on call at night and my husband was gone for a conference, there was no problem [with the children], our neighbor had a key. Then both sets of doors were open into the hallway and the children ran in and out. And she kept an eye on them and we did the same for her. [...] And all of this ended when the lawyer in our yard bought a BMW. Then it was over. (Interview quoted in Wohlrab-Sahr et al., 2009, pp. 271–272)

Even after the end of socialist secularization drives, the question of life after death remained irrelevant to this woman, although it had presumably been a focus of religious mediation in the Protestant and Catholic Christian traditions in which earlier generations of her family had lived. But she, her daughter, and the granddaughter who was four years old when the Berlin Wall fell preserved a sense of mourning for the egalitarian community of socialist East Germany, embodied by the seemingly random association of neighbors in a large building (Wohlrab-Sahr et al., 2009, pp. 214, 272).

These retrospective family interviews, conducted in the early 21st century, echo the "faith in people, in the collective" expressed by the Soviet radio show from 1972. They also mirror the acknowledgement and even celebration of social ties between finite human beings that comes up in interviews with atheists and agnostics in the heavily secularized societies of western Europe, such as late 20th-century Britain, Denmark, and Sweden (Brown, 2009, pp. 176–179; Zuckerman, 2008). In central and western Europe, this concentration on medium transcendence is the result of a centuries-long process of theological and social change whose causes and implications have been debated in detail by historians, philosophers, and social scientists (Asad, 2003; Bruce, 2002; Casanova, 1994; C. Taylor, 2007).

In the Soviet Union, communist activists committed to secularization also faced the legacies of Christianity and other monotheistic religions that focused on Luckmann's level of great transcendence, with divine beings imagined to stand outside of earthly laws of time and space. But in rural areas such as the Volga region, religious mediation began at the level of small transcendence. For example, the walls of a house, creating an experiential divide between inside and outside spaces, might be singled out for ritual attention. Members of the household fed the spirits residing in the corners where walls crossed, and guests saluted them upon entering. The Orthodox Christian custom of placing icons in the "forward corner" across from the door to the house creates a link between the small transcendence of animated walls to the great transcendence of a heavenly hierarchy of saintly and divine beings (Paxson, 2005, pp. 251–263). Elsewhere, I use the term "neighborliness" to describe the small transcendence of transgenerational households and face-to-face communities of neighbors whose small-scale loyalties and enmities were too localized for socialist visions of social solidarity (Luehrmann, 2011b; see also Chau, this volume). In the face of rural neighborliness on one side and the great transcendence of institutionalized and reformist religion on the other (Pasieka, this volume), socialist secularization strengthened and promoted medium transcendence. Communist activists tried to get people to accept and appreciate the social and economic ties that connect human contemporaries to a community with common problems and goals.

In the early decades of Soviet rule this process still involved elevating human agents and groups to a status approaching that of great transcendence. In the purges, for instance, Stalin and the Communist Party were treated as the repositories of historical truth, yardsticks in relation to whom ordinary citizens could be guilty of betrayal without even knowing or intending it (Hellbeck, 2006). There is evidence that Soviet leaders themselves were taken aback by the violence unleashed in the purges and, more generally, the unpredictable consequences of popular mobilizations (Taubman, 2003). As Alexei Yurchak (2006, chapter 2) has pointed out, the Soviet Union after Stalin's death never instituted a new external guarantor of ideological truth and purpose. None of his successors took on this role, shifting responsibility for the continued move toward communism to a prosaic consensus within human collectives, in which fields of intertextuality and practices of citation were the only reliable guides for what was ideologically acceptable and what was not. During this period, any form of mass orchestration that was not framed by a rationalistic, bureaucratic tone risked provoking accusations of a "cult of personality," a phrase that both Khrushchev and Brezhnev used to denounce their respective predecessors (Breslauer, 1982). It was perhaps this fear of evoking associations with a "cult" that made the stiff and formal official meeting the model par excellence for Soviet secular festivities – "almost as though people can think of no other 'Soviet' way of doing things," in Caroline Humphrey's astute observation (1998, p. 399). Cultural workers often lamented the lack of popular appeal of Soviet events, but were also reluctant to abandon rational frameworks and unleash emotions that might prove hard to control (Luehrmann, 2011a).

All this means that the deliberate use of collective effervescence in the Christian Center did not represent a smooth transition from one kind of authoritarian cult to another. Stalin's cult of personality and Pentecostal ways of deciding the "question of leadership" (Engelke, 2007) by reference to divine inspiration were separated by decades of bureaucratic rule where authority presented itself as emanating from sources within society rather than from outside. Where Pentecostals sought to open up human gatherings to the Holy Spirit as a source of great transcendence, Soviet events since Stalin's death had been ever more oriented toward protecting state institutions from anything that might either fragment them or measure them against an external yardstick.

In the struggle to build and maintain society, faith in non-human intentional agents was treated as threatening because it exposed the medium transcendence of social institutions to pressure from above and below. Faith in the laws of science, by contrast, could strengthen the bonds of trust and mutual reliance between humans. Another segment from the atheist radio show from the Mari Republic illustrates how scientific authority could endow interpersonal ties with transcendent strength.

Saved by society

A central theme of Soviet atheism was the struggle between religious faith, portrayed as unfounded and grounded in human isolation, and scientific knowledge, portrayed as emerging from a commitment to human happiness and solidarity. In a radio segment about medicine and religion, a doctor from a small town tells the story of Zina, a saw mill worker and mother of two children. "I remember her joyful laughter when she came to the clinic with other workers [for prophylactic examinations]. Then she did not believe in any god."[3] But Zina became seriously ill and had to spend a lengthy period of time in the hospital, separated from her family and colleagues. Cleaning up her drawers, nurses noticed an Orthodox Christian icon, and the night nurse saw her secretly praying in front of the icon at night. Soon Zina started to refuse the medical interventions her doctors recommended, such as a blood transfusion.

The doctors did not directly challenge Zina's religious beliefs, but started to visit her more often and talk about the successes of Soviet medicine. They also placed another patient in her room who was recovering from a surgical procedure during which she had received a blood transfusion. Hearing that woman's story, Zina soon agreed to a transfusion, and quickly began to recover. When she was released from the hospital, the doctor asked about the icon for the first time. "It's gone," shouted Zina. "Thanks are due to you, Soviet doctors."

A psychologist who explains the case to the radio listeners expounds upon the difference between faith in people and faith in God. The latter, he claims, stems from loneliness, the former from social connections. Her illness separated Zina from her "customary work environment, her circle of [female] friends and acquaintances." Loneliness aggravated the illness at the same time as it made the patient susceptible to religious influences. "The patient was given an icon, suggesting [*vnushiv ei*] that only with that icon's help could she return to her normal life." This icon gave her hope, an experience of transcendence that pointed beyond the temporal and physical bounds of her current illness. "It's a great thing, the faith of the patient in the good outcome of the illness." However, "hope in god has its reverse side: Distrust of people, of the work of their hands and minds." While trust in people ultimately helped Zina to leave her illness behind, faith in forces outside of human society led to fear and other negative emotions, which counteracted the healing process.

In this case report, the interaction between doctor and patient could be likened to an act of confession where Zina gives up her religious isolation and joins the collective of those who have been helped by Soviet science. But in true scientific spirit, the physicians do not wait for Zina to reveal the state of her soul to them. This was a time when even propaganda specialists in the Soviet Union shunned any investigation of deep psychological processes (Benn, 1989). Rather than with a therapeutic conversation or confessional exchange, the persuasive intervention begins with an observation of Zina's behavior: hospital staff members notice the icon and begin to manage Zina's religiosity long before they confront her about it. The cure, characteristically, comes from a human companion, another patient who had a good experience with the procedure that Zina was refusing on religious grounds. Having succeeded in gaining Zina's consent, the doctors first demonstrate the superior powers of their profession before asking her to take a stand on her attachment to icons. By then, she has realized her error, and is ready to thank the true agents of her recovery, "Soviet doctors."

Science in this story is not neutral or merely rational, but its ability to help is strictly grounded in the medium level of interpersonal transcendence. Medical specialists, concludes the biologist who moderates the segment on healing and religion, stand on guard "daily and hourly for the health of every one of us. They give their knowledge, talents and skills for the service of people, and their big, loving human heart. They are representatives of the world's most humane, and at the same time most god-aversive (*bogoprotivnoi*) profession." Medicine is god-aversive because it prevents people from having to take recourse to higher levels of transcendence to gain and protect their health. After the segment, the author and host of the radio show ends with her standard: "Good-bye, we are looking forward to your letters, comrades." The whole broadcast performs an ethos of openness between human partners in which there is no need to confess dark secrets, but the abandonment of errors and bad habits is the result of a combination of rational insight and social authority.

The late Soviet collective remained committed to mutual surveillance and public shaming, techniques that can well be compared to the constitution of authority in some religious groups. But increasingly, sources of guidance and hope were located inside the socialist collective, rather than standing above it. This domestication of authority and the possibility of a general suspicion of all manner of "cults" that came with it ultimately justify the epithet "secular" for Soviet society.

Conclusion: shifting transcendence

I have argued that Soviet socialism did more than merely replace one transcendent authority with another, but rather strengthened a particular level of transcendence at the expense of other possible ways of encountering the limits and permeability of individual existence. Rather than putting human leaders or the spirit of history in the place vacated by former gods, Soviet communists systematically strengthened social and economic ties at a level that went beyond face-to-face communities, but remained limited to human contemporaries. In doing so they not only competed against the great transcendence of institutionalized religion, but also against the localized spirits that animated neighborly loyalties. Soviet society was thus secular in much the same way as Benedict Anderson's (1983) modern nations are secular: both were imagined as finite communities of human contemporaries, constituted by mutual ties and mediations of shared experience, rather than divine will or the benevolence of dead ancestors.

My debt to the theoretical debates around secularization in western Europe notwithstanding, the model of secularity I propose perhaps lends itself more readily to comparisons across the socialist world than ideas of the privatization of religion or the separation of church and state. By focusing on the construction of the social sphere as a newly dominant site of transcendence, it allows for religious others who preach otherworldly salvation as well as those who venerate household hearths and sacred springs. If secularization involves shifts between dominant levels of transcendence, this also means that it is a dynamic process that can move in more than one direction. In some states that were ruled by Communist Parties at some point in the 20th century, there was little time to create the infrastructure of cultural institutions, housing blocs, and economic enterprises that would boost the power of medium transcendence (Evans, this volume). Other countries, such as China, may have gone through comparable shifts between the cult of a leader and violent assaults on older forms of transcendence toward a more routinized concentration on medium transcendence.

In post-Soviet Russia, the resilience of Soviet society-building is palpable, although it also comes under pressure from several sides. Two decades after the Soviet Union's collapse, researchers were still finding evidence of ongoing commitment to the institutional frameworks that developed and sustained interpersonal ties in the Soviet era. "Society work" and "working with people" retained its value among post-Soviet townspeople and villagers (Rogers, 2009, p. 137), and similar to East Germany, the loss of structural supports for this form of society-building could engender communities of regret and nostalgia (Oushakine, 2009).

Socialist visions of society were not devolving back to the fragmentations of neighborliness, but neither was there an overwhelming move to religious revival. Numbers of declared religious believers rose dramatically in the early 1990s, but stabilized around 50 percent from 2000 onward. Fifteen years after the end of atheist propaganda, percentages of unbelievers and atheists remained over 20 percent, and only a fraction of religious believers regularly engaged in religious practices such as liturgical worship or prayer (Furman and Kääriänen, 2006, pp. 48, 54;

Filatov and Lunkin, 2006). Even a well-established religious institution such as the Russian Orthodox Church had only limited success in its lobbying efforts under the governments of Presidents Boris Yeltsin and Vladimir Putin (Papkova, 2011). At the same time, religious organizations of all denominations often relied on the didactic skills and cultural and economic infrastructures left behind from Soviet times (Luehrmann, 2005; Rogers, 2009, chapter 6; Wanner, 2007). The Ioshkar-Ola Christian Center, for example, was located in the building of a former cinema, originally constructed in honor of the 22nd congress of the Communist Party of the Soviet Union in 1961, where communism was declared to be within reach of living generations.

The Soviet way of ordering the social sphere shaped the material conditions of collective worship, and also the way in which local officials understood the newly emergent religious diversity. In Marii El, city and regional officials had a clear preference for the three "traditional" religions of the republic, which could be made to correspond with the three main ethnic groups: "Russian" Orthodox Christianity, "Mari" Paganism, and "Tatar" Islam. Protestant groups that proselytized across ethnic lines aroused suspicion (cf. Pelkmans, 2009). Although everyone knew that there were Christian Tatars and Buddhist Russians, the schema of ethnic religions allowed officials to treat religion as serving the social order rather than exposing it to the demands of extrasocial forces.

Although they had to reckon with the continuing strength of medium transcendence, religious movements also forged new connections between the great and small levels. The teachings of the Christian Center emphasized individual responsibility *and* submission to divinely inspired clergy. They thus resembled the lessons of other early 21st-century reform programs in various parts of the world that mixed appeals to higher powers with ideas of individual responsibility and self-management (Rudnyckyj, 2010; Sullivan, 2009; Zigon, 2011). Where Soviet secularity had privileged the level of the social as the locus and agent of historical development, these programs sought to bring about change through direct connections between the small transcendence of individual experience and great, otherworldly forces. Human collectives were demoted to mere side effects of encounters between divine inspiration and individualized responses that included voluntary submission to "prophetic" pastors.

Twenty years after the end of Soviet socialism, such attempts to relativize the constraints of the social order remained the domain of minority religious groups, jointly dismissed as fanatics by atheists and adherents of mainstream denominations. It remains to be seen if new

Was Soviet Society Secular? 151

connections between small and great transcendence signal a larger shift away from secularization, in Russia or elsewhere in the post-Communist world.

Notes

1. *Priglashaem k razgovoru*, written by Antonina Aleksandrova, March 24, 1972 (Mari Republican Radio Sound Archives, Ioshkar-Ola, tape no. 809).
2. Like many anthropologists working on postsocialist Russia and Eastern Europe, I refer to the ideology promoted by followers of Marx, Engels, and Lenin as "communism," while using terms like "socialism" and "socialist societies" to describe the social conditions of states ruled by communist parties. Officially, none of these states were communist, but merely moving toward it. Considering the negative ring that the term "communism" still has in English, it is helpful to adopt the distinction between the ideal goal and historically existing conditions (Verdery, 1996, p. 235n2).
3. *Priglashaem k razgovoru*, March 24, 1972.

Part II
Creative Destruction

8
Apologetics of Religion and Science: Conversion Projects in Contemporary China

Dan Smyer Yu

Introduction

In the ongoing scholarly debate concerning the unprecedented religious revitalizations in contemporary China, it is commonly agreed that religions in China are not merely in a process of revitalization but have entered a state of rapid growth and transformation. The phrases "late socialism," "market socialism," "red capitalism," and "post-Communism," are frequently used to emphasize the diminishing public popularity of Communism in China. However, little research has recognized an unintended, but ostensibly synthetic, relationship of Communism with religion in China since the mid-20th Century. This social phenomenon of religion in China deserves a more complex analysis which can no longer only rest on assumptions of the once purely antagonistic relationships between religion and Communism, and religion and science as if these concepts and the social realities that they have (re)produced were entirely mutually exclusive and antithetical domains.

Since the turn of the 21st Century there have emerged fresh scholarly perspectives emphasizing the complexity of religious revivals in China. A growing number of scholarly works attribute the causal conditions of the increasing religious populations to state policy shifts (Overmyer, 2003), economic globalization (Yang, 2009a; Cao, 2011), the proliferation of information technology (Smyer Yu, 2008), local community building efforts (Chau, 2005), and individual theurgical needs (Fan and Whiteheads, 2005). Concerning the relationship between religion and Communism, my argument is that Communism has been *destructively creative* to religion in the history of the PRC and it continues to bear characteristics of a pseudo-religion or a belief system that utilizes modern science as its apologetic instrument to compete with traditional religious systems in 21st-century China.

Situated in the current public discourse of religion and science in China, my argument attempts to underscore a highly pronounced pattern among religious adherents and advocates of atheism: that the apologetics of religion appear scientific and the apologetics of science-focused atheism appear religious. The latter's "religiosity" is not measured by its doctrines but rather by its ideological fervor and self-claimed "belief" with an emotional tone that is no less intense than religiously-induced emotional currents. At present the "religiosity" of the state is sanctioned by scientism which treats science as "omniscient, omnipotent, and the bearer of man's salvation" (Hua, 1995, p. 15). Communism in China is no longer expressed in the Maoist "theocracy" (Kipnis, 2001, p. 35) in a militant fashion; however it continues to engage in its conversion project, competing with world religions in the guise of what Chinese statesmen call "the socialist spiritual civilization" and "socialist harmony," both of which emphatically pronounce the imperative position of the "Marxist approach to religion" and "scientific atheism" (Lu and Gong, 2008). In this regard, the opposing constituencies of religion and the Chinese state's scientific atheism defend their positions with what could be termed "scientifically argued religiosity."

Bearing these observations in mind I address the destructive-creative nature of Chinese Communism with my interpretation of Communism's religiosity and case studies of Christianity and Buddhism. In the case of Christianity I intend to address the religiosity of Chinese Communism in its formal similarity with Christianity and how its "monotheistic" style of iconoclasm has "cleared" the social space of religion for the overwhelming return of Christianity. The Buddhist case is intended to underscore how Buddhists' skillful employment of modern scientific rhetoric, as a form of its dialogue with the state's scientism, supports the reconstruction of the social legitimacy of Buddhism with a self-claimed scientific validity.

The encounter of communist religiosity and Christianity in China: where do the numbers lead us?

Recent official statistics report five million Catholics and 16 million Protestants in China (UFWD, 2002a). In their recent publication Ashiwa and Wank cite from the Information Office of the State Council showing that in 1997 China had ten million Protestants and four million

Catholics. In Jacqueline Wenger's comparative study of official and underground Protestant churches, her figures show ten to 14 million in 1997 and 15 million in 2003 (Wenger, 2004, p. 169). In Richard Madsen's estimate, there are 20 million Protestants and 12 million Catholics (Madsen, 2003, p. 469). In Nanlai Cao's *Constructing China's Jerusalem* he estimates, "There may be more than sixty million Protestant Christians (twelve million registered) in China today" (Cao, 2011, p. 5). Since most of us appear to reference the Chinese state's religious population census, mainly from the State Administration for Religious Affairs, the United Front Work Department, and the Information Office of the State Council, the variance does not seem too large being between two and four million since the turn of the 21st Century. Among the figures that are unavailable are those indicating the number of Christians attending home and underground churches. In this paper I work with figures commonly acknowledged among scholars and the different agencies of the Chinese state.

Scholars commonly agree that there were approximately 700,000 to one million Christians, mainly Protestants, in 1949 (Aikman, 2003; Wenger, 2004; Madsen, 2003). In comparison with the current census of 16 million, the increase of approximately 15 million within the last half a century does compel us to reconsider the deeper and bigger picture of the exponential growth of Christianity. The number of Christians growing from three million in 1983 to 17 million in 2003 in Ryan Dunch's findings is truly astonishing (Dunch, 2008, p. 169). It shows the growth of the Christian population in China starting right after China initiated its economic reforms rather than in the missionary era from the mid-1800s to the mid-1900s. I am not suggesting that the Chinese state's policy shift deserves full credit for this unprecedented growth, but neither do I entirely align myself with the commonly discerned causes of the growth, that is, the "death of Communism" (Cao, 2011, p. 5; Dirlik, 1994, p. 75); religious constituencies' resistance to Communist rule (MacInnis, 1996); and the impact of the market economy (Yang, M. 2008, p. 28). They do not convince me enough as being the only bases of the return and flourishing of Christian communities, whether registered or underground.

Christianity had entered China through European missionaries before Communism; however, its delayed growth parallels with the development of Chinese Communism. It appears that Christianity's massive growth has rather been materialized under Communist rule. Of interest is the fact that even with the presence of missionaries before 1949, the Christian population was 700,000 when the Nationalist state did not have a militant policy to suppress all religions; whereas since 1949 the number has increased over 20 times without the presence of missionaries. Why were missionaries so ineffective? What did Communism offer to Christianity besides its destructive campaigns? What seeds did these campaigns plant for contemporary Chinese Christians' reaping the harvest of their spiritual abundance and ecclesiastic growth?

A glimpse of pre-1949 Christianity

In Mayfair Yang's critique of Protestantism, missionaries contributed to the construction of a religion-superstition dichotomy, which is inherently rooted in European Protestant Reform and the Enlightenment thought (2008, p. 13). The inception of the idea of superstition then permitted a biased understanding of human religious practices, some of which were parsed into the category of religion and others which were labeled magic, witchcraft, shamanism, or divination, etc., all of which were lumped together by missionaries as superstitions. "Superstition" was not merely an innocuous class of religious practices but was (is) markedly stigmatized. These so-called superstitions were (are) undesirable from the Christian monotheistic theological perspective. In my reading of Western missionaries' writings in late Qing and early Republic eras I also see the same pattern in missionary writings. The titles of missionary publications then vividly expressed this sentiment of the religion-superstition and the West-China dichotomies:

> *Ways That Are Dark* (Walshe, 1886); *New Forces in Old China* (Brown, 1904); *A Maker of the New Orient* (Griffis, 1902); *How England Saved China* (Macgowan, 1913); *New Thrills in Old China* (Hawes, 1913); *The Cross and the Dragon or Light in the Broad East* (Henry, 1885); *The Uplift of China* (Smith, 1907).

Like their colleagues expanding the dominion of Christendom in Africa, missionaries working in China were also operating with what the Comaroffs call the "agentive mode" of modernity (1991, p. 22). Missionaries' close association with colonial powers, especially those embracing Protestantism, met resentment from the Chinese then (Dunch, 2002, p. 308).

Christian converts in the early 1900s already had a taste of Communist religiosity when they encountered the militant, Communism-influenced youth (Zhao and Duan, 2009, p. 10). In making peace with Communist anti-Christian sentiment, Chinese Christians prior to the establishment of the PRC took initiative to distance themselves from Western missionaries by forming its own native association known as the Three Self

Patriotic Movement (TSPM). In the meantime, its founders and early veterans attempted to recognize theological and formal similarities between Christianity and Communism. In the narrative of his conversion experience, the late Wu Yaozong (吴耀宗1893–1979), one of the leading indigenization proponents and founders of TSPM, remarked that Jesus and Karl Marx "all have fiery passions advocating social justice and a new world for humankind with their prophetic visions...They are all faithful to their beliefs and are willing to die for them" (recited from Zhao and Duan, 2009, p. 440). This attempted alliance failed after the founding of the PRC. TSPM has been fully under the control of the state. Chinese Christianity had to undergo the destructive manifestation of Communists' "fiery passions" before it could taste the fruit of current rapid growth.

Delayed growth of Christianity on the soil of Communist religiosity

The religiosity and the ideology of Marxism in the PRC are entwined such that the discussion of one cannot leave out the other. In this sense the idea of religiosity cannot be reserved only for traditional religious practices. Religiosity here refers to both a collectively cultivated psychological state and a set of patterned social behaviors with clear doctrinal volitions to outwardly project the ideals of a given ideology for the purpose of restoring the wholesomeness of an original state or of welcoming an ultimately ideal world. This type of religiosity produces an "intersubjective psychic field" or a "transpersonal [s]elf" (Corbett, 1996, p. 25) as the communally united identity of the individuals with the same belief. It promotes collectively what Geertz calls the "powerful, pervasive, and long-lasting moods and motivations in men" (Geertz, 1973, p. 88). Religiosity in this sense, whether manifested as individual religious experiences or collective ceremonial performances, can be seen as the routines of the moral and spiritual preparation for a given prophesied new birth of the entire society or humankind.

Understood in this religious sense Marxism, Communism, and Maoism were synonymous with each other. Their syncretic combination was, and is, a "political religion" of China (Zuo, 1991), with a messianic future toward which to project, worshipping Mao as the deified charismatic authority, and ordained a national conversion project on behalf of Communism. It is not exaggerating to state that this political religion was, in fact, the state religion of China, whose conversion project was fully carried out through all possible ways and means at the disposal of the Communist statecraft, that is, the education system, administrative units, the military, the police force, broadcasting, cinema, mobile loud speakers, personal testimonies, massive public rallies, and Maoist study groups for young and old alike. The Party, the state, the nation, and the people had to be united as one undivided vessel for the Communist message.

This grand conversion project of the Chinese Communist Party, undertaken during the first three decades of the PRC, was markedly destructive to traditional Chinese forms of religion. The category of superstition continued to be a stigma but was no longer set apart from religion as during the late Qing and early Republic eras; instead religion and superstition became synonymous by the mandate of the Party and among the populace. The suppression and destruction of religious practices and ideologies, no matter how widespread or localized, materialized Marx's vision for a religion-free society with "human self-consciousness as the highest divinity" (Zuo, 1991, p. 100). The most destructive part of the melodrama of this conversion project was the Cultural Revolution during which the nation of China experienced a form of "emotional ecstasy" (Zuo, 1991, p. 100) or a trance-like, fanatic state of consciousness. Murray N. Rothbard plainly puts it, "Marxism is a religious creed" (1990, p. 125) regardless of the fact that it ironically denounced religion as an illusion and the opium of the masses (Marx, 1973, p. 13). The Chinese version of Marxism did not deviate from its European source but rather manifested itself as such in particular because of its millennial nature.

From my fieldwork with Christians, mostly Protestants in Beijing, I find their conversion processes, especially those converts aged between 40 and 55, are centered on redemption, guilt, and existential-spiritual bewilderment. A churchgoer in his mid-50s shared with me his conversion story. He was the oldest among his three siblings whose parents were Party members. None of his family members were Christians. His conversion to Christianity evidently has been a "deconversion" from his Communist belief as well as a recovery from his own destructive acts in the past, especially his fanatic participation in the Cultural Revolution as a Red Guard and his publicly denouncing his parents as "anti-revolutionaries." This narrative is a prototype of Christian conversion among many of his peers. According to him his pre-Christian conversion to Communism took place in one of eight of Mao's charismatic rallies with thousands of Red Guards in Tiananmen Square in the autumn of 1966, the year marking the beginning of the Cultural Revolution. In his recollection, everyone was jumping and shouting "Long Live Chairman

Mao" in the square. He didn't notice he had lost his shoes until after the rally ended, but he truly felt he was part of something important. In his narrative, the charismatic, messianic traits of Chinese Communism centered upon the personality of Mao are overt.

In Tu Wei-ming's critique of Maoism, he remarks, "the pervasive destruction affected millions, yet the real culprit behind the scenes of death and desperation was unnamed. Such was the sinister force of this ideological holocaust!" (Tu, 1996, p. 151). Thus, a person during the Cultural Revolution could be both a victim and a victimizer, or a victim and an agent, which "illustrate[s] a whole series of paradoxes about power, agency, complicity, and rebellion in the evolution of state-society relations" (Kipnis, 2003, p. 280). It was the agency of Communism that possessed the Party members and many common Chinese. The Cultural Revolution was not a war of the state against people but one instigated by the state which the people perpetrated against the people with violence spurred by differences in their exegeses of Maoism and Communism. The whole nation was enchanted and mobilized by Marx's eschatology – the promise that there would be a last day of suffering for the masses and the dawn of Communist millennium, a "secularized Kingdom of Heaven on earth (Rothbard, 1990, p. 123).

The Marxist millennial vision under Mao's charismatic authority found prime soil in which to grow. Its religiosity manifested as lofty belief in the Party and the nation. This is the collective experience of Marxism in China and Eastern Europe over 40 years ago: the Communist Party was "divinely ordained as a means to realize the nation's goals" and "as the highest value of the working class" (Nowak, 2011, p. 163). Communism was incontestably the state religion of China. Its format bore similar, militant, characteristics of monotheistic religions: xenophobia toward other belief systems, an absolutely required devotion to the object of worship, theocratic mandate through charismatic authority such as Mao (Kipnis, 2001, p. 35), the dualistic split of self and other, and doctrinal justification for both physical and symbolic violence.

Resembling Christianity, as TSPM founders like Wu Yaozong observed, the Chinese Communist conversion project also obsessively relied on its proclaimed alliance with the suffering masses. In actually working with the masses on the individual level, this alliance was rather conditional in the sense that the suffering individual's body/soul had to proclaim absolute allegiance to the Party and make full commitment to the Communist vision. Thus the body was required to undergo mass rallies and class struggle sessions demonstrating devotion (along with everyone else) to the Communist mission, while the soul was mandated to participate in and conform to Party-led thought-work (*sixiang gongzuo* 思想工作). The disciplining of the body and the re-mapping of the mind were an integral process of Communist conversion. This ideological religiosity of Chinese Communism resembles what Foucault calls a "*régime du savoir*" (Foucault, 1995, p. 201), which refers to how power produces subjects via knowledge. In this case Communism and its messianic persuasion were deployed as a "technology of the soul" (Foucault, 1995, p. 30) in re-mapping the minds of its new subjects. Conscious, reflective cognizance of Communism soon became reflexive and unconscious shown in uniform social behaviors and idiomatic use of political language. In Bourdieu's term, it eventually became a "habitus" which is "the product of the work of inculcation and appropriation necessary in order for those products of collective history, the objective structures to succeed in reproducing themselves" (Bourdieu, 1977, p. 85).

On September 2, 1986, Mike Wallace, of CBS' 60 Minutes, asked Deng Xiaoping what he meant by "going to see Marx." Deng did not answer directly but said, "I'm a Marxist. Marxism, in another word, is called Communism" (Baidu.com). The intra-Communist phrase "Going to see Marx" is a euphemism for dying or death; however, it has become a contemporary idiom and a classic line in TV shows and films uttered by characters of Communist veterans on their deathbeds or at a heroic and dangerous moment on a battlefield. Several decades after the Chinese Communist revolution and political campaigns, Marx has become a lord of the netherworld, guarding the gate of afterlife.

I share the same view as scholars such as Rothbard (1990) and Berki (1983), and consider that Marxism is not merely a political ideology; instead, its core belief is Marx's vision of the Communist, messianic paradise on earth. Class struggle, or other such forms of conflict engaged in for the sake of manifesting Communism's ideals, are the means not the end of its belief. The path of Marxism in China has demonstrated its religiosity: the leader of the Party was deified as the god of a religion (Kipnis, 2001). The immanence of this religiosity is an integral part of the corporate body of the Party, which, as Albert James Bergesen points out, "represents a situation where symbolizations of the corporate nation have penetrated and merged with the structure of ordinary reality" (1978, p. 22). The Cultural Revolution ended over three decades ago; however, the religiosity of Marxism continues, often reflexively.

Obviously the fanatic Communist campaigns of the past did clear the social landscape of religion. Its iconoclasm toward native and foreign religions brought about their destruction but also prepared the groundwork for the eventual return and flourishing growth of Christianity. It is noteworthy that when the Chinese state re-acknowledged the cultural and social validity of religions, it only gave legitimacy to world religions but not to folk and popular religions, that is, fortune telling, feng shui, and magic performances (UFWD). Christianity's competition from these traditional Chinese religious constituencies is now almost absent. Meanwhile the Chinese state continues to advocate scientism in governing the religious affairs of its citizens, making an effort to disassociate superstition from world religions while continuing to stigmatize traditional religious forms and new popular religions (Bergesen, 1978). This preferential state policy admittedly rests itself on the initial Chinese Communist vision starting from Chen Duxiu that "science will replace religion." To point out again, "science" in this context is synonymous with scientism as aforementioned in the sense of its "theological" disposition to "save China." Along with China's adoption of market economy with the imprint of Protestant values (Cao, 2011), such policy and its ideological disposition historically rooted in Marxist scientism undoubtedly favors the growth of Christianity as contemporary Christians have little competition from traditional folk religions.

Scientific apologetics of Buddhism: renewing the Buddhist discourse of religion and science

Both Communists and Christians were responsible for introducing the idea of superstition against folk religious practices in the modern history of China. The Communist suppression of Buddhism in the past was based on its inclusion of Buddhism in the category of superstition. Temples and monasteries bore much of the destructive measures of the state, becoming popular targets of ill-informed young revolutionaries like Red Guards. While the iconoclasm of Communist scientism inadvertently laid the groundwork for the current rapid growth of Christianity in China, its legacy seems to recede in people's memory; however, in the 21st Century "being scientific" in China is a social norm. One does not need to believe in Communism or a religion, but being scientific is equivalent to progress (*xianjing* 先进) and civilization (*wenming* 文明). In the meantime the Party, to strengthen its ruling position, continues to promote Marxist scientific atheism and proselytize its citizens with numerous state-funded projects which I will address in the last segment of the chapter. The Party's mission apparently appears like a competitor to traditional religious systems.

In this context, an emerging number of contemporary Chinese Buddhist teachers are engaged in the discourse of religion and science as a destigmatization process, as many practicing Buddhists feel that symbolic violence of Communist scientific atheism has done more damage to Buddhism than its physical violence. Many of them hold the view that temples and monasteries could be quickly rebuilt; however, it takes longer time to clear the misrepresentation of Buddhism as superstition on people's minds. I see a dual pattern of contemporary Buddhists' engagement with the state's scientism and scientific atheism. On one hand it is obviously a destigmatization process. On the other hand, by employing scientific rhetoric Buddhism is winning converts from Party members and younger generations of Chinese citizens who have gone through professional trainings in China's modern higher education system.

While many monasteries report economic gains from receiving both domestic and international tourists, the lay constituency, especially younger and more educated members, is taking leadership in exploring ways to recover Buddhism from the pejorative, stigmatizing image of superstition levied against it during the first three decades of the PRC. Numerous private Buddhist websites host forums or threaded discussions on Buddhism and science. They have become a formidable social space of Buddhists, attracting attention from scholars of Buddhist studies and administrators of religious affairs. The ongoing discourse on Buddhism and science is both a renewal of the intra-Buddhist interest initiated in the early Republic era and a modern attempt to re-brand Buddhism as a rational religion. Many Buddhists actively involved in this discourse are what I call "modern Buddhist apologetics" who use scientific language to advocate Buddhist teachings in an effort to re-establish Buddhism as a science of the mind, as contemporaneous and equal to modern science. However, in practice many Buddhists continue with their non-rational, devotional behaviors among themselves. The public representation of Buddhism as a science of the mind does not fully correspond to private practices of Buddhists for a variety of personal interests. The subtext of such public self-representation, in my ethnographic observation, is mostly a self-defense mechanism as well as a conversion strategy.

Scientific representation of Buddhism

Web forums on Buddhism and science are popular sites in contemporary China. Many Buddhist dialogues and debates with science, in most instances, have two noticeable trends. One is the attempt to prove how scientific Buddhism is. Another is to represent Buddhism in the rhetoric of Marxist scientific perspective of religion, an integral part of the state ideology, so as to make Buddhism look politically correct and thus ideologically non-threatening to the state. Both trends appear to demonstrate Buddhism as a rational religion or a thought-system rather than a blind faith. In addition to renewing the discourse of Buddhism and science initiated by earlier generations of Dharma masters and prominent lay practitioners, both trends characteristically defend Buddhism by citing the works of modern scientists of Buddhist faith and reinterpreting or simply co-opting Marxist critique of religion in defense of Buddhism.

Dorzhi Rinpoche and Khenpo Sonam Darje, two contemporary Tibetan Dharma teachers who have a large number of Han Chinese patrons, are among the leading Buddhist apologetics in China who utilize Marxist terms in their effort to reestablish the social legitimacy of Buddhism. Both teachers have obviously developed a textual strategy when they address Buddhism's modern scientific relevance. Their citations from the works of Marx and Engels are directed toward their effort to recast Buddhism in scientific terms as well as to reclaim religious freedom as a social right. These are the frequently cited quotations of Marx and Engels in their texts:

Marx –
"Dialectic materialism in Buddhism has reached a fine degree" (Sonam Darje, 2000a, p. 166).
"Religion is a theory about the totality of the world, and includes principles of all sorts" (Sonam Darje, 2000b, p. 190).
"Everyone should have the opportunity to realize his or her religious needs, just as one has to fulfill corporal needs without the interference of police" (Sonam Darje, 2000b, p. 195).
Engels –
"Human's dialectic thinking reached its maturity at the Buddha Sakyamuni's time" (Sonam Darje, 2000a, p. 191).
"Buddhists are at the higher stage of rational thinking" (Sonam Darje, 2000a, p. 190; Dorzhi, 1998, p. 405).

Dorzhi Rinpoche went a step further in representing Buddhism as a type of atheism that shares some commonality with Marxist scientism, remarking, "As soon as science appears, religions perish with the exception of Buddhism...Other religions usually accept the existence of 'god,' but Buddhism criticizes this 'god' to start with; thus, its death has utterly no impact on Buddhism" (Dorzhi, 2000, p. 110). Both Tibetan lamas are well versed in the history of modern Chinese Buddhist history as they also reference Han Chinese Dharma Masters in the Republic era. Their apologetic position is the same as their Han Chinese counterparts who invoke prominent Buddhist scientists in support of the rational aspect of Buddhism.

Both Dorzhi Rinpoche and Khenpo Sonam Darje are the most popular Tibetan lamas winning Chinese converts. Dorzhi Rinpoche's *Wisdom Arising from Compassion* is one of the Buddhist best sellers in China. The jacket of its first edition marketed it as "a book for Buddhists as well as for intellectuals, scientists, cadres, and Party Members" (Dorzhi, 1998). In my work with him, I notice that many of Chinese Buddhist converts come from these social classes (Smyer Yu, 2011, p. 125). Khenpo Sonam Darje spent time particularly documenting over 200 cases of Chinese intellectuals' conversion to Buddhism in his two-volume publication titled *The White Caps of Wisdom Ocean* (Sonam Darje, 2000b). In contemporary China he is said to be the Tibetan lama attracting the largest number of Chinese converts.

In the publications of these Tibetan lamas, and Chinese Buddhist teachers and lay advocates, the most frequently cited Buddhist scientists include You Zhibiao, Wang Jitong, Wang Shouyi, and Shen Jiazhen. Among these Buddhist scientists of Chinese origin, You Zhibiao's "Scientific Viewpoint of Buddhism" is widely circulated in the cyberspace of China. You Zhibiao attended Harvard University, specializing in radio engineering. Upon his return to China, he was appointed as a professor at Zhejiang University. He defended Buddhism as a "pure rational religion" (You, n.d.) and stated the negation of the existence of soul as a commonality of Buddhism and science.

Professor Chen Bing of Sichuan University, one of the most active scholars facilitating the Buddhism-science dialogue, highlights You in his "A Reflection on the Interface of Buddhist Studies and Science" (Chen, 2008) foremost as a modern scientist. Like his Buddhist-scholar peers, Chen also reiterates the most frequently cited statements of You, such as "Buddhism...is a superb science" and "Some parts of Buddha Dharma can be explained with science, while other parts surpass science" (Chen, 2008). In Chen's apologetic appraisal of Buddhism, You's writings obviously appear to be a scientific index for the purpose of emphasizing Buddhism as a rational religion free from superstition.

Wang Jitong is another Buddhist scientist often cited by Chen Bing and his scholarly peers. Wang's publications in the Republic era such as "Buddhism and Science" and "A Comparative Study of Buddhism and Science" (Chen, 2008) are referenced in the same apologetic manner claiming the scientific spirit of Buddhism. Wang's statement, "Every religion except Buddhism did not start with scientific methods" (Chen,

2008), is another quotation popular with Chinese Buddhist supporters who wish to highlight Buddhism's empirical experiment with the mind and the body in relation to the material world. It is one of the building blocks for contemporary Buddhist apologetics to claim Buddhism as "an applied science" (Chen, 2008).

Other contemporary scientists and scientifically-minded Buddhists, such as Niu Shiwei of the Chinese Academy of Science, Jiang Jinsong of the Chinese Academy of the Social Sciences, and He Bing (an actor), rigorously defend Buddhism's compatibility with modern science (Jiang and He, 1999). It is widely noted that the contemporary general public in China is losing confidence in Communism as a belief system; whereas modern science, which the Communists have promoted for over half a century, has become a national *habitus* in the Bourdieuan sense (Harker, Mahar, and Wilkes, 1990, p. 78). In other words, the Chinese Marxist habitus has engendered its own social language with a set of modern scientific glossaries, which, in fact, dominates the thought-activities of the Chinese populace in relation to religion. This social language, more often than not, operates in an unconscious fashion, and resembles what Bourdieu calls doxa as the "universe of the undisputed" (Bourdieu and Wacquant, 1992, p. 168). It gave justification to extensive mob violence in the physical sense in the past, and is still capable of repeating the past if needed.

In many ways, the current Buddhist revitalization is the continuation of Taixu's "Buddhist Revitalization Movement" of the 1920s in the sense of reclaiming Buddhism from the stigma of superstition. The difference between the two Buddhist revitalizations lies in a more complex political context. In the Republic era, the exegeses of science among Buddhist apologetics came from diverse modern Western philosophical traditions as shown in the works of Taixu, Liang Qichao, and You Zhibiao. However, in contemporary China the Marxist scientific perspective dominates the public discourse of Buddhism and science in addition to its state-sanctioned ideological position. Thus making Buddhism appear "politically correct" and "scientifically enticing" is an integral part of the current Buddhist apologetics' mission.

Infrared Communism and its "long-term" conversion project

Communist religiosity manifested its symbolic and physical violence to both Christianity and Buddhism in the past; however its formal similarity with Christianity inadvertently favors Christianity's growth in China as it continues to limit the returning of popular religious practices of China. The entrance of Christianity and Communism into China occurred in the same historical background. In my view, their antithetical relationship has been expressed in the salvation-oriented, monotheistic appearance of their religiosities. Communism, although it is not a conventional religious tradition, is anti-religious in nature; however, its self-edification as the only way of saving the world makes itself look like a "monotheistic" system except that its atheism replaces theism. Like the doctrine of Christianity, Chinese Communism also has little acceptance for different religious worldviews and practices. Regardless of the fact that Christians suffered from persecutions during the first three decades of the PRC, this aspect of Communism has worked in the advantage of Christianity in China: Communist scientism in the past severely paralyzed Christianity but also swept away most of Christianity's native competitors. Likewise, Buddhism is also undergoing a rapid growth. Its use of modern scientific language for destigmatizing itself from the label of superstition is also winning converts from cultural and political elites of China. This is an unprecedented conversion phenomenon in the history of Chinese Buddhism.

Communist religiosity, in the meantime, is not dying as the Chinese Communist Party continues to propagate it in more acceptable ways to the Chinese populace. In his study of contemporary China's architecture and ideology, Mihai Cracium sees the continuation of state ideology in China's urban high rises. He addresses the current manifestation of Chinese Communism as an "infrared Communism" which is "a covert strategy of compromise and double standard, a preemptory reversal of history that links 19th-century idealism with the realities of the 21st century" (Cracium, 2001, p. 69). It is noticeable that Chinese Communism has entered this invisible spectrum as the state often addresses its ideological matters in the terms of "socialist civilization" and "harmonious society" rather than the overt Communist terms of the pre-reform era. In September 2009 the state formally propagated a new project called "the Sinification, Contextualization, and Popularization of Marxism" (news.cn). Its fundamental goal is to continue to let Marxism and the vision of its ideal future world to grow roots in China. This new project of the Party is applauded by many of its members as "the sacred mission of the Chinese Communist Party members" (Chen, 2012, p. 53).

On the religious front, the Research Center for Contemporary Critical Ethnic and Religious Issues at Minzu University of China and the Institute for the Marxist Approach to Religion at the Chinese Academy of the Social Sciences, are the most active state-funded research institutions which have produced volumes of their research results concerning how to reposition Marxism as the guiding principle for the religious affairs of Chinese citizens. Unlike the extremist era of the Cultural Revolution, Marxist scholars in these institutions appear passionate about Marxist ideals but also appear reasonable toward the pluralizing trend of religion in China. Mou Zhongjian, a leading Marxist scholar, writes, "our socialism should be the most tolerant -ism toward religion" (Mou, 2009, p. 9). This tolerating position does not mean a fundamental ideological shift from the past intent to destroy religion to the present protection of religious freedom. It reflects the Party's recognition of religion's "long-term nature" (*changqixing* 长期性) which, according to the former President of China Jiang Zemin, means that "The time for the final demise of religion may be much more remote than the time for the disappearance of class and state" (Mou, 2009, p. 10).

The Party's Marxist approach to religion is gradually generating a more tolerating environment for religion as observed by numerous scholars. However, in both the practical and theoretical senses this Marxist approach to religion bears a similar appearance as the Communist national conversion project of the past but couched in more civil and rational language. If different religious traditions are reviving and growing in China, so too is the religiosity of Chinese Communism in the garment of Marxism and scientific socialism. The Party's new project for exploring fresh exegetical angles of Marxist perspective on religion is rekindling the intra-Party interest in the first generation Communists' fervor for the eventual replacement of religion with science (Patterson, 1969, p. 20). Instead of finding fresh Marxist perspectives many contemporary Marxist scholars and research-oriented administrators cannot help but regressing to Marx's antithetical stance toward religion. The only noticeable difference from the anti-religious position of the Party during the Mao era is that this group of state-funded scholars rarely use the word "Communism"; instead "scientific atheism" and "scientific socialism" dominate the theme of this new state project for further Sinifying Marxism. Nomenclatures of Marxism, Communism, and socialism are different, but in essence they are synonymous to each other in this context. They are fundamentally an antithesis to religion, attempting to revitalize a Communist scientism whose ideological quintessence has been popularized with this century-old cliché, "Only science can save China" (只有科学才能救中国). While the rhetoric of Communism bores the public, "being scientific" rarely does; instead it continues to be a cultural norm of the PRC especially in the context of China's ongoing modernization project and its emergence as a global economic and geopolitical power. This is where the Party and its Marxist scholars and policy analysts find public confidence; thus it is also the entrance point for reintroducing Communist beliefs to the public but in the language of science.

The idea of science in the Party's Marxist approach to religious affairs is diametrically opposite to religion as current leading Marxist scholars continue to assert (Mou, 2009; Gong, 2008). Gong Xuezeng, a prominent Marxist scholar, defines science as a knowledge system which "accurately reflects the origins of the natural world and human society" and is founded upon "materialism especially [Marx's] dialectic materialism" (2007). His definition deviates from the common understand of science as a system of knowledge concerning the physical or material world gained through observation and experimentation, which had no direct leaning toward one particular political ideology. According to Gong and his peers, religion opposes science because it bases itself on "supernatural power as the determinant of the natural world and human society" (Gong, 2007). Religion then is again reduced as "a delusion of the mind" (Gong, 2007, p. 1). Thus, the notion of science in this fresh, low profile, but well-funded, campaign for promoting Marxism is imbued with Marxist atheism as an inherent belief of the Party. Although this atheism is attributed with a "scientific nature" (Gong, 2007) in a rational manner, it is nevertheless colored with what Dan Chun, another leading Marxist scholar, calls "the religious emotion of atheists" which originates from scientific atheists' ultimate hypothesis concerning the non-existence of divinity or any power beyond the human-perceived empirical realm (Dan, 2007). Dan Chun remarks, "although we have always emphasized science and Enlightenment thought when we doubt and negate theism, we do not deny that scientists and philosophers also possess religious emotion" (Dan, 2007). This "religious emotion" of Chinese Marxists is a product of modern secularism which "offers a teleology of religious decline and can function as a self-fulfilling prophecy" and whose spiritualism appears "truth-seeking, experimental in nature" (van der Veer, 2009, p. 1101).

Among Western scholars when Chinese Communism is recognized as a political religion (Zuo, 1991; Kipnis, 2001; Yang, 2009b), it is closely associated with the deification of Mao (Zuo, 1991), the theocratic rule of the Party (Kipnis, 2001), and the previous fanatic belief of Communist Party members (Yang, 2009). In the studies of Post-Mao China this image of Communism as a political religion has receded into the background of China's recent history. However, Communist scientism embedded in the Maoist political religion has moved forward with the current modernization project of the state. On the folk level the nostalgia for Mao and Maoism has evolved into a local religion of Shaoshan, Mao's hometown (tianyayidu.com, 2011) and "a primitive totem worship" elsewhere in China (Hubbert, 2006, p. 146). Among contemporary China's Marxist intellectual elites, their predecessors' "intellectual and emotional attachment to science-as-doctrine" and "science worship" (Kwok, 1965, p. 16 recited from Kipnis, 2001, p. 34) is being renewed through the rational expressions of their scientific atheism as well as in the midst of the new popular fervor celebrating China's rising as a global power.

The relationship of state and religion in China is frequently researched by scholars. In most instances, they are separated in both theoretical and practical terms. It is true that the state has a record of persecuting religion; thus, it is natural that it is seen as an opposing force to religion. However, observing the manifestations of religiosity from what Xinzhong Yao and Paul Badham propose as "the religious experience" of the Chinese (2007), what is found is that both religious and non-religious [science believers] constituencies possess their respective religiosities; thus it is given that scientific atheists also have their "religious mentality" (Yao and Badham, 2007, p. 162). In this regard it could be said that scientific atheism is the state religion of China. The separation of state and religion, as the state proposes, only refers to the separation of traditionally understood religious systems, that is, Christianity and Buddhism, from the state but not the separation of the state from scientific atheism as a soteriological ideology and the Communist belief in a messianic coming of a remote future.

Furthermore, scientific atheism, as the state religion or the religiosity of the state, has found its popular acceptance whether consciously or unconsciously. In early 2010, Wang Zuo'an, the current director of China's State Administration for Religious Affairs, proposed Chinese media's political "desensitization of religion (*zongjiao tuimin* 宗教脱敏)" (christiantimes.cn, 2010). This proposal quickly received positive feedback from religious constituencies. However, the media has had little response to his proposition. Instead, political desensitization of religion has quickly evolved into an appeal of religious individuals and scholars who are sympathetic to the marginalized social position of religion. Li Xiangping, a professor of religious studies at the Eastern Normal University, writes in his blog acknowledging the returning and diversification of religion in China but also pointing out reasons why religion is still marginalized, "First scientism is re-ignited. This type of discourse, on the contrary, wants to elevate scientism again to the status of divinity. Second the ideological return to so-called materialism once again negates all religious beliefs" (2010).

In the last few years the Chinese state's Marxist indigenization project started seeing its first successes in the popular realm of China. The civil appearance of the religiosity of Marxism/Communism continues with the state's resourceful and skillful support. Confidence in modern science as a cultural norm of contemporary China continues to saturate both religious and non-religious populations through consumerism, nationalistic sentiment, and even in religious adherents' debates with atheism, as shown in the case of Buddhists earlier. Thus religiosities of scientific atheists and traditional religious practitioners are entwined in the language of modern science. Similar to how the late Professor Fei Xiaotong viewed the ethnic diversity of China over half a century ago, religion in China is also conforming to the model of "diversity in unity." The "unity" is the ideological framework of China's scientific atheism.

9
Perun vs Jesus Christ: Communism and the Emergence of Neo-paganism in the USSR

Victor A. Shnirelman

Soviet anti-Westernism and a birth of Neo-paganism

Soviet politics was very inconsistent, and the results were inconsistent as well. In this chapter, I will show how a promotion of "scientific atheism" unintentionally caused a revival of paganism. I will address the following themes: how exactly did Neo-paganism converge with Soviet ideology? How did it diverge from it? Were those divergences a further development of Soviet ideas, or were they a fundamental break from them? What was the authorities' attitude towards neo-pagan activity? What place did the neo-pagans occupy within the Soviet system? What was the attitude of Soviet intellectuals towards Neo-paganism?

From the 1960s on, there was a growth of interest in ethnicity in the USSR, including in traditional rituals and ceremonies, as well as ethnic roots, which, with respect to Russian nationalism, meant the early Slavs. This perspective produced a mythic view of the remote past, looking back to when the Slavs were not spoiled by external evil agents and enjoyed their own "Vedic" faith. Russian nationalists manifested great enthusiasm towards the faked *Book of Vles* (Tvorogov, 1990; also see Shnirelman, 1998a; 2011). As is well known, ethnic identity supported by several attributes is much stronger than if supported by only one or two. Ethnic nationalists usually view the world through ethnic glasses and identify religion with ideology. One can achieve this in two ways – either through the naturalization of a world religion or through the development of one's own ethnic faith. Many Russian Neo-pagans made the second choice and turned to paganism as ideological support for Russian nationalism.

Soviet ideology waged an uncompromising war against universal religions. This struggle was based on two arguments – one Marxist ("religion justifies exploitation") and another xenophobic ("religions exercise a corruptive alien influence"). Early propaganda emphasized the first argument, but after the antagonist social classes had disappeared, the first argument lost its appeal; in contrast, the importance of the second one increased. As the authorities feared the "corruptive effect" of Western culture, they did their best to oppose it with native culture, emphasizing the idea of cultural originality.

Finally, since the period of late Stalinism onwards, authorities began to foster anti-Semitism, which increased after 1967. At that time, the authorities recollected that Christianity developed out of Judaism and began to criticize both the Bible and Judaism from a xenophobic and anti-Semitic point of view. In certain republics (Ukraine, Armenia, and the Republics of the Volga region) local intellectuals manifested the same rejection of Christianity as Russian nationalists did. What is noteworthy is that Christianity was rejected mostly from the point of view of ethnic nationalism rather than for atheist reasons. Christianity was opposed to a highly romanticized view of the pre-Christian past, which allegedly had its own "positive (*svetloe*) worldview."

All of this resulted in ambivalence among Russian nationalists. On the one hand, they were against the communist regime, but on the other, they were statists, that is, they stood for the integrity of Russia and against both regional separatism and the West. At the same time, they struggled to maintain the ethnic Russian culture and resisted the dissolution of ethnic Russians into the "new Soviet entity." Similarly, Russian paganism was also in a dual position. From the point of view of patriotism, it supported the authorities, but with respect to religion and ethnic Russian nationalism, it stood against them.

In this context, "A Word to the Nation" is noteworthy. Issued in samizdat in 1970, this text became the first manifesto of ethnic Russian nationalism ("A Word to the Nation," 1971; "Slovo natsii," 1981). The document supported the authoritarian regime and complained that the Soviet policy of affirmative action infringed the (ethnic) Russian people's rights. While using racist arguments, its author demanded that (ethnic) Russians be provided with the status of ruling nation. The radical right-wing spirit of the document has already been pointed out (Yanov, 1987, pp. 155–165). Indeed, its aspiration to save industrial civilization from the "colored" is reminiscent of the pamphlets that were popular in Germany at the turn of the 1930s (Hermand, 1992, p. 129).

A year later, another document was promoted by samizdat. The "Letter to Solzhenitsyn" reproduced anti-Semitic stereotypes of late Stalinist propaganda: it claimed that Zionists had seized power in the USSR and that the "true history" of the ancestors of the ethnic Russian was intentionally hidden from the general public (Agursky, 1975, pp. 205–218).

As later came to light, the first document was written by Anatoly M. Ivanov (Skuratov) and the second one – by Valery N. Emelianov. Both of them made a great impact on the ideology of the political wing of Russian Neo-paganism, which strives for the establishment of an (ethnic) Russian authoritarian regime. Since the very late 1980s on, many Russian radicals advocated chauvinist and racist ideas. Many of these radicals developed their arguments on behalf of Russian paganism and furiously attacked "Jewish Christianity."

Russian Neo-paganism occupies a special place among the New Religious Movements. Its peculiarity is a search for ethnic Russian identity, which has met strong challenges and suffered heavy losses, first, during the period of building the "new Soviet entity" in the Soviet Union, and then in post-Soviet Russia. In my view, Russian Neo-paganism should be analyzed in the context of ethnic nationalism and identity crisis. It has Soviet roots and proves to be, on the one hand, a by-product of late Soviet ideology, and on the other, a peculiar result of the intellectual activity of those alarmed by the miserable future of the Russian people. That is why, in contrast to their Western counterparts, the Russian Neo-pagans focus mostly on social issues rather than the development of personality. They cultivate ethnocentrism rather than individualism.

In their search for spirituality, urban intellectuals have restored some obsolete ideas. While being well trained and respectful towards scholarship, Soviet intellectuals appreciated the occult, which combined ideas ranging from the Theosophy of Helene Blavatsky up to contemporary New Age ideas. There were radical ideas among them, including those reviving Nazi heritage and aspiring to adapt it to contemporary demands. In particular, Russian Neo-pagans adopted various types of swastikas as the key symbol of their identity and faith. This contradicted Soviet ideology, but found some support in the Committee for the State Security (*Komitet Gosudarstvennoi Bezopasnosti*), which, in the 1970s and 1980s, was also searching for a solution to the ideological crisis.

The Soviet path to paganism

It is not easy to say when exactly Neo-paganism became popular among Russian nationalists. In the early 1960s there were a variety of opinions among political prisoners about the major failing of the state, be it Soviet or pre-Soviet. Some people accused the Soviet authorities for moving away from Leninist dogma, others stood against communists and glorified the pre-revolutionary Russian Empire, while still others marked the beginning of Russia's decline with the "westernizing" reforms of Peter the Great and romanticized Moscovite Rus'. Finally, there were also those who blamed the Jews for introducing Christianity to Rus' and thereby destroying the "great pre-Christian cultural heritage." One of these was Alexei Dobrovol'sky, one of the founding fathers of Russian Neo-paganism.[1]

Meanwhile, bizarre as it may seem, a restoration of pagan rituals had been sponsored by Soviet officials themselves since the late 1950s onwards. The initiative developed from local activists who suggested shaping and promoting new secular rituals and festivals as an important part of the anti-religious campaigns (Kampars and Zakovich, 1967, pp. 33–34; Kryvelev, 1963, pp. 16–17). The early 1960s were marked with a new anti-religious campaign aimed at traditional beliefs and festivals. At the same time, in June 1963 the Meeting of the Central Committee of the Communist Party of the Soviet Union (CC CPSU) warned against "spontaneous and drifting" activity in the process of the "dying off of religious aberrations." Then, in November an Ideological Commission of the CC CPSU demanded an intensification of atheist education, in particular, through the formation and introduction of new secular festivals and ceremonies. The Commission worked out the "Measures for an intensification of atheist public education" that were approved by the CC CPSU in January 1964. They argued that new festivals and ceremonies were very important from an ideological point of view because they affected people's emotions rather than only reason. This was once again confirmed by the Decree "On intensification of atheist public education" issued by the CC CPSU on 16 July 1971 (Klimov, 1964; Rudnev, 1964, pp. 3–5; 1982, p. 3; Stepankov, 1964).[2] Evidently, this initiative promoted not only anti-religious propaganda but a struggle against "Westernization" as well, which demanded the promotion of Russian symbols. For example, Komsomol leaders were to confront the twist with "motions that were characteristic of a Russian dancing style," and a dancing team "Lebedushka" (*she-swan*) was formed in the mid-1960s that re-produced a Russian folk dancing style (Mitrokhin, 2003, p. 249).

There were other key innovations in the mid-1960s that marked an important shift in the development of Soviet culture. People began to manifest high interest towards Russian folklore and peasant culture (including vocabulary), and pictures of churches became fashionable. Some observers noted that the "cultural code" changed, and

"Motherland," "nature," "the people" became the key words; the very term of "the people" acquired new, ethnic, meaning, and people began to cultivate a "tribal memory" as well as a "tribal consciousness." Thus, the "Soviet people...began differentiating into [separate] nations" (Vail' and Genis, 1988, p. 217). Indeed, it is at this time that the ideological basics of many ethno-national movements began to develop (Simon, 1991).

Communist, Soviet, Komsomol and Trade-Union organizations as well as a whole army of ethnographers and museum workers were responsible for the realization of new trends in atheist propaganda. Councils for promoting and implementing new socialist rituals were established in the 1960s in many republics within various bureaucratic structures, from the Councils of Ministers down to village administrations, including collective farms (Brudny, 1968, pp. 83–84; El'chenko, 1976, pp. 61–73; Kampars and Zakovich, 1967, pp. 229–232; Kryvelev, 1977, pp. 36–45). The new rituals and ceremonies were introduced by numerous scientific-methodological and cultural-enlightenment centers run by Party and Trade-Union officials, and this activity enjoyed all possible support from the urban and rural Soviets of deputies. Whereas mainly enthusiasts (cultural club workers) were engaged in this activity in the 1960s, the Higher Trade-Union school began to systematically train instructors in "folk festivals and ceremonies" in the 1970s. Paradoxically, this activity was part of the atheist education curriculum, and courses in "scientific atheism" became obligatory in universities from 1964 onwards.

The Soviet anti-religious policy was very contradictory. On the one hand, many traditional peasant festivals were banned in the 1960s as religious ones. On the other, alarmed by negative demographic trends in the countryside, the authorities wanted to improve the situation with an introduction of special festivals for youngsters (Tul'tseva, 2011, pp. 69–70).

At the same time, Soviet ritual specialists were aware that it was impossible to shape new ceremonies from nothing. Their suggestion was to use traditional festive forms well known to local people. They hoped that, over time, the religious content of the festival would disappear and, as a result, the rites would maintain their national shape, while at the same time developing "socialist content" (Kryvelev, 1977, p. 43; Lobacheva, 1973, pp. 22–24). Some authors argued that the festivals have already lost their former religious content (Kampars and Zakovich, 1967, p. 37; Kaloev, 1971, pp. 294–295). At the same time others were concerned that a revival of old folk festivals and rituals would be accompanied by a growth of religious attitudes (Sukhanov, 1973, pp. 229–230). Indeed, the situation proved to be much more complicated. While being able to control both an arrangement of ceremonies and their shape, Soviet officials could not control people's minds, that is, they could not control people's interpretation of the "new rites." The propagandists themselves sometimes provided people with ideas, which encouraged interpretations that diverged very far from a "socialist way of thinking." This activity was sometimes "misunderstood as giving an ideological sanction to the old holidays and thereby increasing their vitality" (Lane, 1981, p. 237).

Perhaps, "an exultation honoring nature and the solstice" was perceived as less ideologically dangerous than the worship of Jesus Christ and the Virgin to Soviet officials.[3] Indeed, specialists in "scientific atheism" argued that numerous folk festivals and rites were initially associated with traditional economic life and seasonal changes rather than with religion. They claimed that folk rituals developed in the "atheist background" and were used by religion for its own gains only much later (Balashov, 1965; Brudny, 1968, pp. 3–13, 23–31; Kampars and Zakovich, 1967, pp. 120–122, 129; Kryvelev, 1963, pp. 16–17; Sukhanov, 1973, pp. 31–34, 51, 233–234). Yet, professional ethnographers and certain Soviet philosophers did not agree. They argued that pre-Christian rituals and festivals also had a religious nature (Petukhov, 1969, p. 275; Ugrinovich, 1975, pp. 66–82) and that traditional rituals were closely linked with dominant religions (Lobacheva, 1973, pp. 15–16). Thus, they argued, it was impossible to extract anything non-religious out of them. It was also not easy to inject them with new "socialist" meaning.

Nonetheless, specialists in "scientific atheism" used to contrast "folk rites" to "religious rites." They usually associated the former with the "vital interests and requirements of both person and society," and the latter with the mercenary interests of the ruling class; the former with a romanticized view of life in the democratic East Slavic society as though slavery was unknown there, and the latter with a subjugation of people that was approved by Christianity. They deliberately identified religion with only universal religions or at least associated it with a stratified society. Thus, they presented their own activity as a restoration of the original folk culture that was persecuted by the Church for centuries. From this perspective "scientific atheism" demanded that religion be analyzed in the context of class oppression. Hence, if there was no class struggle, then there was no religion in prehistoric society. Thus, paganism, including Slavic paganism, had to be viewed as an important part of the original folk culture rather than as religion (El'chenko, 1976,

p. 8; Kampars and Zakovich, 1967, pp. 94, 102; Klimov, 1964; Rudnev, 1982, pp. 5–8, 21, 97, 119, 146; 1989, pp. 101, 108; Sarsenbaev, 1965, pp. 89–91; Tul'tseva, 1985, pp. 4, 93, 100–102, 126). Therefore, some specialists called for a restoration of the images of pagan gods as "artistic images" (Tul'tseva, 1985, p. 168).[4]

One of the most ardent advocates of the new rites was V. A. Rudnev, an assistant professor of the Leningrad High Trade-Union school, an active member of the Leningrad City Commission on civic rituals and a member of the Methodological council for the propaganda of atheist knowledge in the Leningrad branch of the All-Union "Znanie" (Knowledge) Society. His case is instructive as he was one of those who, for dozens of years, occupied themselves with implementing the Party's decrees adopted between the 1960s and 1970s. Aware that it was difficult to create something from nothing, he turned to, in particular, materials on folk, mostly ethnic Russian, traditional rituals. Thus, he came to the pre-Christian heritage of the Eastern Slavs, where he found a rich depository of folk culture appropriate for organizing various calendric festivals, including the "Seeing-off of Winter."[5]

This sort of activist taught the general public that old folk traditions were less religious and deserved to be restored and maintained as a valuable cultural heritage. While doing this, they emphasized the allegedly high cultural level and great spiritual achievements of the Eastern Slavs in the pre-Christian period. At the same time, they accused Christianity of destroying the traditional life of the people, and treated it as reactionary. The complex history of the development of world religions was reduced and simplified. They argued that these religions were always and everywhere brutally forced upon people against their will, even though people "wanted to maintain their originality and free-thinking" (Rudnev, 1982, pp. 5, 92; 1989, pp. 3, 105, 110).

These activists did not hesitate to interpret folk heritage as they wanted to, and ascribed to pagan faith that which was alien to it. For example, with a reference to Procopius of Caesarea, Rudnev put forward the very dubious idea that monotheism existed among the Eastern Slavs in the pre-Christian period. While mentioning, in passing, that the early Jews allegedly made human sacrifices, he revived the accusation of blood libel. At the same time, he failed to note that, as is well known, human sacrifices were practiced by the Eastern Slavs (Rudnev, 1982, pp. 17; 1989, pp. 17, 106). At the height of this rite-creating activity, a pagan festival of the summer solstice, Ivan Kupala (or Ligo in Latvia), was widely restored as a rite of the "Russian birch" to be celebrated on June 22–24 (Brudny, 1968, pp. 37–39, 94–100; El'chenko, 1976, p. 54; Kampars and Zakovich,

1967, pp. 95–102, 133–134; Rudnev, 1982, p. 156; also see: Lane, 1981, pp. 135–136). All these ideas, including erroneous ones, were appreciated and picked up by the Russian Neo-pagans later on.

In the Soviet period, this "paganism" justified the Communist regime, helped authorities to struggle against the monotheist religions and recognized atheism as a special sort of faith (Shneider, 1993; see also Falikov, 1989). A passion for paganism was growing side by side with an interest in folk culture, and propagandists intentionally taught people that pagan faith and rituals had to be viewed as valuable cultural heritage strictly connected to ethnic identity. The Communist authorities not only tolerated these attitudes, but even deliberately promoted them in the face of the coming 1000th anniversary of the Baptism of Rus'. Suffice it to say that in some regions of the USSR directors of the collective farms were obliged to arrange festivals charged with pagan spirit. According to M. Novikova, to the surprise of the general public, the anniversary of the Baptism of Rus' was met with the ninth wave of "pagan faith" (Novikova, 1991, pp. 243, 245).

Drastic changes in science fiction by the Russian nationalist writers in the early 1970s were another factor affecting the development of pagan faith. Whereas under the thaw of the 1960s Soviet science fiction looked ahead to the bright future and focused on the development of communist society, a passionate interest in the remote past emerged in the 1970s which was welcomed by the new director of the "Molodaia Gvardiia" Publishing House, Russian nationalist V. N. Ganichev. The Publishing House began to issue popular almanacs "Secrets of the Centuries" and "Along the Roads of Millennia" containing articles with bizarre depictions of the early Slavic past that greatly diverged from all plausible scholarly hypotheses. Firstly, the remote Slavic ancestors were depicted as nomadic pastoralists who roamed between the Carpathian Mountains and China: this image legitimated the Russian claim to all the territory of the former Russian Empire. Secondly, Slavic roots were pushed as far back into prehistory as possible. Thirdly, the early Slavs were presented as though they played a major part in Classical and Early Medieval history. This literature promoted an idea of the "Aryan nature" of the Slavs and intensively discussed pre-Christian beliefs (Shnirelman and Komarova, 1997; Shnirelman 2008; 2012, pp. 50–74). Komsomol leaders appreciated this trend as a way to attract youngsters. Soon they enriched it with fantasies of Big Foot and UFOs and began to arrange special searching teams consisting of Komsomol members. They believed that this might turn youngsters away from urgent social and political problems and re-direct their energy to the "secrets of the remote past," which were discussed from an occult perspective rather than grounded in any scholarship.

The aforementioned ideological campaigns and other activities took place in the period when Soviet authorities began to realize that official ideology was in crisis. This was first understood by the KGB, which began searching for new ideologies already in the 1970s. One of their suggestions was to revive right-wing nationalist Black Hundred ideas, which were based on anti-Semitism (Iakovlev, 1998; Polikarpov and Shelokhaev, 1998, pp. 10–11; Strel'nikov, 1998). Noteworthy, side by side with fantasies about the "Slavic-Aryans" the "Molodaia Gvardiia" Publishing House published books aimed against "International Zionism," which were suffused with anti-Semitic attitudes. This activity was supported by certain members of the CC CPSU (Bondarenko, 2002). All of this material was enthusiastically mastered by the first Neo-pagans. This is why a blend of anti-Christianity with anti-Semitism, which is characteristic for their worldview, is no accident. Scholars have already documented the racism in their publications (Dallam, 2014; Ivakhiv, 2005; Kaganska, 1986; Kavykin, 2007; Mitrokhin, 2003, pp. 414–415; Shnirelman, 1998a; 1998b; 2007; Shnirelman and Komarova, 1997).

There was one more driving force, namely a doubtful activity of the Ministry of Defense, which in the 1980s, began to create a so-called, "psychotronic weapon," (*psikhotronnoe oruzhie*) which would enable mind control over the enemy (Antonov, 1998; Krugliakov, 2008; Krugliakov et al., 2008; Shleinov, 1998).[6] Visionaries, astrologists, and occult scholars were invited to take part in their experiments. However, the golden time for this sort of specialist began at the turn of the 1990s, when, due to TV shows, they attracted the general public for several years. There was even a team of psychic specialists (*extrasensii*) in President Yeltsyn's administration, where they made up part of the security service between 1992 and 1996. They were responsible for the astrological predictions for the President. At that time, the Ministry of Defense had a special laboratory, where they tried to use astrology for military goals. A man who called himself a "descendant of Egyptian priests" served as a consultant in both the Ministry of Defense and the space industry. There were similar services in other ministries and even in the Russian Parliament (Aleksandrov et al., 2003; Krugliakov, 1998; Kuzina, 2005; Mikhailichenko, 2002; Parkhomenko, 1995; Shavlokhova and Sokolov-Mitrich, 2005; Svetlova, 2006). This bizarre development was launched by the People's Academy of Energy and Information, established in Moscow in 1980, which embraced numerous occult scholars, healers, astrologists, and the like.

The "Russian God," Aryans, and a "struggle against infidels"

Mass Soviet propaganda about Russia's pagan heritage was a success, as the very nature of the atheist way of life in the USSR encouraged pagan and occult attitudes (Dunaev, 1998). A sociological survey of non-traditional religions carried out in the 1980s demonstrated that new, post-atheist denominations were growing like mushrooms between the 1970s and 1980s. An attentive observer describes an aggressive rejection of both Christianity and Judaism, accompanied by the accusation that these religions destroyed the Russian state and subjugated the peoples of the world, coupled with the dream of restoring the "Pan-Aryan (Russian) pantheon [of gods]," capable of consolidating the Russians in their struggle against Evil forces (Epstein, 1991). Patriotism and nationalist ideas made up the core of this paganism. These ideologies overwhelmingly dominated neo-pagan ideas to the extent that they have erased a rich set of ancient gods and celebrated only the impersonal "Russian God." According to the same author, this "poor religion" lived by "hope rather than memory" (Epstein, 1991), a position which was closely associated with a Messianic stance.

Former atheists appreciated this sort of religion because, on the one hand, they were by no means fascinated with the complex dogmas and rituals of the traditional monotheist religions, which seemed too complicated for them, and on the other, they were attracted to occult ideas, which were highly dynamic and were framed in relation to scholarly knowledge (Epstein, 1993). This attitude towards religion was common in Russia, especially in the provinces, during the 1990s (Ushakova, 2003). For example, according to a sociological survey carried out in the city of Tambov in the mid-1990s, the great majority of local youth, who manifested their religiosity believed in God as the Highest Reason. They viewed religion and an impersonal God as an attractive source of morality at the period when science, art, and politics were stigmatized by journalists as very dubious activities (Borisenko, 1996, pp. 126–129).

"Critical notes of the Russian man on the patriotic journal of 'Veche'," issued in 1973, was one of the first manifests of Russian Neo-paganism. Its author was the aforementioned Valery Emelianov, an expert in the Near East, who once served as Khrushchev's assistant.[7] In accordance with contemporary Soviet propaganda the article demonized "International Zionism." Christianity and Islam were called the "daughter branches of Judaism" invented in order to subjugate all of humanity to Jewish rule. The author believed that "Christianity in general and Russian Orthodoxy in particular...were created to erase all the original and national, to turn all believers into rootless cosmopolitans." Russians were invited to replace Russian Orthodoxy with the worship of Slavic pagan gods and to "finish with Russian Orthodoxy as a pre-chamber of Jewish slavery." At the same time, the author called the Bolsheviks the only force able to rescue the world from the "Zionist plot" ("Kriticheskie zametki," 1975; see also Dunlop, 1983, p. 267; Verkhovsky and Pribylovsky, 1996, p. 9).

To put it briefly, this article contained all the elements of the future ideology of radical Neo-pagans: an absolute hatred towards Jews, a mystic fear of the "Zionist plot," a rejection of Christianity as the "Jewish religion," a call for the revival of the original ideology of Slavic-Russian paganism side by side with a loyalty to Bolshevik ideals.

Emelianov developed all these ideas in his book "De-Zionization" that was first published in Arabic in the Syrian daily *al-Baas* in 1979 by President Hafez Asad's order. In those days the book was also distributed in Moscow in numerous photocopies that made it seem as though it was published in Paris. Among illustrations one could see reproductions of Konstantin Vasiliev's drawings, which showed the struggle of Russian warriors against evil forces. The central one was a picture named "Ilya Muromets wins the victory over the Christian plague," which ever since has been popular among Russian Neo-pagans.[8]

The emergence of a Neo-pagan stance among the audience of the samizdat journal *Veche* was no accident. Indeed, one of its activists was A. M. Ivanov (Skuratov) who, in his youth, received historical training. In *Veche* he collaborated with some other advocates of "pre-Christian Slavic ideology," namely N. G. Bogdanov and K. A. Vasiliev (Pribylovsky, 1998b). In the 1970s, they actively forged basic ideas and symbols for radical Russian Neo-paganism, which, by contrast to many of its Western counterparts, based itself on the Nazi racial myth (Agursky, 1975; Poliakov, 1996, pp. 139–140; Shnirelman, 2015). In the 1980s, certain Russian writers became obsessed with a search for this pre-Christian heritage, and nostalgia about Aryanism merged with racism.

A "Readers' Club" (*Obshchestvo knigoliubov*) (RC) emerged in the early 1980s, which soon received a name of "Pamiat." Members of the Moscow branch of the "All-Russian society for maintenance of historical and cultural sites and monuments" and people from the circle of the artist Ilia Glazunov made up the core of it. In the early 1980s the RC's members were obsessed with Neo-paganism and a neo-pagan view of the past, which provided Russians with the idea that they were the earliest people in the Earth. This was confirmed by one of the RC's founders, Emelianov (1929–1999), who claimed that "Pamiat'" was established as a pagan, anti-Christian organization (Emelianov, 1994). In June 1983 Valery Skurlatov successfully gave a talk on the faked "Book of Vles" at their meeting.

The RC's leaders were devoted members of the Communist Party of the Soviet Union and ardent advocates of the Soviet Empire's integrity. At that time they were proud of the label "national communists" and almost entirely rejected Russian Orthodox and monarchic values. Their Neo-paganism was represented by a mix of Slavic pagan beliefs and vulgarized Hindu teachings. The pamphlets "De-Zionization" by Valery Emelianov and "The Christian Plague" by Anatoly Ivanov (Skuratov) served the major sources of knowledge (Mitrokhin, 2003, pp. 555–556; Moroz, 1992, pp. 71–72; Pribylovsky, 1992, pp. 165–166; Solovei, 1991, p. 18; Verkhovsky and Pribylovsky, 1996, pp. 9–10). To put it differently, between 1970 and 1985 future Neo-pagans proved to be a part of the Soviet Russo-centric patriotically minded intelligentsia, who enjoyed some support in the Central Committee of the CPSU and dreamt of "national socialism" for the Russian people (Bondarenko, 2002).

Many of the future founder-fathers of Russian Neo-paganism took an active part in the campaign against "International Zionism" launched by the Soviet authorities after 1967 (Dunlop, 1983, pp. 267–268; Korey, 1995; Laqueur, 1993, p. 107 ff.; Nudel'man, 1979, p. 39 ff.; Vishnevskaia, 1988; Yanov, 1987, pp. 141–144). They gave lectures for students and workers and also issued books which sharply criticized Zionism from patriotic positions. For example, Emelianov taught in the Institute of Foreign Languages and several other educational institutes including the Higher Party School. While serving as a lecturer for the Moscow City branch of the CPSU in the early 1970s, he gave public talks unmasking the "Kike-Masonic plot" (Nudel'man, 1979, pp. 36–37). These lectures stopped only after an official protest by the American Senator Javitz to the Soviet Ambassador A. Dobrynin in 1973 (Vishnevskaia, 1988, p. 85). Valery Skurlatov gave a course on "Criticism of the Zionist ideology" at the University of Peoples' Friendship between 1983 and 1985 (Mitrokhin, 2003, pp. 412–414). The philosopher Viktor N. Bezverkhy taught Marxism-Leninism in the Leningrad State University and several other civic and military colleges. In 1981 he took an oath to "devote all his life to a struggle against Judaism – the bloody enemy of the humanity." This oath written in blood was found in his apartment during a search in 1988. He taught his favorite students racial and anti-Semitic theories calling for the deliverance of humanity from the "defective offspring" of mixed marriages. Around 1979, Bezverkhy began developing the idea of the "Volkhv club," which was to include Nazi-style para-military groups. At the same time, he drew on his knowledge about the working of the Gestapo in order to compile files on Jewish intellectuals in Saint-Petersburg (Lisochkin, 1988; Solomenko, 1993; Verkhovsky, Papp, and Pribylovsky, 1996, pp. 242–243; see also Shnirelman, 1998a).

It seems that it was just a struggle against "International Zionism" that drove all these activists to their furious criticism of Christianity, a discourse within which anti-Semitism blended with a search for pre-Christian Slavic ancestors identified as the "Aryans." For example, in his "Anti-Zionist" book published in 1975 Skurlatov accused the Vedic Aryans of racism and provided these "white-skin and blue-eyes patriarchal pastoralists" with a negative image (Skurlatov, 1975, pp. 7–8). Yet, the following year he turned around and began to advertise the "Book of Vles." As he identified the Aryans with the ancient Russes his attitude towards them drastically changed, and since that time, he has consistently called them "light-bearers" (Shnirelman and Komarova, 1997).

These ideas were interpreted in his own way by A. F. Shubin-Abramov, one of the first academicians of the self-declared Russian Academy of Sciences, Arts, and Culture established in 1992. He called himself a "student of the Teachers" and promoted an "ancient Russian Pan-Human Alphabet" of 147 signs that, he claimed, developed over 7,500 years ago. He claimed, "We, the Russians, created all truthful, moral and beautiful things on the Earth with the help of the forefathers' language" (Beliakova, 1994; Solovieva, 1992). Since 1979, he has argued that this alphabet contained significant "Vedic knowledge," which has been once given to humans by the Creator, or the "Teachers." Every single letter allegedly contained important information. As a result, every particular word proved to be an abbreviation which, being "deciphered," provided whole phrases of condensed meaning. Following this esoteric concept, Shubin-Abramov viewed human history as a degradation from the Golden Age down to contemporary decline and decay. He argued that over time some letters have been lost because of the intrigues of "evil agents." He believed that, for a "revival of the Fatherland," one has to come back to the original alphabet. And he occupied himself with that task as a Chair of the public organization called "Pan-Human Alphabet" (Shubin-Abramov, 1996). His ideas have been picked up by many Russian Neo-pagans over the last 20 years.

Yet, the Soviet mainstream by no means accepted all the Neo-pagans. Some of them were considered dissidents and from time to time were prosecuted. The aforementioned Ivanov (Skuratov) was one of them who greatly influenced the formation of a new Russian nationalism between 1970 and the late 1980s.[9] Ivanov got interested in the "Aryan worldview" rather early. Being in exile in the early 1980s, he conducted comparative religious studies to elucidate its major points. At that time, he, firstly, depicted the "Aryans" as more evolved than any other people, and secondly, represented the "Semites" as their eternal enemies. He dated the beginning of the "Aryan resistance against Semitic dominance" to the Early Holocene, placed the center of this resistance in Russia and claimed that the Slavs maintained a "purity of Indo-European nature" to a great extent (Ivanov (Skuratov), 2007, pp. 24–26, 28–29, 36–38). While glorifying the pre-Christian worldview of the "Aryans," he found a religion of the opposite nature among the "Semites" and complained that "unfortunately it took root among us in the form of Christianity" (Ivanov (Skuratov), 2007, pp. 40–44). He claimed that "under the banner of the Jewish God" the "Aryans" had no chance to revive and successfully struggle against Zionism (Ivanov (Skuratov), 2007, p. 83).

While blaming the "aliens" for all of the Russia's misfortunes, Ivanov saw a way to "liberation" through the awakening of an "Aryan (Nordic) consciousness" among the Russians and their return to the "Aryan worldview." Christianity with its "Semitic God" posed an obstacle to this liberation. It is noteworthy that this did not make Ivanov entirely reject Christianity, as do many Neo-pagans. In fact, he wanted to come back to its roots, which he identified with Zoroastrianism rather than with Judaism (Ivanov (Skuratov), 2007, p. 143). He meant an "Aryan Christianity," which some German chauvinists tried to develop in the 1920s and 1930s. At the same time, while Ivanov stigmatized the "civilization corrupted by the Jews," he expected an arrival of an alternative religion from the "preceding Aryan cycle," and valued the "Aryan worldview" much higher than Christianity (Ivanov (Skuratov), 2007, p. 320).

The life trajectory of Alexei A. Dobrovol'sky (volkhv Dobroslav, 1938–2013) was even more exotic. From his youth he was obsessed with the idea of a "revival of the Russian nation." To achieve this goal he collaborated with monarchists, national-socialists, Russian Orthodox and, for a short period, was a member of the Patriotic organization of "Pamiat." Yet, he was mostly attracted to pagan beliefs, the occult and Nazism. He was prosecuted many times for anti-Soviet activity in the Soviet period. In the beginning of the 1990s he left for the Kirov region and established a pagan community there, which included his own family. From there he managed to simultaneously participate in the Russian national-liberation movement and to develop his pagan teachings. As a result, he is still an important figure among Russian political radicals and is highly respected by Neo-pagans, especially their national-socialist wing.[10]

Over the last ten years he was taken to court several times for radicalism, and some of his books were included on the list of extremist literature in 2007.

The first Russian groups for discussion and promotion of pagan ideas began to take shape in the 1980s. They were either the readers' clubs ("Pamiat" emerged in this way), secret societies ("Volkhv club" in Leningrad), centers for health care (Spiritual union of "Tezaurus" in Leningrad), or folklore-ecological groups (A. V. Riadinsky's group at the tourist center of "Bylina" in the Moscow region, the ecological-cultural center of "Tsaritsyno" in Moscow City, and Moscow pagan community of "Kupala"). Some of them were oriented to folklore, others were oriented to ecology and health, while still others focused on political and social issues. Yet all of them were highly attracted by a pre-Christian Slavic cultural heritage. Many of them manifested negative attitudes towards Christianity, and more frequently than not, these attitudes combined with anti-Semitism. Noteworthy, this stance was not restricted to ethnic Russians. Pagan movements emerged in Latvia and Lithuania already in the 1960s. Then, side by side with Russian pagan communities, their peers began to take shape in the Ukraine, Armenia, and Northern Ossetia in the 1980s. Somewhat later they appeared in the Middle Volga River region (Shnirelman, 1998c; 2001; 2002). Yet, besides an anti-Christian stance, they all manifested ethnic nationalist attitudes, sometimes including the "Aryan ones." Moreover, a development of Neo-paganism was often accompanied by the cultivation of racial views. It is also worth noting that there were many former communist officials among the first pagan leaders.

Conclusions

Thus, Neo-paganism in the territory of the former USSR and, in particular, Russia, was to a major extent a by-product of Soviet national, anti-religious, and cultural politics. While occupying itself with the glorification of remote ancestors, Neo-paganism met the demands of Soviet ethnic nationalisms; while addressing folklore, it implemented officially adopted cultural policy; while developing a tough criticism of Christianity, it spread the ideas of Soviet atheism; while demonizing the Jews, it served the Soviet state anti-Zionism. At the same time, in all these spheres Russian Neo-paganism time and again violated the boundaries of state ideology. Instead of the Slavs it found the "Slavic-Aryans" in prehistory; in the name of folklore it attempted to develop pagan rites; in their criticism of "International Zionism" the pagan ideologists used

Nazi ideas. Therefore, the relationships between the founder-fathers of Russian Neo-paganism and the Soviet state were not without problems. The most radical pagan leaders were persecuted from time to time. Nonetheless, if necessary, the Soviet authorities resorted to their help to promote their own atheist and anti-Western ideas. In addition, the Neo-pagans enjoyed support from certain Russian intellectuals (writers, journalists, artists), who shared their attitudes. Sometimes they enjoyed the protection of Komsomol leaders and even some members of the CC CPSU, who appreciated the "Russian idea."

Most of all, Neo-paganism was a product of the Soviet ethno-nationalist project aimed at the worship of the ethnic nation. Indeed, when addressing native gods many Neo-pagans ask them to protect the ethnic nation rather than individual human beings. Indeed, in this paradigm, the nation is much more important than particular human beings. Thus, Neo-paganism in the post-Soviet context is a true ethnic religion focused mostly on the prosperity of the ethnic nation, which means that, in contrast to the 18th and 19th centuries when nationalism sought to be a religion, nowadays it is religion that wants to be nationalism.

Yet, after the collapse of Communist dogma and a new arrival of religion, Russian Orthodoxy has once again occupied its dominant position in society because people associate it with traditional faith, Russian identity, and patriotism. While appealing to ethnic Russian values, Russian Orthodoxy is effectively and successfully winning on the field of nationalism. By contrast, many people view paganism as too archaic and exotic. Nonetheless, paganism is occupying its own niche, modest as it is, in the religious scene of post-Soviet Russia.

Acknowledgment

The project was supported by the Russian Scientific Foundation (no. 14-18-03090).

Notes

1. Barukh Podol'sky (Israel). Personal communication, May 27, 2003.
2. For the introduction of the new rites see: Lane (1981, pp. 45–54).
3. Christel Lane also noted that "holidays of pagan origins are considered more amenable to redefinition and, therefore, more acceptable for inclusion in the Soviet ritual-festive complex than those with Christian or Islamic content." She pointed to the "mistaken belief that pagan ritual is less religious then the Christian variety." In that she found similarities with the Nazi practice. See: Lane (1981, pp. 131, 233).

4. Lane also emphasized that "the selection of a cultural past has frequently been biased in favor of the more remote pagan past rather than the Christian stage of cultural development." See: Lane (1981, p. 238).
5. Enthusiasts from various regions advocated a restoration of this traditional festival known as Maslenitsa devoted to Sun and rooted in the pre-Christian period. See: Balashov (1965, p. 30); Mytskiula (1968, p. 52); Kampars and Zakovich (1967, pp. 87–88, 132–133); Brudny (1968, pp. 31–34, 86–89). For that see: Lane (1981, pp. 132–134).
6. This Cold War interest in occult weapons was not unique to Russia, and existed in both the US and China. See Palmer (2007) on the state development of Qigong in China.
7. For Emelianov see: Verkhovsky, Papp, and Pribylovsky (1996, pp. 263–264); Pribylovsky (1998a); Reznik (1996, pp. 61–82).
8. Ilya Muromets is a well-known knight and defender of Kievan Rus, described in medieval Russian epic poetry.
9. For him see Kheifets (1981, no. 27, pp. 168, 172, 190; no. 28, pp. 157, 160–161, 166–169); Pribylovsky (1998b, p. 21).
10. For him see Rozhdestvenskii (1981–1982, p. 258); Verkhovsky, Pribylovsky, and Mikhailovskaia (1998, pp. 24–25); Lugovoi (1998a, p. 2; 1998b, p. 2); Mitrokhin (2003, pp. 191–198); Shnirelman (2012, pp. 117–119).

10
Conversion to Be: The Christian Encounters of North Korean Migrants in Late Cold War Korea

Jin-Heon Jung

Arjun Appadurai inspires anthropologists to shed light on "one dimension of culture—its orientation to the future" (2004, p. 60). He pinpoints, and I agree, that general definitions of culture in anthropology tend to be associated with kinds of past-ness. On the contrary in his perspective, development, a main theme in economics, is viewed in terms of the progressive "future—plans, hopes, goals, targets" (Appadurai, 2004, p. 60). Drawing on this approach, this paper takes up North Korean migrants' Christian conversion processes in the frame of the past, present, and future.[1] Their conversion is not merely seen as an individual and internal transformation, but rather projected as an emblem of the future transformation of North Korea into liberal capitalism and Christianity. This paper analyzes Korean evangelical "capacity to aspire" in Appadurai's terms. By examining North Korean migrants' conversion narratives, I demonstrate that the seemingly teleological life and social transitions from socialism to liberal capitalism are indeed ambivalent and ambiguous.

North Korea has been and is de facto undergoing multilayered transformations at a rapid pace since the collapse of the Soviet Union. The society is encountering such changes as the hereditary succession of power enforcement for three generations, the failure of currency reform, the nationwide development of a private underground market economy, and increasing numbers of illegal border crossers into China. Externally, North Korean society faces international opposition led by the United States due mainly to North Korea's nuclear weapons development program. Outsiders have been and are assuming that the country is destined to collapse as the former socialist countries did, while also wondering why it has not yet collapsed. It is true that none of the adjacent countries, as well as the Big Powers (China, Russia, Japan, South Korea, the United States, and the European Union), wants to witness a catastrophic collapse of the regime. In such diverse future scenarios, North Korean migrants and their adjustment processes in the South are often considered to be a litmus test of a reunified Korean nation-state.

Since the mid-1990s when North Korean society suffered a famine, the number of those who came by way of China to South Korea increased at a rapid pace. Statistics show that more than 80 percent of North Korean migrants identified themselves as Christian when they arrived in South Korea in the late 1990s up until now (Chung, 2009; Jeon et al., 2010). Most North Korean border crossers rely on underground aid and railroads provided by South Korean missionaries and Korean-Chinese Christians in China and en route to South Korea. In their "Christian passage," as I call it, Christianity helps migrants rationalize their internal transformation and physical relocation in religious terms. Considering a complex series of these migrants' personal trajectories in respect to the geopolitical specificities aforementioned, this ethnography attempts to raise, rather than definitively answer, questions about the relationship between religion and communism and capitalism through microanalysis of the migrants' narratives. Their narratives reveal the politics of language that is redirecting, silencing, and yet mobilizing the testifiers and the listeners alike to respond to God's calling for national and world missionization.

The body of this article is divided into three parts. The first provides a brief historical review of the relationship between Christianity and communism in the context of the Korean division. The second discusses the similarities and differences some of the migrants discover between Christianity and Juche ideology, the North Korean official ruling philosophy, and their southern counterparts' responses. The third part analyzes North Korean conversion narratives as a window through which light is shed on the evangelical national and global aspirations (i.e. a Christianized reunified nation and world evangelization). I conclude with a summary and further research questions on North Korean politics and religion.

Christianity, communism and national division

Heon-ik Kwon suggests that "The history of the global Cold War consists of a multitude of these locally specific historical realities and variant human experiences" (Kwon, 2010b, p. 7), and it is in this sense I want to situate North Korean migrant issues in an ongoing history of the

Korean Cold War. In particular, I stress that North Korean migrants' conversion to Christianity and their narratives must be contextualized as a perpetual process of comparisons over time and space on personal, collective, and institutional levels. Korean division history and its consequences can be more understandable in light of politico-religious differentiation entailed in both North Korean and South Korean human subject-making, a core element of the Korean Cold War cultural projects. The politico-religious differentiation, however, has stood – if ironically – alongside the shared insistence of Korean ethnic homogeneity (Cumings, 2007; Lee, 2006; Shin, 2006). For South Korea, the human project has been one with Christian humanist hues and always defined against the logic of North Korea's "secular" socialist subjects. In turn, for North Korea the project has been one of defining a subject against the Western/American-inflected subject. My aim here is not to establish the epistemological truths of these subject projects but to appreciate them as important cultural projects.

From comrade to enemy: Christianity and communism in colonialism and national division

As a brief history of the relationship between Protestantism and communism, this part asserts mainly two points. First, the relationship between Christianity and communism as main forces in the Korean national independence movement was neither contradictory nor antagonistic; one could be both Protestant and socialist. If not always, both sides of leadership often cooperated in anti-Japanese independence movements and new nation-state-making during the first half of the 20th century. Second, thus in practice, the seemingly irreconcilable relationship between the two observed for over half a century should be considered as a historical construct engendered and reinforced in the context of the Cold War–inflicted national division, as is the North Korean policy on religion/Christianity (cf. Hawk and North Korea Study Team, 2005; Wells, 2008).

The rapid rise of Christianity between 1895 and 1910, Kenneth Wells asserts, "can be accounted for by the weakening of the traditional neo-Confucian, yangban [noble class]-dominated social and political structure caused by the Sino- and Russo-Japanese wars and the imposition of the Japanese Protectorate in 1905" (1990, p. 44). It is not surprising to see that Protestant believers were the most active in anti-Japanese movements, from nonviolent massive protests (e.g. 3.1 Uprising in 1919) to various militant resistances (e.g. bombing buildings or assassinating Japanese officials and Korean collaborators, etc.). Communism became another alternative for envisioning an independent nation-state since the early 20th century, but tensions between Korean communists and evangelicals did not emerge on the surface. During the Japanese colonial period (1910–1945) all Koreans, except for collaborators, were oppressed by the colonizer (Lee, 2010, p. 62; cf. Wells, 2008). The two forces led various national independence and enlightenment movements against Japan.

It was not until shortly after the liberation that there emerged large-scale antagonistic clashes between the two, as Korea was divided into two states by the big powers. Between 1945 and 1953, more than one million people (11 to 15 percent of the northern population) migrated to the South, including 35 to 40 percent of the Protestant population in the North (Kang, 2005, recited from Lee, 2010, p. 65). The division process consisted of a massive migration and killing. Both produced separated families and what Koreans call inner wounds (han), that accumulated rather than dissipated since the liberation. Tens of thousands of people who were accused as communists, collaborators, or their family members, were slaughtered on Cheju Island in April 1948, in Yŏsu in October 1948, and in Sinch'ŏn in October 1950,[2] by the Northwest or Sŏbuk Youth, an anticommunism organization formed in the Seoul YMCA under evangelical leadership, the South Korean Army force, and backed by the United States Army Military Government (USAMGIK) (Lee, 2010, pp. 66–69).

Socialist Christian leadership was cooperating in post-liberation nation-state building in the North.[3] After the division, there was a great attempt on behalf of the Protestant leadership at organizing the Christian Socialist Democratic Party (Kidokkyo Sahoe Minjudang). However, the party was soon forcibly dismissed as they were denied participation in a nationwide election that had been scheduled on a Sunday. Rev. Han Kyŏngjik (Han Kyung-Chik), one of the leaders of the party, had to migrate south of the 38th parallel and later established the Yongrak Presbyterian Church, the world's largest Presbyterian congregation. Those who did not migrate to the South were all allegedly executed,[4] sent to concentration camps, or born again as socialist revolutionary subjects under the Chosun Christian Federation (or Chosun Christian League or Christian Association in North Korea), that was first established in 1946.[5]

In post-war North Korea, the anti-American and anti-Japanese fighting spirit was widely fostered in the name of revolutionary nation-state building in competition with the southern "puppet" regime of imperialist America. North Korean wartime stories articulated the brutality of "inhuman" American soldiers and generated both fear and vengeance that were invariably accompanied by American missionaries' supposedly evil deeds.[6] Whether those stories were true or mere state propaganda, it is important to understand North Korean robust anti-Christian/religious sentiments in their own historical experiences, which are in turn reiterated in particular forms of language and narratives.[7] By the terms of performance and practice of language, one could recognize why many North Korean migrants find similarities between South Korean church rituals and systems and what they have been accustomed to in North Korea. The forthcoming subsection thus discusses the practice of North Korean Juche ideology that, Kenneth Wells points out, substituted "ideological terms and symbols for former religious ones," and directly appropriated the "religious forms" (Wells, 2008, p. 3) and thus displaced religion through a "silent" policy, distinctive from the Soviet and Chinese ones.

"We are happy!" man-centric socialist utopia

Through the notion of "theater state" Clifford Geertz sheds light on the politics of culture, as a state can be governed not by force but by symbols and rituals (Geertz, 1980). Drawing on this theory, Korean anthropologist Byung-ho Chung analyzes a mechanism of North Korean state power that is legitimized through rituals and symbols rather than police and military forces, to which little preceding social scientific studies pay much attention (Chung, 2010). Chung convinces us that normative daily practices and social interrelations as a series of symbolic rituals construe North Korean subjectivities, a model Juche human or *Chuch'e hyŏng in'gan* in North Korean terms. This cultural approach is distinctively credited when one hears accounts about the similarities and differences between Juche ideology and Christianity from North Korean migrants, and is crucial in discussing what is "brainwashing" and what is "conversion" for people like North Korean migrants.

Before delving into the migrants' accounts, it is worth introducing some key characteristics of North Korea that are by and large portrayed as monolithic and homogeneous entities in various English articles and books. Nonetheless, social scientists have struggled to find an analytical frame for better understanding the North Korean power system; a guerilla state model, a dynasty model, a cooperation model, a totalitarian model, and a dictatorship model are some examples that are applied to what most news media call "the most closed socialist society" (see Wada, 1998; Cumings, 2005; Kimura et al., 2001; Myers, 2010 for more discussions). Although each model theory deserves a great deal of attention, my primary concern lies not in the state system itself, but in the accounts of the people in their own terms.

By definition, Juche ideology claims to be a man-centric philosophy different from the materialistic Marxism.[8] The infinite entitlement of man as "the best qualified and most powerful being" (Kim J.-i., 1996, p. 2) who can dominate and transform the world is also a model Juche human. The "man's movement" in the Korean modern historical context can also be characterized as anti-imperial, self-reliant nation-state building. The North Korean Juche human is an individual who serves national sovereignty, which is represented by the Workers Party. The North Korean Constitution Article 63 manifests "In the Democratic People's Republic of Korea the rights and duties of citizens are based on the collectivist principle, 'One for all and all for one'." In order to maintain their "own" hegemonic spirit of men-centric, anti-imperial collective self, ideology education for all people becomes imperative. Scholars in political science and international relations have wondered how the weakest of the former socialist countries has survived, and how the weakest of the Six Party members (US, Russia, China, Japan, North and South Koreas) seems to dominate the relationship (see Kim, 2006). For the Juche citizen-subjects, it is ideology itself that is a force:

> The most serious lesson of the collapse of socialism in several countries is that the corruption of socialism begins with ideological corruption, and that a break-down on the ideological front results in the crumbling of all socialism's fronts and ends in the total ruin of socialism. (Kim J.-i., 1995)

It is so-called "ideology education" (*sasang haksŭp*) that is required of all people in North Korea. Throughout life in schools, workplaces, the small and large organizations that people belong to, North Koreans come to internalize a strong sense of national pride and self-respect. North Korean migrants often testify that they considered themselves as extended family cared for by Father Kim Il Sung and his son Kim Jong Il, and because of their unique revolutionary spirit against imperialists (i.e. the US and Japan) their country and people are all admired by foreign countries.

Myung-hee, who was in her mid-30s when we met in 2007, once described the ways that her parents practiced Juche Idea during her church testimonial:

> My parents were really serious about following the party and the leader comrade [Kim Il Sung]. As they learned, the first thing they did in the morning was clean the portrait of Kim Il Sung on the wall, with what we called "sincerity cloth" which they made themselves with luxurious fabric. While they were doing that, they prayed, "Let me live clean today as the great leader Kim Il Sung teaches us." In schools, they conduct ideology education in order to raise the loyalty of students toward the great leader Kim Il Sung for about thirty minutes before class, including singing songs together.

North Korean children at school seem to internalize the loyalty to the leader with words and songs like "We are happy!" and "Thank you dear Father Kim Il Sung (now Kim Jong Il)!" They learn how to shape their mouth and eyes, to make a cheerful voice, and to move rhythmically as learned when they are singing songs that are mainly about the great leader. For B. R. Myers, the North Korean worldview is summarized as follows: "The Korean people are too pure blooded, and therefore too virtuous, to survive in this evil world without a great parental leader" (Myers, 2010, p. 15). This rather cynical interpretation is partly true when dealing with normative North Korea, which is by no means homogeneous, timeless, and monolithic. What makes an ontological analysis about North Korea more interesting is when we pay attention to what North Korean migrants narrate about their experiences and knowledge of their home country, in particular, Juche ideology or as it is often called, *Kimilsungism*.

I often witnessed that many North Korean migrants are surprised at the fact that there are similarities between the doctrine and operation system of North Korea and the South Korean Church. For instance, the Ten Commandments of Moses are equivalent to the Ten Point Principle for Solidifying the Party's Monolithic Ideological System. Memorizing key speeches and lessons of Kim Il Sung and Kim Jong Il is like reading the Bible, self-criticism like a religious testimonial, and a daily cell meeting not dissimilar from Bible studies are just some examples.

Intimate enemies: encounter, comparison, and the conversion to Christianity of North Korean migrants

One may be curious how former socialist subjects interpret and accept the concept of God as Christians do. For North Korean migrants who first encounter the Bible, the story of Jesus Christ is equivalent to Kim Il Sung, as I was told numerous times, "When I read the first few pages of the Bible, I found that the book is totally understandable. If you replace Jesus with Kim Il Sung or Kim Jong Il or vice versa, there is nothing difficult to understand."[9] This analogical understanding of the Christian God may be acceptable at first, as most Korean-Chinese pastors and missionaries I met with in China, who were taking care of the migrants at secret shelters, appreciated this point as a great advantage for the introduction of Christianity. That is, the descriptions of God and Jesus' works as sacred, absolute, and mysterious in the Bible are similar to what North Korean migrants had learned and believed as that which Kim Il Sung and Kim Jong Il did, and were doing, for the Korean nation.

This comparison between God and their former leaders is, however, intrinsically problematic from the South Korean Christian perspective, and is immediately followed by a critical question about "brainwashing" being different from a religious "conversion." The term of brainwashing is nearly always tied to what the socialist or totalitarian parties are doing to the relatively "innocent" people, as George Orwell illustrates in his famous novels, 1984 and Animal Farm.[10] While there is a partly true assumption that North Korean people are oppressed and controlled by "brutal" state forces, it is through language, symbols, and rituals that the mythology of Kim Il Sung and his family has been created and enacted in North Korea (Chung, 2010).

For instance, Man'gyŏngdae, Kim Il Sung's birthplace, and other designated historical/symbolic sites demonstrate his and his family members' revolutionary achievements for the Korean nation. By placing the ruler in the center as the ultimate symbolic power and model human being, people are mobilized into "becoming a human fortress and shield" for the Great Leader, who is equivalent to Juche spirit and "our own" socialism. "Konghwaguk inmindŭl," or North Korean people, should be ones who "lead an independent and creative life as masters of the state and society" (Kim J.-i., 1992, p. 1). From early childhood, North Koreans are led to this socio-political life, which can be achieved and developed through organizational life, and is more valuable than a physical life inherited from parents. It is said that the socio-political life leads you to the eternal life, while the physical body will eventually disappear.

Those who find the similarities between Kim Il Sung in the state propaganda materials and Jesus Christ in the Bible tend to show two different reactions, although both are indeed two sides of the same coin. First is disenchantment with the Juche ideology and thus their fatherland, and second is a suspicion of Christianity that to them also looks like a false ideology just like Kimilsungism. The first reaction of disenchantment with their previous belief system is different from what Max Weber defines as central to becoming "modern" by rationalization. Instead, the migrants are mobilized to deny Kim Il Sung and Kim Jong Il as mere human beings and further "evil" dictators, while accepting the Christian God and Jesus as true and incomparably superior over any other supernatural powers. So are those who resist "listening to God's words" via missionaries. I will elaborate more on the responses of South Korean missionaries to these North Korean migrants shortly.

The second similarity the migrants point out is between the Ten Commandments of Moses (the Decalogue) and the North Korean Ten Principles for the Establishment of the One-Ideology System (the Ten Principles).[11] I will not analyze these two sets of principles in detail in this paper, but it is enough to say that North Korean migrants point out the similarity between these two sets of principles in terms of the fundamental role and the form, whether it is coincident or not. Primarily, just as the Decalogue is conceived and practiced in Judaism and most Christianity, the Ten Principles are highest over the socialist constitution and laws that all people should follow in North Korea. Once violated, you could be punished, just as you would on the Christian Judgment Day. In North Korea not only you, but all your family members, could be purged. Of course, there are significant differences in practice between these two principles according to the migrants. One North Korean migrant Christian and activist for the freedom of North Korea wrote in Korean on an internet website, "When I didn't read the Bible properly, I first considered the Ten Commandments, the apostolic creed, and the Lord's Prayer negatively, which in turn ironically recall to me the Ten Principles. [...] But Jesus is so generous that he loves his enemies [...] dies on the cross to save his disciples [...] showing infinite love, self-sacrifice, devotion, universal ethics, daily regulations, and common virtues that we are following."[12] In similar ways, North Korean migrant Christians come to find distinctive differences between the two sets of principles in terms of not only the contents but also the ways that each principle is realized on an individual basis.

This leads to the third similarity that is related to the practices of the belief in Christianity and Juche ideology on an institutional level. It includes religious confession, cell group meetings, group Bible study, regular worship, Bible reading, minister's sermons about the Bible during Sunday church services; self-criticism, work or village unit meetings, constant social education, memorizing the Great leader's teachings, and so on in North Korea. One of my North Korean migrant interlocutors pointed out, "Because the church operation system is so similar to the one in the North, and we were fed up with such strict ways of life, this is one of the main reasons why some northerners are hesitant to go to church. They don't want to be controlled, but be free as long as we now are in the free south." This account raises a significant set of questions about what "being free" or freedom and religious freedom (voluntary or "agentively submissive" in Saba Mahmood's terms (2001)) vs compulsory practices of belief mean in the context of North Korean individual migrants' life trajectories and in envisioning a social transformation in North Korea. These are the questions that North Korean migrants' conversion processes imply, and that some converts found answers to on their own terms or, as they often precisely claim, by divine power.

Consequently the processes of encounter, comparison, and conversion of North Korean migrants to Christianity are not unilinear. These processes consist of constant and complex negotiations with knowledge, experiences, and human interactions with their counterparts, who include ethic Korean missionaries in China and South Korea, and for illegal border crossers – police agents.

Brainwashing or conversion

I consider Christianity as a primary intra-ethnic "contact zone" (Pratt, 1992) in which similar yet different sets of language, knowledge, ethics, and values are encountered, shared, and negotiated in diverse scales. The perspective of "contact zone" shows us that it is Christianity that is intolerant to coexistence with others, which are always the subject of missionary work. Previously, I have demonstrated tensions between Christianity and communism in the history of Korean division, and that North Korean migrants discover some similarities between the two antagonistic peers. Some of them come to realize significant differences as well. Interestingly, for South Korean Christians, comparisons between the two are unacceptable, as is discussing the similarities and differences between the two ideologies/religions.

Ethnographic vignettes of the responses of South Korean and other ethnic Korean missionaries provide insight into North Korean migrants' conversion processes in light of the firm evangelical stance against communism. When I first went to the Yanbian Korean-Chinese Autonomous Prefecture in the summer of 2000 to collect data about North Korean refugee children in the area, I met with a South Korean pastor and professor who had been working with the refugees for some time. Although I introduced the main purpose of the trip and my meeting with him, he seemed to keep assuming that I was a potential missionary, and at end of our long conversation, gave me this final advice: "Do not even think of converting them to Christianity. It is almost impossible because they are fully colored with Juche ideology. Instead, just help them by providing their daily needs." He emphasized that he had made all possible efforts to introduce them to the Christian God while helping more than 500 North Korean famine refugees, and that it is naïve to believe that they understand the Bible well enough through comparisons with Juche ideology, or by replacing Kim Il Sung with God or Jesus. In his account, and the accounts of many other South Korean Christians I met with, as long as a North Korean migrant compares Christianity to Juche ideology or Kimilsungism, s/he cannot be Christian. Based on his own experiences, he concluded to help rather than missionize the refugees.

His account can be also understood in the particular historical and geopolitical context. In this time period, namely the late 1990s and early 2000s, in the Sino-North Korean border area where most North Korean border crossers concentrated in search of food, South Korean missionary work and humanitarian aid activities for the border crossers were less organized. Some new converts among the Korean-Chinese considered running a secret shelter or orphanage as an emerging business to attract the flow of South Korean Christian monetary funds and materials.

In 2007, when I went to this area in China, large numbers of secret shelters and churches that had housed North Korean refugees had been forced to shut down by the Chinese police, yet some remained open in secret. Nonetheless, there was a similar account about North Korean migrants' transformations. One Korean-American missionary who was managing his own secret shelters in the mountain area expressed to me that "They cannot adjust to either Chinese or South Korean capitalist society unless their brain is taken out, washed completely, and put back as new." In his account, "they" continued to recall Juche ideology and practice Juche habits (habitus in Bourdieu's term) while learning the Bible and practicing Christian rituals in his shelters for years. He said thus that since their brains (he called it gol, in North Korean vocabulary) were washed with Juche ideology, they needed to be first re-washed with nothing, and then Christianity, and new capitalist habits could be learned.

One may say that this missionary's account sounds more radical than others. Yet he expressed his thought in local vocabularies with less concern for his "missionary" status than for his human rights activist status as he was operating a secret mission in a very dangerous geopolitical condition. As such, it was not unusual to hear almost identical accounts from South Korean Christians who were working for North Korean new arrivals in South Korea. These South Korean Christians are, in my perspective, representing Korean evangelicalism that dominates the nature of Korean Protestantism and emphasizes religious spirituality (*yŏngsŏng*) and salvation (*guwŏn*) on the level of the individual and revival experiences as a form of ritual on the level of the collective church (Buswell and Lee, 2006). Above all, they do not accept Juche ideology as similar to other religions (e.g. Islam, Buddhism, Hinduism, etc.) or legitimate ideologies with which they could have an inter-religious conversation. The Christian Council of Korea (CCK), the largest association of Korean Protestant denominations, does not officially consider the Christian Federation in North Korea as their legitimate counterpart for inter-Korean Christian dialogue, although each individual church or denomination had been partnered with the latter, and beginning in the early 2000s until recently, the latter officially invited the CCK to establish a partnership.

In these larger historical and institutional contexts, it is significant to take into account the process of North Korean migrants' conversion to Christianity as a complex series of negotiations and interactions. The process occurs internally and externally. One element that makes the process more complex is the lack of opportunity for having "open-minded" conversations as well as interactions between North Korean migrants and their southern counterparts. The term "open-minded" refers to what both my North and South Korean interlocutors call an "invisible barrier," which is often metaphorically used to express North and South Korean cultural differences in secular terms. From the standpoint of South Korean evangelicalism, this barrier amounts to inherent difficulties for "complete" conversion to Christianity and even the impermeability of God's words to North Koreans.

Nonetheless, there are North Korean migrants who convert to Christianity and who claim to be God's chosen. Some become pastors and missionaries and thus claim a leadership role in evangelizing North Korea and beyond. Converting to Christianity does not merely mean following the South Korean Christian order of things, but rather brings us to question what Korean Christianity, Christian language, and Christian conversion mean in the context of the late Cold War Korean peninsula. The following section examines North Korean conversion narratives as a window through which we can seek answers to these questions.

Conversion narratives in contact perspective

By the idea of "contact zone," this chapter has scrutinized the power-imbued encounters, negotiations, and reconfigurations of new selves and meanings of life between established Christians and former socialist subjects in the zones where the Christian God is believed to work for a greater plan. What is significant in the forms and processes of the interpersonal contacts is the presence and intervention of God, a supernatural actor, and its (would-be) adherents' belief in it. This religious aspect has received much less scholarly attention in discussions of the dynamics of diversifying contact zones (Askins and Pain, 2011; cf. Clifford, 1997, pp. 188–219; Linke, 2006; Schorch, 2013). Extending the idea which Pratt articulated in the context of post-colonial frontiers, museums (Clifford, 1997; Schorch, 2013), art projects (Askins and Pain, 2011), states (Linke, 2006), bus stops, and parks in cities (a research project in progress at the Max Planck Institute), to name a few, all appear to be cross-cultural contact spaces between different actors and cultures. Contacts are made in and through places, which are however in flux, mediated, and experienced. Religious conversion often takes place on a route construing contacts in particular time and space just as St Paul encountered on his way to Damascus, rather than completed as a single event.

As of June 2014, the Ministry of Unification of South Korea reports that the number of North Korean migrants in South Korea is 26,854, and 70 percent of them are female.[13] My empirical data suggest that the women account for about 70–80 percent of North Korean Christian migrants (more than 80 percent of the newcomers aforementioned). Different from South Korea and elsewhere, where females outnumber the males in church congregations, it is unlikely to say that North Korean migrants' conversion to Christianity is gendered, but rather reflects the gender ratio of the North Korean migrant population. It is notable that records indicate a gradual decline of the number of regular churchgoers among migrants. Main reasons include the characteristics of their occupations (e.g. service sectors like restaurant, beauty shop, construction sites, etc.), and oftentimes experiences of discrimination in church. The stalemate of growth, and further, the decline of the Christian population in South Korea has continued since the 1990s, while the size and scope of mega-churches gets bigger and bigger, which a Pentecostal theologian Young-Gi Hong (2003) dubs the McDonaldization of Korean churches.

North Korean migrant converts' testimonies in faith demonstrate the distinctive nature of Christian conversion in a larger contemporary context and inspire us to foresee what a post-division inter-religious/

ideological dialogue would look like. They manifest the experienced Great Famine (1995–1998), everyday lives in the North, and the stunning agonies they underwent as a stateless people in China, and ultimately how God saved and called the migrants for greater plans such as saving others and national evangelization. I highlight North Korean migrants' conversion narratives as a performance hosted largely by conservative churches from which they often receive financial and social benefits. In return, the migrant narratives serve to provide spiritual and often ethical inspiration for audiences by relating tales of suffering, miracles, national evangelization, and human rights (Jung, 2013). In this light, their testimonials in faith are a form of ritual, generating "the dual effect of the conversion, the strengthening of their faith and the transformation of their lives" (Stromberg, 1993, p. 3).

It is not unusual in South Korean evangelical churches to invite popular preachers, laypersons, and new converts to listen to their testimonies in faith. Different from an altar call, that is widely practiced at the apex of the worshiping services, the guest testifiers make the profession of their faith while highlighting specific moments and events that led them to convert to Christianity or revitalize their faith before the church congregation. Each testimony in faith tends to take around 50 minutes or a little longer. North Korean adult migrants who had received formal school education in North Korea are good at articulating their opinions, at least according to most of their southern counterparts. However, my years-long field research among them suggests that they are extremely wary of having our conversations recorded either on a notebook or a voice recorder. Exceptions are rare unless they are compensated or volunteer for a talk in specific situations. This tendency originates not only from the previous lived experience in the North where state surveillance is severe, says a former officer in the Korean (read North Korean) People's Army. My empirical data also suggest that it is a learned strategy as a result of critical experiences of police interrogations on their perilous journeys to and in South Korea. Grace, as I call her here, was also so rigorous to the off-record preference that I had to erase files in my digital voice recorder even though the informal conversation we had for the first time at her church was not properly recorded.

However, Grace became a seasoned speaker, delivering her testimonial in faith before South Korean Christians. Elsewhere I analyze her conversion narrative at length with focus on disjuncture and contradictions between our personal conversations and her formulaic testimony in faith (Jung, 2013). For instance, Seoul, where she encountered social discrimination at workplace and church, where her North Korean friends lost their government subsidies through fraud, and where young migrants faced such unexpected violence as bullying and dispiritedly lagged behind at school, appears in her testimony as "Canaan," in a Biblical term. As such, most of the North Korean migrant converts' testimonials I witnessed in church-sponsored events demonstrate a stark contrast between the suffered past in the North and the blessed present in the South in evangelical vocabularies. On the contrary, aforementioned negative socio-cultural encounters experienced while living in capitalist Seoul, taken into account in our personal conversations, are nearly completely silenced in such religious accounts.

When considered as a "contact zone," what they articulate and they silence reflects indeed the ways in which the migrant individuals interpret, appropriate, and respond to the present power structures and power-imbued predicaments within which they are positioned. The considerable number of testimonies of North Korean famine survivors published in international news media and human rights reports of transnational organizations should be treated similarly. In such institutional settings as evangelical churches, Special Envoy for North Korean Human Rights in the United State, and the UN Commission of Inquiry on Human Rights, to name a few, the migrants are mobilized and often required to configure suffering as spatially and temporally Other (i.e. in the past and in North Korea), and to preclude the possibility of describing the present-day sufferings that they undergo in South Korea or such liberal host societies as the United States.[14] As such, my analyses of Grace's and other North Korean migrant converts' lengthy testimonies in faith evoke that the evangelical Protestant vocabularies that they acquire through institutional training and articulate in church settings translate their current life in capitalist societies like Seoul, South Korea, into the "blessed life."

Their religious accounts are likely to serve to reproduce the binary opposition between the "poor" and "evil" North and the "prosperous" and "blessed" South, as propagated by the South Korean state during the Cold War era. It is an indisputable reality at the present time. However, I punctuate earlier that the integral role of the divine actor, the Christian God, in constituting their conversion passage should be taken into consideration. What is remarkable in their conversion narratives is indeed the ways in which such human mediations and critical assistance provided by Korean-Chinese, South Korean, or Korean-American missionaries are nearly erased or devalued. Alternatively, it is no other than God who appears in such virtual forms as Jesus Christ's bleeding face, a voice from the heaven, dense dawn fog blinding border guards, a light guiding a path in a darkest night, and so forth, to lead the desperate asylum seekers to a safer place. Namely, God chose them to become born again as a valuable servant for a greater cause, a reunified Christianized Korean nation. It is also the nature of evangelical discipline that enables the migrant converts to place their personal relationship with God in the center, while putting the human and institutional caring efforts aside in enunciating their conversion passages. This manifests their claim of the leading role in God's greater plan for national evangelization. Grace ends her testimony with accounting her aspiration in great conviction that she is called to work for lost souls such as North Korean refugees, the poorer people she came across while passing through Southeast Asian borders, and whatever God leads her to do.

Conclusion

I have tried to articulate the relationship between religion/Christianity and communism in the context of the Korean modern history of colonialism, the devastating Korean War, and a half-century of national division. In turn, their conversion is arguably intertwined within the larger historical context and in relation to modern state-building in North and South Korea that is both mirrored and competitive.[15] I have demonstrated that North Korean migrants compare Juche ideology and Christianity when they encounter the Bible and church practices. The similar aspects of the two belief systems they discover serve to ease some of them into accepting Christianity at first, while hindering others from further approaching Christianity. In response to this tendency of comparison among North Korean migrants, some Korean-Chinese missionaries argue that it is good to teach the migrants in this way because of the similarities. In contrast, the South Korean evangelical standpoint disallows any attempt to "compare" the Christian God and Kim Il Sung, since the latter is merely idolatry that cannot in any way be equated with the ultimate true God. The last section analyzed the nature of North Korean conversion narratives that constitute their Christian passage, as I call it, intertwined with a complex network of underground missionary and brokering activities aimed at North Korean missionization. And yet I highlighted that their testimonies in faith serve to legitimize their religiosity and leading role in the national and global mission directly granted by God. In this spirit, this chapter asserts that North Korean migrants' conversion to Christianity may neither be a precursor of Christian and South Korean capitalist triumph over the socialist North, nor a mere mimicry of the deep-seated anti-communist political religiosity. It is rather a symptom of the post-division era in Northeast Asia where both rigid and hybrid forms of power and ideas are contacted and contested, as are the supernatural forces claimed to be behind them.

This work was supported by the Academy of Korean Studies Grant funded by the Korean Government (MEST) (AKS-2011-AAA-2104). The author is grateful to the participants in the workshop, "Religion and Communism: Comparative Perspectives from Asia and Europe" convened by Justine Quijada and Tam T. T. Ngo at the Max Plank Institute in Goettingen, Germany.

Notes

1. I call those who fled from North Korea to China, South Korea, and other countries for various reasons as North Korean migrants, refugees, and border crossers alternately and in accordance with context.
2. As Timothy Lee briefly points out in his book, the Sinchŏn massacre where more than 35,000, a quarter of the town's population, were killed in a month, has recently received popular attention thanks to Hwang Sŏgyŏng (Hwang Sok-yong, 2001)'s novel *Sonnim* (The Guest) in which Hwang indicates that Communism and Christianity are all merely guests – foreign elements disturbing a host family (i.e. the Korean nation). In light of the term *sonnim* that used to be a figurative expression for smallpox caused by a ghost possession in local folk religion (i.e. shamanism), the guests are also seen as ghosts in need of a local healing ritual to make it leave the patient's body, the Korean peninsula. Meanwhile, Pablo Picasso painted "Massacre in Korea" (1951) based on the Sinchŏn incident.
3. Kenneth Wells asserts "The relation of Protestants to socialism was rather complex. The founder of the first Korean socialist and then Communist party, in 1918, was a Protestant, Yi Tonghwi, while the Communist Manifesto was translated into Korean by another Protestant activist, Yŏ Un-hyŏng" (Wells, 2008, p. 8).
4. According to an official record announced by the Korean Church Martyrs Missionary Association (KCMMA) in 2001, about 90 percent of Protestant martyrs (191 by 2001) were executed by Communists between 1945 and 1953 (see Kang, 2007).
5. In the same vein, all other preexisting religions including Buddhism and Ch'ŏndogyo (religion of the heavenly way, a grassroots indigenous religion that first emerged in the late 19th Century), began to lose or give up their structural foundations through land and education reform at a rapid pace at the beginning of North Korean state building (Wells, 2008).
6. For instance, American missionaries' "unforgettable" atrocities that appeared in school textbooks are as follows: an American imperialist who came to Korea under the guise of a missionary let his dog attack a young Korean boy who picked an apple from the ground of his orchard, and then inscribed "thief (*Tojŏk*)" with hydrochloric acid on his forehead; American missionary doctors took organs from Korean patients and sold them to the US, and so on.

Wartime stories about the US army's merciless killings of innocent Koreans include that a group of people were all killed as they hid in church building believing that US bombers would not drop bombs on a church. Such stories are not only reiterated in class or workplaces, but also exhibited virtually in the places where such "brutality" took place. North Koreans repeatedly visit the sites like the Sinchŏn museum where the massacre occurred as mentioned in footnote 2, to rearm their anti-American sentiment.

7. Under the banner of "Our own way!" anti-imperialism in general and anti-Americanism in particular are intrinsically blended in the concept of Juche. Recorded in a 1999 video by a non-governmental relief agency at work in North Korea, a six or seven year-old boy was asked to say something to South Korean students. In a decisive voice he speaks as if having been prepped: "What I just wanted to say to South Korean friends (Namjosŏn dongmu-dŭl) is that let us kick imperial Yankees out of our country as soon as possible and study and play together." At the heart of this young boy's formulaic account is a strong sense of blood purity among ethnic Koreans and North Korean national pride. North Koreans in North Korea "officially" believe that their country is a true independent state which has never been afraid of, but rather always stands against, "imperial" America.

8. "Marxist philosophy raised, as its major task, the clarification of the essence of the material world and the general law of its motion, whereas the Juche philosophy has raised, as its important task, the elucidation of man's essential characteristics and the law of social movement, man's movement. Therefore, the Juche philosophy is an original philosophy which is fundamentally different from the preceding philosophy in its task and principles" (Kim J.-i., 1996, p. 2).

9. I first encountered this sort of account when carrying out intensive field research collecting substantial data about North Korean children's health conditions for a South Korean non-governmental organization at Yenji, the capital city of the Korean-Chinese Autonomous Prefecture in summer 2000, when tens of thousands of North Korean border crossers were wandering around in search of food.

10. Probably different from his own intention, George Orwell's *Animal Farm* was translated into Korean and published in Korea as the first foreign language edition by the United State in 1948 when the conflicts between socialists and their counterparts were escalated. Since then, Kim Il Sung, the founder of North Korea, has been portrayed as a huge pig rather than regular man in South Korean anti-communist cartoons.

11. The Ten Principles are as follows, excluding three to five sub-regulations of each principle:
    1. We must give our all in the struggle to unify the entire society with the revolutionary ideology of the Great Leader Kim Il Sung.
    2. We must honor the Great Leader comrade Kim Il Sung with all our loyalty.
    3. We must make absolute the authority of the Great Leader comrade Kim Il Sung.
    4. We must make the Great Leader comrade Kim Il Sung's revolutionary ideology our faith and make his instructions our creed.

5. We must adhere strictly to the principle of unconditional obedience in carrying out the Great Leader comrade Kim Il Sung's instructions.
6. We must strengthen the entire party's ideology and willpower and revolutionary unity, centering on the Great Leader comrade Kim Il Sung.
7. We must learn from the Great Leader comrade Kim Il Sung and adopt the communist look, revolutionary work methods and people-oriented work style.
8. We must value the political life we were given by the Great Leader comrade Kim Il Sung, and loyally repay his great political trust and thoughtfulness with heightened political awareness and skill.
9. We must establish strong organizational regulations so that the entire party, nation and military move as one under the one and only leadership of the Great Leader comrade Kim Il Sung.
10. We must pass down the great achievement of the revolution by the Great Leader comrade Kim Il Sung from generation to generation, inheriting and completing it to the end.
More information and stories are introduced at the following link: http://www2.law.columbia.edu/course_00S_L9436_001/North%20Korea%20materials/10%20principles%20of%20juche.html.
12. http://www.ffnk.net/board/bbs/board.php?bo_table=user_column&wr_id=56&page=3.
13. The number of North Koreans that arrived in South Korea by 2014 June, Ministry of Unification, S. Korea.

	~'98	~'01	'02	'03	'04	'05	'06	'07	'08	'09	'10	'11	'12	'13	14.6 (TNTV)	Sum
Male	831	565	510	474	626	424	515	573	608	662	591	795	404	369	131	8,078
Female	116	478	632	811	1272	960	1513	1981	2195	2252	1811	1911	1098	1145	601	18,776
Total	947	1043	1142	1285	1898	1384	2028	2554	2803	2914	2402	2706	1502	1514	732	26,854
Female Rate	12%	46%	55%	63%	67%	69%	75%	78%	78%	77%	75%	70%	72%	76%	82%	70%

http://www.unikorea.go.kr/index.do?menuCd=DOM_000000101007001002 (accessed on July 19, 2014).
14. The number of North Korean migrants in western countries where they are entitled to claim refugee status and protection increases since the United States enacted the North Korean Human Rights Act in 2004, followed by some European countries consecutively. It was reported that several of them committed suicide in the United States until recently, while S. J. Lee, an anthropologist who recently carried out extensive interviews with those who settle down in United Kingdom, addressed that they showed a much higher degree of satisfaction with life in UK than those who are in South Korea, and that the reasons should be analyzed in the near future (at a closed seminar in Seoul, 2013).
15. After the Korean War, both North and South Korea had to rebuild everything from the ashes. For instance, South Korean militant regimes (1960–1980s) were driving the economic development-first policy with an anti-communist

line that oppressed basic human rights. In the North, material well-being was equally emphasized as a supreme national task. The "Great Supreme Leader" Kim Il Sung promised three meals a day with a bowl of white rice and a beef or other meat soup, or *i pap e koki kuk*, which was only enjoyed by the ruling *yangban* (nobility) class in the feudal times or by the Japanese colonizers and collaborators. Different from "liberal" South Korea, however, under the banner of "Let's live on our own way!" justifying Juche socialist philosophy, North Korean politico-economic reforms have run parallel with idolization of the leader (see Cumings, 1991; 2004).

11
The Role of Religious Art in Post-Communist Russia
Clemena Antonova

The following chapter will consider some aspects of the role of Orthodox religious art in post-Communist Russia. It will be shown that the connection between art and religion that the Bolsheviks had attempted to sever was re-established during and after the Gorbachev era. At the same time, the religious art of the past, just as Russian religious philosophy from the 19th and early 20th centuries, was burdened with the task of filling in the ideological vacuum left by the collapse of Communism. In this chapter, I will suggest that while these expectations have largely proved fruitless, the approach towards religious art as a visual model of the unity between religion and secularism could lead into a more promising direction. This is where Russian religious philosophy could prove useful.

Section 1 will consider Bolshevik cultural policy on religious art in the larger framework of policies on religion. I suggest that the general thrust of Soviet strategies on religious art throughout the Communist period was defined at the time and can be described as an attempt to strip art of its religious connotations. Thus, Orthodox art was removed from its original context in monasteries and churches into newly founded museums in order to turn cult images into secularized, aesthetic objects. Soviet re-contextualization of art followed the implications of Lenin's position as outlined in his *Plan for Monumental Propaganda*.

Section 2 will look at the revived interest in religious art after 1989 alongside the re-discovery of Russian religious philosophy from the end of the 19th century and the beginning of the 20th century. It will be suggested that Pavel Florensky's (1882–1937)[1] works in particular had a direct impact on this renewed Post-Soviet fascination with the Orthodox icon. My focus will fall on Florensky's essay "The Church Ritual as a Synthesis of the Arts," which he wrote in response to Lenin's *Plan*. In this work, the Russian author opposes the Soviet concept of the museum, in which art is dissociated from its religious context, to the church in which art works as part of an organic whole. Florensky's notion of the church and the religious art it houses is as the space that bridges and overcomes the divide between this and the other world.

The present paper will address the relevance of ideas developed in Russia at the beginning of the 20th century to the situation after *perestroika*. Can the icon play a crucial role in modernity as writers such as Pavel Florensky were suggesting? Can religious art, by offering a model that overcomes the divide between religion and secularism, help fill in the ideological vacuum left by the end of Communism?

Bolshevik cultural policy on religious art

Cultural policy on religious art after the October Revolution in 1917 was a direct result of Bolshevik policies on religion. In 1993, Richard Pipes, a major Russian historian, remarked that "in histories of the Russian Revolution, religion receives little if any attention" (Pipes, 1993, p. 337). Even now most general histories do not include a section on religion and research on this subject is published in more specialized volumes.[2] This is surprising not only because religion is such a vital part of human life in general, but also because in the Russian case in particular it could have very well been "the Achilles' heel of the Soviet regime" (Bourdeaux, 1995a, p. 4). According to one view, the failure of Soviet policy on religion is among the major factors that contributed to the collapse of the Soviet system (Bourdeaux, 1991; 1992). This chapter will consider the case of religious art, an almost completely neglected problem, as an illustration of the Soviets' strategies in their struggle with religion.

The position of Marxist-Leninism on religion and the Church can be summarized in the popular expression, which both Marx and Lenin used: "Religion is the opium of the people." Already in 1905, Lenin had explained that "religion teaches those who toil in poverty all their lives to be resigned and patient in this world, and consoles them with the hope of reward in heaven." Thus he concludes:

> As for those who live upon labour of others, religion teaches them to be charitable in earthly life, thus providing a cheap justification for their whole exploiting existence and selling them at a reasonable price tickets to heavenly bliss. Religion is the opium of the people. Religion is a kind of spiritual intoxicant, in which the slaves of capital drown their humanity and their desires for some sort of decent human existence. (Lenin, 1905)

In this view, religion, a remnant of feudalism, becomes the ideological weapon of capitalism, just as the Church is the bastion institution of the old order. Therefore, religion can have no place in a Socialist society, and atheist propaganda throughout the Soviet period, from Lenin to the early days of Gorbachev, was a constant motif in policy-making (Lenin, 1926; Shakhnovich, 1961). However, what was to be done about religion? This is where one notices a variety of views within the Party. Marxist-Leninist theory holds that, with the development of economic forces, religion will naturally disappear. As Lenin said at one point, religion will be "steadily relegated to the rubbish heap by the normal course of economic development" (Lenin, 1926). However, even though there were promising signs, it became clear that the disappearance of religion altogether would not happen spontaneously in the foreseeable future. Already after the February Revolution, reports were suggesting that Russian prisoners of war in German camps ceased to attend church service in huge numbers once attendance was no longer mandatory. There had been other signs of hostility against the Church even before the Bolsheviks took power, but the attachment to religion proved too tenacious.

One line of thought within the Party held the view that religion should be eradicated not by "punishment and repression, but with good schools, Communist propaganda, and Socialist economics" (Daly, 1997, p. 236).[3] Lunacharsky, the Commissar for Enlightenment, maintained that repression would be counter-productive, as "religion is like a nail: if you hit it on the head, you only drive it deeper" (Pipes, 1993, p. 338). He and some others started a movement known as "Bogostroitel'stvo" (God-building), which sought to replace traditional religion with its focus on a divine being with a basically religious belief in mankind as the object of worship. Lenin, however, was deeply distrustful of "God-building," as he was skeptical of the idea that science would prove an alternative to religion.

One is struck by the persistent efforts of Bolsheviks to expose the frauds and misconceptions that religion had been exposing people to for centuries and the almost complete failure of these efforts with believers. A theme that ran through the discussion during the 1926 All-Russian Conference on Anti-Religious Struggle was that an atheist should only explain, bring scientific proof, and people would be convinced. Thus, a participant in the conference cites, in a positive spirit, how "a Communist took an icon into the street and shot it with a rifle", demonstrating in this way that "you see, nothing is going to happen to me. God has not punished me" (Hecker, 1933). The incident recalls an episode in Dostoevsky's *The Brothers Karamazov*, where the old Karamazov spits on the icon of his wife and the message is the same "you see, nothing is going to happen to me." In either case, the effect on believers was very different from the intended one. This, however, would hardly have come as a surprise to Lenin, who represented another position within the Party, which was much more hardline. As was characteristic of Lenin, he took account of changing circumstances and adapted his strategies and priorities in response. The resolution passed at the Twelfth Party Congress in 1923, that atheists refrain from offending the sensibilities of believers since ridicule only intensifies "religious fanaticism," by no means implied giving up the struggle against religion (Pipes, 1993, p. 358). It just meant pursuing militant atheism through other means, which were very much dictated by circumstances.

Up to 1922, the policy of the Soviet government followed a more or less soft line in regard to the Church. On January 26, 1918, a decree of the separation of the church from the state and schools from the church was issued. Just as in the aftermath of the French Revolution, the property of the Church was nationalized.[4] The Bolsheviks had another, much more urgent problem on their hands which threatened their very existence. At least up to 1921, they were heavily engaged in the Civil War (1918–1921) against the White forces. It was well known that many of the clergy were sympathetic to the White cause and some were even fighting in their ranks. The Bolsheviks won and in the meantime the ground was laid for a charge that became common two years later: the priests and their sympathizers were associated with counter-revolutionary activity.

Soviet ideologues were quick to take advantage of another historical circumstance. The country, already devastated by both internal and external wars, was hit by a famine with almost unprecedented force. On June 26, 1921, the government came out with a warning that 25 million people in the Volga region faced starvation. Foreign organizations were asked for help and a number of measures were launched. It is in this context that the confiscation of church valuables was undertaken. The widely accepted view is that the famine was used as a pretext to justify an assault on the church and true purpose of the sale of church valuables was political rather than philanthropic (Daly, 1997, p. 238; Pipes, 1993, p. 347). This is probably true in the sense that the confiscation could have been put off for some time, but in the long run it was inevitable. Lenin's *Plan for Monumental Propaganda* had clearly implied it already in 1918 in respect to religious art (see below).

The genuine crisis before the Soviet government also represented an opportunity for discrediting the Church which was too good to be missed. The authorities set out to expropriate all movable Church property of value, including religious art, allegedly to use it in the struggle against the famine. In December 1921, Trotsky joined Litvinov to coordinate the sale of this property abroad in order to get funds and food for the hunger-stricken provinces. The press, in the meantime, was busy reporting on the scale of the crisis, which had led to incidents of cannibalism. In this atmosphere, any unwillingness on the part of the Church to surrender valuables could be easily interpreted as counter-revolutionary activity, sabotaging the new regime. That there was such unwillingness is undeniable, though not because the Church refused to help in the famine relief on principle. On January 6, 1922, the Patriarch encouraged believers to donate valuables, although not consecrated items. The following month he endorsed this statement by declaring the surrender of consecrated vessels to be sacrilegious and threatened those guilty of the offence with excommunication. Throughout March, all over Russia there were cases of popular resistance to the removal of church property (Freeze, 1995). The government took the view that these incidents had been organized by the high clergy, and it was at this point that there was a shift in Soviet policy towards the Church, which up to then had refrained from open repression. In the period between the spring of 1922 and the spring of 1923, 44 religious leaders were executed and 346 received prison sentences of one to five years on charges of resisting the requisition of church valuables. This policy was openly sanctioned by Lenin in his letter to the Politburo of March 19, 1922, which says that "the greater the number of reactionary bourgeoisie and reactionary clergy that we manage to execute in this affair, the better" (Pipes, 1993, p. 352). As has been noticed, a "large portion of the valuable objects seized from churches found their way not to the hungry but into museums" (Fletcher, 1965, p. 251). While this proves that the hunger crisis was not the only reason for the confiscation, it is also very much in the spirit of Lenin's general position on art and religion.

Years later, Lunacharsky remembered a conversation he had with Lenin in the winter of 1918–1919. Lenin had commented on the role of art "to help the education and the bringing up of the new generations" and had cited in this context Campanella's *The City of the Sun*. The walls of Campanella's utopian city were covered with frescoes, which served an educational purpose.[5] The ideas that Lenin had discussed with Lunacharsky came out in a concrete form in his *Plan for Monumental Propaganda*, the main focus of which fell on new works of art which contemporary artists would create in the context of a victorious Socialist revolution. In this sense, it is not surprising that most critical literature on the subject deals with this aspect of Lenin's *Plan* (Bowlt, 1978; Lodder, 1993; Neiman, 1960). What is rarely noticed is the position on the religious art of the past, which is the main topic of this chapter. As Lenin told Lunacharsky a list needed to be worked out "of those ancestors of Socialism or its theoreticians and fighters, but also outstanding names in philosophy, science, art, etc., who even without having a direct relationship to Socialism, were genuine heroes of culture" (Lunacharsky, 1933, pp. 232–233). The works of those artists on the list were to be preserved. Preservation was an important part of the *Plan*, and Soviet achievements in conservation are a good witness to that. One of the concrete outcomes of Lenin's position was the removal of religious art from its original context in monasteries and churches to public museums and art galleries.

That there was actual physical destruction of works of art in the early Soviet period cannot be denied. The decree issued on April 12, 1918, concerns the "demolition of monuments, erected in honour of the tsars and their servants and the creation of projects for monuments of the Russian Socialist Revolution." However, the demolition of tsarist monuments had always been made with the qualification that all those of artistic value should be preserved. Preservation meant re-contextualization, that is, what was preserved was the actual work itself, while its meaning was intentionally transformed. Thus, an Orthodox icon would be perceived differently depending on the context in which it is viewed, that is, whether it is placed in a church or in a museum.

Lenin and the Bolsheviks discovered nothing new when they employed a strategy of re-contextualization. After the French Revolution, special depots were created in Paris to hold artistic objects until it was determined which ones would be disposed of and which ones would be housed in the newly created public museums (Haskell, 1993, p. 237). In Soviet Russia, a number of religious works, such as Andrey Rublev's *Holy Trinity* icon, probably Russia's most famous medieval image, thus found their way into museums and galleries.

To divest images of their religious associations became a primary task for the new regime, a task which was, moreover, seen as part and parcel of the struggle against superstition and ignorance. It proved to be uphill work, as holy images had become an organic aspect of Russian identity. As Robin Cormack has noticed in several of his works, the cult of images became a permanent feature of Eastern Orthodox identity (1997, p. 43). This is important for our purposes, because the continuity between the "Second" (i.e. Constantinople) and the "Third Rome" (i.e. Moscow) is perhaps nowhere as pronounced as in the deeply felt attachment to sacred images, which frequently took the same form. In Tolstoy's *War and Peace*, the icon of the Smolensk Mother of God is treated very much like a medieval *palladium*, that is, a public cult object recognized by all. It is carried along with the Russian army and paraded in procession before battle in a manner recalling, for instance, the role played by the legendary image of Christ of Edessa during the Persian attack on Constantinople in 544. Soldiers and officers bow in front of the image (i.e. the medieval *proskynesis*) and kiss it (i.e. the ancient *aspasmos*). We read of the old General Kutuzov, who "went to the icon, sank heavily on his knees and bowed to the ground" and then "put out his lips in a naive, child-like way and kissed the icon, and again bowed down" (1968, p. 919). The example is revealing because it shows that the attachment to images was not limited to the uneducated, as Marxism-Leninism implied, but permeated all strata of society – peasant soldiers, as well as aristocratic officers and generals. This is the population that the Bolsheviks had come to rule over.

It is a testament to the power of images that the religious icon remained an object of remarkably stable allegiance among people with a variety of political views. Even those sympathetic to the Soviet regime felt alienated when faced with shows of disrespect to sacred icons. The evidence given below describes what must have been a wide-spread attitude. A Voronezd reader wrote to the journal *Narodnoe prosveshchenie* (Popular Enlightenment) in 1928:

> My teacher in junior class, meeting me sixteen years after I left school, wept and told me that she is even afraid to live and work in the present time. She has no regrets for Tsar – he drove her fiancé into the grave and so she is still unmarried at forty. But the icons that they [mostly members of the Komsomol, the Party organization for the youth, and the Militant Atheist League] threw out of school – this was more than she could bear. (Fitzpatrick, 1992, p. 112)

The Bolsheviks' view of religion as a dark superstition, muddling the minds of people, seemed to find no better confirmation than popular attitudes towards holy images. Since the theology of the image, worked out in the context of the Iconoclastic Controversy in Byzantium (8th–9th centuries), was inaccessible to the average believer, he/she almost automatically invested images with supernatural powers. In Russia, as in Western Europe, images were believed to cry, to shed blood, to have the ability to cure the sick, etc. There is a famous episode at the time of Catherine the Great during a terrible plague that had taken the lives of thousands in Moscow. At the order of the Empress, the kissing of icons was temporarily forbidden as a measure against the spread of the disease. This enlightened decision led to what is known as the Plague Riot (1771), during which there were hundreds of victims, including the Archbishop who had read out the decree. The people expected salvation from their icons and saw no need for doctors, whom they threatened to kill (Alexander, 1989, pp. 154–157; Pares, 1953, p. 259). In this respect, things had not changed much by the time of the Bolsheviks. The story of the village which soon after the October Revolution wrote to the government asking for a portrait of "the new sovereign Revoljutsia" rings quite true (Pares, 1953, p. 490). Apart from political ignorance on part of the peasants, it is also revealing about the role that images played in Russian society.

The Bolsheviks energetically set out to combat such beliefs. The attempts to demonstrate "frauds" behind the miraculous powers of icons and relics were nothing new in Russian history. Peter the Great was known to have been fond of finding out the secret mechanisms in the back of icons which were responsible for the "tears, blood," etc. This failed to produce the expected result, a loss of faith, and instead confirmed the popular idea that the Tsar was the Antichrist. The Bolsheviks do not appear to have been more successful, when they uncovered "miraculously preserved" saints' bodies which turned out to be wax effigies.[6] The strength of popular religiosity and the failure of Soviet policies on religion are illustrated by the reaction of an old peasant who told an American visitor: "Our holy saints disappeared to heaven and substituted rags and straw for their relics when they found that their tombs were to be desecrated by the nonbelievers. It was a great miracle" (Pipes, 1993, p. 346). A strictly rationalistic approach would, no doubt, interpret that as a stubborn, unthinking reaction which would call for further efforts at "raising the cultural level" (a favorite expression of Lenin's).

The role of religious art in a time of crisis

In 2004, an event that attracted enormous attention in Russia was the return from the United States of one of the most sacred Orthodox icons, that of the Mother of God of Tikhin. According to legend, this was an image painted by St Luke, which was taken to Constantinople in the 5th century. After the fall of Byzantium under the Ottomans in 1453, the icon somehow found itself in Russia. Many incidents throughout the medieval period allegedly prove that the Mother of God of Tikhin was a miracle-working icon. During the Second World War it was sent by a Russian bishop to the United States in order to be protected from the Nazis. Its return to Russia became an occasion for national celebration and was officially attended both by the Patriarch and by President Putin (Garrard and Garrard, 2008, p. 198).

Obviously a radical transformation of attitude had taken place in post-Communist Russia. However, if one wants to fix a moment in time which marked the turning point from state-sponsored atheism to deep respect and re-consideration of Orthodox traditions at the official level, one would need to go back to the Gorbachev era. At the beginning of his presidency, Gorbachev had promised, as all his predecessors, a "decisive and uncompromising struggle against all manifestations of religion and a strengthening of atheist propaganda" (Gabel, 2005, p. 458). Indeed, there is little doubt that Gorbachev himself was "a confirmed atheist" (Dziewanovski, 1997, p. 367), but as it became clear in the next several years he was even more committed to his program of *perestroika*. This is why it is under Gorbachev, for the first time in several decades, that "every aspect of religion began to flourish with vigour" (Bourdeaux, 1995b, p. 114). It is well known that a great boost for the revived interest in religion was presented in 1988, the year of the 1000th anniversary of the baptism of Russia. For many observers, the celebrations for the anniversary marked "a turning point in church-state and church-societal relations" (Chaplin, 1995, p. 97), as for a few weeks "it seemed as though the Communist Party had yielded primacy to Holy Russia, which was being reborn before the eyes of an astonished populace" (Bourdeaux, 1995b, p. 114).

What has been rarely remarked upon is the role of the 1988 anniversary celebrations for attracting attention to Orthodox art. Religious art, which Russians had been used to viewing in museums, was, for the first time in years, considered in its deep links with Orthodox Christianity. A number of measures in the following years re-established the idea that the Bolsheviks had attempted to obliterate, that is, that Orthodox art belongs to Orthodox religion. The new property law of 1990 gave religious communities the right to own buildings. On December 5, 1991, President Yeltsin promised that all "shrines, churches, monasteries and sacred objects" would be returned to "the believers to whom by right they should belong." Two years later, on April 23, 1993, a decree on the transfer of religious structures and other properties to religious organizations was issued. In the meantime, the Russian Orthodox Church showed its appreciation of its artistic heritage. The Bishops' Council issued, in 1992, an appeal to "the people who are occupied with the upkeep of the monuments of Orthodox culture" and stated that "the Church shares this concern and with all its power will assist the revival of cultural heritage" (Chaplin, 1995, p. 106).

All the cited measures sought intentionally and consistently to reverse the trend of Bolshevik cultural policy on religious art described above. The Bolsheviks, as we saw, had attempted to annihilate the religious meaning and associations of images by re-contextualizing them as art. In the post-Communist period, there has been a pronounced trend towards restoring the original, religious connotation of medieval art. This has been evident not only on the level of policy-making, but on the intellectual plane, where it took the form of re-discovering authors, sometimes long forgotten, who had approached religious art from the standpoint of Orthodoxy. Here I will draw attention to Pavel Florensky, one of the main representatives of Russian religious philosophy at the beginning of the 20th century, whose work became gradually available from the late 1960s on, but especially after *perestroika*. The contemporary fascination with Florensky in Russia is, I believe, at least partly due to an idea that runs like a thread through his writings, namely the suggestion that the icon can play a saving role in the crisis of modernity (see below). The question at the end of the 20th and the beginning of the 21st century is if the holy image can once again provide meaning at a time experienced by many as a crisis of values. Evidence of the problem of re-contextualization can be seen in the visitors who have been noticed praying before the Rublev icon in the Tretyakov Gallery in Moscow.

The reception of Florensky is, in many ways, representative of the fate of Russian religious philosophy in post-Communist Russia. In the first years after *perestroika* Florensky was mainly seen as a martyr to Orthodoxy. He was canonized by the Russian Orthodox Church, while in 2004 his photograph was seen hanging, exactly in the manner of an Orthodox icon, in the basement of the Church of St Tatiana the Martyr, the church of the University of Moscow.[7] Florensky had become a priest after his graduation from the Theological Academy in the years before the October Revolution. After being arrested in 1933 and being moved from one labor camp to another, ending at the notorious Solovski, he was executed in 1937. In 2002, the remains of 30,000 victims were found at Toksovo, in the suburbs of St Petersburg. It was reported that Florensky's remains might be among the dead (Titova, 2002).

Florensky's writings in the 1910s and early 1920s organically belong to a trend in Russian religious philosophy, going back to the middle of the 19th century and reaching its developed form with the works of Vladimir Soloviev (1853–1900) at the end of the century. It should not be forgotten, though, that this line of thought, when not completely ignored, has rarely found favor with the Russian Orthodox Church. Florensky's writings stand out within this tradition of ideas in that they constantly approach themes, typical of Russian religious philosophy, through visuality and visual categories. Florensky's interest in the icon is unique and, in my opinion, his works have been a major factor behind the revived interest in religious art in the post-Communist period. For Florensky the icon is important because it is interpreted as a visual model of his religious philosophy,[8] an approach that was especially welcome in the context of the religious revival after 1989.

Florensky's commitment to Orthodoxy is a well-established fact. However, it should be taken into account that, as I have suggested elsewhere (Antonova, 2010a, pp. 73–95), the Soviets did not regard him so much as a religious thinker but as a scientist, especially someone working in the applied sciences. Florensky's original training had been in mathematics and physics, and after the Revolution he naturally went back to the hard sciences. There are more than 20 patents in his name. Tellingly, there had been no question of including him among the list of mostly religiously oriented intellectuals who were exiled in 1922 at the order of Lenin and Trotsky. Even in the 1930s, Florensky had a flat in Moscow given to him by the state to facilitate his work. This is where he was at the time of his arrest. In this sense, it is very likely that Florensky's repression and execution happened within the context of the purges against the technical intelligentsia in 1937.

Admittedly, it has frequently proved impossibly hard to determine why people were arrested and executed during the Stalinist trials, as the absurdity of the charges in so many cases defies human reason (Conquest, 1990 [1968]). During the intense religious revival of the first years after the collapse of the Soviet system, there was an almost exclusive focus on the religious dimensions of Florensky's personality, obscuring the rest of his heritage. This one-sided focus also illustrates the unbounded enthusiasm for the intellectual traditions of pre-revolutionary Russia, which were brought to fill in the ideological and spiritual vacuum left by the collapse of Communism. At the same time, especially more recently, Russian intellectuals have started questioning the ability of pre-revolutionary thought to address contemporary problems, as well as the uncritical reception of early 20th century ideas. A modern Russian historian has critically observed that "we are infected with nostalgia for pre-revolutionary Russia" and that "it is precisely there, in the past, that we stubbornly seek answers to the burning questions of the day" (Azadovski, 1995, p. 85). Anthropologists who did field research in

Russia in the late 1990s noticed "an aspiration to the reconstruction of an idealized, abstract, and invented 'glorious past' of pre-Soviet religious traditions" (Benovska-Sabkova, 2010, p. 95).

The idea that a religious revival was taking place in the late 1980s and early 1990s was meant to draw associations with the "Russian Religious Renaissance"[9] at the beginning of the 20th century. Sometimes, even the same term, that is, "religious Renaissance," has been used (Eliason, 1991). What the art historian Erwin Panofsky remarked about the notion of a Renaissance in the more usual application of the term holds true in the Russian case too. For Panofsky, what is characteristic about medieval "renascences" is that that they were "limited and transitory," while the Italian "Renaissance" with a capital letter was "total and permanent" (Panofsky, 1960 [1957], p. 106). In this sense, the religious ferment that had been started with Gorbachev's *perestroika*, just as the one at the beginning of the 20th century, was a limited affair restricted to extremely small sections of the population and lasting for a relatively short duration of time. All this is familiar, but what is important for our purposes is that the turn to intellectual developments in the early 20th century brought a renewed interest in writings on religious art and specifically in the medieval Russian icon. The question is if early 20th century writings, as Florensky's, can provide solutions to contemporary problems a hundred years later.

Let us consider some recurrent themes in Florensky's theory of the icon. First, the Russian author gives expression to a typical 19th century notion propagated by the romantics, which persists in various guises in the 20th century aesthetic discourse on modernity, namely that art can play a redeeming role in a disintegrating modern culture. Second, he stands out within this line of thought by placing his argument within an Eastern Orthodox context. This is evident not only by the intended associations with writings that form the Eastern Orthodox corpus, but also in his claim that it is the ancient Russian icon – rather than music, as, for instance, with Schopenhauer and Nietzsche – which fulfills the mission of art. The icon as the supreme example of genuine art is essentially symbolic. As such it has the ability to restore the lost "magical" identity between "being" and "thing," which lies at the heart of art.

All these ideas are in the background of Florensky's essay "The Church Ritual as a Synthesis of the Arts," which was written in response to Bolshevik cultural policy on religious art. Florensky wrote his essay in October 1918, that is, a few months after Lenin's *Plan for Monumental Propaganda* came out. In a rush, he published it in 1922 after the Decree on the Confiscation of Church Valuables was issued. According to

Florensky, the Lavra (i.e. a monastery which has been given a special status) of the Trinity in Sergiev Posad, founded in the 14th century by the country's patron saint, Sergius of Radonezh, was "infinitely necessary to Russia" (Florensky, 2002, pp. 110–111). Florensky urged the authorities to preserve it in its original function as a functioning monastery, but also as a treasury of some of Russia's most valuable medieval art. The meaning of an image, Florensky explains, depends not only on its pictorial representation but on the conditions of reception, as well. The church, which is the meeting ground of man and God, of this and the other world, not only in terms of architectural structure but in terms of all the conditions available in a functioning church, is opposed to the art gallery and the modern museum. The former provides the "specific conditions" under which the icon can "live," while in the latter "it dies, or at least it enters a state of anabiosis" (Florensky, 2002, p. 101). Florensky's thesis is that the religious image can only exist in organic unity with its sacred landscape, provided by the music of the choir, the light of the candles, the movement of the priests, in short all the elements that make up the church ritual. The icon, as the supreme example of religious art, needs its natural environment just as a living creature does. Florensky draws an analogy with the new zoo in Hamburg, where animals lived not in cages but in open spaces, designed as close as possible to their natural habitat (Florensky, 2002, p. 102). Once the sacred image, which forms a whole with its environment, that is, the church, finds its place in the modern museum, the "whole" is disrupted. As "there is no reality outside the whole," in the art gallery "we see not icons but merely caricatures of them" (2002, p. 108).

Florensky's essay was written in reaction to contemporary events. It is, therefore, completely legitimate to question the relevance of his ideas at present, quite apart from their possible art historical interest. In my view, if there is relevance, it is not to be sought in a narrow applicability of Florensky's concrete, practical suggestions. In principle, museums now are no closer to returning art to its original contexts as they had been in the 1920s. Florensky's proposal of classical sculpture being put under the open sky is not likely to happen, most fortunately, according to some. But there is a deeper level of meaning in Florensky's theory of the icon. The Orthodox image is put forward as a visual model of organic unity, a unity that brings together religion and culture, religious and secular knowledge, etc. This is why the leitmotif of a "whole," a "synthesis," is so important in Florensky's essay. The idea of unity lies at the heart of Russian religious philosophy from the very beginning. Soloviev called this notion *tsel'noe znanie*, that is, unified knowledge, and from him on it underlies the writings of every major Russian religious philosopher. For Florensky, the icon is the abstract concept of *tsel'noe znanie* made visible and concrete. In this sense, Florensky's theory of the icon is relevant so long as we agree with the contemporary Russian thinker, Mikhail Epstein, for whom "the comprehensive interaction of religion and culture" can and should become "a vital, broadly evident imperative" (Epstein, 1995, p. 293). In other words, what is probably necessary now is not a "religious Renaissance" but the creation of conditions for bringing together the traditions of secular culture and religiosity in the wide sense that had been kept isolated for decades.

Conclusion

This chapter considered the cultural policy on religious art from the very beginning of the Soviet period and at the end, during the Gorbachev era and the first years of post-Communism. This issue was placed within the larger framework of policies and attitudes to religion. It was, thus, suggested that the failure of Soviet strategies on religious art is symptomatic of the failure on religion in general and, ultimately, of the whole system.

Another idea that was put forward was that the religious philosophy of pre-revolutionary Russia can play a constructive role at a time of a crisis so long as it is approached not through the lens of a "religious Renaissance" but through the concept of the unity of culture and religion. Pavel Florensky's ideas on Orthodox religious art can become relevant again if they are understood in this context.

Notes

1. For a biography of Florensky in English, see Pyman (2010). For a short introduction of his ideas, see Antonova (2010b, pp. 73–95).
2. On the history of the Orthodox Church in Russia under the Soviet regime, see Pospielovsky (1984); Marshall, ed. (1971); and Curtiss (1953).
3. Decree of December 1918, cited in Daly (1997, p. 236).
4. For the most part, though, this only legalized seizures of land that the peasants had already conducted on their own (see Curtiss, 1953, p. 46).
5. Lunacharsky, 1933, pp. 232–233. Interestingly, Chagall decided to celebrate the first anniversary of the October Revolution in a similar fashion – by covering the walls of the city of Vitebsk with paintings.
6. In Note 4 to his text, Donald Treadgold notices that this practice seemed to have had "only a limited effect on the faithful" (1987, p. 187). René Fülöp-Miller, too, comments on "the ineffectiveness of Bolshevik attacks" (1968, p. 350).

7. Cited in Graham and Kantor (2009, p. 4). The photograph was later taken down, most probably because the Church realized that St Tatiana had become a meeting place of the so-called Name-worshippers, a religious heresy that Florensky had been associated with.
8. On the relationship between art and theology, as well as religious philosophy, see Victor Bychkov (1993), and Antonova (2010a).
9. The term was popularized by Nicholas Zernov (1963).

12
Chinese Socialism and the Household Idiom of Religious Engagement
Adam Yuet Chau

Religionscape as a suffused presence

The conventional approach to studying the impact of Maoism on the Chinese religious landscape (henceforth "Chinese religionscape," defined here as the totality of the articulations between religious conceptions and practices and their conditions of possibility) focuses on the policies during the Maoist period *directly* and *explicitly* relating to the management, control and suppression of religious institutions, personnel and activities. This includes the analyses of, for example, the establishment of the state bureaucratic organs in charge of the officially recognized religions (Buddhism, Daoism, Islam, Catholicism, Protestantism); the anti-religion/anti-traditionalist policies that aimed at eradicating not only the so-called "feudal superstitions" but also, at the height of the Cultural Revolution in the 1960s and 1970s, the entirety of religion as a domain of social and personal life; the opportunistic deployment of certain religious traditions in the service of international diplomacy (e.g. Buddhism in dealing with Japan and the Buddhist countries of South and Southeast Asia and Islam in dealing with Islamic countries in the Middle East and later in the post-Soviet Central Asia). Part of this approach of course is a description and analysis of how different "religions" responded to the challenges, suppression and manipulation. There are three inter-related problems with such an approach.

First, there are actually no such thing as "different religions" responding to state policies (the "fallacy of misplaced concreteness"). Categories such as Buddhism, Daoism, and even Islam, Catholicism and Protestantism are conceptual fetishes – for the state and some of the religious practitioners, especially the elite, as well as for scholars, especially those in comparative religion – that do not correspond to how people "do" religion on the ground.[1]

The second problem with this approach is what might be called the "fallacy of imputed ontology" [or "fallacy of misplaced circumscribedness"]. In looking at how Maoist religious policies impacted Chinese "religions," one inadvertently, if not necessarily or consciously, posits a pre-existing entity called "Chinese religions" (or a particular religion such as Daoism or Protestantism) that has an ontological autonomy that actually never existed in isolation from the rest of society and polity. The forms and contents of the ways in which the Chinese do religion have always been a product of interactions with the state (and of course broader societal forces and structural elements); therefore, Maoist religious policies have to be seen in the context of a *historically continuous* process of state construction and management of "religious activities."

The third problem with this approach is even more serious. To look at "state-religion" relations is to assume that there is a domain of social and organizational life that can be labeled as "religion," which falls into the trap of state-constructed categories and administrative practices, when such constructions should be deconstructed rather than used as the basis of analysis (i.e. another form of the "fallacy of misplaced concreteness" or perhaps the "fallacy of misplaced/imputed discreteness"?). In a way both the state constructing "religion" as a discrete (and concrete!) domain of social and organizational life and the scholars studying what is going on in this domain are suffering from the lingering legacy of (sociological) functionalism (and its branch in anthropology, structural-functionalism), which will still happily posit a "religious system" (or the so-called "religious sector" in modern China) in any "social organism," even if perhaps less explicitly today among the scholars compared to the heydays of functionalist thinking, though the state continues unabashedly with its own administrative functionalism (see Malarney, 1996). In the past few years there have been a number of scholarly works that engage with the construction of the category of religion in modern China (e.g. many of the articles in two exemplary edited volumes: Ashiwa and Wank, 2009b; M. Yang, 2008; see also Duara, 1991; Goossaert, 2006a; 2006b; 2008; Nedostup, 2010; Overmyer, 2003b; Goossaert and Palmer, 2011), but in most cases the scope of analysis is still restricted to thematic concerns that are ostensibly related to religion.

So what is to be done? It is of course far easier to identify limitations in existing paradigms than coming up with new ones. This chapter is an attempt to come up with some different ways of tackling the issue of understanding Chinese religionscape, not just during the Maoist period but hopefully in other periods and contexts. The first thing we have to recognize is that Chinese religionscape is a *suffused presence* in Chinese society, meaning that whatever we want to recognize as religious practices are inextricably intertwined with *the entirety of Chinese social lives and structural forms*. This is not the same as saying, as C. K. Yang famously argued (1991 [1961]), that Chinese religion is divided into "institutional" and "diffused" forms (in fact I contend that this might have been one of the most misleading formulations on Chinese religion). In other words, I am not suggesting that religious values and practices are diffused into every nook and cranny of society (even if this is the case). Rather, I am arguing that *the structure and transformations of the larger society have determining impact on the very shape of the religionscape*. For example, if the household is a crucial unit of engaging with religious activities by the Chinese, we should expect that there would be more analysis on the shifting nature of the household and how it has impacted religious practices, but so far we have seen very little of this kind of analysis (but I will attempt such an analysis here). What this recognition means is that we have to go beyond the type of state-religion, impact-response analysis and look into *how religious practices articulate with broader societal forces*. So instead of looking at religious policies, one would look at how the most pervasive organizing principles of society operate and how they impact the religionscape. The rest of this chapter is to attempt at this kind of analysis.[2]

The household as basic unit of religious engagement

To put it schematically, the Chinese engage in religious activities at three different levels: the individual, the household and the community. Traditionally anthropologists and historians of Chinese religious life have primarily focused on aspects of communal religious life such as collective rituals and temple festivals. On the other hand, the personal aspects of religious life, admittedly much more difficult to access, have been studied primarily through the lens of discursive productions of elite religious practitioners. But the household has not been the focus of serious investigation, though, I would argue, it is the *most* fundamental unit of religious engagement in Chinese religious life.

The household is the most fundamental unit of religious engagement in Chinese religious life because the household is the most basic political, economic and moral-religious building block of Chinese society. To the extent that an individual engages in religious activities, most of the time he or she is engaging in such activities on behalf of members of the household as an intimate collectivity whose welfare is inter-dependent. There has been a long-held misconception about Chinese religious life, that since women seem to participate more in religious activities they must be more religious (or superstitious, depending on one's attitude towards such activities). But the truth is that most women participate in religious activities on behalf of all members of their households; they are simply representatives of the household as a unit of religious engagement. The same is true when only the names of heads of households are written on the memorials to be sent (through burning) to the celestial court in communal rituals; on these occasions the heads of households do not act as individuals but rather as representatives of their respective households.

The household is also the site of the worship of various deities and spirits (e.g. ancestral and deity worship at domestic altars, the stove god). On the more obvious, basic and prosaic level, the household is host to the stove god (see Chard, 1990; 1995), Heaven and Earth (*tiandi*), the immediate ancestors and perhaps some other common deities found in domestic settings (e.g. the God of Wealth, Guanyin). Usually represented in the form of spirit tablets (*shenzhupai*) on domestic altars, these are some kind of permanent lodgers in the home, to be cared for on a daily basis, usually in the form of incense (freshly offered in the morning), red electric lamps in the shape of candles and offerings that need not be replaced too frequently (e.g. fruits made of wax, biscuits and candies in wrappers). Familiarity has made it unnecessary for the host household members to be too ceremonious in interacting with these deities and ancestors (see Stafford, 2000). Typically the matron of the household (i.e. wife of the head of the household) assumes the responsibility of this kind of "everyday forms of hosting." These minor yet recurrent hosting occasions mirror those minor social hosting occasions (e.g. friends and neighbors dropping by for a visit). At certain nodal points along the lunar calendrical trajectory the family makes more elaborate and special offerings with more ostentatious gestures of being the host to these spirits and deities, collectively or individually, for example, on the first day of the lunar New Year, on the birthday or death anniversary of an immediate ancestor, on the birthday of one of the deities such as Guanyin (somehow extremely generalized deities such as Heaven and Earth, the stove god and the God of Wealth don't have birthdays).

When the village or neighborhood community stages a communal religious festival such as a temple festival or New Year's festival, it is the households that serve as the basic participatory building blocks in the forms of contributing funds and/or labor. In fact, in most communal rituals the households stage their own household-based mini-rituals that are embedded in the larger framework of the communal ritual but are nevertheless expressions of the household idiom of religious engagement. The first section of this article below will look into how the larger societal transformations during the Maoist and reform periods have impacted the nature of the household and its concomitant religious practices.

There is another important aspect of the household that makes it the most basic unit of religious engagement. In Chinese religious life, the most common and most important activities are in the form of households hiring ritual specialists to conduct rituals on behalf of the household, especially at funerals. The overwhelming majority of these specialists-for-hire are not regular members of any larger religious institution and do not live in special dwellings separate from the common people; rather, they are mostly householders themselves who live amongst the people who constitute their clientele base. In contrast with clerics who live collectively in cloisters (e.g. monasteries, nunneries, Daoist belvederes and temples), these religious specialists are atomized, living within the community of their prospective clients but sometimes far removed from other, similar specialists. I have in mind the proverbial *yinyang* master, the *huoju* (or *sanju*) Daoist priest, the spirit medium and other similar types of *householder religious specialists* (or *householder religious service providers*). The second half of this article will examine the advantages of such a form of religious service provision, especially in the context of a potentially hostile political environment.

In other words, we will see that (1) the overwhelming majority of religious activities in Chinese life use the household as the basic unit; (2) most ritual service providers in China are household-based; and (3) a large number, if not the majority, of religious activities in China involve households engaging with ritual specialists who are themselves householders. These observations will establish what can be called the household idiom of religious engagement in contrast with the corporatist idiom (e.g. lineage collective worship, temple festivals) or the individualist idiom (e.g. individuals engaging in personal-cultivational activities).[3]

This chapter lays out a preliminary analysis of the household idiom in Chinese religious practices. I explore the following questions: How does the household idiom work on the side of the ordinary household and on the side of the household-based religious service providers? How have the societal transformations under Chinese socialism (especially the

Land Reform and collectivization during the Maoist period and de-collectivization during the reform period) impacted this idiom? What are the implications for our understanding of Chinese religious history and religious culture when we look at the household idiom more seriously?

The making of the socialist middle peasant and the impact of socialist transformations on the household idiom of religious engagement

The Land Reform of the early 1950s had an inadvertent effect on religious life that very few scholars have remarked on. Traditionally, the funding of temple festivals typically came from rents from temple land as well as richer members of the community (e.g. gentry landlords and merchants). The expropriation of temple property and the political and economic disempowerment of these former patrons of temple festivals meant that these traditional sources of funding ended. However, a new and large class of "socialist middle peasants" came to the fore after the poor peasants were given land (and sometimes houses and extra wives of former landlords). Many of these poor peasants previously couldn't even afford to get a wife and form a family, and therefore were not able to become patriarchs of households and to stage the "hosting" occasions so crucial to a peasant's identity and self-worth (on hosting see Chau, 2004). Nor could they sponsor the temple festivals other than participating in them. But now they emerged as heads of households, newly empowered by the socialist state, and "turned around" and became the real "masters" of their own lives (*fanshen zuo zhuren*).[4] With their new, modest prosperity these socialist middle peasants could also feel that they "owned" the temple festivals because they could sponsor the staging of temple festivals in monetary terms as well. In other words, there was a process of the *democratization of religious life* in the early Maoist period in the wake of Land Reform (i.e. from the late 1940s to the mid-1950s). It was indeed a "honeymoon period" for the former poor but now "middling" peasants (see Friedman et al., 1991).

But all this changed when the Maoist state (overly) enthusiastically embraced and enforced collectivization in the mid to late 1950s. All of a sudden the enhanced "household sovereignty" (Chau, 2004) that the state granted the peasants was taken away from them. The honeymoon ended rather suddenly and unexpectedly. The centrally planned economy vitiated the households and communities of their political economic and socio-cultural basis, which is the very stuff that many religious practices express, confirm and celebrate. The loss of household and communal sovereignty also necessarily meant that there was no more motivation to engage in religious practices as households and communities no longer existed as beneficiaries of these practices.[5]

A large part of the Chinese peasants' "social suffering" (see Kleinman, 1995) during the Maoist commune period came from their inability to host important household event productions as a result of the taking away of their household sovereignty. Even though the Communist Revolution and the Land Reform enabled a great number of heretofore poor peasant men to get wives and form their own (sovereign) families, the irony is that the Party in turn prohibited them from asserting this newly gained sovereignty through hosting funerals and weddings (because, the Party said, it was too wasteful and the rituals were superstitious nonsense). Even though the Party said that the peasants had "flipped back up from being oppressed to become their own **masters**" (fanshen zuo zhuren 翻身做主人), these new masters could not be **hosts** (zhuren 主人). So what the Party did was to host the funerals and weddings on the peasants' behalf! The production team Party secretary would routinely preside over "socialist new style" funerals and weddings with minimal or no banqueting. And because of the severe restriction on travel, the invitation to relatives and friends from outside of the production team vicinities was kept at a minimum, again restricting the assertion of household sovereignty. In other words, the Party usurped the peasant families' (sovereign) right to host on the occasions of major family events. For a Chinese peasant, not being able to host on those important occasions was tantamount to not being fully human. Starving during the Great Leap was mere physical suffering; not being able to host at one's parents' funerals and one's sons' weddings was moral failing and ontological defeat.

A kind of second honeymoon period for Chinese peasants happened during the economic reform period, when the state dismantled the collectivist infrastructure and introduced the household responsibility system, which meant giving back household sovereignty to the peasants (i.e. the peasant patriarchs). This regained sovereignty translated into renewed energy and *jouissance* in "hosting" funerals, weddings and temple festivals (see Chau, 2006a). The revival of the household-based mode of production enabled the revival of household-based mode of event production. But we have to keep in mind that this peasantry of the reform period is no harking back to traditional times (if there is such a thing to begin with) but a direct legacy of the socialist Land Reform. The pervasiveness of the contemporary socialist middle peasantry is illustrated by the elaborateness of funerals for most households except the very destitute. In rural Shaanbei in north-central China, where I did my fieldwork in the mid and late 1990s, most households host, when there is a death in the family, elaborate funerals that last two days. They say that it is an abbreviated version of the *standard* three-day funeral. However, this "standard" funeral they are referring to was, in the pre-Liberation, pre-Land Reform era, the standard funeral for rich landlords only, whereas the poor peasants had the briefest of rituals. In other words, most peasant households today are so "middling" that they can almost host funerals of similar elaborateness as former landlords. This fact has profound implications for religious life in the countryside.

Socialist persecution of religious institutions and appropriation of religious real estate as a boon for the household idiom

The Maoist party-state has been understood as a so-called Leninist state, that is, it is governed by ideological discipline (via disciplinary practices internal to the CCP itself [see Apter and Saich's book on Maoist regime of self-criticism (Apter and Saich, 1995)] as well as outreach disciplinary practices that were pandemic within the entire society) and centralized political organization (via a bureaucratic state fused with the party that acts as its command center at every level). What is less discussed is the Leninist state's inability to tolerate any social organization even when it is not political.

Traditionally Chinese religious institutions included many with strong institutional forms. For example, the Quanzhen school of Daoism was organized as branches of lineages of transmission, as were most of the Buddhist sects. And there were numerous sectarian groups. However, there was a tendency towards decentralization (not only because of the dynastic state's attempt to curtail overly strong religious institutions), so none of the religious groups reached the kind of centralized authority and control wielded by the Catholic Church in pre-modern Europe, the Church of England in Britain, or the Russian Orthodox Church in pre-Revolutionary Russia. But the attitude and accompanying suppressive practices adopted by the Maoist state against the religious institutions resembled the kind of radical anti-clerical stance of the French Revolution and the Russian Revolution, which did face the formidable enemies of the religious establishment (the Catholic Church in the case of 18th century France and the Russian Orthodox Church in the case of early 20th century Russia). So the Maoist state constructed a strawman enemy called "clerical authority" (or "power of the gods") (*shenquan*) to justify their suppressive, and often violent, measures against religious institutions and personnel, when these measures seemed out of proportion to the power that these religious institutions and personnel actually wielded, not to mention that the overwhelming majority of religious personnel were household-based religious service providers without any institutional base. The real reason behind the severe suppression of religious institutions during the Maoist period is a general intolerance of *any* social institution outside the orbit of the party-state. In other words, more than the *religiousness per se* of Chinese religious institutions, it was their *institutionality* that invited severe suppression.[6]

Not unlike religious institutions in the more familiar case of Western Christianity (with the Catholic Church being the most exemplary), traditionally Chinese religious institutions were also avid accumulators of real estate (see Fisher, 2008; Gates, 1999). In addition to monastic grounds proper with their grand buildings (including temple halls and dormitories for monks and nuns) and large courtyards, large Buddhist and Daoist monastic centers owned large expanses of land, collecting rents on farm lands and urban rental properties (in addition to being exempt from taxation). Some of these properties were granted by imperial favor; some were expropriated from other, rival religious institutions (for example, when one sect gained imperial favor at the expense of another that lost favor or was persecuted); some were donated by devotees; and some were straightforwardly purchased in the property market by astute estate managers. The smaller temples had at least some land dedicated to raising funds (usually through rent collection) for the annual temple festivals and other festivities (as well as temple maintenance and repairs and the hiring of any resident cleric). The native place associations almost always had deities from their native places enshrined in dedicated halls within the native place association compounds and staged annual festivals celebrating their deities' "birthdays."

Religious real estate suffered a big blow during the late Qing movement to turn temple properties into schools and/or fund local education with temple income (*miaochan xingxue*) (see Goossaert, 2006a) (though most schools were owned and run by local lineages and communities, so it wasn't an issue of state expropriation of property). The Republican government continued with a similar program, though this time more aggressive in expropriating religious real estate, though because of war disruptions and the short-livedness of their regime on the mainland the impact was not sustained (see Nedostup, 2010). It was really the early Maoist period that spelled the end of religious real estate. During the Land Reform of the early 1950s, land and property of all "evil landlords" were forcibly redistributed to poor peasants. Land and property owned by temples, native place associations, guilds and communities were either taken away by various government agencies hungry for offices and turf or redistributed. Anyone resisting or protesting was met with the harsh "dictatorship of the proletariat." As a result there was no longer a physical site on which to celebrate the deities' birthdays, now that the temple grounds and halls had turned into schools, government offices, factories, etc. Even today in urban China many long-standing primary and secondary schools sit on the former grounds of temples. Again we see that it was not so much the *religiousness* of the temples that invited Maoist "wrath" but rather their *status as property owners* (and consequentially as political economic actors).

The persecution of religious institutions and the appropriation of religious real estate obviously dealt a great blow to all forms of institutionalized religious life. However, it had unintended consequences for the household idiom of religious engagement. One would imagine that the elimination of larger and more powerful religious institutions might open the space up for household-based ritual specialists. Of course while institutional religion was being persecuted, household-based ritual specialists were also being persecuted. There was the famous "campaign against spirit mediums" (*fanwushen yundong* 反巫神运动) launched by the Communist government as early as during the Yan'an days (1930s), and once in power the Communist government continued with their efforts to stamp out these "superstitious" cheats and tried to reform them into productive citizens of the new society. However, because of the de-centralized and relatively private nature of household-based ritualists (more on this below), the attacks on them were far less thorough when compared to those on temples, lineages and major cult centers.

Interestingly, the household-based ritualists' homes sometimes even became the refuge of deities that were driven out of their temples. During my fieldwork in Shaanbei I came across a spirit medium in a village. He was an elderly man and had, by that time, already passed most of the work to his son. He proudly told me how, during the height of the Cultural Revolution, the Azure Cloud Immortal had to flee his abode (temple) situated in the town of Shenmu because the red guards were destroying his temple. So he took in the Azure Cloud Immortal as an additional tutelary deity (on top of the Red Cloud Immortal, which was a female deity, and the True Lord of Fire). When he or his son went into trance, one of the three tutelary deities would come down to possess the spirit medium. He said that because he was a poor peasant and had good relations with local cadres (because he had cured the illnesses of their family members, among other kinds of help) he was never persecuted. In fact he even practiced during the Cultural Revolution, though more discreetly. In the 1990s the urban devotees of the Azure Cloud Immortal wanted to rebuild the temple (though in a different site since the old temple ground was still occupied by government offices) and invite the deity back to Shenmu City. But since the deity had become quite used to life in the countryside he apparently didn't want to go back, at least not yet at the time of my fieldwork. Even though this is an isolated case, one can imagine that similar cases of refugee deities must have been quite widespread during the Maoist period; in other words, the deities didn't get destroyed or disappear; they simply changed residence and continued with their lives, though admittedly far less glamorously than before. And the key to their survival was the household idiom of religious service provision.

Household-based ritual service providers, or, the advantages of being atomized

Traditionally, there have always been many more religious service providers who are household-based than institutionally based. The most common institutionally based religious specialists included Buddhist monks, Quanzhen Daoist priests and Confucian academicians (if they served as Confucian ritualists). On the other hand, household-based religious specialists include spirit mediums, yinyang masters, Zhengyi Daoist priests, ritual masters (*lisheng*), magical healers (see Dorfman, 1996), ceremony directors, sectarian ritualists (see DuBois, 2005; Jones, 2004; Johnson, 2010), ancestral worship ritualists (e.g. the Confucian clan ritual officiants analyzed in Jing, 1996), householder Buddhist "monks," votive offering (*zhizha*) makers (e.g. makers of *wangye* boats), incense and candle makers, story-tellers, opera singers, cooks, ritual dramatists, fortune tellers, divination poem decipherers, temple caretakers, professional corpse handlers (in Cantonese areas; see Watson, 1988), professional funeral wailers, corpse beauticians, statue makers, mural painters, etc. (see Hayes, 1985).[7] It is true that at certain points in Chinese history the Buddhist sangha and the Daoist Quanzhen Order were very sizable, but such hyper-institutional expressions were never long-lived, as they were always subject to the whims of Chinese emperors (often the key patron and protector), shifting state policies and persistent critiques of the Confucian literati-official elite.

Because grassroots householder religious service providers were never registered, it is extremely difficult to arrive at any estimate of the overall size of this broad category of people for any historical period in late imperial China or today (see Goossaert, 2000). It is tempting to speculate that at any point in history, for any one religious cleric officially affiliated with a monastery or temple (even counting the small temple resident clerics), there must have been ten or more householder religious service providers dispersed among the people. These are the unsung heroes (or villains depending on one's perspective) in Chinese religious history. Because they rarely compose any texts – many of them are indeed illiterate or barely literate – or contribute to any religious discourse that will be recorded for posterity, their stories and significance are easily forgotten, overlooked, or erased. However, in the local scheme of things, their presence and service is crucial to the mental, physical, "spiritual" and social health of local individuals, households and communities. But why do so many religious service providers adopt the household idiom (as a business model)? What are the advantages of the household idiom for them?[8]

The structural advantages of the household idiom are many: ease of internal management (including transmission); ease of engagement with a largely household-based clientele; flexibility in forming larger ad hoc groups of ritualists if necessary; and low profile hence protection against state and elite suppressions.

The household (*jia, hu*), according to Hill Gates, is the key product of, as well as player in, the twin modes of production (tributary and petty capitalist) whose tango-like articulation has characterized China's political economic landscape in the past 1000 years (see Gates, 1996). Given the strictures and incentives provided by the Chinese state (*the key player in the tributary mode of production*), "Chinese people had no choice but to organize themselves as *jia*.... [It] was the legitimate social instrument with which to wrest a living from a hard world" (Gates, 1996, p. 103). Not happy with being merely tax-paying, corvée-bearing direct producers, most Chinese households also engage in petty capitalist activities in the market (commercial as well as labor) to advance comparative advantages and to better fulfill ideologically salient cultural goals (e.g. making enough money to find wives for all of one's sons). Frequent co-operations with other households notwithstanding, Chinese households are fundamentally individualistic (what Victor Nee calls "peasant household individualism"; see Nee, 1985; see also Croll, 1986/87). Therefore householder religious service providers can be seen as just one type of petty capitalists (see Gates, 1999), and their specialization and niche marketing no different from strategies adopted by householder craftsmen and shopkeepers.

The householder religious service provider acts as an owner-operator of his family business, using the home as base and following petty capitalist principles in all matters of importance (see Creed, 2000). He uses his family members and close kin as helpers and treats his son (or sons) as a target of expertise transmission and eventual succession (agnatic nephews are often suitable too). He benefits from the considerable trust obtained within this familial atmosphere and the power of a patriarch. He also enjoys the freedom, autonomy and flexibility of an owner-operator. It is said that the Chinese like to be their own boss (see Hsiung, 1996) because then one will not get bossed around by others.

Another advantage of the household idiom for religious service providers is the fit in terms of scale between the specialist and his or her clientele, which is overwhelmingly household-based. Despite the fact that the personal as well as the communal are important dimensions of Chinese religiosity, the household remains the most salient site in which most Chinese "do" religion (on "doing religion" see Chau, 2006a; 2006b; 2011b). In other words, the household is *the most basic unit of religious or ritual engagement*. Dispersed into the ocean of Chinese households and adopting the household idiom themselves, these grassroots religious service providers fit snuggly in the midst of their clients. The clients feel most comfortable approaching them as they have built up neighborly relationships over time (sometimes over generations) (this is especially true in the case of spirit mediums, yinyang masters and huoju Daoists). Even though most Chinese are not averse to visiting large temples and praying to very powerful deities (e.g. Buddha, Guanyin, Jade Emperor), engaging with and hiring clerics stationed in these large temples is another matter. Because these temples and monasteries had extensive land endowment and substantial rent and donation income (or in today's China the clerics are salaried), the clerics felt little inclined to provide regular ritual service to the "small people." Hence their attitude to the common people tended to be condescending, aloof, if not callous and rude. (The salaried clerics of major temples and monasteries in the People's Republic of China (PRC) tend to have similar attitudes.) The householder ritualists, on the other hand, are usually models of good personal and business relations, for their livelihood depends on good *guanxi* (social relations).

The advantages of formal affiliation with a large and translocal religious organization were not lost to most householder religious service providers. But with the prestige and security of belonging to a famous temple or monastery inevitably comes the pain of organizational and religious discipline. For the Zhengyi huoju Daoists, they preferred getting accredited by the Daoist authorities and being left alone. (One may see the Longhushan Daoist ordination system as a religious franchise, except that the individual practitioners had a lot more freedom compared to a real franchised merchant.) A huoju Daoist priest may belong to a Daoist lineage and this may be very important to his identity, but it would not be relevant for his capacity to serve his clients. Similarly, spirit mediums in some parts of China might form "families" based on master-disciple relationships, but except for some collective rituals and group duties such as doing pilgrimages each spirit medium worked by him- or herself (see Li, 1948).

Yet the most crucial advantage of the household idiom is that it allows the householder religious specialists to assume a very low profile to operate under the radar screen of the authorities. Larger religious institutions often draw too much attention to themselves, and often their spectacular success will eventually lead to their perhaps equally spectacular downfall (as the Chinese phrase has it: *shuda zhaofeng*, or, "a tree, if too big, will surely draw storms and destruction to itself"). Householder religious service providers are, thanks to the household idiom, pre-adapted to suppression (be it from the state authorities, Confucian elites or rival religious specialists such as the big temple clerics and sectarians). Dispersed among the people, a householder ritualist takes advantage of his familiarity with his home turf and makes friends with local state agents such as the local police (who are most likely his neighbors and clients) to avoid harsh treatment during oppressive times. Though recognized by the state as an average householder just as his neighbors, he avoids getting taxed for the money he makes in the ritual market, partly because the state refuses to recognize his trade as legitimate (as taxation connotes recognition and approval) and partly because the tax officials probably have no idea that he exists or their families are themselves his loyal clients. And when times are really bad (e.g. at the height of Maoist anti-superstition campaigns), he can simply put aside his special trade and pick up farming again. For the householder religious specialists, there can be no such thing as *huansu* (forceful return to non-religious/clerical life by state policies targeting religious clerics; literally "returning to the ordinary [world]") because their very existence is already so ordinary and not very religious to begin with. When forcefully "returned to the ordinary world," most monks, nuns and Daoist priests would have lost their means of ritual production such as scriptures, sutras, musical instruments, deity scrolls and murals, ritual implements and the very ritual space itself (often confiscated by the authorities or destroyed). On the other hand, the householder ritualists must have over the centuries perfected the art of storing and hiding their ritual paraphernalia to prevent theft and confiscation attempts; and because their ritual space is flexible and protean the state cannot take it away from them. Many of the householder ritualists' prized possessions were destroyed during the "Smashing the Four Olds" campaign during the Cultural Revolution (see Dean, 1993, pp. 43–45), yet much have survived as well, thanks partly to the resilience and tactics of the countless different kinds of householder religious service providers. In the post-Mao era, many householder ritualists replenished any lost ritual manuals by borrowing and copying from others (this despite the traditional tendency to keep family manuals as well-guarded secrets). It is interesting to note that in the past decade or so the Daoist Association, working with the Religious Affairs Bureau, has attempted to register huoju priests (Dean, 2009; Lai Chi-Tim, 2003. To what extent this effort has been successful is unclear. One can guess that many if not most huoju Daoist priests would not choose to register for fear of official control and interference.

The tight control exerted by the party-state on institutionalized religions such as Buddhism and Daoism in today's China despite their legality shows the extreme vulnerability of the corporatist idiom. In a curious reversal of fortunes, during the reform era, it is the members of the official Daoist temples who are complaining about the lack of financial income, because they are under a lot of restrictions that prohibit them from conducting rituals outside of the temples (and there are fewer clients who would commission rituals to be conducted at the temples rather than at their own homes or villages). On the other hand, the dispersed householder priests in suburban and rural areas are enjoying a brisk business as never before. The officially affiliated priests (i.e. the big temple clerics) even make use of intermediaries to find ritual work outside of their temples to make money (D. Yang, 2005).

The discursive construction of the "superstition specialist households" (*mixin zhuanyehu*) during the reform era

In the past two decades or so the Chinese official media have often reported on the social ills posed by the many so-called "superstition specialist households" (*mixin zhuanyehu*) active in rural China. According to these media portrayals, these superstitious specialist households contribute to the re-surfacing of "feudal superstitious grime" (*fengjian mixin chenzha fanqi*), and that grassroots-level cadres and the Public Security Bureau should be vigilant and try to crack down on these undesirable elements.

By superstition specialist households the authorities seems to be referring to all kinds of people who make a living doing what are considered superstitious activities in the popular religious realm. These include fortune tellers, *fengshui* masters, spirit mediums, ritual healers, uncertified Daoist priests, folk musicians who play at weddings and funerals, story-tellers, opera singers and orchestra members of private folk opera troupes performing at temple festivals, makers of votive paper offerings, printers of hell bank notes, full-time temple caretakers, etc.[9] Many of these are precisely what I have labelled "household-based ritual service providers."

Continuing to use the label "superstition" to refer to the activities yinyang masters and spirit mediums are engaged in, the authorities may sound like they are reviving the virulent Maoist anti-superstition campaigns. However, except in a few locales where such anti-superstition attitudes are occasionally turned into concrete action (e.g. demolition of temples, banning of lavish funerals, leveling of conspicuously large graves on supposedly valuable farmland), most of the talks of cracking down on superstition remain at a rhetorical level. Most local cadres not only tolerate apparently superstitious activities but even encourage and participate actively in them (see Chau, 2006a). The central government has so far avoided using Maoist-era campaign-style strategies to deal with the "superstition boom."

Even though the term *mixin* (superstition), imported as a modern neologism from Japan, has been in use in China for a century by now, the term *zhuanyehu* (specialist household) seems to be a new, reform-era invention. After the long Maoist suppression of private businesses of all sorts (from 1950s to 1970s), privately owned and operated businesses finally came back in the 1970s and flourished thereafter, contributing significantly to China's dynamic economic growth in the past two decades or so. Most of these businesses are very small, family operations, continuing a long tradition in Chinese political economic history of what Hill Gates calls petty capitalist enterprises (Gates, 1996). Along with the slogan "To get rich is glorious," new terms such as *getihu* (private business households), *zhuanyehu*, *xiangzhen qiye* (village and township level enterprises), and *chengbao* (contract enterprises) came into vogue. The term *getihu* became especially ubiquitous. *Geti* (private, independent) is of course in contradistinction with *jiti* (collective), the latter referring to the Maoist collectivization of farming, industrial and other kinds of production, goods distribution and even consumption (e.g. in the extreme form of collective canteens during the Great Leap Forward). In the Maoist era, *geti* was considered petty bourgeois (*xiaozichanjieji*) or of peasant consciousness (*xiaonong xixiang*) and thus politically suspect; it smacked of selfishness and immorality while *jiti* connoted morality and revolutionary civic-mindedness. During the reform era, the overall socioeconomic atmosphere is a sea change from that of the Maoist era; now the most important and celebrated qualities in a person are self-initiative, a spirit of adventure and risk taking, flexibility (*linghuo*), a keen sense of market opportunities, sociability (including skills in banqueting and drinking – key to building and maintaining *guanxi* with business partners and political patrons), imagination, management and negotiation skills, personal flair and charisma, skills in talking and persuading, etc. These are necessary qualities for successful entrepreneurs. In addition to these qualities, one would be even more "of the reform spirit" if one specializes in a particular trade or profession, that is, if one becomes a "specialized household" (*zhuanyehu*). The term *zhuanye* connotes professional, expert, dedicated trade. The money-making, commercial aspect of these professionals is highlighted, so much so that ironically an even more professional (in the sense of full-time pursuit and professional accreditation), certified Daoist priest or Buddhist monk who draws a salary from the Daoist or Buddhist Association but does not sell his service for money would not even be included in this *zhuanyehu* category (the same goes for the Muslim *ahongs*, Protestant ministers and Catholic priests).

Though sardonic and condemning in tone, "superstition specialist household" as an appellation in fact willy-nilly puts the different kinds of religious service providers in the larger categories of *getihu* and *zhuanyehu* that are not only legitimate but even celebrated in reform-era China. Indeed, most of these religious service providers have the same qualities mentioned above that are crucial for successful entrepreneurs. However, curiously, the authorities continue to consider householder religious service providers as "people who gain without laboring" (*bulao erhuo zhe*). In the current political economic climate, to make money and get rich is glorious, but not if it is through mongering superstition or engaging in otherwise morally dubious activities (such as regularly selling one's blood for money), so the party-state argues.

An important fact to keep in mind about the category *zhuanyehu* is that even though the term *hu* refers to households, in reality it sometimes refers to an individual entrepreneur alone, not necessarily including his or her household members. The reason why the authorities still prefer to use the term household as a shorthand (i.e. a metaphor) reveals the extent to which the household idiom has become a hegemonic idiom in statist mentality, that is, the household being the state's most basic unit of engagement with society for as long as China has had a household registration system (*huji*).

Conclusions

The revival of household-based political economy and the cash nexus during the post-Mao reform era has provided the material and socio-structural basis for the revival of Chinese petty capitalism (Gates, 1996; also D. Yang, 2005) and its concomitant household-based petty religiosity. This has provided a fertile ground for the flourishing of householder religious service providers as well as household-based religious engagement. The vitality of the household idiom of religious engagement will probably persist for as long as the household remains the key structural component of the Chinese political economic, social and moral order.

Following from the above analyses, we can arrive at the following conclusions. *First*, religious practices in China do not constitute a discrete realm independent from the larger structures of society; rather, because of the diverse idioms of religious engagements at the individual, household and institutional levels, religion has a suffused presence in Chinese society (i.e. religion being thoroughly penetrated by societal forms and forces). Changes in the structural composition in the larger society will therefore have profound impacts on the ways in which people "do" religion, which means that analyses of religious change cannot avoid looking at larger societal transformations. *Second*, the impact of Chinese socialism on religion has issued far more from the ways in which it transformed the overall societal structures than from anti-religion policies. Since the household is such a central idiom in religious engagement in Chinese religious culture and Chinese socialism has had such an immense impact on the nature and make-up of the household, it is imperative that we examine closely how such transformations of the household have brought about transformations in the ways in which people "do religion."

Notes

1. Elsewhere I have developed a schema of five "modalities of doing religion" that I believe can help us better understand how people do religion in China and in other contexts (see Chau, 2006a; 2009; 2011b).
2. I have drawn inspirations for this approach from the works of scholars like Hill Gates (e.g. Gates, 1996) and Robert Weller (e.g. Weller, 2000), who have

both looked at the intimate links between religious conceptions and practices and larger societal forces.
3. This also contrast sharply with the usual mode of religious engagement in Christianity, where individual worshippers constitute a congregation that supports collectively a priest or equivalent, and where the believers engage with God, at least in theory, as individuals.
4. Incidentally, the resistance to the radical terms of the Marriage Law of the same period has to be seen in the context of this sudden emergence of socialist middle peasant patriarchy.
5. Not to mention the fact that as all resources were centrally planned and their uses and distribution were centrally conceived and coordinated, there was simply no room for local communities or individual households to marshal any significant amount of material resources for religious practices (which in China traditionally meant the intense amassing of a large amount of stuff, especially food items but also alcohol, tobacco, incense, spirit money and firecrackers).
6. It is true that the Chinese Communist regime was hostile to religion *tout court*, but one can say that it was never against religion as a spiritual force; instead, its anti-religion policies relied on a political economic theory of religion.
7. One may object to calling opera singers, story-tellers, folk musicians and mural painters "religious specialists," though they might warrant such an appellation because traditionally the themes of their art were very much related to popular religion.
8. Most of them probably never "chose" the household idiom because it was simply the only idiom available to them.
9. Other terms for these people include *mixin zhiyezhe* (superstition professionals) and *mixin zhiye fenzi* (superstition professional elements).

13
Awkward Secularity between Atheism and New Religiosity in Post-Soviet Kyrgyzstan

Mathijs Pelkmans

Introduction

The term "chaos" has the dubious honor of being one of the terms that has been used most frequently to characterize the post-Soviet condition of the 1990s, both by those who lived through the period and by those who observed and wrote about it (e.g. Manning, 2007; Nazpary, 2002; Pelkmans, 2012). In the post-Soviet Central Asian republic of Kyrgyzstan, where I have carried out several research projects over the past 15 years, the locally preferred term was *bardak*, which the dictionary translates as chaos but also as brothel, thus nicely allowing moral judgment to be woven into expressions of frustration. When people used the term chaos they were often talking about post-Soviet conditions: the declining standards of living, the deteriorating infrastructure, the privatization of law, and the monetization of patronage networks, or *blat* (cf. Ledeneva, 1998). But apart from highlighting existential uncertainties and dissatisfactions, the term also pinpointed epistemological conundrums. The official truths that together represented "communist ideology" had lost their institutional backing and were challenged by new sets of ideas. In order to illustrate the destabilizing character of this process let me cite from a conversation in the late 1990s with a befriended academic and former communist party member, someone who presented himself as being "not religious." The previous day he had watched, on his regular TV channel, a US-produced documentary demoting evolutionary theory. The documentary had presented scientific evidence stating that the world could only be several thousand years old, and used this to uphold the strength of intelligent-design theory. "It is amazing," he told me, "all those years I had assumed that evolution was a fact, but now it turns out that it was just atheist propaganda." What interested me in this incident were not the specific strengths or weaknesses of either theory, but rather the reclassification of the "fact" of evolution into Soviet "propaganda" precisely because it happened in such an ad hoc manner. It illustrated that because *all* previously acquired knowledge had potentially been propaganda (in the sense of having *deliberately* been distorted), knowledge itself had become tremendously unstable.

The quotation also raised several other sets of questions. First, what happened to atheism? Did atheism really simply evaporate? Or was the "fact" of evolution (and more broadly scientific atheism) perhaps never completely accepted as factual? This question refers to the complex issue of how deeply atheist ideology had been able to penetrate the minds of Soviet citizens. In other words, if we can speak of "evaporation" at all, what is it that evaporated? This set of questions requires engagement both with the reality of "actually existing atheism" and with its legacy in the 1990s and beyond. These issues are important, first because the "secularity" of Soviet society continues to be subject of debate, and secondly because of the tendency to brush the legacy of atheism aside. Ironically, this last point becomes clear when looking at the books and articles that carry atheism in their title and deal with the post-socialist world. In those cases the title is never in the format *"Atheism After...,"* but always in the format *"After Atheism."* So we have David Lewis's (2000) *After Atheism: Religion and Ethnicity in Russia and Central Asia*, Paul Froese's (2004) "After Atheism: An analysis of Religious Monopolies in the Post-communist World," or for example Sergei Filatov's (2008) "Orthodoxy in Russia: Post-atheist Faith." This tendency may be justified if "atheism" is meant to refer to the Soviet state project, to the institutionalized ideology with its own clergy, publications, and links to other state agencies; that part of "atheism" did indeed disappear, even if not completely.[1] But all too often this tendency has also implied that other aspects and meanings of atheism are either overlooked or supposed to have evaporated as well: atheism as the absence of belief in God, or more actively as the denial of God. Renewed attention is warranted to both the legacies of the atheist project, and to the continuing existence of unbelief.

A second set of questions emerges from this discussion, namely how the distinction between the religious and the secular should be understood. In more empirical terms, how are the secular and the religious imagined and defined in an environment that some have characterized as "post-post-religious" (Peel, 2009)? Problematically, though, the term secular does not have a direct translation in Russian, the lingua franca of the region (neither does it have a direct translation in Kyrgyz). The Russian term that most closely approximates "secular" is *svetskii* or "worldly," but I have only heard Orthodox Christian Clergy and Protestant "believers" use the term, which limits its usefulness. Instead of "worldly" I would suggest that the most relevant translation of "secularism" in relation to Soviet Central Asia would be "socialism," but to get to that point we need to start with another term: atheism. The term atheism offers a direct contrast with religion, and it continues to be used by citizens attempting to clarify their stance towards past and present ideologies. The following two quotations are taken from conversations in 2003 and 2004 with people in Kok-Jangak, a small town in Southern Kyrgyzstan. The contradictions in these statements are particularly insightful.

1. The first quotation is from a conversation with the local imam, whom I asked why so few middle-aged men attended the Friday prayers: "The problem is that they [men between 40 and 60 years old] still have an atheist worldview." He added that it was basically hopeless to argue with these men, because they refused to accept the truth.
2. These same middle-aged men sometimes agreed with such assessments, and it was not uncommon that they positively referred to themselves as "the last Soviet generation." However, this did not mean that they also considered themselves unbelievers, or as one man told me: "We just *pretended* to be atheists, but in our hearts we always believed".
3. Sometimes the previous two contrasting views merged, such as in the following statement by a middle-aged Kyrgyz woman in a neighboring town: "Look, we are atheists, but of course we all believe in God." She later elaborated: "We are atheists. Yes, we are Muslims but let me explain. We are all Muslim people – Kazaks, Kyrgyz, Uzbeks, Turkmen, Tajiks. We were born Muslims. That's it." (quoted in McBrien and Pelkmans, 2008)

Although the idea of an Atheist Believer, or an Atheist Muslim, might appear as a contradiction in terms, in fact it straightforwardly conveys an attempt to position oneself at some distance from both the Soviet antireligious stance and the definitions of Islam advanced by piety movements that were becoming increasingly influential in the early 2000s. The awkward juxtaposition of the categories "atheist" and "believer" also highlights that these categories have unstable meanings. This instability is at least partly caused by the fact that the men and women cited above were simultaneously responding to Soviet and post-Soviet frames of reference. In the following I will discuss the awkward position of those who find themselves in between atheism and religiosity and illuminate how this position relates to shifting frames of reference.

Soviet atheism and the secular

The topic of Soviet atheism and its relation to the secular is so huge such as to require book-length discussions (such as Luehrmann, 2009). Here I only aim to coin in a few thoughts. I start with a short discussion of two books on religion and atheism in Kyrgyzstan, both of which were published in the early 1990s, and which show remarkable congruence *and* divergence.

In 1991, before August of that memorable year,[2] Abdyldaev, a Kyrgyz philosopher and scholar of atheism, published his *From the History of Religion and Atheism in Kyrgyzstan* (in Russian). The book contains a detailed history of the successes of the anti-religious struggle, as well as the various obstacles that had to be overcome. His tone is often jubilant, and towards the end of his book he writes that "at present we have an entire battery of functioning people's universities of atheism" (1991, p. 110), delivering graduates, *propogandisty–ateisty*, who are prolific in their activities. For example, the 90 atheist teachers in one province of Kyrgyzstan gave a total of 2,221 lectures on atheism in the year 1986–1987 (1991, pp. 116–117). He acknowledges that the atheist project is by no means completed, and lists the familiar problems such as the use of crude and offensive techniques (1991, p. 109; see also Ro'i, 1984, p. 31). But he envisions a bright future in which religion will have withered away, and he proposes that this goal will be faster reached if atheist activists engage more seriously with the philosophical basis of their project and proceed in non-confronting manners, for example by promoting non-religious rituals (1991, pp. 126–127).

Only two years later in 1993, another Kyrgyz scholar, Anara Tabyshalieva published *Belief in Turkestan: Essays on the History of Religion of Central Asia and Kazakhstan* (in Russian). The book traces the history of various religious traditions, and has a chapter titled "Soviet times." In it she argues that "secularization was realized in almost intractable ways, it progressed in bits and pieces, and always had a 'shock' character" (1993, p. 108). She mentions the closure of mosques and churches, the change of alphabet, the *hujum* or unveiling campaigns, and the Terror of the 1930s when believers were equated with Trotskyites and imperialist spies (1993, pp. 112–115) as aspects of this long and erratic struggle against religion. While Abdyldaev focuses on the anti-religious efforts, Tabyshalieva writes more about the effects, and especially the failure to inculcate atheist worldviews. For example, she discusses the paradox that cheap literature on atheism often functioned to trigger interest in religion (1993, p. 116; see also Exnerova, 2006, p. 106; Kendzior, 2006), and the cynical question that emerged in the minds of the enlightened intelligentsia: "did we have the pure atheism or did we perhaps [only] get its imitation?" (1993, p. 121). Tabyshalieva concludes her chapter by stating that "the renaissance of religiosity turned out to be the unexpected answer to the long and indifferent domination of atheism, to the social disruption and economic disappointments that were chaotically produced, and most importantly to the loss of belief in a communist or a socialist future" (1993, p. 122).

These two texts could hardly be at once more similar and more different. They largely converge in their assessment of how the atheist project progressed – checkered, that is – and in its limitations. However, the normative evaluation of this project and the projections into the future could hardly be different: the expectation that ultimately the atheist project would succeed, versus the view that atheism was a thing of the past, taken over by new religiosity. Tabyshalieva's text, appearing only two years after the collapse of the Soviet Union, is an early example of how the atheist project started to be bracketed off, as part of what Verdery has called an "orgy of historical revisionism" (1999, p. 112). In subsequently locally published books on religion there is not even space for the Soviet atheist project, authors instead quickly jumping from pre-Soviet to post-Soviet times (see for example Chotaeva, 2004). This may be partly because "the new thing" always seems more relevant, but is also informed by the need to overcome the Soviet period and the related argument that because the atheist project had failed it was no longer relevant. However, instead of allowing ourselves to be restricted by the misleading – because too simplistic – question of success versus failure, we may more fruitfully focus on what the atheist project actually produced.

This brings us to the topic of Soviet secularism. Atheism and secularism should certainly not be conflated, and many scholars have argued that the Soviet atheist project failed to produce a secular society, for at least three reasons: (1) Soviet society was not secular because communism was a religion in and of itself; (2) Soviet society was not secular because it did not have a public sphere that allowed for open communication, while the private sphere was itself politicized, thus making it impossible to speak of the privatization of religion; (3) Soviet society was not secular because its citizens didn't accept atheism. Sonja Luehrmann has extensively, and critically, discussed these arguments in her PhD dissertation (2009), and I will therefore keep my discussion limited. She shows that the arguments suffer from a problematic equation of secularism with liberalism, and convincingly suggests that a state-directed, politically charged environment can still produce forms of secularism as "a view of exclusively contemporary human sociality" (2009, p. 15). However, point 3 about the extent to which Soviet citizens internalized atheist messages remains unresolved. Luehrmann focuses on didacticism, and shows how the atheist teachers themselves acquired didactic skills and appropriated parts of the atheist message. Left unexplored in her discussion, however, is how people who were neither active as atheist teachers nor actively involved in religious communities of various kinds engaged with and were affected by atheist ideology.

Referring back to the quoted statements about atheism, I think that the men's insistence that they had never embraced "atheism" should be taken seriously, but so should the imam's suggestion that these same men displayed an "atheist worldview" (if we don't interpret atheism too literally, that is). The issue is not to decide whether or not atheist messages were accepted or rejected, but to understand how the Soviet project (of which atheist messages were a part) affected people's understanding of, and disposition towards, what became seen as "religion."

The point about never having embraced atheism refers to the frustrated attempts of Soviet authorities not only to combat religion, but to identify it in the first place. Although during the 1930s and 1950s, in particular, the Soviet regime waged extensive anti-religious campaigns in which religious leaders were prosecuted and most mosques and madrasahs were shut down, it was far less successful in eradicating many aspects of religious expression and identity that were part of everyday life. In fact, even while the Soviet regime successfully combated certain public manifestations of religion, it ironically also encoded religious identities through its nationality politics. As Karpat has shown for Soviet Central Asia more generally, the appeal of newly created national categories derived (in part) from "the incorporation of many elements of the religious culture in the emerging 'national' cultures [which gave] the adherents of the latter a sense of the historical continuity, strength, and durability of their cultures" (1993, p. 416). Vice-versa, the incorporation of religious elements in conceptualizations of ethnicity, nationality, and culture also enshrined the position of Islam. As Shahrani writes in an article on identity dynamics in Central Asia: "The modern concept

250 *Mathjis Pelkmans*

of nationalities has provided 'legitimate' basis through which some of the most critical traditional notions of Muslim Turkestani identities and loyalties are communicated, and in which traditional values are reinvested" (1984, p. 35, emphasis original).[3] By the end of the Soviet period, national identity was intimately tied to Muslimness, but a Muslimness which had been stripped of much of its "spiritual" content and could thusly be made compatible with Soviet ideals (Shahrani, 1995). Conversely, the processes allowed for an environment where self-avowed atheists could actively claim to be Muslims.

The contradicting point, about the men nevertheless displaying an "atheist worldview," is equally important. I will offer some examples from the same middle-aged men that I already talked about. At some point we were discussing their views of the local "unregistered Baptist" community. The Soviet media, school teachers, and other official communications had always portrayed these Baptists in an extremely negative light, using the derisive terms *sekt* (sect) and *fanatiki* (fanatics). Talking about this, Nurbek, one of my acquaintances remarked: "I never believed the stories that the Baptists would sacrifice one of their children on a special holiday and would then eat the child, I never believed that. But I did believe in the stories that once a year they would retreat and partake in a secret sexual orgy." The anecdote was intentionally humorous, but also indicated that Nurbek used to perceive forms of self-avowed religiousness as being out of the ordinary – intriguing, abnormal – and moreover that he had internalized those aspects of anti-religious propaganda that were in line with already held desires, fears, or ideas.

Equally telling is that, apart from exotic stories and fantasies about "sects" and "fanatics," religion rarely came up as a significant topic when these men talked about their lives during the Soviet period. They recounted their school years, their first loves, their period in the army, and their jobs in the coalmine. All these were meaningful experiences, but religion was absent from them. Indeed, during my first extensive stays in Kyrgyzstan (in 1995 and 1998–1999) I hardly ever had conversations about religion, or encounters in which Islam was more than "a part of our culture." Gardaz's (1999) description of an "ice-cold atheist wind blowing through Kyrgyzstan" is a cheap caricature, but nevertheless underscores that in the 1990s "religion" was not an important issue for many urbanites. The oxymoron of "atheist believers" which I coined in the introduction of this chapter bespeaks the fruitlessness of trying to decide whether the "atheist" project was or wasn't accepted, because it was simultaneously accepted and rejected.

Post-Soviet challenges

Whether or not Kyrgyz citizens accepted atheist messages, their ideas about what it meant to be Muslim were formed in dialogue with anti-religious discourses and policies. These ideas lost their accepted meaning in the 1990s. In this section I will first discuss how the position of people who present themselves as "not religious" is being challenged, and then move to a discussion of how these same people respond to the new assertions of religiosity that have become increasingly visible in Kyrgyzstan over the last decade.

* * *

The first challenge that the "not religious" faced was that after the 1990s their conduct was no longer always sufficient to qualify as a Muslim. During Soviet times it had been sine qua non that Kyrgyz men would drink vodka; alcohol consumption was intertwined with ideas of masculinity and an important ingredient in assertions of hospitality. Although most men continued these practices, they were increasingly criticized for doing so. Similarly, if during the Soviet period it was assumed that only the very old would pray (and rarely in a mosque), this too changed. I already mentioned that the imam of Kok-Jangak tried to convince middle-aged men to pray, but they turned out to be insensitive to his arguments. As the imam told me: "they always have excuses, and they always think that they know it better, telling me that the Kyrgyz had never prayed in mosques. But this is not about being Kyrgyz, this is about Islam. Islam is one and Kyrgyz is another."

The imam was not the only one who attempted to disentangle religion and culture, and thus to undo a connection that had been reinforced under Soviet rule. Local Tablighi circles became increasingly active in the 2000s.[4] They not only invited inhabitants to start praying, but also addressed false conceptions of Islam in their teachings and criticized for example funerals and weddings, which were deemed un-Islamic. Moreover, newly pious Muslims started to transform life-cycle rituals into "religiously pure" events. For example, by abolishing "traditional" wedding parties, prohibiting serving alcohol, reinforcing gender segregation, and inviting wedding speakers, these newly pious Muslims challenged the formerly agreed upon notions of what was Islamic and what was not (McBrien, 2006). Specifically, they disconnected being Muslim from being Kyrgyz, stressing the supranational character of Islam rather than its relation to culture and national identity. But although in some locations in Southern Kyrgyzstan such newly pious assertions made significant headway, in Kok-Jangak this was hardly the case. Local residents explained this by referring to the town's history as a mining-town – a former beacon of socialist modernity – and that therefore the mindset of its inhabitants was more "cultured" and modern. For example, they pointed out that whereas they had been to "Islamic" funerals in other settlements, in Kok-Jangak such funerals had taken place only a couple of times, and these had been talked badly about.

* * *

One important legacy of "atheism" is that it provided citizens with a vocabulary to respond to religious authorities. My acquaintances drew on a repertoire of received wisdom, much of which had its roots in Soviet times. Kadyr, for example, would repeatedly tell me the Kyrgyz saying that "one should listen to what the mullah says, but not do as he does" as a way to underline that a lot of this self-avowed religiosity was simple pretense. At other times he would point at one of the first post-Soviet imams, who had received money to build a mosque, but instead used it to furnish his own house.

Kadyr also continued to find value in controlling religion and lamented the idea of freedom of religion. "Maybe such freedom is a good thing in Western Europe, but here it is dangerous, our people are not suited for it. Look at Uzbekistan. If Karimov [the president] did not repress the fanatics, we would have an Islamic state as a neighbour within no time. Maybe here [in Kyrgyzstan] it is a bit better, because our people are less fanatic than Uzbeks...but still..." He continued by criticizing the presence of a small group of Tablighis in town, asserting that "they don't work and they can only think about religion – they always tell you the same thing. For us [at this point his wife had joined him, and she agreed with the following point] this is just really revolting (*protivnyi*)". The problem flared up when two of their children started to display interest in Islam. Their two sons (twins of 10 years old) had secretly joined some neighborhood kids to the meetings organized by Tablighis at the local mosque. When Kadyr found out about this he gave his sons a lecture, but knowing that this might not be enough (at least for the twin who was most intrigued) he made sure to keep his sons busy with tasks when the Tablighi meetings were taking place.

Inhabitants like Kadyr who saw themselves as "not religious" were clearly disturbed by the new assertions of devotion. In conversation they would often express opinions similar to those of Kadyr, and stereotype the Tablighis, along with other new religious groups such as Pentecostals, as zombies, fanatics, and extremists. It was also clear that the encounters with the imam and with Tablighis were discomforting precisely because "the truth" had become unstable. With anti-religious discourse having lost the institutional backing it enjoyed during Soviet times, attempts to discredit the authoritative basis of newly active religious movements had become even more critical. For example, "not religious" inhabitants insisted that leaders of new religious movements used brainwashing techniques and offered payments to attract followers (see also McBrien and Pelkmans, 2008). The anxieties and tensions expressed by the "not religious" are reflective of the larger cosmological shifts that accompany dramatic changes in constellations of power and state ideology.

Final reflections

How does the history and legacy of state-atheism in the Central Asia contribute to the discussion of religious-secular distinctions and the way that citizens position themselves in relation to those distinctions? In this chapter I focused on citizens who define themselves as "not religious" Muslims. These citizens on the one hand denounced Soviet atheism, but this was accompanied by a fear of what was seen as excessive religiosity, something which they identified in many of the "new" religious currents that gained ground in the country since the late 1990s. These criticisms of excessive religiosity inadvertently linked back to atheist ideology. In a previous publication (McBrien and Pelkmans, 2008) I used an example that I still find very telling. In 2002 Kyrgyzstan's daily newspaper *Vechernyi Bishkek* published a series of articles on the presumed detrimental effects of both Christian and Muslim "extremism." One of these articles incorrectly cited Marx: "Karl Marx was right after all when he announced: 'Religion is the opium of the people! Sweet, intoxicating, and mysterious. In small quantities it is medicine. In large quantities it is poison'." Clearly the newspaper viewed the success of new Christian and Muslim movements as an undesirable and dangerous development, one that poisoned the youth and turned them into spiritual drug-addicts. Marx of course never made the qualifying statements that when taken in small quantities religion can be a medicine. On the contrary, he criticized the soothing quality of institutionalized religion, that is, the small dose, while acknowledging the transformative potential of Luther's reformation.[5] Oblivious to such nuances, the newspaper twisted Marx through their drug metaphor in order to defend what was called "folk" or "liberal" Islam, while depicting the new religious movements as dangerous and detrimental. And instead of being atheist revolutionaries of which Marx would have approved, these new "post-atheist" self-proclaimed heirs of Marx simply aimed to retain the religious status quo in which religious and ethnic categories were tightly entwined. This example, in addition to the ones presented earlier in this paper, show the difficulty of finding a balance between Soviet and newly pious understandings of religion.

The denouncement of what are seen as extreme forms of Islam and Christianity are stark instances of the need to distance oneself from the new religiosity. But what about the relation with atheism? A seemingly innocent joke, which has travelled across the former Soviet Union, may be insightful. It is about a young anti-religious teacher who is sent to the mountains to lecture the herdsmen about evolution. When the teacher has finished his lecture in which he had explained that our human forefathers descended from apes, one of the older herders raises his voice: "This is all very well, and I am willing to accept that *your* forefathers were apes, as long as it is clear that *mine* were decidedly human." The anecdote may be interpreted as ridiculing the atheist perspective and conveys the message that the atheist project failed to convince down-to-earth citizens. However, the anecdote may also be interpreted as ridiculing the old man as a remnant of an outdated worldview. Uncertainty remains about what is true, about what is fact and what is propaganda. I hope to have made clear that the legacy of the atheist project, and the continued existence of unbelief, if not militant disbelief, should not be brushed under the table. Those who are "not religious" continue to struggle to find a position between these two extremes.

Notes

1. For example, the "Councils for Religious Affairs" that were created in 1965 have their contemporary successors in many of the post-Soviet Republics, such as the Kyrgyz "State committee for religious affairs."
2. Judging from the book's final paragraph, the manuscript must have gone to press not long after October 9, 1990, when *Pravda* published the new law "About freedom of consciousness and religious organization." Abdyldaev mentions that although this law may change the relationship with some facets of atheism, it was decided to publish the manuscript in its then-existing form.
3. Soviet authorities bemoaned this intertwining of religious and national affiliation, as in the following quote from the *obkom* secretary of Osh province (*oblast*) in Southern Kyrgyzstan: "some people suggest that a person who observes Islamic rites, demonstrates thereby 'respect' for his nation, and in deviating from them insults it" (cited in Ro'i, 1984, p. 36).

4. Tablighi refers to the Tablighi Jamaat, a conservative Islamic piety movement which has its origins in 1920s India, and has been active in Kyrgyzstan since the early 1990s (see also Ismailbekova and Nasritdinov, 2012).
5. Although admiring the revolutionary power of Luther's reformation, Marx retained his ambivalence as reflected in his statement, "if Protestantism was not the true solution it was at least the true setting of the problem" (Marx, 1844 [1975], p. 182).

References

Abdyldaev, M. (1991) *Iz istorii religii i ateizma v Kyrgyzstane*. Bishkek: Ilim.
Agursky M. (1975) "Neonatsistskaia opasnost' v Sovetskom Soiuze," *Novyi Zhurnal* (New York) 118: 205–218.
Aikman, David (2003) *Jesus in Beijing: How Christianity Is Transforming China and Changing the Global Balance of Power*. Washington, DC: Regnery.
Al-Azmeh, Aziz (1993) *Islams and Modernities*. London: Verso.
Aleksandrov E. B., V. L. Ginsburg, E. P. Krugliakov, and V. E. Fortov (2003) "Akademiki protestuiut protiv zasilia lzhenauki v rossiiskoi armii." *Izvestiia*, October 14, 2003, http://www.inauka.ru/false/article36533. Accessed in November 2004.
Aleksandrova, Antonina (1972) *Priglashaem k razgovoru*, March 24, 1972 (Mari Republican Radio Sound Archives, Ioshkar-Ola, tape no. 809.
Alexander, John T. (1989) *Catherine the Great: Life and Legend*. New York and Oxford: Oxford University Press.
Anderson, Benedict (1983) *Imagined Communities: Reflections on the Origin and Spread of Nationalism*. London: Verso.
Anon. (1971) "A Word to the Nation." *Survey* 17.3: 191–199.
Anon. (1975) "Kriticheskie zametki russkogo cheloveka o patrioticheskom zhurnale 'Veche.'" In M. Agursky ed., *Neonatsistskaia opasnost' v Sovetskom Soiuze*. pp. 219–227.
Anon. (1981) "Slovo natsii." *Veche* 3: 106–131.
Anon. (2005) "Hujinto zongshuji guanyu gojian shehuizhuyi hexieshehui de youguan lunshu" 胡锦涛总书记关于构建社会主义和谐社会的有关论述, *Dangjian* 党建 3–4: 5–10.
Antonov O. (1998) "Vooruzhennye nechistye sily – 3." *Novaia gazeta*, November 30 –December 6, 1998: 15.
Antonova, Clemena (2010a) *Space, Time, and Presence in the Icon: Seeing the World with the Eyes of God*. Farnham: Ashgate Publishers.
—— (2010b) "Changing Perceptions of Pavel Florensky in Russian and Soviet Scholarship," especially section "Intellectual Biography." In O. Sergei and B. Costica eds, *In Marx's Shadow: Knowledge, Power, and Intellectuals in Eastern Europe and Russia*. Lanham: Lexington Books, pp. 73–95.
Appadurai, Arjun (2004) "The Capacity to Aspire: Culture and the Terms of Recognition." In V. Rao and M. Walton eds, *Culture and Public Action*. Stanford: Stanford University Press, pp. 59–84.
Apter, David E. and Tony Saich (1995) *Revolutionary Discourse in Mao's Republic*. Cambridge, MA: Harvard University Press.
Armstrong, Charles K. (1995) "Centering the Periphery: Manchurian Exile(s) and the North Korean State," *Korean Studies* 19: 1–16.
—— (2003) *The North Korean Revolution, 1945–1950*. Ithaca, NY: Cornell University Press.
Asad, Talal (1993) *Genealogies of Religion: Discipline and Reasons of Power in Christianity and Islam*. Baltimore: Johns Hopkins University Press.

References

——— (2003) *Formations of the Secular: Christianity, Islam, Modernity*. Stanford: Stanford University Press.
Ashiwa, Yoshiko and David L. Wank (2009a) "Making Religion, Making the State in Modern China: An Introductory Essay." In Y. Ashiwa and David L. Wank eds, *Making Religion, Making the State: The Politics of Religion in Modern China*. Stanford: Stanford University Press, pp. 1–21.
Ashiwa, Yoshiko and David. L. Wank (2009b) (eds) *Making Religion, Making the State: The Politics of Religion in Modern China*. Stanford: Stanford University Press.
Askins, Kye and Rachel Pain (2011) "Contact Zones: Participation, Materiality, and the Messiness of Interaction," *Environment and Planning D: Society and Space* 29: 803–821.
Azadovski, Konstantin (1995) "Russia's Silver Age, Yesterday and Today: Questions in the Void." In Heyward Isham ed., *Remaking Russia: Voices from Within*. Prague: Institute for EastWest Studies and London: M. E. Sharpe, pp. 79–90.
Azimov, P. (1962) "Prazdnik radostiu dorog." *Izvestiia*, August 24: 3.
Badone, Ellen (1990) (ed.) *Religious Orthodoxy and Popular Faith in European Society*. Princeton: Princeton University Press.
Baidu.com "What Is the Content of Mike Wallace's Interview with Deng Xiaoping?" www.zhidao.baidu.com. Accessed in January 2014.
Balashov, D. (1965) "Traditsionnoe i sovremennoe." *Nauka i religiia* 12: 26–30.
Bays, D. (2003) "Chinese Protestant Christianity Today." *The China Quarterly* 174: 488–504.
Beliakova, N. E. (1994) "Uroki drevnerusskogo. Vseiasvetnaia gramota: 1000 let zabveniia." *Za russkoe delo* 2: 2–3; 3: 3; 4: 3; 5: 2.
Bender, Ryszard (1992) "Pierwsza wojna światowa i Polska niepodległa." In J. Kłoczowski ed., *Chrześcijaństwo w Polsce. Zarys przemian 1966–1979*. Lublin: Towarzystwo Naukowe Katolickiego Uniwersytetu Lubelskiego, pp. 507–552.
Benn, David Wedgwood (1989) *Persuasion and Soviet Politics*. Oxford: Basil Blackwell.
Benovska-Sabkova, Milena (2010) "Strategies of the Russian Orthodox Church in the Context of the Religious Revival in Russia." In Chris Hann ed., *Religion, Identity, Postsocialism*. Halle: Max Planck Institute, pp. 95–98.
Berdyaev, Nicholas (1932) *The Russian Revolution: Two Essays on Its Implications in Religion and Psychology*. London: Sheed & Ward.
Bergesen, Albert James (1978) "A Durkheimian Theory of 'Witch-Hunts' with the Chinese Cultural Revolution of 1966–1969 as an Example," *Journal for the Scientific Study of Religion* 17.1: 19–29.
Berki, R. N. (1983) *Insight and Vision: The Problem of Communism in Marx's Thought*. London: J. M. Dent.
Bhargava, Rajeev (2010) *The Promise of India's Secular Democracy*. Delhi: Oxford University Press.
Billioud, Sébastien (2007) "Confucianism, 'Cultural Tradition,' and Official Discourse in China at the Start of the New Century," *China Perspectives* 3: 50–65.
Billioud, Sébastien and Joël Thoraval (2009) "Lijiao: The Return of Ceremonies Honouring Confucius in Mainland China: The Contemporary Revival of Confucianism," *China Perspectives* 4: 82–100.
Bizot, François (2000) "La place des communautés du Nord-Laos dans l'histoire du bouddhisme d'Asie du Sud-Est," *Bulletin de l'Ecole française d'Extrême-Orient*, Tome 87.

Bjork, James (2010) "Bulwark or Patchwork?: Religious Exceptionalism and Regional Diversity in Postwar Poland." In Bruce R. Berglund ed., *Christianity and Modernity in Eastern Europe*. Budapest: Central European University Press, pp. 129–158.

Blagov, Sergei (1996) *The Cao Dai and Hoa Hao in Vietnam*. Unpublished MS., 1996.

Bocheński, Józef Maria (1932) "Problem katolicyzmu w Polsce." *Droga* 9, pp. 771–785.

Bondarenko, V. (2002) "'Russkii Orden' v TsK partii: mify i real'nost'. Beseda s predsedatelem Soiuza pisatelei Rossii Valeriem Ganichevym." *Russkoe voskresenie*, July 2002, http://www.voskres.ru/articles/rusorden.htm. Accessed in December 2011.

Bong Souvannavong (1960) *Doctrine Lao ou Socialisme Dhammique (Sangkhom Dhammadhipatai) pour le instauration de la Paix*. Genéve (Suisse): Imprimerie Atar.

Borisenko, N. (1996) "Religioznost' molodezhi." In: *Fenomen provintsii. Problemy intelligentsii*. Tambov. Vyp. 4. pp. 126–129.

Boudarel, Georges (1991) "L'insertion du pouvoir central dans les cultes villageois au Vietnam." In Alain Forest et al. eds, *Cultes Populaires et Societes Asiatiques*. Paris: L'Harmattan, pp. 87–146.

Bourdeaux, Michael (1991) *The Gospel's Triumph over Communism*. Minneapolis: Bethany House.

—— (1992) *The Role of Religion in the Fall of the Soviet System*. London: Centre for Policy Studies.

—— (1995a) "Introduction." In M. Bourdeaux ed., *The Politics of Religion in Russia and the New States of Europe*. New York and London: M. E. Sharpe, pp. 3–12.

—— (1995b) "Glasnost and the Gospel: The Emergence of Religious Pluralism." In M. Bourdeaux ed., *The Politics of Religion in Russia and the New States of Europe*. New York and London: M. E. Sharpe, pp. 113–128.

—— (1995c) (ed.) *The Politics of Religion in Russia and the New States of Europe*. New York and London: M. E. Sharpe.

Bourdieu, P. (1977) *Outline of a Theory of Practice*. Cambridge: Cambridge University Press.

Bourdieu, P. and Wacquant, L. (1992) *An Invitation to Reflexive Sociology*. Cambridge: Polity.

Bouté, Vanina (2008) "Cultes aux Espirits et Boudhisme chez les Phounoy du Nord-Laos." In Yves Goudineau and Michel Lorrillard ed., *Recherches Nouvelles sur le Laos*. Vientiane-Paris: École française d'Extrême-Orient, pp. 579–595.

Bowlt, John (1978) "Russian Sculpture and Lenin's Plan for Monumental Propaganda." In Henry Millon and Linda Nochlin eds, *Art and Architecture in the Service of Politics*. Cambridge, MA: MIT Press, pp. 182–194.

Bradley, Mark P. (2000) *Imagining Vietnam and America: The Making of Postcolonial Vietnam, 1919–1950*. Chapel Hill, NC: University of North Carolina Press.

Breslauer, George (1982) *Khrushchev and Brezhnev as Leaders: Building Authority in Soviet Politics*. London: George Allen & Unwin.

Brettell, Caroline (1990) "The Priest and His People: The Contractual Basis for Religious Practice in Rural Portugal." In Ellen Badone ed., *Religious Orthodoxy and Popular Faith in European Society*. Princeton: Princeton University Press, pp. 55–75.

Brown, Arthur Judson (1904) *New Forces in Old China: An Unwelcome but Inevitable Awakening*. New York: Fleming H. Revell Company.
Brown, Callum (2009) *The Death of Christian Britain: Understanding Secularization, 1800–2000*. Second edition. London: Routledge.
Brown, MacAlister and Joseph J. Zasloff (1986) *Apprentice Revolutionaries: The Communist Movement in Laos, 1930–1985*. Stanford, CA: Hoover Institution Press.
Bruce, Steve (2002) *God Is Dead: Secularization in the West*. Oxford: Blackwell.
Brudny, V. I. (1968) *Obriady vchera i segodnia*. Moscow: Nauka.
Buchowski, Michał (2001) "Communism and Religion: A War of Two Worldview Systems." In Iva Doležalova, Luther H. Martin, and Dalibor Papoušek eds, *The Academic Study of Religion During the Cold War. East and West*. New York: Peter Lang Publishing, pp. 39–57.
Burdziej, Stanisław (2005) "Religion and Politics: Religious Values in the Polish Public Square since 1989," *Religion, State & Society* 33.2: 165–174.
Buswell Jr., Robert E., and Timothy S. Lee (2006) (eds) *Christianity in Korea*. Honolulu: University of Hawaii Press.
Bychkov, Victor (1993) *The Aesthetic Face of Being: Art in the Theology of Pavel Florensky*. Crestwood, New York: St. Vladimir's Seminary Press.
Cai, Yongshun (2004) "Irresponsible State: Local Cadres and Image Building in China," *Journal of Communist Studies and Transition Politics* 20.4: 20–41.
Calhoun, Craig, Mark Juergensmeyer and Jonathan van Antwerpen (2011a) (eds) *Rethinking Secularism*. Oxford: Oxford University Press.
——— (2011b) "Introduction." In Craig Calhoun, Mark Juergensmeyer and Jonathan van Antwerpen eds, *Rethinking Secularism*. Oxford: Oxford University Press, pp. 3–30.
Cao, Nanlai (2011) *Constructing China's Jerusalem: Christians, Power, and Place in Contemporary Wenzhou*. Stanford: Stanford University Press.
Casanova, Jose (1994) *Public Religions in the Modern World*. Chicago: University of Chicago Press.
——— (2001) "Civil Society and Religion: Retrospective Reflections on Catholicism and Prospective Reflections on Islam," *Social Research* 68.4: 1041–1080.
——— (2009) "The Secular and Secularisms," *Social Research* 76.4: 1049–1066.
Chaplin, Vsevolod (1995) "Church and Politics in Contemporary Russia." In Michael Bourdeaux ed., *The Politics of Religion in Russia and the New States of Europe*. New York and London: M. E. Sharpe, pp. 95–112.
Chard, Robert L. (1990) "Master of the Family : History and Development of the Chinese Cult to the Stove." PhD Dissertation, University of California, Berkeley.
——— (1995) "Rituals and Scriptures of the Stove Cult." *Ritual and Scripture in Chinese Popular Religion: Five Studies*. Berkeley, CA: Chinese Popular Culture Project, pp. 3–54.
Chari, Sharad and Katherine Verdery (2009) "Thinking between the Posts: Postcolonialism, Postsocialism and Ethnography after the Cold War," *Comparative Studies of Society and History* 51.1: 6–34.
Chatterjee, Partha (2006) "Fasting for Bin Laden: Problems of Secularization in India." In David Scott and Charles Hirschkind eds, *Problems of the Secular Modern: Talal Asad and His Interlocutors*. Stanford: Stanford University Press, pp. 57–74.

Chau, Adam Yuet (2004) "Hosting Funerals and Temple Festivals: Folk Event Productions in Rural China." "http://www.tandfonline.com/toc/raan20/ current"Asian Anthropology 3: 39–70.

―――― (2005) "The Politics of Legitimation and the Revival of Popular Religion in Shaanbei, North-Central China," *Modern China* 31.2: 236–278.

―――― (2006a) *Miraculous Response: Doing Popular Religion in Contemporary China*. Stanford: Stanford University Press.

―――― (2006b) "Superstition Specialist Households?: The Household Idiom in Chinese Religious Practices," *Min-su ch'ü-i* (*The Journal of Chinese Ritual, Theatre, and Folklore*) 153: 157–202.

―――― (2008) "The Sensorial Production of the Social." *Ethnos* 73.4: 485–504.

―――― (2009) "Expanding the Space of Popular Religion: Local Temple Activism and the Politics of Legitimation in Contemporary Rural China." In Yoshiko Ashiwa and David Wank eds, *Making Religion, Making the State: The Politics of Religion in Contemporary China*. Stanford: Stanford University Press, pp. 211–240.

―――― (2010) "Mao's Traveling Mangoes: Food as Relic in Revolutionary China," *Past and Present*. Supplement 5.

―――― (2011a) (ed.) *Religion in Contemporary China: Revitalization and Innovation*. London: Routledge.

―――― (2011b) "Modalities of Doing Religion." In David A. Palmer et al. eds, *Chinese Religious Life: Culture, Society, and Politics*. Oxford: Oxford University Press, pp. 67–84.

―――― (2012) "Efficacy, Not Confessionality: Ritual Polytropy at Chinese Funerals." In Glenn Bowman ed., *Sharing the Sacra: The Politics and Pragmatics of Inter-communal Relations around Holy Places*. Oxford and New York: Berghahn Books, pp. 79–96.

Chen Bing (2008) "A Reflection on the Interface of Buddhist Studies and Science," *Buddhism Online*. http://news.fjnet.com/fjlw/200807/t20080725_77589.htm.

Chen Fashui (2012) "On the Formation and Development of Chinese Marxism's Historical Characteristics," *Journal of Liaoning University*, 40.3: 53–59.

Cheng, Grace Ming-Hui (2002) "'Culture for Development and Development for Culture Is the Ideology of the Day': The Politics of Culture in Vietnam's Post-1986 Transition," PhD dissertation, University of Hawaii, 2002.

Chotaeva, Cholpon (2004) *Ethnicity, Language and Religion in Kyrgyzstan*. Tohoku University.

Christiantimes.cn (2010) "Media Must 'Desensitize' Religion," http://www.christiantimes.cn/?action=View&id=308.

Chrypinski, Vincent (1990) "The Catholic Church in 1944–1989 Poland." In Sabrina Pedro Ramet ed., *Catholicism and Politics in Communist Societies*. Durham, NC: Duke University Press, pp. 117–141.

Chung, Byung-ho (2009) "Between Defector and Migrant: Identities and Strategies of North Koreans in South Korea," *Korean Studies* 32: 1.

―――― (2010) "Kŭkchang kukka Pukhan ŭi sangjin kwa ŭirye" (Symbol and Ritual in the Theater State North Korea), *T'ongil munjeyŏn'gu* 54: 1–42.

Çınar, Alev (2005) *Modernity, Islam and Secularism in Turkey: Bodies, Places and Time*. Minneapolis: University of Minnesota Press.

Çınar, Alev et al. (2012) "Introduction: Religious Nationalism as a Consequence of Secularism." In Alev Çınar, Srirupa Roy, and Maha Yahya eds, *Visualizing Secularism and Religion: Egypt, Lebanon, Turkey, India*. Ann Arbor, MI: Michigan University Press, pp. 1–24.

Clifford, James (1997) *Routes: Travel and Translation in the Late Twentieth Century.* Cambridge & London: Harvard University Press.
Comaroff, John L. and Jean Comaroff (1991) *Of Revelation and Revolution: Christianity, Colonialism, and Consciousness in South Africa.* Chicago: The University of Chicago Press.
Conquest, Robert (1990 [1968]) *The Great Terror: A Reassessment.* London: Hutchinson.
Corbett, Lionel (1996) *The Religious Function of the Psyche.* New York: Brunner-Routledge.
Cormack, Robin (1997) *Painting the Soul: Icons, Death Masks, and Shrouds.* London: Reaktion Books.
Cracium, Mihai (2001) "Ideology: Shenzhen." In Chuihua Chung, Jeffrey Inaba, Rem Koolhaas and Sze Tsung Leong eds, *Great Leap Forward.* Cambridge, MA: Harvard Design School.
Creed, Gerald W. (2000) "'Family Values' and Domestic Economies," *Annual Review of Anthropology* 29: 329–355.
Croll, Elisabeth (1986/87) "New Peasant Family Forms in Rural China," *The Journal of Peasant Studies* 14: 469–499.
Cumings, Bruce (1981) *The Origins of the Korean War: Liberation and the Emergence of Separate Regimes, 1945–1947.* Princeton: Princeton University Press.
—— (1991) *The Two Koreas: On the Road to Reunification?* Durham, NC: Foreign Policy Association. Duke University Press; Politics, History, and Culture Series.
—— (2004) *North Korea: Another Country.* New York: The New Press.
—— (2007) "Kim Jong Il Confronts Bush – and Wins. A New Page in North-South Korean Relations," *Le Monde Diplomatique,* October.
Curtiss, John (1953) *The Russian Church and the Soviet State, 1917–1950.* Boston: Little, Brown.
Dai Dai Tam Ky Pho Do (1966) *Thanh Ngon Hiep Tuyen.* Tay Ninh: Toa Thanh Tay Ninh.
Dallam, M. W. (2014) "Race and Ethnicity." In G. D. Chryssides and B. E. Zeller eds, *The Bloomsbury Companion to New Religious Movements.* London: Bloomsbury, pp. 295–299.
Daly, Jonathan (1997) "'Storming the Last Citadel': The Bolshevik Assault on the Church, 1922." In Vladimir Brovkin ed., *The Bolsheviks in Russian Society. The Revolution and the Civil Wars.* New Haven and London: Yale University Press, pp. 235–270.
Dan Chun (2007) "On Scientific Atheism: A Tradition of Enlightenment," http://www.kxwsl.com/ReadNews.asp?NewsID=2377.
Darczewska, Katarzyna (1989) *Katolicyzm we współczesnym społeczeństwie polskim: o niektórych uwarunkowaniach i postawach.* Wroclaw: Zakł. Nar. im. Ossolińskich.
Das, Veena and Deborah Ann Poole (2004) (eds) *Anthropology in the Margins of the State.* Santa Fe: School of American Research Press.
David-Fox, Michael (2011) "Opiate of the Intellectuals? Pilgrims, Partisans, and Political Tourists," *Kritika* n.s. 12.3: 721–738.
Dhammikamuni, D. P. (2010) *Buddhism in Laos: A Study from the Ancient up to the Present.* Bangkok: Healthy Heart Press (in Lao; title also given in English).
—— (c. 2010) *Buddhism and Democracy: Theravada Buddhist Perception,* (no press details), Wat Obmabuddhavas, Savannakhet City, Laos.

Dean, Kenneth (1993) *Taoist Ritual and Popular Cults of Southeast China*. Princeton, NJ: Princeton University Press.

——— (2009) "Further Partings of the Way: The Chinese State and Daoist Ritual Traditions in Contemporary China." In Yoshiko Ashiwa and David Wank eds, *The Politics of Religion in China*, Stanford: Stanford University Press, pp. 179–210.

Demick, Barbara (2009) *Nothing to Envy: Ordinary Lives in North Korea*. Spiegel & Grau.

Denney, Stephen (1990) "The Catholic Church in Vietnam." In Sabrina Pedro Ramet ed., *Catholicism and Politics in Communist Societies*. Durham, NC: Duke University Press, pp. 270–296.

——— (2008) "Religion and Dissent in Vietnam," *Journal of Interdisciplinary Studies*, 18.1: 136–152.

De Treglode, Benoit (2002) *Heros et Revolution au Viet Nam*. Paris: Harmattan.

DeVido, Elise (2007) "Buddhism for This World: The Buddhist Revival in Vietnam, 1920 to 1951 and Its Legacy." In Philip Taylor ed., *Modernity and Re-enchantment: Religion in Post-Revolutionary Vietnam*. Singapore: ISEAS, pp. 250–297.

Dirlik, Arif (1994) *After the Revolution: Waking to Global Capitalism*. Hanover, NH: University Press of New England [for] Wesleyan University Press.

Dobbelaere, Karel (2002) *Secularization: An Analysis at Three Levels*. Bruxelles: PIE Lang.

Dorfman, Diane (1996) "The Spirit of Reform: The Power of Belief in Northern China," *Positions: East Asia Cultures Critique* 4.2: 253–289.

Dorzhi (1998) *Wisdom Arising from Compassion*. Gansu, China: Gansu Nationality Publishing House.

——— (2000) *Dependent Co-Arising of Causes and Conditions as an Essence of Buddhadharma*. Chengdu, China: Sichuan Nationality Press.

Dragadze, Tamara (1993) "The Domestication of Religion under Soviet Communism." In Chris Hann ed., *Socialism: Ideals, Ideologies and Local Practice* (ASA Monographs No. 31). London: Routledge, pp. 148–156.

Dror, Olga (2007) *Cult, Culture and Authority: Princess Lieu Hanh in Vietnamese History*. Honolulu: University of Hawaii Press.

Duara, Prasenjit (1991) "Knowledge and Power in the Discourse of Modernity: The Campaigns Against Popular Religion in Early Twentieth-Century China," *Journal of Asian Studies* 50.1: 67–83.

——— (2008) "Religion and Citizenship in China and the Diaspora." In Mayfair Mei-hui Yang ed., *Chinese Religiosities: Afflictions of Modernity and State Formation*. Berkeley: University of California Press, pp. 43–65.

DuBois, Thomas David (2005) *The Sacred Village: Social Change and Religious Life in Rural North China*. Honolulu: University of Hawaii Press.

Dudek, Antoni and Ryszard Gryz (2003) *Komuniści i Kościół w Polsce (1945–1989)*. Kraków: ZNAK.

Duiker, William (1976) *The Rise of Nationalism in Vietnam*. Ithaca, NY: Cornell University Press.

Dunaev, S. (1998) "Okkul'tnyi renessans: ot bezbozhiia k bes-bozhiiu," *Nezavisimaia gazeta* 21: 14.

Dunch, Ryan (2002) "Beyond Cultural Imperialism: Cultural Theory, Christian Missions, and Global Modernity," *History and Theory* 41.3, October: 301–325.

——— (2008) "Christianity and 'Adaptation to Socialism.'" In Mayfair Mei-hui Yang ed., *Chinese Religiosities: Afflictions of Modernity and State Formation*. Berkeley: University of California Press, pp. 155–178.

Dunlop, John B. (1983) *The Faces of Contemporary Russian Nationalism*. Princeton, NJ: Princeton University Press.

Dunn, Elizabeth (2004) *Privatizing Poland: Baby Food, Big Business, and the Remaking of Labor*. Ithaca, NY: Cornell University Press.

Dutournier, Guillaume and Ji Zhe (2009) "Social Experimentation and 'Popular Confucianism': The Case of the Lujiang Cultural Education Centre," *China Perspectives* 4: 67–80.

Dutton, George, Jayne Werner and John Whitmore (2012) (eds) *Sources of Vietnamese Tradition*. New York: Columbia University Press.

Dziewanovski, M. (1997) *A History of Soviet Russia and Its Aftermath*. Fifth edition. Upper Saddle River, NJ: Prentice Hall.

Eberts, Mirella (1998) "The Roman Catholic Church and Democracy in Poland," *Europe-Asia Studies* 50.5: 817–842.

Eisenstadt, S. N. (2000) "Multiple Modernities," *Daedalus* 129: 1.

Ekaphone Phouthonesy (2005) "Science and Religion," *Vientiane Times*, May 6.

El'chenko Iu, N. (1976) *Novomu cheloveku – novye obriady*. Moscow: Izdatel'stvo politicheskoi literatury.

Eliason, Lynn (1991) *Perestroika of the Russian Soul: The Religious Renaissance in the Soviet Union*. Jefferson, NC and London: McFarland.

Elliott, David W. P. (2003) *The Vietnamese War: Revolution and Social Change in the Mekong Delta 1930–1975*. Armonk, NY: M. E. Sharpe.

Emelianov, V. N. (1994) "Nastoiashchaia 'Pamiat' zhiva," *Russkaia pravda* 3: 3.

Enders, Kristen (2011) *Performing the Divine*. Copenhagen: NIAS Monograph Series.

Engelke, Matthew (2007) *A Problem of Presence: Beyond Scripture in an African Church*. Berkeley: University of California Press.

Epstein, Mikhail N. (1991) "Put' v pustyne," *Nezavisimaia gazeta*, October 9, p. 8.

—— (1993) *Novoe sektantstvo: tipy religiozno-filosofskikh umonastroenii v Rossii (70–80-e gg. XX v.)*. Holyoke: New England Publishing Co.

—— (1995) *After the Future*. Amherst, MA: University of Massachusetts Press.

Evans, Grant (1991) "Reform or Revolution in Heaven: Funerals among Upland Tai," *The Australian Journal of Anthropology* 2.1: 81–97.

—— (1993) "Buddhism and Economic Action in Socialist Laos." In C. M. Hann ed., *Socialism: Ideals, Ideologies and Local Practice*. London: Routledge, pp. 123–141.

—— (1998a) "Secular Fundamentalism and Buddhism in Laos." In Oh Myung-Seok and Kim Hyung-Jun eds, *Religion, Ethnicity and Modernity in Southeast Asia*. Seoul: Seoul National University Press.

—— (1998b) *The Politics of Ritual and Remembrance: Laos since 1975*. Chiang Mai: Silkworm Press.

—— (2002) *A Short History of Laos: The Land in Between*. Sydney: Allen & Unwin.

—— (2004) *Laos: A Situation Analysis and Trend Assesment*. Writenet Report by Grant Evans commissioned by United Nations High Commissioner for Refugees, Protection Information Section (DIP).

Evrard, Olivier (2008) "Atténuation et Perpètuation des Frontières Ethniques: Notes sur la 'Taïsation' des Populations Khmou du Nord Laos. " In Yves Goudineau and Michel Lorrillard eds, *Recherches Nouvelles sur le Laos*. Vientiane-Paris: École française d'Extrême-Orient, pp. 533–558.

Exnerova, Vera (2006) "Caught between the Muslim Community and the State: The Role of Local Uzbek Authorities in Ferghana Valley, 1950s–1980s," *Journal of Muslim Minority Affairs* 26.1: 101–112.

Falikov, B. Z. (1989) "Neomistitsizm v SSSR." In D. E. Furman and Father Mark ed., *Na puti k svobode sovesti*. T.1. Moscow: Nauka, pp. 478–492.

Fan Lizhu and James D. Whiteheads (2005) "Fate and Fortune: Popular Religion and Moral Capital in Shenzhen," *Journal of Chinese Religion* 32: 83–100.

Feng Hongping 丰鸿平 (2005) "Quanqiu jikong: zhengzhi huayu toushiwenlu" 全球祭孔: 政治话语投石问路, *Nanfang dushibao* 南方都市报, September 27.

Fernando, Mayanthi (2010) "Reconfiguring Freedom: Muslim Piety and the Limits of Secular Law and Public Discourse in France," *American Ethnologist* 37.1: 19–35.

Feuchtwang, Stephan (2001) "Remnants of Revolution in China." In C. M. Hann ed., *Post-socialism: Ideals, Ideologies, and Practices in Eurasia*. London: Routledge, pp. 196–215.

Filatov, Sergei (2008) "Orthodoxy in Russia: Post-atheist Faith," *Studies in World Christianity* 14.3: 187–202.

Filatov, Sergei and Roman Lunkin (2006) "Statistics on Religion in Russia: The Reality behind the Figures," *Religion, State and Society* 34.1: 33–49.

Fisher, Gareth (2008) "The Spiritual Land Rush: Merit and Morality in New Chinese Buddhist Temple Construction," *The Journal of Asian Studies* 67.1: 143–170.

Fitzpatrick, Sheila (1992) *The Cultural Front: Power and Culture in Revolutionary Russia*. Ithaca, NY and London: Cornell University Press.

Fletcher, William (1965) *A Study in Survival. The Church in Russia, 1927–1943*. New York: SPCK.

Florensky, Pavel (2002) "The Church Ritual as a Synthesis of the Arts." In Pavel Florensky and N. Misler ed., *Beyond Vision: Essays on the Perception of Art*. London: Reaktion Books, pp. 93–113.

Foucault, Michel (1976) *Histoire de la sexualité. Vol. 1*. Paris: Gallimard.

——— (1984) "Truth and Power". In Paul Rabinow ed. *The Foucault Reader*. New York: Pantheon Books, pp. 51–75.

——— (1995) *Discipline and Punish*. New York: Vintage Books.

Fox, Tom (2011) "Ho Chi Minh City Cardinal on Church Growth in Vietnam," *National Catholic Reporter* on-line blog, February 19. http://www.ncrobline.org/blogs/thomas-c-fox.

Freeze, Gregory (1995) "The Counter-Reformation in Russian Orthodoxy. Popular Response to Religious Innovation, 1922–1925," *Slavic Review* 54: 305–339.

Friedman, Edward, Paul G. Pickowicz and Mark Selden (1991) *Chinese Village, Socialist State*. New Haven, CT: Yale University Press.

Froese, Paul (2004) "After Atheism: An Analysis of Religious Monopolies in the Post-communist World," *Sociology of Religion* 65.1: 57–75.

Fülöp-Miller, René (1968 [1928]) *The Mind and Face of Bolshevism: An Examination of Cultural Life in Soviet Russia*. New York: A. A. Knopf.

Furman, Dmitrii and Kimmo Kääriänen (2006) *Religioznost' v Rossii v 90e gody XX-nachale XXI veka*. Moscow: OGNI TD.

Gabel, Paul (2005) *And God Created Lenin: Marxism and Religion in Russia, 1917–1929*. Amherst and New York: Prometheus Books.

Gal, Susan and Gail Kligman (2000) *The Politics of Gender after Socialism*. Princeton: Princeton University Press.

Gardaz, Michel (1999) "In Search of Islam in Kyrgyzstan," *Religion* 29.3: 275–286.

Garrard, John and Carol Garrard (2008) *Russian Orthodoxy Resurgent: Faith and Power in the New Russia*. Princeton and Oxford: Princeton University Press.
Gates, Hill (1996) *China's Motor: A Thousand Years of Petty Capitalism*. Ithaca, NY: Cornell University Press.
—— (1999) "Religious Real Estate as Indigenous Civil Space," *Bulletin of the Institute of Ethnology (Academia Sinica)* (Special Issue in Honor of Professor Li Yih-yuan's Retirement (I)): 313–333.
Geertz, Clifford (1973) *The Interpretation of Cultures*. New York: Basic Books.
—— (1980) *Negara: The Theartre State in Nineteenth-Century Bali*. Princeton, NJ: Princeton University Press..
Gentile, Emilio (1990) "Totalitarianism and Political Religion," *Journal of Contemporary History* 25.2–3: 229–252.
Giao-Hoi Phat Giao Hoa Hao (1966) *Sam Giang Thi Van – Toan Bo cua Duc Huynh Phu So* (Complete Edition of Prophecies and Sermons of Prophet Huynh Phu So). An Hanh: Ban Pho Thong Giao Ly Trung Uong.
Giddens, Anthony (1991) *The Consequences of Modernity*. Cambridge: Polity
Giebel, Christoph (2001) "Museum Shrine: Revolution and Its Tutelary Spirit in the Village of My Hoa Hung." In Hue Tam Ho Tai, *The Country of Memory*. Los Angeles: University of California Press, pp. 77–105.
Gillis, John R. (1994) (ed.) *Commemorations: The Politics of National Identity*. Princeton, NJ: Princeton University Press.
Göle, Nilufer (2006) "Europe's Encounter with Islam: What Future?" *Constellations* 13.2: 248–262.
—— (2008) "Secularism Is a Women's Affair," *New Perspectives Quarterly* 25.2: 35–37.
Gong Pengcheng龚鹏程 (2008) *Beiming xingji* 北溟行记, Shanghai: Shanghai renmin chubanshe.
Gong Xuezong (2007) "A Few Questions about Science and Religion," http://www.kxwsl.com/ReadNews.asp?NewsID=2375.
—— (2008) "On Guiding Religion to Be Compatible with Socialist Society." In Lu Dajie and Gong Xuezeng eds, *Marxist Approach to Religion and Contemporary Religions in China*. Beijing: Minzu Publishing House, pp. 205–224.
Goody, Jack (2004) *Islam in Europe*. Cambridge: Polity Press.
Goossaert, Vincent (2000) "Counting the Monks: The 1736–1739 Census of the Chinese Clergy," *Late Imperial China* 21.2: 40–85.
—— (2005) "Les fausses séparations de l'État et de la religion en Chine, 1898–2004." In Jean Bauberot and Michel Wieviorka eds, *De la séparation des Églises et de l'État à l'avenir de la laïcité*, Paris: L'aube, pp. 49–58.
—— (2006a) "1898: The Beginning of the End for Chinese Religion?" *Journal of Asian Studies* 65.2: 307–335.
—— (2006b) "State and Religion in Modern China: Religious Policies and Scholarly Paradigms," *Bulletin of the Institute of Modern History, Academia Sinica* 54: 169–210.
—— (2008) "Republican Church Engineering: The National Religious Associations in 1912 China." In Mayfair Mei-Hui Yang ed., *Chinese Religiosities: Afflictions of Modernity and State Formation*. Berkeley: University of California Press, pp. 209–232.
Goossaert, Vincent and David A. Palmer (2011) *The Religious Question in Modern China*. Chicago: The University of Chicago Press.

Goscha, Christopher (2002) "La guerre par d'autres moyens: reflexions sur la guerre du Viet Minh dans le Sud-Vietnam de 1945 a 1951," *Guerres mondiales et conflits contemporains* 206: 29–57.

Gottschalk, Peter (2013) *Religion, Science and Empire: Classifying Hinduism and Islam in British India*. Oxford: Oxford University Press.

Grabowska, Mirosława (2001) "Religijność i Kościół w procesie transformacji w Polsce." In Edmund Wnuk-Lipiński and Marek Ziółkowski eds, *Pierwsza dekada niepodległości. Próba socjologicznej syntezy*. Warszawa: ISP PAN, pp. 169–180.

Graham, Loren and Jean-Michel Kantor (2009) *Naming Infinity: A True Story of Religious Mysticism and Mathematical Creativity*. Cambridge, MA and London: Belknap.

Griffis, William Elliot (1902) *A Maker of the New Orient*. New York: Fleming H. Revell Company.

Grimshaw, Mike (2011) "Encountering Religion: Encounter, Religion, and the Cultural Cold War 1953–1967," *History of Religions* 51.1: 31–58.

Gurian, Waldemar (1952) "Totalitarian Religions," *Review of Politics* 14.1: 3–14.

Habermas, Jürgen (1962) *Strukturwandel der Öffentlichkeit: Untersuchungen zu einer Kategorie der bürgerlichen Gesellschaft*. Neuwied/Berlin: Luchterhand.

Halemba, Agnieszka (2015) *Negotiating Marian Apparitions: The Politics of Religion in Transcarpathian Ukraine*. Budapest: Central European University Press.

Halfin, Igal (2009) *Stalinist Confessions: Messianism and Terror at the Leningrad Communist University*. Pittsburgh: University of Pittsburgh Press.

Hann, Chris (2000) "Problems with the (De)Privatization of Religion," *Anthropology Today* 16.6: 14–20.

——— (2001) (ed.) *Post-socialism: Ideals, Ideologies, and Practices in Eurasia*. London: Routledge.

——— (2006) *The Postsocialist Religious Question: Faith and Power in Central Asia and East Central Europe*. Munster: LIT Verlag.

——— (2010a) "Introduction: Broken Chains and Moral Lazarets: The Politicization, Juridification and Commodification of Religion after Socialism." In Chris Hann ed., *Religion, Identity, Postsocialism: The Halle Focus Group 2003–2010*. Halle/Saale: The Max Planck Institute for Social Anthropology, pp. 1–21.

——— (2010b) *Religion, Identity, Postsocialism: The Halle Focus Group 2003–2010*. Halle/Saale: The Max Planck Institute for Social Anthropology.

Hann, Chris and Mathjis Pelkmans (2009) "Realigning Religion and Power in Central Asia: Islam, Nation-State and (Post)Socialism," *Europe-Asia Studies* 61.9: 1517–1541.

Harding, Susan Friend (1987) "Convicted by the Holy Spirit: The Rhetoric of Fundamental Baptist Conversion," *American Ethnologist* 14: 167–181.

——— (2000) *The Book of Jerry Falwell: Fundamentalist Language and Politics*. Princeton and Oxford: Princeton University Press.

Harker, Richard, Cheleen Mahar and Chris Wilkes (1990) (eds) *Introduction to the Work of Pierre Bourdieu: The Practice of Theory*. London: Macmillan.

Haskell, Francis (1993) "The Musée des Monuments Français." In *History and Its Images*. New Haven and London: Yale University Press, pp. 236–252.

Hawes, Charlotte E. (1913) *New Thrills in Old China*. New York: Hodder & Stoughton.

Hawk and North Korean Study Team (2005) *"Thank You Father Kim Il Sung": Eyewitness Accounts of Severe Violations of Freedom of Thought, Conscience, and Religion in North Korea*. US Commission on International Religious Freedom.
Hayden, Jacqueline (1994) *Poles Apart: Solidarity and the New Poland*. London: Routledge.
Hayes, James (1985) "Specialists and Written Materials in the Village World." In David Johnson et al. eds, *Popular Culture in Late Imperial China*. Berkeley, Los Angeles, and London: University of California Press, pp. 75–111.
Hecker, Julius (1933) *Religion and Communism: A Study of Religion and Atheism in Soviet Russia*. London: Chapmen and Hall Ltd.
Hellbeck, Jochen (2006) *Revolution on my Mind: Writing a Diary under Stalin*. Cambridge, MA: Harvard University Press.
Henry, B. C. (1885) *The Cross and The Dragon*. New York: Anson D. F. Randolph and Company.
Hermand, Jost (1992) *Old Dreams of a New Reich: Volkisch Utopias and National Socialism*. Bloomington: Indiana University Press.
Hirsch, Francine (2005) *Empire of Nations: Ethnographic Knowledge and the Making of the Soviet Union*. Ithaca, NY: Cornell University Press.
Ho Chi Minh. (1977) *Selected Writings*. Hanoi: Foreign Languages Publishing House.
Hong, Young-Gi (2003) "Encounter with Modernity: The 'Mcdonaldization' and 'Charismatization' of Korean Mega-Churches," *International Review of Mission* 92: 239–255.
Hours, Bernard et Monique Selim (1997) *Essai d'Anthropologie Politique sur Le Laos Contemperain: Marché, socialisme, et genies*. Paris: L'Harmattan.
Hsiung, Ping-chun (1996) *Living Rooms as Factories: Class, Gender, and the Satellite Factory System in Taiwan*. Philadelphia, PA: Temple University Press.
Hua, Shiping (1995) *Scientism and Humanism: Two Cultures in Post-Mao China (1978–1989)*. Albany: State University of New York Press.
Hubbert, Jennifer (2006) "(Re)collecting Mao: Memory and Fetish in Contemporary China," *American Ethnologist* 33.2: 145–161.
Hue Tam Ho Tai (1983) *Millenarianism and Peasant Politics in Vietnam*. Cambridge: Harvard University Press.
Hu Jintao 胡锦涛 (2005) "Zai shengbuji zhuyao lingdao ganbu tigao goujian shehuizhuyi hexie shehui nengli zhuanti yantaoban shang de jianghua" 在省部级主要领导干部提高构建社会主义和谐社会能力专题研 班上的 话, http://www.china.com.cn/chinese/news/899546.htm. (last accessed March 17, 2015)
Hu Lianhe 胡联合, Hu Angang 胡鞍钢 and Wang Lei 王磊 (2006) "Yingxiang shehui wending de shehui maodun bianhua taishi de shizheng fenxi" 影响社会稳定的社会矛盾变化态势的实证分析, *Shehui kexue zhanxian* 社会科学战线 4: 175–185.
Humphrey, Caroline (1998) *Marx Went Away – But Karl Stayed Behind*. Ann Arbor, MI: University of Michigan Press.
—— (2002a) "Shamans in the City." In *The Unmaking of Soviet Life: Everyday Economies after Socialism*. Ithaca, NY: Cornell University Press, pp. 202–221.
—— (2002b) "Stalin and the Blue Elephant: Paranoia and Complicity in Postcommunist Metahistories," *Diogenes* 49.2: 26–34.
Huntington, Samuel P. (1991) *The Third Wave: Democratization in the Late Twentieth Century*. Norman: University of Oklahoma Press.

Husband, W. B. (1998) "Soviet Atheism and Russian Orthodox Strategies of Resistance, 1917–1932," *Journal of Modern History* 70.1: 74–107.

——— (2000) *"Godless Communists": Atheism and Society in Soviet Russia, 1917–1932*. DeKalb: Northern Illinois University Press.

Huynh Kim Khanh (1982) *Vietnamese Communism 1925–1945*. Ithaca, NY: Cornell University Press.

Hwang, Sok-Yong (2001) *Sonnim* (Guest). Seoul, South Korea: Changbi Inc.

Iakovlev, A. N. (1998) "Rossiiskikh fashistov porodil KGB." *Izvestiia*, June 17, p. 5.

Information Office of the State Council of the People's Republic of China (1997) *White Paper: Freedom of Religious Belief in China*. Beijing.

International Crisis Group (2006) *Perilous Journeys: The Plight of North Koreans in China and Beyond*.

Ishii Yoneo (1986) *Sangha, State and Society: Thai Buddhism in History*. Honolulu: University of Hawaii Press.

Ismailbekova, Aksana and Emil Nasritdinov (2012) "Transnational Religious Networks in Central Asia: Structure, Travel, and Culture of Kyrgyz Tablighi Jama'at," *Transnational Social Review* 2.2: 177–195.

Ivakhiv, Adrian (2005) "Nature and Ethnicity in East European Paganism: An Environmental Ethic of the Religious Right?" *Pomegranate* 7.2: 194–225.

Ivanov (Skuratov), A. M. (2007) *Rassvety i sumerki ariiskikh bogov: rasovoe religiovedenie*. Moscow: Belye Al'vy.

Jackson, Peter A. (2003) *Buddhadasa: Theravada Buddhism and Modernist Reform in Thailand*. Chiang Mai: Silkworm Books.

Jammes, Jeremy (2010) "Divination and Politics in Southern Vietnam: Roots of Caodaism," *Social Compass* 57.3: 357–371.

Jellema, Katrin Louise (2007) "When You Drink from the Stream, Remember the Source: Moral Landscapes of Memory in a Northern Vietnamese Village," PhD dissertation, University of Michigan.

Jeon, W.-t. (2007) *Saram-ŭi T'ongil ttang- ŭi T'ongil* (Unification of People, Unification of Land). Seoul, South Korea: Yonsei University Press.

Jeon W.-t. et al. (2010) *T'ongil sirhŏm kŭ 7 yŏn: Bukhan ital jumin ŭi namhan sari paepŏl yŏn'gu* (7 years of Unification Experiment: Panel Study of North Korean Migrants' Life in South Korea). Seoul: Hanul Ak'ademi.

Ji Zhe, (2004) "Buddhism and the State: The New Relationship," *China Perspectives* 55: 2–10.

——— (2005) "Confucius, les libéraux et le Parti. Le renouveau du confucianisme politique," *La Vie des Idées* 2: 9–20.

——— (2008) "Tianxia, retour en force d'un concept oublié. Portrait des nouveaux penseurs confucianistes," http://laviedesidees.fr/Tianxia-retour-en-force-d-un. html. (last accessed March 17, 2015)

——— (2011) "Buddhism in Reform-Era China: A Secularised Revival?" In Adam Yuet Chau, ed., *Religious Revitalization and Innovation in Contemporary China*. London: Routledge, pp. 32–52.

Jiang Jinsong and He Bing (1999) "Taixu's Scientific Worldview," *The Voice of Dharma* 11: 3–11.

Jing, Jun (1996) *The Temple of Memories: History, Power, and Morality in a Chinese Village*. Stanford: Stanford University Press.

Johnson, David (2010) *Spectacle and Sacrifice: The Ritual Foundation of Village Life in North China*. Cambridge, MA: Harvard University Asia Center.

Jones, Stephen (2004) *Plucking the Winds: Lives of Village Musicians in Old and New China*. Leiden: CHIME.
Jung, Jinheon (Jin-Heon) (2013) "Narrativization of Religious Conversion: 'Christian Passage' of North Korean Refugees in South Korea," *Hankukonomunhwa* 50: 269–288.
Kaganska, M. (1986) "The Book of Vlas: The Saga of Forgery," *Jews and Jewish Topics in Soviet and East European Publications*. Jerusalem, vol. 4: 3–27.
Kahin, George McT. (1987) *Intervention: How America Became Involved in Vietnam*. New York: Anchor Books.
Kaloev, B. A. (1971) *Osetiny*. Moscow: Nauka.
Kampars P. P. and N. M. Zakovich (1967) *Sovietskaia grazhdanskaia obriadnost'*. Moscow: Mysl'.
Kang I.-c. (2005) "Han'guk Kaesin'gyo Pan'gongjuŭi ŭi hyŏngsŏng kwa jaesaengsan (Formation and Reproduction of Korean Protestant Anticommunism)." *Yŏksapip'yŏng* 70: 40–63. Seoul, South Korea: Yŏksapip'yŏngsa.
——— (2007) *Han'guk ŭi Kaesin'gyo wa Pan'gongjuŭi: Posujŏk Kaesin'gyo ŭi chŏngch'ijŏk haengdongjuŭi t'amgu* [Korean Protestantism and Anti-communism: An Examination of Conservative Protestantism's Political Activism]. Seoul, South Korea: Chungsim.
Kaplonski, Christopher (2008) "Show Trials and State Power in the 1930s," *American Ethnologist* 35.2: 321–337.
Karpat, K. (1993) "The Old and New Central Asia," *Central Asian Survey* 12.4: 415–425.
Kavykin O. I. (2007). *"Rodnovery." Samoidentifikatsiia neoiazychnikov v sovremennoi Rossii*. Moscow: Institut Afriki.
Keane, Webb (1997) "Religious Language," *Annual Review of Anthropology* 26: 47–71.
——— (2010) "Marked, Absent, Habitual: Approaches to Neolithic Religion at Çatalhöyük." In Ian Hodder ed., *Religion in the Emergence of Civilization: Çatalhöyük as a Case Study*. Cambridge: Cambridge University Press, pp. 187–219.
Keith, Charles (2012) *Catholic Vietnam: Church, Colonialism, and Revolution, 1887–1945*. Berkeley: University of California Press.
Kendzior, Sarah (2006) "Redefining Religion: Uzbek Atheist Propaganda in Gorbachev-Era Uzbekistan," *Nationalities Papers* 34.5: 533–548.
Khamtan Thepbouali (Maha) (1975) *Buddhism and the Lao Revolution*. From private papers.
Khamyad Rasdavong (Maha) (2006) *The History of Buddhism in Laos*. Vientiane: Xangkhou Press.
Khana Khōsanā 'Ophom Sūnkāng Phak (Laos). (2004). *Salup songkhām pasāson phāitai kānnamphā khǫng Phak Pasāson Pativat Lāo 1945–1975*. Vientiane: Khana Khōsanā 'Ophom Sūnkāng Phak.
Kharkhordin, Oleg (1999) *The Collective and the Individual in Russia: A Study of Practices*. Berkeley: University of California Press.
Kheifets M. (1981) "Russkii patriot Vladimir Osipov," *Kontinent* 27: 159–214.
Kim Jong-il (1992) "Socialism Is the Life of Our People". Talk with the Senior Officials of the Central Committee of the Workers' Party of Korea. November 14. E-library of North Korean official website. http://www.korea-dpr.com/lib/558.pdf

——— (1995) "Giving Priority to Ideological Work Is Essential for Accomplishing Socialism." E-Library of North Korean official website, http://www.korea-dpr.com/lib/101/pdf.

——— (1996) "The Juche Philosophy Is an Original Revolutionary Philosophy." E-Library of North Korean official website, http://www.korea-dpr.com/lib/108.pdf.

Kim, S. (2006) *The Two Koreas and the Great Powers*. Cambridge and New York: Cambridge University Press.

Kim, Suk-Young (2010) *Illusive Utopia: Theater, Film, and Everyday Performance in North Korea*. Ann Arbor, MI: University of Michigan Press.

Kimura, Mitsuhiko, Makoto Okamura and Koji Futagami (2001) "An Interpretation of the North Korean Regime," *The Journal of The Korean Economy* 2.1: 183–200.

Kipnis, Andrew (2001) "The Flourishing of Religion in Post-Mao China and the Anthropological Category of Religion," *The Australian Journal of Anthropology* 12.1: 32–46.

——— (2003) "The Anthropology of Power and Maoism," *American Anthropologist* 105.2: 278–288.

Kleinman, Arthur (1995) *Writing at the Margin: Discourse between Anthropology and Medicine*. Berkeley: University of California Press.

Klimov, E. (1964) *Novye obychai i prazdniki*. Moscow: Profizdat.

Korey, William (1995) *Russian Antisemitism, Pamyat, and the Demonology of Zionism*. Chur: Harwood Academic Publishers.

Kosing, Alfred (1987) *Wörterbuch der marxistisch-leninistischen Philosophie*. Third edition. Berlin: Dietz.

Kourilsky, Grégory (2006) *Recherches sur L'Institut Bouddhique au Laos (1930–1949)*. Mémoire de Master, EPHE.

Krugliakov, E. P. (1998) "Rossiia snova vo mgle?" *Nezavisimaia gazeta*, May 6, p. 16.

——— (2008) "Shtrikhi k portretu 'akademika' Akimova," *V zashchitu nauki* 3: 77–82.

Krugliakov, E. P. et al. (2008) "Predislovie," *V zashchitu nauki* 3: 5–8.

Kryvelev, I. A. (1963) "O formirovanii i rasprostranenii novykh obychaev i prazdnikov u narodov SSSR," *Sovetskaia etnografiia* 6: 16–24.

——— (1977) "Sovremennye obriady i rol' etnograficheskoi nauki v ikh izuchenii, formirovanii i vnedrenii," *Sovetskaia etnografiia* 5: 36–45.

Kubik, Jan (1994) *The Power of Symbols against the Symbols of Power: The Rise of Solidarity and the Fall of State Socialism in Poland*. University Park, PA: Pennsylvania State University Press.

Kula, Marcin (2003) *Religiopodobny komunizm*. Kraków: Nomos.

Kurczewska, Joanna (2005) "National Identities Vis a Vis Democracy and Catholicism (The Polish Case after 1989)," *Polish Sociological Review* 4.152: 329–349.

Kuzina, S. (2005) "'Psi-sluzhba' zashchishchala Kreml' ot porchi," *Komsomol'skaia pravda*, January 6–14, p. 6–7.

Kwon, Heonik (2006) *After the Massacre: Commemoration and Consolation in Ha My and My Lai*. Los Angeles: University of California Press.

——— (2008) *Ghosts of War in Vietnam*. Cambridge: Cambridge University Press.

——— (2010a) "North Korea's Politics of Longing," *Critical Asian Studies* 42: 3–24.

——— (2010b) *The Other Cold War*. New York: Columbia University Press.
——— (2013) "The Korean War and Sino-North Korean Friendship," *The Asia-Pacific Journal* 11.31.4, August 12.
Ladwig, Patrice (2008) "Between Cultural Preservation and This-Worldly Commitment: Modernization, Social Activism and the Lao Buddhist Sangha." In Yves Goudineau and Michel Lorrillard eds, *Recherches Nouvelles sur le Laos*. Vientiane-Paris: École française d'Extrême-Orient, pp. 465–492.
Lafont, Pierre-Bernard (1982) "Buddhism in Contemporary Laos." In Martin Stuart-Fox ed., *Contemporary Laos*. St Lucia: University of Queensland Press, pp. 148–162.
Lai Chi-Tim (2003) "Daoism in China Today, 1980–2002," *The China Quarterly* 174: 413–427.
Lai, Hongyi Harry (2003) "The Religious Revival in China," *Copenhagen Journal of Asian Studies* 18: 40–64.
Lane, Christel (1981) *The Rites of Rulers: Ritual in Industrial Society – The Soviet Case*. Cambridge: Cambridge University Press.
Laqueur, Walter (1993) *Black Hundred: The Rise of the Extreme Right in Russia*. New York: Harper Collins.
Ledeneva, Alena (1998) *Russia's Economy of Favours: Blat, Networking and Informal Exchange*. Cambridge: Cambridge University Press.
Lee, S.-j. (2006) *The Making and Unmaking the Korean National Division: Separated Families in the Cold War and Post-Cold War Eras*. Doctoral Dissertation, University of Illinois at Urbana-Champaign.
Lee, Timothy S. (2010) *Born Again: Evangelicalism in Korea*. Honolulu: University of Hawaii Press.
Le Hong Ly va Nguyen Phuong Cham (2008) *Su bien doi cua ton giao tin ngung o Vietnam (The Transformation of Religions and Religious Belief in Vietnam Today)*. Hanoi: The Gioi.
Lemon, Alaina (2008) "Hermeneutic Algebra: Solving for Love, Time/Space, and Value in Putin-Era Personal Ads," *Journal of Linguistic Anthropology* 18.2: 236–267.
Lenin, V. I. (1905) "Socialism and Religion," *Novaia zhizn'* December 16.
——— (1926) *Religiia, tserkov i partii (Religion, the Church and the Party)*. Moscow.
Lewis, Bernard (1993) *Islam and the West*. Oxford: Oxford University Press.
Lewis, David (2000) *After Atheism: Religion and Ethnicity in Russia and Central Asia*. Surrey, England: Curzon Press.
Li Fan 李凡, (2011), "Jidujiao zai dangdai Zhongguo de fazhan" 基督教在当代中国的发展, http://www.world-china.org/bookdownload2/基督教在当代中国的发展.pdf (last accessed March 17, 2015)
Lindquist, Galina (2005) "Healers, Leaders and Entrepreneurs: Shamanic Revival in Southern Siberia," *Culture and Religion* 6.2: 263–285.
——— (2006) *Conjuring Hope: Healing and Magic in Contemporary Russia*. New York: Berghahn Books.
Linke, Uli (2006) "Contact Zones: Rethinking the Sensual Life of the State," *Anthropological Theory* 6.2: 205–225.
Lisochkin I. (1988) "Neispovedimy puti 'vedizma'," *Leningradskaia Pravda*, December 22, p. 3.
Li Wei-Tsu (1948) "On the Cult of the Four Sacred Animals (Szu Ta Men) in the Neighbourhood of Peking," *Folklore Studies* 7: 1–94.

Li Xiangping (2010) "Debates on the Social Function of Religion in Media," http://lxp0711.blog.hexun.com/59039919_d.html.
Lobacheva, N. P. (1973) "O formirovanii novoi obriadnosti u narodov SSSR," *Sovetskaia etnografiia* 4: 14–24.
—— (1975) *Formirovanie novoi obriadnosti uzbekov*. Moscow: Nauka.
Lodder, Christina (1993) "Lenin's Plan for Monumental Propaganda." In Matthew Bown ed., *Art of the Soviets: Painting, Sculpture and Architecture in a One-party State, 1917–1992*. Manchester: Manchester University Press, pp. 16–33.
Luce, Don and John Sommer (1969) *Vietnam: The Unheard Voices*. Ithaca, NY: Cornell University Press.
Luckmann, Thomas (1985) "Über die Funktion der Religion. " In Peter Koslowski ed., *Die religiöse Dimension der Gesellschaft: Religion und ihre Theorien*. Tübingen: Mohr-Siebeck, pp. 26–41.
Lu Dajie and Gong Xuezeng (2008) (eds) *Marxist Approach to Religion and Contemporary Religions in China*. Beijing: Minzu Publishing House.
Luehrmann, Sonja (2005) "Recycling Cultural Construction: Desecularisation in Postsoviet Mari El," *Religion, State & Society* 33.1: 35–56.
—— (2009) "Forms and Methods: Teaching Atheism and Religion in the Mari Republic, Russian Federation," PhD dissertation, University of Michigan.
—— (2011a) "Wunder ohne Wunder. Die Säkularisierung des Staunens in der sowjetischen Atheismuspropaganda unter Chruščev und Brežnev." In Alexander Geppert and Till Kössler eds, *Wunder. Poetik und Politik des Staunens im zwanzigsten Jahrhundert*. Frankfurt: Suhrkamp, pp. 395–418.
—— (2011b) *Secularism Soviet Style: Teaching Atheism and Religion in a Volga Republic*. Bloomington: Indiana University Press.
Lugovoi, E. (1998a) "Satanizm ili 'volkhovanie'," *Sovety Baby Iagi* 1.10: 2.
—— (1998b) "Bez sroka davnosti: predatel'stvo," *Sovety Baby Iagi* 2.11: 2.
Lunacharsky, Anatolii (1933) "Lenin o monumental'noi propaganda" (Lenin on Monumental Propaganda). *Literaturnaia gazetta* 4–5, January 29.
Luther, Martin (1991 [1523]) "On Secular Authority." In Harro Hopfl ed. and trans. *Luther and Calvin on Secular Authority*. Cambridge: Cambridge University Press, pp. 1–46.
Macgowan, J. (1913) *How England Saved China*. London: Adelphi Terrace.
MacInnis, Donald (1996) "From Suppression to Repression: Religion in China Today," *Current History* 95: 284–289.
Mack, Arien (2009) (ed.) "Special Issue: The Religious-Secular Divide: The U.S. Case," *Social Research* 76.4.
Madan, T. N. (1998) "Secularism in Its Place." In Rajeev Bhargava ed., *Secularism and Its Critics*. Delhi: Oxford University Press.
Madsen, Richard (2003) "Catholic Revival during the Reform Era," *The China Quarterly* 174, Religion in China Today, June, pp. 468–487.
—— (2009) "Back to the Future: Pre-modern Religious Policy in Post-secular China," http://www.fpri.org/articles/2009/03/back-future-pre-modern-religious-policy-post-secular-china (last accessed March 17, 2015).
—— (2011) "Secularism, Religious Change, and Social Conflict in Asia." In Craig Calhoun, Mark Juergensmeyer and Jonathan Van Antwerpen eds, *Rethinking Secularism*. Oxford: Oxford University Press, pp. 248–269.
Mahmood, Saba (2001) "Feminist Theory, Embodiment, and the Docile Agent: Some Reflections on the Egyptian Islamic Revival," *Cultural Anthropology* 16.2: 202–236.

——— (2006) "Secularism, Hermeneutics, and Empire: The Politics of Islamic Reformation," *Public Culture* 18.2: 323–347.
Main, Izabela (2004) *Trudne świętowanie. Konflikty wokół obchodów świąt państwowych i kościelnych w Lublinie (1944–1989)*. Warszawa: Trio.
Majka, Józef (1968) "The Character of Polish Catholicism," *Social Compass* 15: 185–208.
Malarney, Shaun (1996) "The Limits of 'State Functionalism' and the Reconstruction of Funerary Ritual in Contemporary Northern Vietnam," *American Ethnologist* 23.3: 540–560.
——— (2002) *Culture, Ritual and Revolution in Vietnam*. New York: Routledge.
——— (2007) "Festivals and the Dynamics of the Exceptional Dead in Northern Vietnam," *Journal of Southeast Asian Studies* 38.3: 505–537.
Manning, Paul (2007) "Rose-Colored Glasses: Color Revolutions and Cartoon Chaos in Postsocialist Georgia," *Cultural Anthropology* 22.2: 171–213.
Marody, Mirosława and Sławomir Mandes (2006) "On Functions of Religion in Molding the National Identity of Poles," *International Journal of Sociology* 35.4: 49–68.
Marr, David (1981) *Vietnamese Tradition on Trial, 1920–1945*. Berkeley, CA: University of California Press.
——— (1986) "Religion in Contemporary Vietnam." In R. F. Miller and T. H. Rigby eds, *Religion and Politics in Communist States*. Canberra: The Australian National University, pp. 123–133.
Marshall, Richard (1971) (ed.) *Aspects of Religion in the Soviet Union, 1917–1967*. Chicago: University of Chicago Press.
Martin, David (2002) *Pentecostalism: The World Their Parish*. Oxford: Blackwell.
Martin, Terry (2001) *The Affirmative Action Empire: Nations and Nationalism in the Soviet Union, 1923–1939*. Ithaca, NY: Cornell University Press.
Marx, Karl (1963) *Contribution to a Critique of Hegel's Philosophy of Right*. In *Early Writings*, ed. Thomas Bottomore. London: Watts.
——— (1973) *On Society and Social Change*. Neil J. Smelser, ed. Chicago: the University of Chicago Press.
——— (1844 [1975]) "Contribution to the Critique of Hegel's Philosophy of Law: Introduction." In *Marx and Engels Collected Works*. Moscow: Progress Publishers, pp. 175–187.
——— (2002 [1843]) "On the Jewish Question." In John Raines ed., *Marx on Religion*. Philadelphia: Temple University Press, pp. 44–70.
McBrien, Julie (2006) "Listening to the Wedding Speaker: Discussing Religion and Culture in Southern Kyrgyzstan," *Central Asian Survey* 25.3: 341–357.
McBrien, Julie and Mathijs Pelkmans (2008) "Turning Marx on His Head: Missionaries, 'Extremists,' and Archaic Secularists in Post-Soviet Kyrgyzstan," *Critique of Anthropology* 28.1: 87–103.
McDaniel, Justin Thomas (2008) *Gathering Leaves and Lifting Words*. Chiang Mai: Silkworm Books.
McHale, Shawn F. (1995) "Imagining Human Liberation: Vietnamese Buddhists and the Marxist Critique of Religion, 1920–1939," *Social Compass* 42.3: 329–344.
——— (2002) "Mapping a Confucian Past and Its Transition to Modernity." In Benjamin A. Elman, John B. Duncan and Herman Ooms eds, *Rethinking Confucianism: Past and Present in China, Japan, Korea and Vietnam*. Los Angeles: UCLA Asian Pacific Monograph Series, pp. 397–430.

——— (2004) *Print and Power: Confucianism, Communism and Buddhism in the Making of Modern Vietnam*. Honolulu: University of Hawaii Press.

Mikhailichenko, B. (2002) "Proritsatel' v pogonakh," *Moskovskie novosti*, January 8–21, p. 42.

Mitrokhin, N. A. (2003) *Russkaia partiia. Dvizhenie russkikh natsionalistov v SSSR, 1953–1985 gody*. Moscow: Novoe literaturnoe obozrenie.

Moroz, Ye. L. (1992) "Bortsy za 'Sviatuiu Rus' i zashchitniki 'Sovietskoi Rodiny.'" In *Natsional'naia pravaia prezhde i teper'*, part 2, issue 1, ed. R. Sh. Ganelin. Saint-Petersburg: Institut sotsiologii RAN, pp. 68–96.

Mosse, George. (1991) *Fallen Soldiers: Reshaping the Memory of World Wars*. Oxford: Oxford University Press.

Mou Zhongjian (2009) *Exploring Religion*. Beijing: Religion & Culture Press.

Myers, B. R. (2010) *The Cleanest Race: How North Koreans See Themselves – And Why It Matters*. New York: Melville House.

Mytskiula, P. (1968) "O sovremennykh obychaiakh," *Kommunist Estonii* 4: 48–58.

Nandy, Ashis (1988) "The Politics of Secularism and the Recovery of Religious Tolerance," *Alternatives* 13: 177–194.

Nazpary, Joma (2002) *Post-Soviet Chaos: Violence and Dispossession in Kazakhstan*. London: Pluto Press.

Nedostup, Rebecca (2010) *Superstitious Regimes: Religion and the Politics of Chinese Modernity*. Cambridge, MA: Harvard University Press.

Nee, Victor (1985) "Peasant Household Individualism," *International Journal of Sociology* 14.4: 50–76.

Neiman, M. (1960) "Iz istorii leninskogo plana monumental'noi propaganda" (From the History of Lenin's Plan for Monumental Propaganda). In *Stanovlenie sotsialisticheskogo realizma v sovetskom izobrazitel'nom iskusstve*, Moscow.

News.cn (2009) "Promoting Sinification, Contextualization, and Popularization of Marxism," http://news.xinhuanet.com/theory/2009–10/27/content_12336587.htm.

Ngo, Tam T. T. (2009) "The 'Short-waved Faith': Christian Broadcastings and the Transformation of the Spiritual Landscape of the Hmong in Northern Vietnam." In K. G. Francis Lim ed., *Mediated Piety: Technology and Religion in Contemporary Asia*. Leiden: Brill, pp. 139–158.

——— (2010) "Ethnic and Transnational Dimensions of Recent Protestant Conversion among the Hmong in Northern Vietnam," *Social Compass* 57.3: 332–344.

——— (2011) "The New Way: Becoming Protestant Hmong in Contemporary Vietnam," PhD dissertation, Department of Social and Cultural Anthropology, Vrije University Amsterdam.

Nguyen, Lien Hang T. (2012) *Hanoi's War: An International History of the War for Peace in Vietnam*. Chapel Hill: University of North Carolina Press.

Nguyen, Minh Quang (2005) *Religious Issues and Government Policies in Viet Nam*. Ha Noi: The Gioi.

Ninh, Kim (2002) *A World Transformed: The Politics of Culture in Revolutionary Vietnam. 1945–1965*. Ann Arbor, MI: University of Michigan Press.

Nivelle, Pascale (2009) "'Caonima': le clip qui fait la nique à Pékin," *Libération*, March 14.

Novikova, M. (1991) "Khristos, Veles – Pilat. 'Neokhristianskie' i 'neoyazycheskie' motivy v sovremennoi otechestvennoi kul'ture," *Novyi mir* 6: 242–254.

Nowak, Leszek (2011) "Paradoxes of Social Consciousness under Socialism," *Studies in Soviet Thought* 43.2, Polish Philosophy at Crossroads, March 1992, pp. 159–168.
Nudel'man, R. (1979) "Sovremennyi sovetskii antisemitism. Formy i soderzhanie." In *Antisemitizm v Sovetskom Soiuze. Ego korni i posledstviia.* Ierusalim: Biblioteka "Aliia," pp. 24–52.
Oh, Dae-hyung and Kyung-ho Ha (1989) *Dangŭi ryŏngdomite ch'angjakgŏnripdoin daeginyŏmbidŭlŭi sasangyesulsŏng* (The Ideological-artistic Quality of Great Monumental Objects Created and Erected under the Leadership of the Party). Pyongyang: Chosun Art Press.
Oushakine, Serguei (2009) *The Patriotism of Despair: Nation, War, and Loss in Russia.* Ithaca, NY: Cornell University Press.
Overmyer, Daniel (2003) "Religion in China Today: Introduction," *The China Quarterly* 174: 307–316.
Paert, Irina (2004) "Demystifying the Heavens: Women, Religion, and Khrushchev's Anti-Religious Campaign, 1954–64." In Melanie Ilič, Susan E. Reid, and Lynne Attwood eds, *Women in the Khrushchev Era.* Basingstoke: Palgrave Macmillan, pp. 203–221.
Palmer, David (2007) *Qigong Fever: Body, Science and Utopia in China.* New York: Columbia University Press.
—— (2008) "Heretical Doctrines, Reactionary Secret Societies, Evil Cults Labeling Heterodoxy in Twentieth-Century China." In Mayfair Mei-Hui Yang ed., *Chinese Religiosities: Afflictions of Modernity and State Formation.* Berkeley: University of California Press, pp. 113–134.
—— (2009) "China's Religious Danwei: Institutionalising Religion in the People's Republic," *China Perspectives* 4: 17–30.
Panofsky, Erwin (1960 [1957]) *Renaissance and Renascences in Western Art.* London and New York: Harper & Row.
Papkova, Irina (2011) *The Orthodox Church and Russian Politics.* New York: Oxford University Press.
Pares, Bernard (1953) *A History of Russia.* Revised edition. London: Knopf.
Park, Hyun Ok (2005) *Two Dreams in One Bed: Empire, Social Life, and the Origins of the North Korean Revolution in Manchuria.* Durham, NC: Duke University Press.
Parkhomenko, S. (1995) "Bashnia Merlina," *Moskovskie novosti* 29: 8–9; 31: 18–19.
Pasek, Zbigniew (2006) "State and Local Governments Policies towards New Religious Movements in Poland, 1989–2004." In Irena Borowik ed., *Religions Churches and Religiosity in Post-communist Europe.* Kraków: Nomos, pp. 181–191.
Pasieka, Agnieszka (2015) *Hierarchy and Pluralism: Living Religious Difference in Catholic Poland.* Palgrave Macmillan.
Patterson, George (1969) *Christianity in Communist China.* Waco: Word Books.
Paxson, Margaret (2005) *Solovyovo: The Story of Memory in a Russian Village.* Bloomington: Indiana University Press.
Peel, J. D. Y. (2009) "Postsocialism, Postcolonialism, Pentecostalism." In M. Pelkmans ed., *Conversion after Socialism: Disruptions, Modernisms and Technologies of Faith in the Former Soviet Union.* New York: Berghahn Books, pp. 183–199.
Pelkmans, Mathijs (2009) (ed.) *Conversion After Socialism: Disruptions, Modernisms, and Technologies of Faith in the Former Soviet Union.* New York: Berghahn.

────── (2012) "Chaos and Order along the (Former) Iron Curtain." In H. Donnan and T. Wilson eds, *The Blackwell Companion to Border Studies*. Malden, MA: Wiley Blackwell, pp. 269–282.

Pelley, Patricia (2002) *Post-Colonial Vietnam: New Histories of the National Past*. Durham, NC: Duke University Press.

Peperkamp, Esther (2010) "Business and God in Saxony: Life Histories and Moral Narratives of Christian Entrepreneurs." In Chris Hann ed., *Religion, Identity, Postsocialism: The Halle Focus Group 2003–2010*. Halle/Saale: The Max Planck Institute for Social Anthropology, pp. 85–87.

Peris, Daniel (1998) *Storming the Heavens: The Soviet League of the Militant Godless*. Ithaca, NY: Cornell University Press.

Petukhov, A. (1969) "Bumazhnye tsvety," *Novyi mir* 6: 272–277.

Pham Quynh Phuong (2009) *Hero and Deity: Tran Hung Dao and the Resurgence of Popular Religion in Vietnam*. Chieng Mai, Thailand: Mekong Press.

Pham Van Minh (2002) *Vietnamese Engaged Buddhism: The Struggle Movement of 1963–1966*. Westminster, CA: Van Nghe.

Phan, Peter (2014) "Christianity in Vietnam Today, 1973–2013, Contemporary Challenges and Opportunities," *International Journal for the Study of the Christian Church* 14: 1.

Phoumi Vongvichit (1969) *Laos and the Victorious Struggles of the Lao People Against U.S. Neo-Colonialism*. Hanoi: Neo Lao Haksat Editions.

Phra Santisouk Phetphouvong (2004) "Buddhist Teachings and Life," *Pasason* August 16 (in Lao).

Pipes, Richard (1993) *Russia under the Bolshevik Regime*. New York: Vintage Books.

Piwowarski, Władysław (1968) "The Image of the Priest in the Eyes of Parishioners in Three Rural Parishes," *Social Compass* 15: 235–249.

────── (1976) "Industrialization and Popular Religiosity in Poland," *Sociological Analysis* 37.4: 315–320.

Plamper, Jan (2010) *Alkhimiia vlasti. Kul't Stalina v izobrazitel'nom iskusstve*. Moscow: Novoe literaturnoe obozrenie.

────── (2012) *The Stalin Cult: A Study in The Alchemy of Power*. New Haven, NJ: Yale University Press.

Poliakov, L. (1996) *Ariiskii mif. Issledovanie istokov rasizma*. St.-Petersburg: Evraziia.

Polikarpov, V. V. and V. V. Shelokhaev (1998) "Iz sledstvennykh del N. V. Nekrasova 1921, 1931 i 1939 godov," *Voprosy istorii* 11–12: 10–48.

Porter, Brian (2001) "The Catholic Nation: Religion, Identity, and the Narratives of Polish History," *The Slavic and East European Journal* 45.2: 289–299.

Pospielovsky, Dimitry (1984) *The Russian Church under the Soviet Regime, 1917–1982*, 2 vols. Crestwood and New York: St. Vladimir's Seminary Press, 1984.

Powell, David E. (1975) *Antireligious Propaganda in the Soviet Union: A Study of Mass Persuasion*. Cambridge: MIT Press.

Prapod, Assavavirulhakam (2010) *The Ascendancy of Theravada Buddhism in Southeast Asia*. Seattle WA: University of Washington Press.

Pratt, Mary Lousie (1992) *Imperial Eyes: Travel Writing and Transculturation*. New York and London: Routledge.

Pribylovsky, V. V. (1992) "Pamiat'" In R. Sh. Ganelin ed., *Natsional'naia pravaia prezhde i teper'*. Chast' 2, vyp.2. Saint-Petersburg: Institut sotsiologii RAN, pp. 151–170.

—— (1998a) "Russkie iazychniki," *Ekspress-khronika*, February 21.
—— (1998b) "Novye iazychniki – liudi i gruppy," *Russkaia mysl'*, April 30–May 6, p. 21.
Pyman, Averil (2010) *Pavel Florensky: A Quiet Genius*. London: Continuum.
Quijada, Justine Buck (2009) "Opening the Roads: History and Religion in Post-Soviet Buryatia," PhD dissertation, Department of Anthropology, University of Chicago.
—— (2012) "Soviet Science and Post-Soviet Faith: Etigelov's Imperishable Body," *American Ethnologist* 39.1: 138–154.
Quinn-Judge, Sophie (2002) *Ho Chi Minh: The Missing Years: 1919–1941*. Berkeley, CA: University of California Press.
Rajtar, Małgorzata (2010) "'Heaven on Earth': Conversion and Morality in Eastern Germany." In Chris Hann ed., *Religion, Identity, Postsocialism: The Halle Focus Group 2003–2010*, Halle/Saale: The Max Planck Institute for Social Anthropology, pp. 89–92.
Ramet, Sabrina Pedro (1990) *Catholicism and Politics in Communist Societies*. Durham, NC: Duke University Press.
—— (1998) *Nihil obstat: Religion, Politics, and Social Change in East-Central Europe and Russia*. Durham, NC: Duke University Press.
Reynolds, Craig J. (2006) *Seditious Histories: Contesting Thai and Southeast Asian Pasts*. Washington: University of Washington Press.
Reznik, Semen (1996) *The Nazification of Russia: Anti-Semitism in the Post-Soviet Era*. Washington, DC: Challenge Publications.
Riegelhaupt, Joyce (1984) "Popular Anti-clericalism and Religiosity in Pre-1974." In Eric R. Wolf and Herbert H. Lehmann eds, *Religion, Power and Protest in Local Communities*. Berlin u.a.: Mouton, pp. 93–116.
Riesebrodt, Martin (2007) *Cultus und Heilsversprechen: Eine Theorie der Religionen*. Munich: Beck.
Ro'i, Yaacov (1984) "The Task of Creating the New Soviet Man: 'Atheistic Propaganda' in the Soviet Muslim Areas," *Soviet Studies* 36.1: 26–44.
Rogers, Douglas (2005) "Introductory Essay: The Anthropology of Religion after Socialism," *Religion, State and Society* 33.1: 5–18.
—— (2009) *The Old Faith and the Russian Land: A Historical Ethnography of Ethics in the Urals*. Ithaca, NY: Cornell University Press.
Roguska, Beata (1999) *Kościół w III Rzeczypospolitej*. Komunikat z badań (CBOS).
Rothbard, Murray N. (1990) "Karl Marx: Communist as Religious Eschatologist," *The Review of Austrian Economics* 4: 123–179.
Roy, Olivier (2007) *Secularism Confronts Islam*. New York: Columbia University Press.
Rozhdestvenskii S. D. (1981–1982) "Materialy k istorii samodeiatel'nykh politicheskikh ob'edinenii v SSSR posle 1945 goda." In *Pamiat'*, Moskva-Parizh,1981–1982, 5: 226–283.
Rudnev V. A. (1964) *Kommunisticheskomu bytu – novye traditsii*. Leningrad: Znanie.
—— (1982) *Obriady narodnye i obriady tserkovnye*. Leningrad: Lenizdat.
—— (1989) *Drevo zhizni: ob istokakh narodnykh i religioznykh obriadov*. Leningrad: Lenizdat.
Rudnyckyj, Daromir (2010) *Spiritual Economies: Islam, Globalization, and the Afterlife of Development*. Ithaca, NY: Cornell University Press.

Rutherford, Danilyn (2008) "The Enchantments of Secular Belief." Religion and Culture Web Forum, Martin Marty Center, University of Chicago Divinity School. http://divinity.uchicago.edu/martycenter/publications/webforum/archive.shtml (last accessed October 19, 2011).
Sangren, P. Steven (1984) "Traditional Chinese Corporations: Beyond Kinship," *Journal of Asian Studies* 43: 391–416.
——— (2000) *Chinese Sociologics: An Anthropological Account of the Role of Alienation in Social Reproduction*. London: The Athlon Press.
Sarsenbaev, N. S. (1965) *Obychai i traditsii v razvitii*. Kazakhstan: Alma-Ata.
Saykham Champaouthoum (2004) "The Lao People and Buddhism," *Pasason*, August 3 (in Lao).
Schorch, Philipp (2013) "Contact Zones, Third Spaces, and the Act of Interpretation," *Museum and Society* 11.1: 68–81.
Schütz, Alfred (1962) "Symbol, Reality, and Society." In *Collected Papers, vol. 1: The Problem of Social Reality*. The Hague: Martinus Nijhoff, pp. 287–356.
Schütz, Alfred and Thomas Luckmann (1989 [1983]) *The Structures of the Life-World, vol. 2*. Richard Zaner and David Parent trans. Evanston, IL: Northwestern University Press.
Service, Robert (2002) *Lenin: A Biography*. Cambridge, MA: Belknap.
Shahrani, Nazif M. (1984) "'From Tribe to Umma': Comments on the Dynamics of Identity in Muslim Soviet Central Asia," *Central Asian Survey* 3.3: 27–38.
——— (1995) "Islam and the Political Culture of 'Scientific Atheism' in Post-Soviet Central Asia: Future Predicaments." In M. Bourdeaux ed., *The Politics of Religion in Russia and the New States of Eurasia*. Armonk, NY: Sharpe, pp. 273–292.
Shakhnovich, M. (1961) *Lenin i problemy idealizma. Kritika religii v trudakh V. I. Lenina*. Moscow.
Shavlokhova, M. and D. Sokolov-Mitrich (2005) "Materi protiv Grabovogo," *Izvestiia*, September 26, p. 1.
Shin, G.-W. (2006) *Ethnic Nationalism in Korea: Genealogy, Politics, and Legacy*. Stanford University Press: Studies of the Walter H. Shorenstein Asia-Pacific Research Center.
Shleinov, R. (1998) "Vooruzhennye nechistye sily – 2." *Novaia gazeta*, November 16–22, p. 7.
Shneider, G. (1993) "Ot ateizma k iazychestvu." In: M. N. Epstein. *Novoe sektantstvo: tipy religiozno-filosofskikh umonastroenii v Rossii (70–80-e gg. XX v.)*. Holyoke: New England Publishing Co., pp. 144–148.
Shnirelman, Victor A. (1998a) *Russian Neo-pagan Myths and Antisemitism*. Jerusalem: The Hebrew University of Jerusalem (ACTA no. 13).
——— (1998b) "Vtoroe prishestvie ariiskogo mifa," *Vostok* 1: 89–107.
——— (1998c) *Neoiazychestvo i natsionalizm. Vostochnoevropeiskii areal*. Moscow: IEA.
——— (2001) "Nazad k iazychestvu? Triumfal'noe shestvie neoiazychestva po prostoram Evrazii." In V. A. Shnirelman ed., *Neoiazychestvo na prostorakh Evrazii*. Moscow: Bibleisko-Bogoslovsky Institut, pp. 130–169.
——— (2002) "'Christians, go home!': A Revival of Neo-Paganism between the Baltic Sea and Transcaucasia (an overview)," *Journal of Contemporary Religions* 17.2: 197–211.
——— (2007) "Ancestral Wisdom and Ethnic Nationalism: A View from Eastern Europe," *Pomegranate* 9.1: 41–61.

——— (2008) "Vozvrashchenie ariistva: nauchnaia fantastika i rasizm," *Neprikosnovennyi zapas* 62: 63–89.
——— (2011) "Zhizn' i sud'ba fal'shivki: 'Vlesova kniga' v sotsial'nom interiere." In A. E. Petrov and V. A. Shnirelman eds, *Fal'sifikatsiia istoricheskikh istochnikov i konstruirovanie etnokraticheskikh mifov*. Moscow: Institute of Archaeology, pp. 115–144.
——— (2012) *Russkoe Rodnoverie: neoiazychestvo i natsionalizm v sovremennoi Rossii*. Moscow: Bibleisko-Bogoslovsky Institut.
——— (2015, in press) *Aryiskii mif v sovremennom mire*. Moscow: NLO.
Shnirelman, V. A. and G. A. Komarova (1997) "Majority as a Minority: The Russian Ethno-nationalism and Its Ideology in the 1970–1990s." In H.-R. Wicker ed., *Rethinking Nationalism and Ethnicity: The Struggle for Meaning and Order in Europe*. Oxford: Berg, pp. 211–224.
Shubin-Abramov, A. F. (1996) *Bukovnik Vseiasvetnoi Gramoty*. Moscow: n. d.
Simon, Gerhard (1991) *Nationalism and Policy toward the Nationalities in the Soviet Union*. Boulder: Westview.
Siripanyo, Bhikku S. (2009) *Buddhist Education*. Prathammakhan Press, Thailand: Khon Kaen (in Lao).
Skurlatov, V. I. (1975) *Sionizm i aparteid*. Kiev: Izdatel'stvo Politicheskoi Literatury Ukrainy.
Slezkine, Yuri (1996) "The USSR as a Communal Apartment or How a Socialist State Promoted Ethnic Particularism." In R. Suny and G. Eley eds, *Becoming National*. Oxford: Oxford University Press, pp. 203–238.
Smith, Arthur H. (1907) *The Uplift of China*. New York: The Presbyterian Department of Missionary Education.
Smith, Jonathan Z. (1998) "Religion, Religions, Religious." In Mark C. Taylor ed., *Critical Terms for Religious Studies*. Chicago: University of Chicago Press, pp. 269–284.
Smolkin-Rothrock, Victoria (2010) "'A Sacred Space Is Never Empty': Soviet Atheism, 1954–1971," PhD dissertation, Department of History, University of California, Berkeley.
Smyer Yu, Dan (2008) "Living Buddhas, Netizens, and the Price of Religious Freedom." In Li Zhang and Aihwa Ong eds, *Privatizing China: Socialism from Afar*. Ithaca, NY: Cornell University Press, pp. 197–213.
——— (2011) *The Spread of Tibetan Buddhism in China*. London: Rouledge.
Socialist Republic of Vietnam (1992) Ban Ton Giao cua Chinh Phu. *Cac Van Ban cua Nha Nuoc ve Hoat Dong Ton Giao*. Ha Noi: Ban Ton Giao.
——— (1995) *The Constitutions of Vietnam: 1946–1959–1980–1992*. Hanoi: The Gioi.
Solomenko E. (1993) "Adolf Hitler v Sankt-Peterburge," *Izvestiia*, June 10, p. 5.
Solovei V. D. (1991) "'Pamiat'': istoriia, ideologiia, politicheskaia praktika." In A. V. Lebedev ed., *Russkoe delo segodnia. Kn.1. Pamiat'*. Moscow: TsIMO IEA RAN, pp. 12–95.
Solovieva, T. (1992) "RA – Russkaia Akademiia, ili est' li proroki v svoem Otechestve," *Den'*, January 10–18, p. 1.
Sonam Darje (2000a) "A Scientific Treatise on Buddhism." In *A Treasure House of Buddhist Faith*. Hong Kong: Hong Kong Chinese Culture Publishing House, pp. 145–302.
——— (2000b) *The Whitecaps on the Ocean of Wisdom*. Hong Kong: Chinese Culture Press.

Stafford, Charles (2000) *Separation and Reunion in Modern China*. Cambridge: Cambridge University Press.
Stepankov, V. I. (1964) *Novye prazdniki i obriady – v narodnyi byt*. Moscow.
Strassberg, Barbara (1988) "Changes in Religious Culture in Post War II Poland," *Sociological Analysis* 48.4: 342–354.
Strel'nikov, K. (1998) "Rassudku vopreki, naperekor stikhiiam ... ," *Russkaia mysl'*, July 16–22, p. 10.
Stromberg, Peter G. (1993) *Language and Self-Transformation: A Study of the Christian Conversion Narrative*. Cambridge [England]: New York: Cambridge University Press.
Suh, Dae-Sook (1995) *Kim Il Sung: The North Korean Leader*. New York: Columbia University Press.
Sukhanov, I. V. (1973) *Obychai, traditsii, obriady kak sotsial'nye iavleniia*. Gor'ky: Volgo-Viatskoe knizhnoe izdatel'stvo.
Sullivan, Winnifred Fallers (2005) *The Impossibility of Religious Freedom*. Princeton, NJ: Princeton University Press.
―――― (2009) *Prison Religion: Faith-Based Reform and the Constitution*. Princeton, NJ: Princeton University Press.
Suny, Ronald (1993) *The Revenge of the Past: Nationalism, Revolution and the Collapse of the Soviet Union*. Stanford: Stanford Univesity Press.
Svetlova E. (2006) "Kukhonnaia psikhoterapiia." *Moskovskii komsomolets*, September 29, p. 5.
Swearer, Donald K. (2009) *The Buddhist World of Southeast Asia*. Second edition. Chiang Mai: Silkworm Books.
Tabyshalieva, Anara (1993) *Vera v Turkestane (Ocherk istorii religii Srednei Azii i Kazakhstana)*. Bishkek: Kommerchesko-izdatel'skaiâ firma "Az-Mak".
Tambar, Kabir (2009) "Secular Populism and the Semiotics of the Crowd in Turkey," *Public Culture* 21.3: 517–538.
Tambiah, S. J. (1977) *World Conqueror and World Renouncer: A Study of Buddhism and Polity in Thailand against a Historical Background*. Cambridge: Cambridge University Press.
Taubman, William (2003) *Khrushchev: The Man and His Era*. New York: Norton.
Taylor, Charles (1989) *Sources of the Self*. Cambridge, MA: Harvard University Press.
―――― (2007) *A Secular Age*. Cambridge, MA: Belknap.
Taylor, Phillip (2004) *Goddess on the Rise: Pilgrimage and Popular Religion in Vietnam*. Honolulu: University of Hawaii Press.
―――― (2007) (ed.) *Modernity and the Reenchantment of Religion in Post-Revolutionary Vietnam*. Singapore: ISEAS.
Thich Nhat Hanh (1967) *Vietnam: Lotus in a Sea of Fire*. New York: Hill and Wang.
Tianyayidu.com (2011) "Chairman Mao in Shaoshan has Become a God," http://tianyayidu.com/article-a-243519.html.
Titova, Irina (2002) "The 'Russian da Vinci' May Be among the Remains," *St. Petersburg Times*, October 1.
Tolstoy, Lev (1968) *War and Peace*. London: Penguin Classics.
Topmiller, Robert J. (2002) *The Lotus Unleashed: The Buddhist Peace Movement in South Vietnam, 1964–1966*. Lexington: University of Kentucky Press.
Tran Van Giau (1975) *Su Phat Trien cua Tu Tuong o Viet Nam tu The Ky XIX den Cach Mang Thang Tam*. Tap II. Hanoi: Nha Xuat Ban Khoa Hoc Xa Hoi.

Treadgold, Donald (1987) *Twentieth Century Russia*. Eighth edition. Boulder, CO: Westview Press.

Tri Hai (1938) "Vi sao ma phai chan hung phat gia" (Why We Must Revive Buddhism). *Duoc Tue* [The Torch of Buddhism], February 20.

Truong Chinh (1985) "De cuong ve van hoa Viet Nam" (Theses on Vietnamese Culture). In *Mot chang duong van hoa: Tap hoi uc va tu lieu ve De cuong van hoa cua Dang va doi song tu tuong van nghe, 1943–1948*. Hanoi: Nha Xuat Ban Tac Pham Moi.

—— (1977) "Marxism and Vietnamese Culture." In *Selected Writings*. Hanoi: Foreign Languages Publishing House, pp. 212–296.

Tu, Wei-ming (1996) "Destructive Will and Ideological Holocaust: Maoism as a Source of Social Suffering in China," *Daedalus* 125.1, Social Suffering (Winter, 1996): pp. 149–179.

Tul'tseva L. A. (1985) *Sovremennye prazdniki i obriady narodov SSSR*. Moscow: Nauka.

—— (2011) "Russkii prazdnik i demografiia v 20 – nachale 21 veka," *Etnograficheskoe obozrenie* 4: 64–74.

Tumarkin, Nina (1983) *Lenin Lives! The Lenin Cult in Soviet Russia*. Cambridge: Harvard University Press.

—— (1994) *The Living and the Dead: The Rise and Fall of the Cult of World War II in Russia*. New York: Basic Books.

Turner, Bryan S. (2009) "Evangelism, the State, and Subjectivity." In Julius Bautista and Francis Khek Gee Lim eds, *Christianity and the State in Asia: Complicity and Conflict*. London and New York: Routledge, pp. 18–35.

Tvorogov, O. V. (1990) "Vlesova kniga." In *Trudy Otdela Drevnerusskoi Literatury*. T. 43. Leningrad: Nauka, pp. 170–254.

Ugrinovich, D. M. (1975) *Obriady. Za i protiv*. Moscow: Politizdat.

United Front Work Department (UFWD) (2002a) "The Current State of Religion in China," http://www.zytzb.cn/publicfiles/business/htmlfiles/tzb2010/wdzj/200911/574214.html.

—— (2002b) "What Is the Difference between Religion and Superstition?" http://www.zytzb.cn/publicfiles/business/htmlfiles/tzb2010/zhishi/200911/574197.html.

United States Department of State (2010) "International Religious Freedom Report, Country Report for Vietnam, September 13, 2011," Washington, DC. Available at http://www.state.gov/g/drl/rls/irf/2010_5/index.htm.

Ushakova, Iu. (2003) "Atipichnaia religioznost' v postsovetskoi Rossii," *Novyi mir* 9: 131–149.

Vail', P. and A. Genis (1988) *60-e: mir sovetskogo cheloveka*. Ann Arbor, MI: Ardis.

van der Veer, Peter (2009) "Spirituality in Modern Society," *Social Research* 76.4, Winter 2009: pp. 1097–1120.

—— (2001) *Imperial Encounters: Religion and Modernity in India and Britain*. Princeton, NJ: Princeton University Press.

—— (2011) "Smash Temples, Burn Books: Comparing Secularist Projects in India and China." In Craig Calhoun, Mark Juergensmeyer and Jonathan VanArtwerpen eds, *Rethinking Secularism*. New York: Oxford University Press, pp. 270–281.

Verdery, Katherine (1996) *What Was Socialism and What Comes Next?* Princeton, NJ: Princeton University Press.

—— (1999) *The Political Lives of Dead Bodies: Reburial and Postsocialist Change*. New York: Columbia University Press.
Verkhovsky, A. and V. Pribylovsky (1996) *Natsional-patrioticheskie organizatsii v Rossii*. Moscow: Institut experimental'noi sotsiologii.
Verkhovsky, A., A.Papp, and V. Pribylovsky (1996) *Politicheskii extremizm v Rossii*. Moscow: Institut experimentalnoi sotsiologii.
Verkhovsky A., V. Pribylovsky and E. Mikhailovskaia (1998) *Natsionalism i ksenofobia v rossiiskom obshchestve*. Moscow: Panorama.
Vermander, Benoît (2009) "Religious Revival and Exit from Religion in Contemporary China," *China Perspectives* 4: 4–15.
Vishnevskaia, Iu. (1988) "Pravoslavnye, gevalt!" *Sintaksis* 21: 82–101.
Voegelin, Eric (1993 [1938]) *Die politischen Religionen*, Peter J. Opitz ed. Munich: Wilhelm Fink.
Wada, Haruki (1998) *Kita Chōsen: Yūgekitai kokka no genzai* (North Korea's Partisan State Today). Tokyo: Iwanami Shoten.
Walshe, W. Gilbert (1886) *Ways That Are Dark: Some Chapters on Chinese Etiquette and Social Procedure*. Shanghai: Kelly and Walsh, Limited.
Wang Gungwu (2002) "State and Faith: Secular Values in Asia and the West." In Eric Hershberg and Kevin W. Moore eds, *Critical Views of September 11: Analyses from around the World*. New York: New Press, pp. 224–242.
—— (2003) "Secular China," *China Report* 39.3: 305–321.
Wanner, Catherine (2007) *Communities of the Converted: Ukrainians and Global Evangelism*. Ithaca, NY: Cornell University Press.
Wanner, Catherine (2012) (ed.) *State Secularism and Lived Religion in Soviet Russia and Ukraine*. Washington, DC and Oxford: Woodrow Wilson Center Press/ Oxford University Press.
Warner, Michael, Jonathan VanAntwerpen and Craig Calhoun (2010) (eds) *Varieties of Secularism in a Secular Age*. Cambridge: Harvard University Press.
Watson, James L. (1988) "Funeral Specialists in Cantonese Society: Pollution, Performance, and Social Hierarchy." In James L. Watson and Evelyn S. Rawski eds, *Death Ritual in Late Imperial and Modern China*. Berkeley and London: University of California Press, pp. 109–134.
Weber, Max (1947) *The Theory of Social and Economic Organization*, Talcott Parsons ed. New York: The Free Press.
Weller, Robert P. (2000) "Living at the Edge: Religion, Capitalism, and the End of the Nation-State in Taiwan," *Public Culture* 3: 477–498.
Wells, Kenneth M. (1990) *New God, New Nation: Protestants and Self-Reconstruction Nationalism in Korea 1896–1937*. Honolulu: University of Hawaii Press.
—— (2008) "The Place of Religion in North Korean Ideology." In Susan Pares and J. E. Hoare eds, *Korea: The Past and the Present*. Folkestone, Kent: Global Oriental, pp. 248–264.
Wenger, Jacqueline E. (2004) "Official vs. Underground Protestant Churches in China: Challenges for Reconciliation and Social Influence," *Review of Religious Research* 46.2: 169–182.
Werbner, Richard (1998) "Smoke from the Barrel of a Gun: Postwars of the Dead, Memory, and Reinscription in Zimbabwe," In Richard Werbner ed., *Memory and Postcoloniality*. London: Zed, pp. 71–102.
Werner, Jayne (1974) "Catholics in South Vietnam," *Commonweal*, November.

—— (1976) "The Cao Dai: The Politics of a Vietnamese Syncretic Religious Movement," PhD dissertation, Cornell University.
—— (1980) "Vietnamese Communism and Religious Sectarianism." In William S. Turley ed., *Vietnamese Communism in Comparative Perspective*. Boulder, CO: Westview Press, pp. 107–137.
Wines, Michael (2009) "A Dirty Pun Tweaks China's Online Censors," *New York Times*, March 11.
Winiarczyk-Kossakowska, Małgorzata (2010) Kościół bierze państwo (interview by Jacek Żakowski). *Polityka*, January 9.
Winter, Jay (1995) *Sites of Memory, Sites of Mourning: The Great War in European Cultural History*. Cambridge: Cambridge University Press.
Wohlrab-Sahr, Monika, Uta Karstein, and Thomas Schmidt-Lux (2009) *Forcierte Säkularität: Religiöser Wandel und Generationendynamik im Osten Deutschlands*. Frankfurt: Campus.
Woodside, Alexander (1976) *Community and Revolution in Modern Vietnam*. Boston: Houghton Mifflin.
Xu Ben 徐贲 (2005a) "Zhongguo de 'xinjiquanzhuyi' jiqi moshi jingxiang" 中国的 "新极权主义"及其末世景象, *Dangdai zhongguo yanjiu* 当代中国研究 91: 4–26.
—— (2005b) "Gonggong zhenshi zhongde shehui hexie" 公共真实中的社会和谐, *Kaifang Shidai* 开放时代 5: 109–116.
—— (2008) "'Gaige kaifang': hefaxing weiji de xiaojie yu zai xingcheng" "改革开放": 合法性危机的消解与再形成, *Dangdai zhongguo yanjiu* 当代中国研究3: 34–45.
Yang, C. K. (1991 [1961]) *Religion in Chinese Society: A Study of Contemporary Social Functions of Religion and Some of Their Historical Factors*. Prospect Heights, IL: Waveland Press.
Yang, Der-Ruey (2005) "The Changing Economy of Temple Daoism in Shanghai." In Fenggang Yang and Joseph B. Tamney eds, *State, Market, and Religions in Chinese Societies*. Leiden: Brill, pp. 113–148.
Yang, Fenggang (2005) "Lost in the Market, Saved at MacDonald's: Conversion to Christianity in Urban China," *Journal for the Scientific Study of Religion* 44.4: 423–441.
—— (2008) "The Red, Black, and Gray Markets of Religion in China," *China Agricultural University Journal of Social Sciences Edition* 25.4, December, pp. 93–122.
—— (2009a) "Religion in China under Communism: A Shortage Economy Explanation," *Journal of Church and State, doi:10.1093/jcs/csp042*.
—— (2009b) "Cultural Dynamics in China: Today and in 2020." A paper presented at an NBR conference titled "China 2020: Future Scenarios," Airlie Center, VA, February 15–17, 2007.
Yang, Mayfair Mei-Hui (2000) "Putting Global Capitalism in Its Place: Economic Hybridity, Bataille, and Ritual Expenditure," *Current Anthropology* 41.4: 477–509.
Yang, Mayfair (2008) (ed.) *Chinese Religiosities: Afflictions of Modernity and State Formation*. Berkeley: University of California Press.
Yanov, A. (1987) *The Russian Challenge and the Year 2000*. Oxford: Basil Blackwell.
Yao, Xinzhong and Paul Badham (2007) *Religious Experience in Contemporary China*. Cardiff: University of Wales Press.

You Zhibiao (n.d.) "Scientific Viewpoint of Buddhism," http://www.jcedu.org/fjwh/kx/kxg1.htm.

Young, Glennys (1997) *Power and the Sacred in Revolutionary Russia: Religious Activists in the Village*. Pennsylvania: Pensylvania State University Press.

Yu Jianrong 于建嵘 (2010a) "Yali weiwen de zhengzhixue fenxi: Zhongguo shehui gangxing wending de yunxing jizhi," 压力维稳的政治学分析——中国社会刚性稳定的运行机制, *Zhanlüe yu guanli* 战略与管理 4: 55–60.

―――― (2010b) "Zhongguo jidujiao jiating jiaohui hefahua yanjiu" 中国基督教家庭教会合法化研究, *Zhanlüe yu guanli* 战略与管理 2: 16–22.

Yurchak, Alexei (2006) *Everything Was Forever, until It Was No More: The Last Soviet Generation*. Princeton, NJ: Princeton University Press.

Zaremba, Marcin (2001) *Komunizm, legitymizacja, nacjonalizm. Nacjonalistyczna legitymizacja władzy komunistycznej w Polsce*. Warszawa: Instytut Studiów Politycznych PAN, Wydawnictwo TRIO.

Zernov, Nicholas (1963) *The Russian Religious Renaissance of the Twentieth Century*. London: Darton, Logman and Todd.

Zhao Litao (2010) "Religious Revival and the Emerging Secularism in China." In Michael Heng Siam-Heng and Ten Chin Liew eds, *State and Secularism: Perspective from Asia*. Singapore: World Scientific, pp. 301–317.

Zhao Shiling and Duan Qi (2009) *Christianity in China: Contextualized Wisdom*. Beijing: Religion & Culture Press.

Zheng, Mao (2008) "Jade Buddha Temple MBA Alumni Celebrating with Their Shanghai Jiaotong University Peers," http://www.sjtu.edu.cn/news/shownews.php?id=17839.

Zigon, Jarrett (2011) *HIV Is God's Blessing: Rehabilitating Morality in Neoliberal Russia*. Berkeley: University of California Press.

Zubrzycki, Geneviève (2001) "'We, the Polish Nation': Ethnic and Civic Visions of Nationhood in Post-Communist Constitutional Debates," *Theory and Society* 30.5: 629–668.

Zuckerman, Phil (2008) *Society without God: What the Least Religious Nations Can Tell Us About Contentment*. New York: New York University Press.

Zuo, Jiping (1991) "Political Religion: The Case of the Cultural Revolution in China," *Sociological Analysis* 52.1 (Spring, 1991): 99–110.

Index

Abdyldaev, 247, 248, 254n2
abortion, Poland, 76, 79–80, 90n6
American War in Vietnam, 30, 39, 41–2, 117–18, *see also*
Vietnam War
animism, 55, 65, *see also* paganism
anticlericalism, 82, 86, 88, 91n17
anti-imperialism, 29, 37, 56, 207n7
anti-colonialism, 14, 21–2, 30, 36, 41–2, 114, 118, 122, 129
anti-Japanese imperialism, 112–14, 192–3
see also decolonization
anti-Semitism, 91n16, 174–5, 181, 184–5, 187
ARVN (Army of the Republic of Vietnam), 39, 41
Aryans, Slavic-, 181, 182, 185–7
atheism, 3–7, 245, 246
atheist believers, 246, 250
atheist Catholic, 78, 85
atheist Muslim, 246
atheist secularism, 3–7
assuming communism like a religion, 10–12, 140–3, 145, 150, 155–63, 167–70
assuming communism represses religion, 8–10
assuming religion an expression of national identity, 13–15, 29–49, 54–67, 173–88, 244–54
as historical project, 15–19
Azure Cloud Immortal, 234–5

baptisms, 52n88, 73, 76, 83, 180, 218
Berlin Wall, 95, 144
Bolsheviks
cultural policy on religious art, 211–17
removal of Church property, 213–14
role of religious art in time of crisis, 217–23

see also religious art; Soviet society; Soviet Union
Bourdieu, Pierre, 162, 167, 200, *see also* habitus
brainwashing, North Korea, 194, 197, 199–201
Brezhnev, Leonid Il'ich, 141, 146
Buddhism
in China, 24, 92–4, 99, 100, 107, 156, 163–8, 171, 225, 239
Christianity and, 8, 59, 64, 94, 156, 167–8, 171
in Laos, 22, 54–69
in North Korea, 201, 206n5
revitalization, 167
in Russia, 2, 150
scientific apologetics of, 163–4
scientific representation of, 164–7
Taoism and, 19, 68n2, 92–3, 99, 107
in Vietnam, 32–5, 40–1, 47, 51n53

Cambodia, Pol Pot, 8, 54
Cao Dai
Anti-colonial religious movement, 21, 49n13, 50n24
declared illegal, 53n90
dismantling, 51n50, 52n84
relations with Viet Minh, 50n35
spirit possession, 49n12, 52n86
Vietnam, 30–7, 39–40, 42, 45, 46–7
Casanova, Jose, 3, 5, 15–16, 86
Catholicism, 7
China, 92, 107, 225
Poland, 6, 22, 71–4, 76–8, 83–7, 88, 90n9–10
Vietnam, 30, 31, 35–40, 47, 48
CC CPSU (Central Committee of the Community Party of the Soviet Union), 176, 181, 184, 188
CCP (Chinese Communist Party), 93, 94, 96–100, 102, 105, 107, 109, 110n4, 110n6, 160, 161, 168, 170, 232

Cemetery of Revolutionary Martyrs,
      126, 128, 129
censorship, 75, 100–101, 174–80, 182,
      194, 197
charismatic authority, North Korea,
      130–2, see also cult of personality
China
   authority without authenticity, 95–8
   axis of state limitation on religion,
      104–8
   Christianity (pre-1949), 158–9
   Christianity and communist
      religiosity, 159–63
   Confucianism, 98–101
   contemporary, 92–5
   encounter of communist religiosity
      and Christianity in, 156–8
   Falungong movement, 93, 104–7
   harmony slogan, 98–101
   house churches, 11, 104, 107, 157
   infrared communism and
      conversion project, 167–72
   neo-totalitarian politics, 101–4,
      105, 109
   political slogans, 97–8
   post-ideological politics of PRC,
      95–8
   public sacrifice and staged power,
      101–4
   religionscape, 225–7
   revitalization of, 155–6
   rigid stability of, 104–8
   river crabs, 98–101
   scientific apologetics of Buddhism,
      163–4
   scientific representation of
      Buddhism, 164–7
   secularization without secularism,
      108–10
   Tiananmen Square, 95–6, 160
   underground churches, 104,
      107, 157
   see also PRC (People's Republic of
      China)
Chinese Academy of Social Sciences,
      167, 168–9
Christianity
   Buddhism and, 8, 59, 64, 94, 156,
      167–8, 171

Catholic Church, 70–89, 232–3
   in China, 24, 93–4, 107, 156–63,
      167–9, 171, 233, 243n3
   communist religiosity and, in
      China, 156–8
   conversion narratives, 202–5
   delayed growth of, in Communist
      China, 159–63
   Eastern Orthodox, 25, 136, 140,
      145, 147, 150, 183–4, 186, 188,
      215, 218–22, 232, 235, 246
   encounter of communist religiosity
      and, in China, 156–8
   Islam and, 93, 94, 254
   Jewish origins of, 175
   in Laos, 64, 67
   North Korea, 12, 190–2, 194, 196–9,
      199–201, 206n2
   in Poland, 71–88
   relationship with state, 15–16, 23,
      94, 99, 101, 140, 155, 171, 188,
      191
   religious engagement, 243n3
   in Russia, 136, 145, 150, 174–6,
      178–9, 181–3, 185–7, 218
   in South Korea, 191–2, 194,
      196–203, 205
   in Vietnam, 30, 35, 40, 45, 47–8
civic religion, see state ritual
Cold War, 3, 6–7, 14
   Christianity conversions, 201
   Korean War, 112–13, 117, 191–2
   grieving families in Vietnam, 45
   North Korea, 24–5, 191–2, 204
   occult weapons, 189n6
   South Korea, 24–5, 192, 204
   Vietnam War, 112–13, 117
colonialism
   Indochina, 31–5
   Korea (Japanese colonialism),
      112–15, 117–19, 129
   Laos, 54–6, 59
   Vietnam, 48–9
commemoration
   China, 101
   North Korea, 23, 112–13, 115–17,
      120–3, 127, 129, 132–3n1
   Poland, 90n5
   Vietnam, 1, 23, 44-5

communism
  colonial Indochina, 31–5
  in China, 92, 94, 97, 155–63, 167–72
  in Laos, 54, 60, 62, 65
  in Kyrgyzstan, 248
  in North Korea, 191–3, 199, 205
  in Poland, 71–80, 85–8
  in Russia, 134–6, 140–3, 145, 150, 151n2, 173, 210–11, 220
  in Vietnam, 30–1, 41–2, 48
communist ideology, 88
  atheism, 2
  comparison to religion, 10–12, 135
  and scientism of China, 94
  shared vision of modernity, 17
  socialism, 21
  transcendence, 23
Communist Manifesto (Marx and Engels), 54
Communist Party, 8, 18–22, 244
  Chinese (CCP), 93, 94, 96–100, 102, 105, 107, 109, 110n4, 110n6, 160, 161, 168, 170, 232
  Indochinese (ICP), 30, 31, 32, 35, 38, 41, 43, 44, 49n5–6, 50n24
  Laos, 22
  North Korea, 118, 206n3
  Poland, 8, 22–3, 70–8
  Soviet Union, 135, 141, 145, 150, 176, 184, 218
  Vietnam, 30, 39–42, 49n3
communist secularization, 3, 12, 15–18, 109, 135, 145, 149, 151
Confucian ethics/virtues, 32, 43, 94, 100, 129
Confucianism, 49n16, 49n6, 55, 68n2, 93, 98–102, 104, 106, 110n7
  ethics/virtues, 32, 43, 94, 100, 129
  Festival of Confucian Culture, 102, 104, 110n12
Constructing China's Jerusalem (Cao), 157
conversions, 20
  in China, 156, 159–62, 164, 166–9
  Christian conversions, 13, 67, 160, 190, 192, 196–9, 201–2, 205
  in Laos, 61, 67, 68n7, 69n18
  in North Korea, 190–2, 194, 196–201, 202–5
  in Poland, 84
  post-mortem, 84
  in Soviet society, 136
  in Vietnam, 45
cult of personality
  Ho Chi Minh, 30, 43–5, 48
  Kim Il Sung, 114–24, 132, 197–8
  Mao, 161
  Marx as a deity, 162
  Stalin, 146
Cultural Revolution, 2, 8, 24, 37, 54, 93, 102, 160–2, 169, 225, 234–5, 239

Daoism, 225–6, 229, 232–3, 235, 237–41
decolonization, 38–9
Deng Xiaopeng, 21, 99, 100, 162
"De-Zionization" (Emelianov), 183, 184
Dobrovol'sky, Alexei A., 176, 186
Doi Moi
  resurgence of religion under, 29–30
  Vietnam, 30, 39, 43–4, 46–8

Emelianov, Valery, 175, 182–4
Engels, Friedrich, 54, 151n2, 165
Enlightenment, 4, 15, 34, 158, 170, 177, 193, 212, 216
ethno-national identity, 8, 13–15
  in China, 92, 159, 230, 238
  in Kyrgyzstan, 249–51
  in Laos, 55, 57–8, 63–5, 67
  in North Korea, 116–17, 191
  in Poland, 74, 78, 85–6, 89, 90n9–10
  in USSR. 173, 175, 180, 188, 215, 221
  in Vietnam, 41–4, 47–8

Fallen Soldiers (Mosse), 116
Falungong, 93, 104–7
feudalism, 28, 212
feudal superstition, 8, 225, 239
Florensky, Pavel, 25, 210, 211, 219–23, 224n7
folk culture, 10, 178–80
Foucault, Michel, 9, 136, 162
French colonialism
  in Laos, 54–6. 59
  in Vietnam, 29, 48

French Orientalists, 55–6
French Revolution, 213, 215, 232

Geertz, Clifford, 159, 194
globalization, 95, 155
Gorbachev, Mikhail, 210, 212, 218, 221, 223
Graves of Revolutionary Martyrs, North Korea, 114, 118–21, 124, 126, 131–2
Greek Catholics, 73, 81–2, 84

habitus, 104, 162, 167, 200, *see also* Bourdieu, Pierre
Hann, Chris, 3, 6, 8–9, 10–11
harmony, Confucianism, 98–101
Hoa Hao, Vietnam, 30–7, 39–40, 42, 46–7, 50n35, 51n50
Ho Chi Minh, 1–2, 38, 44
  creation of Viet Minh, 35–6
  cult of, 30, 43–5, 48
  Indochinese Communist Party (ICP), 30, 31
Holy Trinity Icon, Rublev, 215, 219
Ho Phap Pham Cong Tac, 36, 37, 46
house churches, China, 11, 104, 107, 157, *see also* Christianity; China
household
  construction of superstition specialist, 239–42
  impact of socialist transformations, 230–2
  political economy, 242
  ritual service providers, 235–9, 242
  socialist middle peasants in China, 230–2
  socialist persecution of religious institutions in China, 232–5
  sovereignty, 230–2
  in Soviet Union, 145, 149
  unit of religious engagement in China, 25, 227–30, 243n5
Humanism, communist, of Soviet society, 134–5
human rights, 41, 48, 107, 200, 203, 204, 208n14, 209n15
Huynh Phu So, 34, 36, 37, 50n23

icons, 20, 27, 127, 145, 147–8, 210–13, 215–23

ICP (Indochinese Communist Party), 30, 31, 32, 35, 38, 41, 43, 44, 49n5–6, 50n24
ideology education, North Korea, 195–6
Immanent Frame project, 15, 26n3
Indochina Wars, 36–7, 42, 50n31, *see also* Vietnam war
International Zionism, 181, 182, 184, 185, 187
Islam, 5, 47, 201
  China, 92–4, 107, 225
  Kyrgyzstan, 25, 244, 246, 249–54
  Soviet society, 150, 182, 188n3
  Tablighis, 251–3, 255n4
Ivanov (Skuratov), Anatoly M., 175, 183–6

Jade Emperor, 32, 49n12, 52n86, 237
Jiang Zemin, 100, 169
Juche ideology, North Korea, 12, 24, 191, 194–8, 200–201, 205, 207n7–8, 209n15
Judaism, 174, 182, 184, 186, 198

Kim Il Sung, 114–15, 119–26, 129–31, 195–8, 200, 205, 207n10, 207–8n11, 209n15
Kimilsungism, 196, 197, 200
Kim Jong Il, 114, 123–5, 130, 131, 195–8
Kim Jong Suk, 124, 125–7, 129–31, 133n2
Kim Jong Suk, Our Mother (song), 126
Kim Jong Un, 132n1
Komsomol, 18, 176–7, 180, 188, 216
Korean War, 112–15, 117–23, 132n1, 205, 208–9n15
Krushchev, Nikita, 141, 146, 182
Kyrgyzstan, 244–7
  national culture in post-Soviet, 25
  post-Soviet challenges, 251–3
  religious movements, 253–4
  Soviet atheism and secularism, 247–50
  Tablighis, 251–3, 255n4

Land Reform, 39, 40, 52n62, 230–3
Lane, Christel, 141, 188n3–4

Laos, 13, 16
 Buddhism, 54–67
 Communist Party, 22
 NLHS (*Neo Lao Hak Sat*), 56–8, 60–1
 NLSS (*Neo Lao Sang Sat*), 57, 62–4
 Royal Lao Government (RLG), 54, 56–7
 secular fundamentalism, 54
 superstition, 66–7
 Theravada Buddhism, 55, 58, 67–8n1
 thevada (angels), 55, 56, 63, 68n11
LBFO (Lao Buddhist Fellowship Organization), 62–3, 65
Lenin, Vladimir, 8, 151n2, 210–15, 220
Leninism, *see* Marxism–Leninism
LPDR (Lao People's Democratic Republic), 59, 62, 63, 64, 66
LPRP (Lao People's Revolutionary Party), 65
Luckman, Thomas, 135, 142–5
Lunacharsky, Anatolii, 212, 214–15
Luther, Martin, 6, 253, 255n5

Manchurian tradition
 heroes of partisan movement, 120–5
 Kim Il Sung, 129–30, 131
 North Korea, 113–20
 see also anti-imperialism; North Korea
Maoism, 19, 96, 99, 100, 159–60, 161, 225–7
Maoist ideology, 24, 30, 96, 110n3, 156
Mao Zedong, 2, 8, 99, 100, 132n1
 Chinese Communism, 169
 Cultural Revolution, 102
 ideology, 8
 Land Reform, 230–2
 party-state, 232–5
 post-Mao China, 94–5, 110n3, 170–1, 239, 242
 rallies, 160–1
 regime, 96, 109
Marx, Karl, 7, 8, 17, 54, 135, 151n2, 159–62, 165, 211, 253–4, 255n5
Marxism
 in China, 96, 99, 159–62, 168–70, 172
 defining religion, 11, 17
 in Laos, 54, 65–6
 in North Korea, 195
 in Kyrgyzstan, 253–4, 255n5
 in Poland, 74
 in USSR, 135, 151n2, 216
 Vietnam, 30, 43–4, 51n37
Marxism–Leninism, 8, 65, 74, 99, 184, 184, 211–12, 216
Max Planck Institute, 3, 20, 202
mediumism, Vietnam, 45, 47–8, 60–1,
 see also spirit possession
medium transcendence, Soviet society, 23, 135, 142–6, 148–50, 195, 212
 human-centric socialist utopia, Korea, 194–6
 see also human-centric-socialist utopia; transcendence
modernity, colonial Indochina, 31–5
"Molodaia Gvardiia" Publishing House, 180, 181
monasticism, 34, 92–3, 140, 163–4, 210, 215, 218, 222, 229, 233, 236–7
Mother of Chosun, 128–30
Mother of Sŏngun (Kim Jong Suka), 125–6
Mother of Vietnam, 127–9
Muslims, 241, 246, 250, 251, 253

national culture, 14, 22, 25, 38, 45, 49, 249, *see also* ethno-national identity
nationalism, 8, 13–14
 anti-colonialism, 14, 21–2, 30, 36, 41–2, 114, 118, 122, 129
 in China, 19, 94–5, 103, 106, 157, 159, 167, 169, 172
 in Kyrgyzstan, 25, 249–51, 254n3
 in Laos, 54–7, 62, 64–5
 in North Korea, 23, 112, 114–19, 123, 125, 128, 131–2, 191–3, 195, 207n7
 in Poland, 70–2, 74, 78, 85–6, 90n6, 90n9–10
 in USSR. 13, 24–5, 173–7, 180–8
 in Vietnam, 1-2, 22, 29–35, 39–49, 53n90
 see also anti-imperialism

290 Index

neo-paganism
 birth of, in Soviet, 173–5
 former USSR and Russia, 187–8
 Russian, 24, 173, 175–6, 180, 182–8
 Soviet path to, 175–81
Neo-totalitarianism, China, 101–4, 105
Ngo Dinh Diem, 39–40, 42
Nguyen Cao Ky, 40, 41
Nguyen Van Thieu, 41, 42
Ninh, Kim N B., 38, 50n24
NLF (National Liberation Front), 30, 39–42, 51n50
North Korea, 112–13, 118, 190–1, 205–6
 achievement of hereditary authority, 130–2
 brainwashing or conversion, 199–201
 Christianity and communism, 191–4
 conversion narratives, 202–5
 conversion of migrants to Christianity, 196–9
 culture of commemoration, 23, 112–13, 117, 121, 123, 133n1
 Graves of Revolutionary Martyrs, 114, 118–19, 120–1, 124, 126, 131–2
 heroic mother, 124–30
 ideology education, 195–6
 Juche ideology, 12, 24, 191, 194–8, 200–201, 205, 207n7–8, 209n15
 Kim Il Sung, 114–15, 119–26, 129–31, 195–8, 200, 205, 207n10, 207–8n11, 209n15
 man-centric socialist utopia, 194–6
 Manchurian tradition, 113–20
 memorials for war martyrs, 120–3
 Mother of Chosun, 128–30
 national division, 191–4
 Ten Principles, 198, 207–8n11
 Workers' Party, 120–2, 126
North Korea People's Army, 114, 119–20, 122–3, 203

October Revolution (1917), 211, 217, 219, 223n5

paganism
 "Mari", 150
 neo-paganism, Soviet, 173–5
 Soviet path to, 175–81
 see also animism

"Pamiat" organization, 183–4, 186–7
People's Army, North Korean, 114, 119–20, 122–3, 203
perestroika, 211, 218, 219, 221
Plan for Monumental Propaganda (Lenin), 210, 213, 214–15, 221
Poland
 abortion, 76, 79–80, 90n6
 anticlericalism, 82, 86, 88, 91n17
 Catholic atheists, 78, 85
 Catholicism, 6, 22, 71–4, 76–8, 83–7, 88, 90n9–10
 church, state and society, 72, 86–8
 communism and Catholicism in, 76–8
 conflict and coexistence, 75, 76–8
 post-communism, 78–86
 religious life under communism, 73–5
 resistance narrative, 22, 74
Pol Pot, 8, 54
PRC (People's Republic of China), 92–3, 107, 155, 237
 Christian persecutions, 168
 founding of, 158–9
 Marxism, 159–60, 169
 post-ideological politics of, 95–8
 public sacrifice, 103
 superstition, 164
 unofficial Christianity, 107–8
 see also China
Property Commission, Poland, 79, 80
Protestantism, 7, 92, 107, 158, 192, 201, 225–6, 255n5, *see also* Christianity
public sacrifice, China, 101–4, 110n12, *see also* state ritual
purges, Communist Party, 2, 121, 136, 139, 141, 145, 220
Putin, Vladimir, 150, 218

Radio Maryja (Catholic radio station), 80
RC (Readers' Club), 183–4
Red Guards, 160, 163, 234
religion, 5
 assuming communist ideology like, 10–12
 China's limitation on, 104–8

religion – (*continued*)
  colonial Indochina, 31–5
  idea of, 4–5
  as national identity, 24, 42, 48, 55, 61, 64–5, 70–2, 74, 78, 85, 90n9, 250–1
  relations between religions, 3, 7, 15, 30, 55, 99, 101, 127, 129–30, 138, 140, 155, 188, 191, 192
  religious marketplace, 18, 96, 109, 163, 190, 236, 238, 241
  religious revival, 45, 51n53, 63–4, 90n5, 92, 94–5, 99, 108, 149, 155, 177, 183, 201, 220, 223, 237–8
religionscape, China, 225–7
Religious Affairs Bureau, 107, 239
religious art
  Bolshevik cultural policy on, 211–17
  destruction of, 215
  Florensky's ideas on, 210–11, 219–23
  Lenin's *Plan for Monumental Propaganda*, 210, 213, 214–15, 221
  post-Communist Russia, 210–11
  religious Renaissance, 221, 223
  role in time of crisis, 217–23
  Rublev's *Holy Trinity* icon, 215, 219
religious institutions, 8, 20–1, 238
  state policies towards, 39, 55, 92–3
  state registration of, 54, 57, 63, 92, 107
  suppression of, 46, 225, 232–5
ritual service providers, households, 235–9
river crabs, China, 98–101
RLG (Royal Lao Government), 54, 56–7
Rublev, Andrey, *Holy Trinity* icon, 215, 219
Rudnev, V. A., 179–80
Russia, *see* religious art; Soviet society; Soviet Union
Russian Neo-Paganism, 24, 173, 175–6, 180, 182–8
Russian Orthodox Church, 150, 218–20, 232

scientific apologetics, Buddhism, 156, 163–4, 164–7
scientific atheism
  China, 9, 156, 163–4, 169–72
  role of science in communist ideology, 59, 148, 156, 212
  Soviet society, 11–12, 173, 177–8, 245
scientific representation
  of Buddhism, 164–7
  of happiness, 194
  intelligent-design theory, 244–5
  of religion, 212
  of rituals and ceremonies, 177
scientism, 94, 156, 163–71
secularism
  atheism as a form of, 3–7
  China, 92–5, 170
  communist secularism, 3, 14, 18, 20, 94
  modern secularism, 94, 170
  secularization without, 12, 23, 108–10
  Kyrgyzstan, 246, 247–50
  Russia, 210–11
  Vietnam, 32–3
  Western secularism, 5–8, 11, 16–17
  see also atheist secularism
secularization, 3, 5, 9, 12, 15–18, 20, 23, 25, 71–2, 86, 93, 95, 108–9, 135, 143–5, 149, 247
separation of church and state, 4, 6–7, 14, 24, 71, 94–5, 109, 111n15, 149, 171, 213
shamanism, 2, 57, 59, 158, 206n2
Sinchŏn massacre, 206n2, 207n6
Skurlatov, Valery, 184, 185
Slavic-Aryans, 181, 182, 185–7
socialist middle peasant, making of, 230–2
Social Science Research Council, 15, 26n3
Soloviev, Vladimir, 219, 222
Sonam Darje, Khenpo, 165, 166
South Korea, 132n1, 191, 207n7, 207n9
  Christian conversion, 203, 205
  Christianity of, 24, 192–4, 196–201
  North Korean migrants, 206n1, 208n13–14
  North Korean migrants in, 202
  post-Korean War, 208–9n15
  war cemeteries, 115, 118–20, 131

Soviet society
  anti-Westernism, 173–5
  communist humanism, 134–5
  confession and faith, 136–41
  levels of transcendence, 141–6
  medium transcendence, 23, 135, 142–6
  from political religion to secular faith, 141–6
  Russian Neo-paganism, 24, 173, 175–6, 180, 182–8
  saved by Soviet society, 146–8
  secularity of, 245
  shifting transcendence, 148–51
  socialist visions of, 149–50
  totalitarianism, 140
Soviet Union
  Communist Party, 135, 141, 145, 150, 176, 184
  doctor and patient interaction, 147–8
  fall of, 2–3, 9, 11, 14, 149, 190, 248
  mat' geroinya, 127
  religion in, 18, 135, 141–2
  Russian Neo-paganism, 175–6
  socialism, 10, 29
  spirit possession, 29, 47, 49n12, 60, 206n2, *see also* mediumism
  Stalin/Stalinism, 2, 8, 139–41, 145–6, 174–5, *see also* cult of personality
  state ritual, 12, 23, 42–3, 78, 89, 101–4, 112, 117–80, 179, 218
  superstition, 14, 24, 33, 38, 58–9, 69n14, 158, 240
  animism, 55
  ideological definition of, 8, 61, 93, 163, 215–16, 225
  campaigning against, 11, 38, 59, 63, 65, 66–7
  legal suppression of, 33, 47, 58, 160, 238, 240
  mediumism, 45, 47–8, 60–1
  stigma of, 158, 163–7, 168
  superstition specialist households, 239–42, 243n9
Swearer, Donald, 65, 68n8, 69n15

Tablighi Jamaat, 251–3, 255n4
Tabyshalieva, Anara, 247, 248

Taoism, Buddhism and, 19, 68n2, 92–3, 99, 107
Ten Principles, North Korea, 198, 207–8n11
thevada (angels), 55, 56, 63, 68n11
Tiananmen Square, 95–6, 160
Tibetan Buddhism, 93, 94
Tomb of the Unknown Soldier, 112, 115
totalitarianism
  Maoist, 96, 110n3
  neo-, of China, 96–7, 101–4, 105, 109
  Soviet, 140
tourism, 102, 103, 107, 109
Trade-Union organizations, 177, 179
transcendence
  great, 23, 142–6, 148
  human and divine, 24
  interpersonal, 148
  levels of, 12, 23, 135, 141–6
  medium, 23, 135, 142–6, 148–50, 195, 212
  shifting, 148–51
Triumphant Zion, 137, 139
Trotsky, Leon, 36, 214, 220, 247
Truong Chinh, 37–8, 50n24, 51n37–8, 51n40
TSPM (Three Self Patriotic Movement), 158–9, 161

underground churches, China, 104, 107, 157, *see also* Christianity; house churches
USSR, *see* Soviet Union

Viet Minh government, 30, 35–7, 39, 50n29, 50n35–6
Vietnam
  Cao Dai, 30–7, 39–40, 42, 45–7
  Catholicism, 30, 31, 35–40, 47, 48
  Communist Party, 30, 39–42, 49n3
  cult of the heroic in war communism, 42–5
  Doi Moi, 30, 39, 43–4
  long wars (1945–1975) and policies, 35–42
  "Mother of Vietnam", 127–9

National Liberation Front, 30, 39–42, 51n50
religion, communism and modernity in colonial Indochina, 31–5
Vietnam War, 57, 112, 117

War and Peace (Tolstoy), 216
war commemoration, *see* North Korea
Weber, Max, 130, 131, 198
Wells, Kenneth, 192, 194, 206n3
White Caps of Wisdom Ocean (Sonam Darje), 166
Wohlrab-Sahr, Monika, 135, 144

Workers' Party
  North Korea, 120–2, 126, 195
  Vietnam, 41
World Buddhist Forum, 93, 108
World War I, 115
World War II, 32, 36, 218
Wu Yaozong, 159, 161

Yellow Emperor, 101–3, 110n12
Yeltsin, Boris, 150, 218
You Zhibiao, 166, 167

Zionism, International, 181, 182, 184, 185–7

CPSIA information can be obtained at www.ICGtesting.com
Printed in the USA
LVOW09*1325090715

445606LV00008B/21/P